Advance Praise for
A Baptist Vision of Religious Liberty & Free and Faithful Politics

In this engaging volume, Aaron Weaver brings together the words, ideas, and energy of James Dunn, one of Baptist's most outspoken (that's an understatement) advocates of and authorities on religious liberty in the American Republic. Through this well-edited collection of his many sermons, speeches, and articles, Dunn's prophetic voice lives on, and none too soon.

—Bill J. Leonard
James and Marilyn Dunn Professor of Baptist Studies
Wake Forest University

The Baptist genealogy on religious liberty in America goes like this: Roger Williams, John Clarke, Isaac Backus, John Leland, J. M. Dawson, and James Dunn. No Baptist in my lifetime cared more deeply and barked more passionately at the intersection of religious liberty and the separation of church and state than James Dunn. Aaron Weaver puts us in his debt for this stockpile of Dunn's words, a gift that will keep on giving to future generations. So important!

—Walter B. Shurden
Minister at Large
Mercer University

Smyth & Helwys Publishing, Inc.
6316 Peake Road
Macon, Georgia 31210-3960
1-800-747-3016
©2018 by Aaron Douglas Weaver
All rights reserved.

Library of Congress Cataloging-in-Publication Data

Names: Dunn, James M., 1932- | Weaver, Aaron Douglas, editor.
Title: A Baptist vision of religious liberty and free and faithful politics :
  the words and writings of James M. Dunn / edited by Aaron Douglas Weaver.
Description: Macon : Smyth & Helwys, 2018.
Identifiers: LCCN 2018015056 | ISBN 9781641730532 (pbk. : alk. paper)
Subjects: LCSH: Baptists--Doctrines. | Freedom of religion--United States.. |
  Liberty--Religious aspects--Baptists. | Church and state--United States. |
  Christianity and politics--United States.
Classification: LCC BX6331.3 .D86 2018 | DDC 261.70973--dc23
LC record available at https://lccn.loc.gov/2018015056

Disclaimer of Liability: With respect to statements of opinion or fact available in this work of nonfiction, Smyth & Helwys Publishing Inc. nor any of its employees, makes any warranty, express or implied, or assumes any legal liability or responsibility for the accuracy or completeness of any information disclosed, or represents that its use would not infringe privately-owned rights.

A Baptist Vision of Religious Liberty & Free and Faithful Politics

THE WORDS AND WRITINGS OF JAMES M. DUNN

AARON DOUGLAS WEAVER, EDITOR

Also by Aaron Douglas Weaver

James M. Dunn and Soul Freedom

CBF at 25: Stories of the Cooperative Baptist Fellowship

*Different and Distinctive but Nevertheless Baptist:
A History of Northminster Baptist Church (1967–2017)*
(with C. Douglas Weaver)

For James Oliver, Miriam Grace, and Hannah Justice

Acknowledgments

While previous books have been written about Dr. James M. Dunn—a biography I wrote titled *James M. Dunn and Soul Freedom* (2011) and a short compilation of Dunn's quotes and sayings, *The Wit and Wisdom of James Dunn* (1999)—until now there has not been a volume that makes available Dr. Dunn's most notable works. A thank you is owed to Smyth & Helwys Publishing for its long-term focus on Baptist identity, soul freedom, religious liberty, and the contribution of Dunn and the Baptist Joint Committee.

Special thanks are also owed to Amanda Tyler and the Baptist Joint Committee for Religious Liberty for granting permission to make available Dunn's "Reflections" columns from the BJC's newsletter, *Report from the Capital*. I also want to extend gratitude to Tanya Zanish-Belcher, director of Special Collections & Archives at Wake Forest University's Z. Smith Reynolds Library. The James M. Dunn Collection at Wake Forest is an incredible compilation of Dunn's personal correspondence, photos, and mementos. Thanks to Ravensworth Baptist Church in Annandale, Virginia, for lending sermon tapes from Dunn's time as interim pastor. How fun to hear Dunn again and transcribe his words!

I am very much indebted to Dr. Bill Leonard and the Estate of James M. Dunn for making available to me previously unpublished writings for inclusion in this volume. I am grateful for the feedback and assistance Dr. Leonard provided throughout the project. I'm also indebted to another fellow Baptist historian, my dad, Doug Weaver, who has been reading my writing and research and giving guidance since I was in elementary school! Writing about Baptist identity, soul freedom, and religious liberty has become something of a family business!

Last but definitely not least, I want to thank my wife, Alexis, for helping me to take on and complete this project in our lively home of two dogs, a pre-k daughter, first-grade son, and newborn on the way. I love you.

Contents

Preface: From the Editor   5
Foreword by Amanda Tyler   9
Introduction: The Life and Ministry of James M. Dunn   11

Chapter 1: Soul Freedom and Baptist Identity   25
    The Baptist Vision of Religious Liberty (1994)   27
    No Freedom for the Soul with a Creed (2002)   33
    Called to Be Perpetually Indignant Prophets (1990)   37
    Real Baptists (1990)   43
    God and Politics (2008)   44

Chapter 2: Reflections on Being Baptist   49
    To Love, To Act, To Trust (1981)   49
    The Font of Freedom (1983)   51
    Soul Freedom and Sola Scriptura (1985)   54
    Separation as the Best Guarantee for Religious Freedom (1991)   57
    Distinctly Baptist (1994)   60
    Equal Privileges: A Hallmark of Baptists (1994)   62
    Helwys's Demand for Religious Freedom for All Troubles Some
        (1998)   65
    Soul Freedom Nothing but a New Name for a Profound Word:
        Faith (2000)   67

Chapter 3: Church-State Philosophy   71
    Religion and Politics: A Proper Mix (1986)   73
    Church and State: Friends or Enemies? (1988)   82
    Standing for Religious Freedom (1994)   85
    Religious Liberty and Church/State Separation Go Hand in Hand
        (1996)   89
    Freedom's Roots: Back to the Bill of Rights' Beginning (2003)   95
    Pluralism: Another Word for Freedom (1998)   105
    Church and State: The Separation of Powers (1981)   110
    A Threatened Heritage (1994)   122

Chapter 4: School Prayer	131
Prayer Amendment: Unneeded, Unwanted, and Unworkable (1982)	133
Secularization, Trivialization, Collectivization (1982)	136
Voluntary Prayer or Required Ritual? (1989)	139
Chapter 5: Tuition Tax Credits and Vouchers	143
Tuition Tax Credit Pottage (1981)	145
Forswear Funnymentalism (and Vouchers) (1991)	149
Public Money for Public Purposes (1994)	152
School Choice: Wrongheaded Reform of Public Education (1996)	154
Chapter 6: RFRA, Equal Access, and Faith-based Initiative	159
Render therefore unto Caesar (1990)	162
Dear Mr. Vice President: Say It Ain't So (1999)	165
Siamese Twins: Freedom of Religion and Freedom of the Press (1984)	167
Downright Silliness of Church-State Revisionism (1985)	169
A Theology for Public Policy (1988)	172
"Separation" Not a Bad Word (1991)	175
How to Mix Religion and Politics (1994)	178
Chapter 7: Congressional Testimony	181
Testimony on the Nomination of William Wilson to Be Ambassador to the Holy See (1984)	183
Testimony on the Nomination of John Ashcroft to Be Attorney General of the United States (2001)	186
Chapter 8: Christian Ethics	193
Ethical Emphases in Galatians (1972)	194
The Ethical Teachings of Jesus: Sunday School Lesson	206
Southern Baptists and Christian Ethics (1976)	210
Chapter 9: Christian Advocacy	223
Lobbying Isn't a Dirty Word (1975)	224
Dealing with Controversial Issues	225
A Christian Lifestyle for Twentieth Century Baptists (1977)	229
How a Pastor Relates to Politics (1970)	238

How to Get the Church into Politics (1970)	243
Jesus and Caesar—Matthew 22:15-22	250

Chapter 10: Speeches and Interviews 255
    After Brokenness . . . Reconciliation (1979) 255
    Religious Right: Wrongly Fundamental and Fundamentally Wrong
      (1981) 259
    Six Simple Axioms (1991) 266
    Religious Freedom Award Response (1999) 274
    Interview with *The Whitsitt Journal* (2000) 277
    Religious Liberty as a Baptist Distinctive (2001) 282

Chapter 11: Sermons 289
    God, How Can I Draw Closer to You? (1969) 289
    Going Forth in His Presence (1972) 295
    The Sin of Certainty—Mark 9:20-24 (1997) 298
    Grace Enfleshed—John 1:1-14 (1997) 304
    Nine-Commandment Christians—John 1:6-15 (1998) ... 307
    It's a Matter of the Heart (1998) 310
    Response Able and Free (1990s) 314
    Where the Spirit of the Lord Is, There Is Freedom (2001) ... 320
    The Word Was Made Flesh (2002) 326
    For Freedom Christ Has Set Us Free (2010) 331
    Give Me Your Yearning to Breathe Free—John 8:31-36 (2013) ... 336

Afterword by Stephen K. Reeves 341
About the Editor 345

From the Editor

"A Texas-bred, Spirit-led, Bible-teaching, revival-preaching, recovering Southern Baptist."

That's Dr. James M. Dunn in his own words. He was definitely all of that, but the quip does not capture the breadth of his different roles in a ministry that spanned seven decades. Dunn was youth minister, music minister, collegiate minister, ethicist, denominational leader, adviser and counselor, author, supply preacher, advocate, and activist ("Christian lobbyist," in his words), and the list goes on.

During much of the second half of the twentieth century, Dunn was the most aggressive Baptist proponent for religious liberty, church-state separation, and political engagement in the United States in his roles as associate director (1966–1968) and director (1968–1980) of the Texas Baptist Christian Life Commission and executive director of the Baptist Joint Committee on Public Affairs (1981–1999).

From his days as a pastor in the mid-1950s until his death in 2015, Dunn was a tireless advocate and activist for soul freedom: the freedom, ability, and responsibility of each individual to respond to God for herself or himself. During his ministry in Texas and Washington, D.C., Dunn established himself as the public heir of E. Y. Mullins and those before him who insisted that an unfettered conscience and uncoerced faith—born out of a direct personal experience of God and without reliance on ecclesiastical leaders—represented the authentic Baptist tradition.

Soul freedom was the key distinctive of Baptists, according to Dunn. It was their greatest contribution to understanding the Christian faith and the essence of Baptist identity. From the time Thomas Helwys boldly proclaimed in 1611 that "the king is not Lord of the conscience," the hallmark of the people called Baptist, Dunn said, is their "dogged determination to be free—free and faithful." For Dunn, being "faithful" entailed dependence on the Bible with a focus on Christ's greatest command to love one's neighbors, on fervent prayer, and on responsibility. He challenged Baptists to respond to pluralism with this faithfulness. Being faithful meant rejecting the theological creedalism of many conservative Christians (and of some liberals too) as well as the political creedalism—the single-issue litmus tests, divisive tactics, and "sin-sizing" approach—that characterized the Religious Right with its overemphasis of or obsession with certain moral issues to the exclusion of a host of other social concerns.

The confession of faith at the heart of Dunn's vision of religious liberty and free and faithful politics was simple but powerful: *Jesus Christ is Lord.* This early Christian confession makes both a political and a theological affirmation. "To say that Jesus is Lord was to register a public protest and declare that Caesar was not Lord," Dunn emphasized. "It's the most dynamic and moral confession of faith because it implies far more than simply what we believe in our head . . . it speaks of a vital way of life."

Being faithful also meant taking action. "If we really believe in soul freedom, our approach to ethics would be far more action-oriented," Dunn told a 1976 gathering of Southern Baptist leaders in Nashville, Tennessee. "Soul freedom allows great liberty for one whose relationship is directly with God. A deep belief in the priesthood of the believer lets one launch out on faith in spite of controversy, opposition, and certain defeat. We are free to fail. We are not free to fail to act."

Throughout his ministry, Dunn developed and displayed a distinctly Baptist approach to advocacy—a vision of religious liberty and free and faithful politics rooted in a Christ-centered theology and ethic that prioritized an unfettered conscience, uncoerced faith, and loving concern for others and embraced the social implications of the gospel. Freedom and justice were inseparable, according to Dunn. His vision was committed to the common good and to equality and respect for the dignity of all people. The *imago Dei*—the image of God in every human being—was kept at the forefront of Dunn's vision.

In 2002, he preached, "It is our commitment to persons made in the image of God that fuels our passion for social justice, for Christian ministry, for evangelism, for ethical behavior. It's our commitment to persons who are made in the image of God and have flesh like the flesh that Jesus took on when he invaded humanity in the person of Jesus Christ. That's what keeps us going."

From 1968 to 1980, as director of the Texas Baptist Christian Life Commission, Dunn taught Baptists in the Lone Star State about the necessity of Christian citizenship, what his mentor T. B. Maston called "applied Christianity." Dunn introduced through his lived example how to practice a free and faithful politics. From immigration reform and environmentalism to women's rights and racial equality, Dunn was an influential advocate for a wide range of pressing social issues.

During his nearly twenty-year-tenure as executive director of the Baptist Joint Committee on Public Affairs (BJC), Dunn advanced religious freedom and defended church-state separation. He aggressively took on the Religious Right with his trademark confrontational style and colorful rhetoric, loudly opposing prayer amendments, voucher proposals, and government funding of religious groups. Dunn found himself at the center of the Southern Baptist Controversy—popularly dubbed the "Battle for the Bible"—that rocked the nation's largest Protestant denomination during the 1980s. The new fundamentalist leaders of his own denomination, represented by the Southern Baptist Convention, attempted to smear his name and silence him. They failed.

In the face of much adversity, Dunn relentlessly championed the religion protections of the First Amendment, leading the BJC to help secure passage of landmark legislation like the Equal Access Act (1984) and the Religious Freedom Restoration Act (1993). The Baptist tradition was true to itself, he believed, when it promoted and supported policies that safeguarded the individual conscience, maximized religious freedom, and insisted that the institutions of church and state remain separate. Dunn strove to remain faithful to this tradition in word and deed. He modeled for multiple generations of Baptists (and many non-Baptists too) how to apply and live out their faith in a manner consistent with the historic Baptist commitment to freedom, reminding them that responsibility "rode piggyback" to soul freedom and required Baptists to speak up and be counted. This paradigm for Christian advocacy—the linking of soul freedom to the social gospel—is an invaluable gift.

During the current tumultuous times as we settle into the twenty-first century, Dunn's vision of religious liberty and free and faithful politics is needed now more than ever. Persistence and resistance in defense of conscience and the pursuit of freedom defined Dunn's life and are central to his legacy. He refused to remain silent, shunned inaction, and never capitulated when freedom was threatened. As he often said, "A threat to anyone's religious liberty is a threat to everyone's religious liberty," echoing Dr. Martin Luther King, Jr.'s powerful refrain, "injustice anywhere is a threat to justice everywhere."

This volume features a selection of the words and writings of James M. Dunn during his years as director of the Texas Baptist Christian Life Commission, executive director of the Baptist Joint Committee on Public Affairs, and professor of public policy at Wake Forest University School of Divinity. The collection includes magazine and newsletter columns, academic journal articles, book chapters, congressional testimony, speeches, chapel addresses, sermons, and even a Sunday school lesson. The earliest entry is a chapel address Dunn gave in 1969, and the latest is a sermon he preached in 2013, two years prior to his death, at the First Baptist Church in America, Providence, Rhode Island. The contents of this volume include Dunn's reflections on a variety of church-state and justice issues and other subjects still of relevance to our current cultural landscape.

To countless Baptists, myself included, James Dunn was an instrumental influence. His wit, wisdom, and fight moved generations of Baptists to better live out our faith, value our freedom, and never take our shared heritage and liberty for granted. It is my hope that this collection of the words and writings of Dr. James M. Dunn will help Baptists and other people of faith, present and future generations, to remember, learn from, and live out his vision of religious liberty and free and faithful politics.

"Soul freedom is the fire that burns in the innards of every true Baptist," said Dunn.

Let's keep that fire burning.

—Aaron D. Weaver, *Editor*

Foreword

"One common characteristic of Baptist saints was their capacity for outrage. Thomas Helwys, Roger Williams, Isaac Backus, John Leland, even the irenic George W. Truett, could be righteously indignant" (Dunn, "Called to be Perpetually Indignant Prophets").

I'd never describe James M. Dunn as irenic, though I, like many others I imagine, count him among the saints of our Baptist heritage. We can thank Dr. Aaron Weaver for this marvelous collection of Dr. Dunn's writings of righteous indignation, spanning his long career as a "Baptist hired hand," as he called himself.

Of course, anyone who ever heard Dr. Dunn speak or had a conversation with him will know that this book is entertaining. To call him an "original" seems banal. His trademark humor and gift of colorful storytelling are present throughout, but there is much more. Reading his columns, speeches, and sermons, one also appreciates his knowledge and love of the Bible, his deep theological understanding, his prophetic voice speaking truth to power, and his ability to use hymn lyrics to great effect.

This book gives the reader numerous opportunities to learn about Dunn's teaching of "soul freedom," for which he is probably best known and admired. It is the theological underpinning of his understanding of religious liberty as well as the continuing work of the Baptist Joint Committee for Religious Liberty, which he led for nearly twenty years at a crucial point in its history.

Even though he may be best remembered for his tireless work defending religious liberty for all, this collection reminds us of his many other passions and contributions to Christian citizenship. Dunn studied ethics under his mentor, T. B. Maston, and lived Maston's "applied Christianity" throughout his life. A passage from a 1972 article seems thoroughly relevant today: "Without freedom there cannot be an authentic ethic. Unless man is in some sense free to choose and is responsible for his actions, his life has really no ethical value" (Dunn, "Ethical Emphases in Galatians"). Dunn gives a powerful response to those who wonder why we continue to insist on religious freedom for all.

How appropriate that this Baptist saint who so loved freedom celebrates his Heavenly Birthday on July 4. Galatians is the key freedom text for him, and specifically Galatians 5:1: "[I]t is precisely for freedom that Christ has set you free." He gives credit where it is due at numerous points to E. Y. Mullins and his *Axioms of Religion*, and Dunn's writings on that seminal work may well introduce it to another generation of Baptists and others.

With freedom, Dunn so often reminded us, comes responsibility. The two are inseparable, he said, like two sides of a coin. This insight led him to advocate for a Christian's duty to actively engage in politics. It is also essential to protecting religious liberty for all, understanding that with freedom comes the responsibility to use it to love your neighbor.

For the thousands of people whose lives Dr. Dunn touched over his remarkable life, this book will also provide an opportunity to sit at the foot of an old friend and mentor. I say that personally, as a fellow "Texican" who learned from Dr. Dunn as a young person when I was an intern at the Baptist Joint Committee in 1998, and later as a staff member just as he transitioned from his position as executive director. You can hear his twang ringing through these pages, and that is a gift in and of itself.

And for me personally as I begin my second year leading the BJC, his written work is inspirational. The courageous truth he preached during times of peril for the BJC and at great personal cost shows what he did for a cause much bigger than himself. In an interview following his retirement from the BJC, he said, "I pray now that survival seems assured, that the BJC will do a far better job of educating Baptists about basic Baptist beliefs on religious liberty than I was able to do." He was far too modest, of course, though I will joyfully accept his charge for our future. His enormous written legacy will continue to aid our efforts as we attempt to live up to the example he set for us all.

—Amanda Tyler
Executive Director
Baptist Joint Committee for Religious Liberty
Washington, D.C.

The Life and Ministry of James M. Dunn

During the depths of the Great Depression, James Milton Dunn was born in Fort Worth, Texas, on June 17, 1932, to William Thomas Dunn, a milkman, and Edith Campbell Dunn. As with most families in segregated Fort Worth during the 1930s, times were tough and financial woes were real. Despite struggles, the Dunn home was a refuge for those with greater needs.

"Seldom a day went by that [my parents] weren't bringing someone into the home to see to it that they had something to eat," Dunn said. The welcome that William and Edith showed to their neighbors, including African-American friends in the racially diverse "borderline community" where the family resided, played a significant role in molding young James's social conscience. They instilled in James a Christian ethic that demanded all people be treated with equal dignity and respect.

The Dunn family was a Baptist family. James's paternal grandparents were Primitive Baptists who became Southern Baptists later in life. As a child and teenager, Dunn attended Evans Avenue Baptist Church, which counted as members numerous faculty, staff, and students of nearby Southwestern Baptist Theological Seminary. For a time, Dunn resisted making a public profession of faith due to his pastor's coercive style of preaching. He recalled that pastor (T. A. Patterson, the father of Paige Patterson who would become one of Dunn's harshest critics years later) made a habit of "trying to scare the hell out of the congregation," particularly the children and youth, with "trap sermons."

After the arrival of a new pastor, Loyed Simmons, twelve-year-old Dunn would "walk the aisle" and be baptized. Simmons, a doctoral student at Southwestern Seminary, often invoked Baptist history from the pulpit and spoke about religious liberty as well as social issues. As a sixteen-year-old, Dunn took part in a study course on Baptist beliefs led by Stewart Newman, a Southwestern professor. Newman introduced Dunn to E. Y. Mullins's landmark book, *The Axioms of Religion* (1908). This book, which scholars contend has done more than any other single work to define

Baptist identity for the twentieth century, was Dunn's first in-depth study of soul competency and the priesthood of all believers—the belief that direct access to God and a relationship with Jesus Christ is for each believer and that every Christian is a minister. Mullins's intense focus on a voluntary, uncoerced personal relationship with Jesus Christ and an unfettered conscience before God would stick with Dunn for the rest of his life.

In 1952, a year prior to his graduation from Fort Worth's Texas Wesleyan College, Dunn accepted a call to vocational ministry. He was nineteen years old. During a revival service, Dunn walked down the center aisle at Evans Avenue Baptist while the congregation sang "Wherever He Leads I'll Go" and told pastor Woody Phelps of his decision. Phelps then announced to the congregation that God was calling Dunn to preach. Dunn quickly corrected his pastor and loudly proclaimed, "No, Dr. Phelps, I didn't say that. God has called me to ministry, but I have no idea what it will be!" The congregation erupted in laughter.

This call to ministry—eventually the ministry of preaching and practicing a free and faithful politics—led Dunn eight miles down the road to Southwestern Seminary, where he received his divinity degree under faculty such as noted theologian James Leo Garrett and pursued a doctorate in ethics under the mentorship of influential Southern Baptist ethicist Thomas Buford Maston. Maston has been hailed as the preeminent shaper of Christian ethics and social concern among Baptists in the twentieth century. His emphasis on "applied Christianity"—applying the gospel to all aspects of life—made his name synonymous with Christian ethics in the Southern Baptist Convention. The pivotal influence of Maston on Dunn, both personally and professionally, cannot be understated.

As a doctoral student, Dunn focused his research on church-state relations. He chose J. M. Dawson as the subject of his dissertation. Dawson, a Baptist statesman and perennial author, was known for his advocacy of social Christianity and his role as the first executive director of the Baptist Joint Committee on Public Affairs (1946–1953). Due in part to the influence of Dawson's writings, Dunn came to realize that ethics could not be divorced from evangelism, nor evangelism from social concern. Personal redemption and social concern belonged together. This notion—a novel idea for many Southern Baptists—would serve as a guiding principle for Dunn's ministry.

Like a typical seminary student, Dunn held several positions in churches while completing his coursework. He began his professional ministerial service in 1954 as the minister of music and youth at First

Baptist Church of Celina. The next year, Dunn left the small rural church for a similar role at First Baptist Church of Weatherford, a larger congregation with a membership of nearly 1,200, where he worked with his future father-in-law, Edwin "Mac" McNeely. McNeely was a leading professor at Southwestern's School of Sacred Music and the interim minister of music at the church.

In 1958, a group of active members at First Weatherford left to start Emmanuel Baptist Church and invited Dunn to serve as the congregation's first pastor. During his three-year tenure there, the new church grew from fifty-seven members to a membership of almost two hundred. A life-changing event also happened while Dunn was pastor at Emmanuel. He married McNeely's daughter, Marilyn, whom he had known since his days in the primary department at Evans Avenue Baptist Church.

After nearly seven years of service in congregational ministry, Dunn became a collegiate minister. For five years, he directed the Baptist Student Union at West Texas State University in Canyon and taught as an adjunct religion instructor. At West Texas State, Dunn was assigned the task of molding college students into Christian leaders as they prepared for careers in local churches, higher education, and the business world. Evangelism and missions were major emphases during his time working with Baptist students.

A turning point in Dunn's ministry came in 1966 with his appointment as associate director of the Christian Life Commission of the Baptist General Convention of Texas. Founded in 1950, the CLC was the brainchild of a small group of Texas Baptists, which included Dunn's mentor, T. B. Maston. Realizing that Texas Baptists had failed to apply Christian principles gleaned from the Bible to all aspects of life—most notably on behalf of racial equality—the CLC was formed to effectively confront social ills. In the years that followed, the ethics agency responded to almost every important issue to trouble American society, including encouraging family planning and giving attention to the growing problems of poverty, world hunger, alcohol abuse, and drug addiction.

Most notably, the CLC backed the controversial desegregation and school prayer rulings of the United States Supreme Court, urged an end to the Vietnam War, and worked to reform the criminal justice system. While the CLC sought to maintain contact with the consensus opinion of Texas Baptists—leading campaigns against liquor, gambling, and obscenity, issues near and dear to the hearts of Baptists in the Lone Star State—the ethics agency did not hesitate to take unpopular positions regarding public school busing, equal rights in housing, and support for sex education.

Less than two years into the job as associate director, Dunn was selected to succeed Jimmy Allen as director of the CLC. For a dozen years at the helm of the increasingly influential CLC, Dunn urged Texas Baptists to embrace their responsibility to participate in the political process as Christian citizens. Promoting an ethic of political engagement motivated by a loving concern for others, Dunn called on his fellow Baptists to be Christian lobbyists. He practiced what he preached, leading the CLC to be more actively involved in public policy debates. Soon enough, the CLC became regarded by lawmakers at the Texas capitol in Austin as one of the most influential organizations in the state.

As director, Dunn continued the Texas Baptist tradition of fighting all legislative efforts to legalize gambling and further the interests of the alcohol industry. He was undoubtedly an influential advocate for a wide range of pressing social concerns, from juvenile justice reform to immigration reform to ensuring equal rights for women and minorities. He also weighed in on more controversial debates, supporting a reform of the state's restrictive abortion laws. At the time, Texas law did not allow for abortion where pregnancies resulted from rape or incest, or in cases where there was strong evidence of severe fetal deformity. Dunn's CLC stressed that Christians could oppose the practice of elective abortion without favoring a constitutional ban on all abortions.

As the Vietnam War was still raging, Dunn urged peace. Also in the late 1960s, under his leadership, Texas Baptists became one of the first Christian groups in the nation to support strict environmental regulations. A tireless supporter of public education, Dunn led the CLC to champion the need for comprehensive sex education and bilingual education while combating efforts to divert money from public schools to benefit private religious education. He spent considerable time lobbying for improved welfare laws to provide a social safety net to the vulnerable in society. He even recruited the help of W. A. Criswell, the fundamentalist stalwart and pastor of First Baptist Church in Dallas, to help lobby for a raise in the welfare ceiling.

Not surprisingly, Dunn and the CLC invested much time in defending church-state separation. His opposition of funding for private religious colleges and universities such as Baylor University raised the ire of other Baptist leaders. Dunn declared that Texas Baptist proponents of tuition grants, which included Baylor president Abner McCall, had compromised the "clarity of our witness for separation of church and state." He asked, "How can you expect us to be true to separation of church and state when our institutions are allowing tuition equalization grants to go to their students?"

Throughout these years, Dunn's advocacy was grounded in a commitment to soul freedom, the foundation of his approach to political engagement and applied Christianity. This ethic was motivated by a loving concern for others and a commitment to furthering the common good. With this distinctly Baptist approach to Christian advocacy, Dunn was following in the footsteps of his forebears such as Thomas Helwys, Roger Williams, and E. Y. Mullins. The Baptist tradition was true to itself, Dunn believed, when it promoted and supported public policies that safeguarded the individual conscience and maximized religious freedom.

Dunn was fortunate to be able to preach and practice a free and faithful politics with little pushback from his Baptist brethren. The cornerstone Baptist distinctive of soul freedom was generally assumed and accepted in Texas Baptist life, according to Dunn. During the 1960s and 1970s, he said, Texas Baptists "did not question 'soul freedom' as basic."

In 1981, at the age of forty-eight, Dunn left the CLC to head the Baptist Joint Committee on Public Affairs, following in the footsteps of his former mentor and the subject of his dissertation, J. M. Dawson. Founded in 1939, the BJC then represented eight Baptist groups (28 million members) in the nation's capital in support of religious liberty and in defense of church-state separation. At the BJC, Dunn would have to change his personal philosophy of staying out of theological battles in order to defend soul freedom, religious liberty, and church-state separation from the fundamentalist faction of the SBC.

Between 1968 and 1980, Dunn had transformed from a mild-mannered, former BSU minister low on confidence to become a nationally known Baptist leader with a reputation for an aggressive but effective style in the public square. He would employ this same aggressive posture against his fundamentalist opponents who sought to censure him and stop the participation of Southern Baptists in the BJC. He did so while doubling down on soul freedom as essential to Baptist identity and to Baptist political engagement.

Dunn took the reins of the BJC as controversy was beginning to erupt within the SBC. During the 1980s, his defense of soul freedom, religious liberty, and church-state separation became pivotal in the Southern Baptist controversy, dubbed the "Battle for the Bible." From the outset, Dunn was a vocal opponent of the so-called Conservative Resurgence, which ultimately gained control of the denomination. He was also one of the primary targets of the emerging fundamentalist leadership.

Upon taking office, Dunn promised an aggressive approach. He certainly delivered, immediately addressing the threat of the Religious Right and warning against a marriage between conservative Christians and the Republican Party. According to Dunn, such a relationship threatened to make religion "the handmaiden of a particular ideology." He said that "God is minimized in any marriage of religion and politics" because "we wind up making God the national mascot and that's civil religion at its worst." In Dunn's opinion, conservative Christians were becoming uncritical supporters of the Republican Party.

Fundamentalist dissatisfaction with Dunn erupted when he attacked President Ronald Reagan's proposal to add a prayer amendment (1982) to the U.S. Constitution—an amendment that proposed to place decision-making power about prayer in public school classrooms in the hands of state legislatures and local school districts. With blunt flair, Dunn exclaimed, "It is despicable demagoguery for the President to play petty politics with prayer. He knows that the Supreme Court never banned prayer in schools. It can't. Real prayer is always free." Dunn questioned whether, in an increasingly pluralistic society, citizens—fundamentalists included—would really want to turn the regulation of religious exercises over to the government. He stressed that mandatory or supervised prayer is antithetical to the Baptist tradition. For Dunn, Reagan's prayer amendment amounted to nothing more than state-sponsored prayer.

Southern Baptist fundamentalists were offended by Dunn's vituperative language directed at Reagan and angered by his public efforts to defeat the prayer amendment. He drew the ire of fundamentalists the following year when he voiced a stinging rebuke of Reagan's social agenda, specifically his proposed Human Life Amendment to constitutionally ban abortion. Dunn bemoaned that "the complex issue of abortion is reduced to the simple cry of 'infanticide' by Mr. Reagan, who would redress 'a great national wrong' in the name of civil religion, making it virtually impossible for mothers to make their own decisions in this very private, very religious matter."

To conservatives, his criticism of Reagan and his reference to mothers making their own choices sounded like a pro-choice position—support for abortion rights. Paige Patterson would later claim that abortion was *the* key issue that led to the SBC's defunding of the BJC in 1991. Whatever the case, Dunn's reticence about his personal view of abortion and his refusal to publicly embrace a pro-life (anti-abortion rights) position was enough to convince fundamentalists that he would never promote or quietly go along with their partisan political agenda. Dunn could not be controlled or silenced, and this further infuriated the fundamentalist leaders.

Dunn worked with Southern Baptist fundamentalists both to promote the Equal Access Act (1983), which supported the rights of religious student groups at public schools, and to oppose the Reagan Administration's appointment of an ambassador to the Vatican. This shared common ground on important church-state issues was not sufficient, however. Following his remarks regarding the prayer amendment, Dunn began to be attacked for his involvement on the twenty-eight-member board of People for the American Way (PFAW). In 1981, PFAW had been founded by controversial television producer Norman Lear alongside Barbara Jordan and a group of distinguished business, religious, and political leaders to counter the growing clout and divisive messages coming from Jerry Falwell, the Moral Majority, and other Religious Right leaders and organizations.

While some Baptists viewed PFAW as a broad-based coalition for First Amendment rights, Dunn's critics were convinced that it was anti-Christian. Paige Patterson, architect of the SBC fundamentalist takeover alongside Houston layman Paul Pressler, said having someone identified with both PFAW and the SBC was "like putting Sodom together with Jerusalem." The strong Catholic presence on PFAW's board, including the president of Notre Dame, Dunn noted, was evidence that PFAW was not out to undermine Christian values.

The smear campaign continued against Dunn, and he soon resigned from the PFAW board in an attempt to calm the criticisms. He did so to no avail. Russell Kaemerling, editor of the popular *Southern Baptist Advocate*, publicly questioned whether Dunn was still sympathetic with the "pornographic smut peddlers, homosexual activists and baby-killing abortionists who make up People for the American Way." Dunn stressed that his decision to leave the board did not signal a retreat from working with groups with different levels of disagreement. Working in coalitions with diverse organization had been an important aspect of Dunn's approach to political engagement since his days at the Texas Baptist CLC. He continued to emphasize that Christians must work with groups from both sides of the ideological spectrum to further the common good and defend religious liberty and church-state separation.

Southern Baptist fundamentalists were attempting to drastically alter the existing relationship between the institutions of church and state through state-sponsored prayer and legislative schemes to provide government aid to religious organizations, according to Dunn. The deliberate attempt on the part of some Southern Baptists was inexcusable, he said. With their support of public monies for sectarian schools and Reagan's prayer amendment, Dunn believed that Southern Baptists had abandoned the Baptist heritage of religious liberty and were not "real" Baptists. Real Baptists, he contended, supported universal religious freedom and embraced church-state separation, which necessitated government neutrality on religious matters.

This guilt-by-association game employed against Dunn was partially successful. From 1982–1983, two SBC state conventions passed resolutions urging the denomination to cut ties with the BJC. Momentum picked up against Dunn and the BJC as Southern Baptist fundamentalists implemented their Conservative Resurgence. They asserted that Dunn was unresponsive to the obvious concerns of rank-and-file Southern Baptists. While the BJC represented multiple Baptist bodies, it was Southern Baptists who carried the financial weight of the organization. "Resurgence" leaders demanded more accountability for their conservative (and partisan) political concerns.

At the 1984 SBC annual meeting, the fundamentalists launched their first big push to withdraw all financial support from the BJC. While this effort barely failed, the push toward severing ties continued unabated. It would take nearly eight years for the SBC to completely defund the BJC. The ties between the two groups were finally and formally severed in 1991. Throughout the defunding fight, Dunn appealed to soul freedom and the centrality of an unfettered conscience and uncoerced faith to Baptist identity. He spoke out against fundamentalism and warned that the gravest contemporary threat to soul freedom came from fundamentalists who were rapidly seizing control of the nation's largest Protestant denomination.

Some have argued that Dunn's language throughout the 1980s was unnecessarily bombastic and his personality too confrontational. Did James Dunn's rhetoric hinder him in the defense of religious liberty in the Southern Baptist Controversy? Perhaps. Surely Dunn's vituperative language against a popular sitting president, such as accusing Reagan of "despicable demagoguery," made him more foes than friends. His attacks on fundamentalism obviously did not sit well with critics. Implying that fundamentalists were like the legalistic critics of the Apostle Paul, whom Dunn dubbed as "Stupid Galatians," likely angered more than a few leaders of the Conservative Resurgence. Yet, as the memoirs of fundamentalist leader Paul Pressler reveal, the desire was always to end the SBC's relationship with the BJC. Dunn's rhetoric was a complicating factor, as were other issues like his refusal to address the subject of abortion and his willingness to work with liberal advocacy organizations like PFAW, but his strong separationist views on church-state matters were primarily why his opponents believed he could never represent them.

Dunn's language reflected who he was, and it showed that he believed it was necessary to fight a vicious threat against a precious Baptist distinctive in soul freedom. Clearly, Dunn did not remain silent or capitulate when he was convinced that conscience was at stake. Instead, he doggedly continued to appeal to soul freedom as the essence of Baptist identity and called Christians to exercise their citizenship, to practice a free and faithful politics undergirded by an unfettered conscience and with the utmost respect for the dignity and equality of all people.

While Dunn's colorful comments could be considered counterproductive at first glance, the power of rhetoric must be taken into consideration. Words can and do inspire. After the SBC severed ties, Dunn and the BJC found themselves in a financial pinch. Over a twelve-month period, the BJC had lost funding of $400,000, which represented more than 50 percent of its budget. Amid these circumstances, Dunn was able to rally moderate and progressive Southern Baptists to give directly to the religious liberty organization. Soon enough, the BJC was once again on firm financial footing, and in the process, Dunn had inspired a new generation of "free and faithful" Baptists aligned with the newly formed Cooperative Baptist Fellowship to become even more passionate about championing religious freedom. Indeed, Dunn's colorful rhetoric was much more of a help than a hindrance to his cause and the mission of the BJC.

The 1990s were a new era for Dunn and the BJC. In this post-SBC era, Dunn focused his energy on numerous church-state battles, including state-endorsed prayer, government funding of religious education and faith-based organizations, and debates over the meaning of the First Amendment's religion clauses. With the election of President Bill Clinton, Dunn found a friend—a "Baptist buddy"—in the White House who shared his vision of religious liberty and church-state philosophy.

"Two Baptists in the White House who understand our history and are committed to religious liberty and the separation of church and state offer bright hope for the future," Dunn wrote about Clinton and Vice President Al Gore following their election. "This administration will clearly oppose the use of public funds for private and parochial purposes and it will not try to tinker with the Bill of Rights to provide government-prescribed prayers for public schools."

Dunn's assessment of President Clinton turned out to be correct. The church-state landscape did indeed change. Clinton made religious liberty a high priority, meeting regularly with faith leaders to discuss ways to further the free exercise of religion. Numerous pieces of legislation were adopted by Congress and signed into law by President Clinton to advance a pro-free exercise agenda. These included the Religious Freedom Restoration Act, the Religious Liberty and Charitable Donation Protection Act of 1998, the International Religious Freedom Act, and the Parsonage Tax Exemption Act. Dunn had his hand in all of these legislative successes. He and the BJC also worked closely with the Clinton Administration to issue two groundbreaking documents to bring clarity to how individuals are allowed to exercise and express their faith in the workplace and in public schools: *Guidelines on Religious Exercise and Religious Expression in the Federal Workplace* and *Guidelines for Religious Expression in the Public Schools*.

Central to the BJC's efforts was the Equal Access Act (1983), which prohibited public schools from discriminating against student groups on the basis of their religious, political, or philosophical viewpoints. In what was a significant victory for Dunn and the BJC, the Equal Access Act withstood a constitutional challenge and was upheld by the U.S. Supreme Court (8-1) in *Westside Community Schools v. Mergens* (1990). Following the *Mergens* ruling, the BJC worked with a coalition of religious groups to develop guidelines to help schools navigate these issues, publishing a booklet addressing a wide range of questions about when student groups could meet and if teachers and outsiders could attend the meetings. These guidelines were distributed to every public high school principal in the United States as well as to school boards, teachers, parents, and religious groups.

Meanwhile, Dunn and the BJC fended off a barrage of school prayer proposals as they did in the 1980s. Shortly after senators Jesse Helms (NC) and Strom Thurmond (SC), both Southern Baptist laymen, introduced school prayer legislation, the *Dallas Morning News* published a 1,700-word profile of Dunn titled "Soul Freedom Fighter: Leader of Baptist Advocacy Group Battles School Prayer Amendment." In response to these proposals, Dunn led the BJC to adopt a statement on school prayer that read,

> Prayer is a holy act that government should not control. We reject the notion that government bureaucrats and public school teachers, who may

not share our faith or any faith, should be entrusted or saddled with our children's spiritual formation. . . . We do not want government telling our children when, where and what to pray. Prayer should be left to churches, families and students themselves.

To refute the popular claim that prayer and God had been kicked out of public schools, Dunn and the BJC led a group of thirty-five religious and civil liberties groups to produce a consensus statement in 1995 on what the law says about religion in public schools. On the subject of school prayer, the document explained that public school students have the right to pray individually or in groups or to discuss their religious views with peers in a nondisruptive manner. After the document's release, President Clinton directed Secretary of Education Richard Riley to provide public school districts across the country with an explanation of the religious expression permitted under the law. Riley's guidelines borrowed heavily from the consensus statement that the BJC helped draft.

During the 1990s, Dunn and the BJC also worked to defeat voucher proposals. In his monthly columns and public speeches, Dunn continued to assail "voucher schemes," arguing that voucher programs were unconstitutional, undemocratic, unfair, uneconomic, and destructive. He also fought off "religious freedom" amendments such as one repeatedly put forward by Rep. Ernest Istook of Oklahoma, a Mormon and Baylor University alumnus. Istook's amendment aimed to open the door to state funding of religious institutions. Dunn lambasted the Istook amendment in a widely read column titled "If You Like Tax-Supported Evangelism, You'll Love Rep. Istook's Proposal." As the Religious Right united behind the Istook amendment, opponents formed the Coalition to Preserve Religious Liberty to coordinate efforts. The BJC co-chaired this coalition, and its efforts were eventually successful as the Istook amendment fell short of the required two-thirds majority needed in the House to pass. Dunn hailed the vote as a victory over what he dubbed the "Religious Tyranny Amendment."

While addressing and searching for a solution to complex church-state issues, Dunn continued to advocate tirelessly on behalf of soul freedom throughout the 1990s. Among Baptists, there was no single individual who wrote and spoke more about the necessity of an unfettered conscience and uncoerced faith than Dunn. He preached soul freedom to all Baptists and practiced a free and faithful politics in the public square. He challenged Baptists to respond to pluralism by being "faithful" rather than creedal. Being faithful, according to Dunn, entailed a greater dependence on the

Bible with a focus on Christ's greatest command to love one's neighbors, on fervent prayer, and on responsibility. As Dunn often said and wrote, "Every freedom carries responsibility piggyback."

Dunn emphasized the centrality of soul freedom to Baptist faith and practice in his column in the BJC's newsletter, *Report from the Capital.* Thousands across the Baptist spectrum read this column each month. He reminded readers that religion is vital in America "precisely because it is voluntary" and that "bona fide Baptists" will always stand for soul freedom and religious liberty. Despite "silly second-guessing," said Dunn, soul freedom is "still vital for Baptists." This common refrain made its way into many of Dunn's sermons, speeches, columns, and other writings throughout the 1990s.

In 1999, Dunn retired from his position as executive director of the BJC after nearly twenty years of service. This was more of a transition than an actual retirement, however. Dunn would leave the position to become a visiting professor at the new Wake Forest University School of Divinity. At a dinner in his honor on October 4, 1999, Dunn's efforts on behalf of soul freedom, religious liberty, and church-state separation were remembered by many notable Baptist leaders. President Clinton attended and paid tribute to his colorful friend. "Our country's a better place because of you," Clinton said. "Our religious liberties are more secure because of you."

Dunn's longtime friend Bill Moyers followed Clinton with a powerful tribute. "James Dunn belongs to a long train of Baptists who have struggled—and often suffered—for a free church in a free state," Moyers said. "Baptists have never had a more savvy master of the legislative process, where the most offensive infringement of religious liberty can be inflicted in fine print no one else bothers to read until it's too late."

At the dinner, Dunn joked to the crowd of more than 275 friends and colleagues that some of the kind words of tribute reminded him of a eulogy. "I am Dunn, but I'm not yet finished," he said. Certainly, Dunn was not done, as he would continue to travel the country speaking in hundreds of pulpits over the next fifteen years. From 2000 until his death on July 4, 2015, Dunn taught students about issues at the intersection of Christianity, ethics, and public policy at Wake Forest's divinity school. In 2011, the James and Marilyn Dunn Chair of Baptist Studies was established at the School of Divinity, and Dunn's longtime friend, Bill Leonard, the school's founding dean, was appointed as the first recipient.

Throughout his professional ministry, spanning seven decades and more than sixty-one years (1954–2015), James M. Dunn offered Baptists a paradigm for engagement in the political arena. He did so as a pastor, ethicist, and activist. He modeled for Baptists how to apply their Christianity in the public square on church-state issues as well as a wide variety of important social issues. He offered a vision of religious liberty and practiced and preached a free and faithful politics grounded in a commitment to an unfettered conscience and uncoerced faith. Dunn personally demonstrated how to fight forces that threaten these biblical freedoms. He taught generations of Baptists (as well as non-Baptists) the importance of soul freedom and the necessity of vigorous support for and defense of religious liberty and church-state separation.

Dunn loudly and persistently called on Baptists to live out their Christian citizenship and become active advocates in their community, state, and nation. "Every Christian a lobbyist" was one of his mottoes. Again, he consistently (and persistently) preached that responsibility "rode piggyback" to soul freedom and required Christians to speak up and be counted.

Dunn's linking of soul freedom to the social gospel (or social justice) is an example worthy of emulation by present and future generations of Baptists. It is a message worthy of consideration for all who profess the early Christian affirmation that *Jesus Christ is Lord*. It is also an example that destroys the claim that a commitment to soul freedom ultimately cripples the ability of Christians to collectively confront the social ills that ail society. Soul freedom, Dunn insisted, required social action and shunned inaction. On countless occasions, he declared, "You could be wrong but you can't be quiet. You can't just up and let the other forces that would hurt people have their way."

Dunn knew his view of freedom was controversial and could be abused. Being Baptist is messy at times. Despite the messiness, Dunn believed being free and faithful is worth the risk because soul freedom is rooted in the nature of God and found in the Bible.

In a day when creedal conformity and partisan politics tends to define Baptists more than ever and when the focus on community often neglects the biblical and historic focus on the individual, Dunn's message of soul freedom still needs to be heard. When those who claim the name "Baptist" question whether Muslims should enjoy religious freedom, and when they align themselves with xenophobic, sexist, and racist voices seeking the restoration of America's greatness, Dunn's vision of religious liberty and free and faithful politics should be re-affirmed, practiced, and loudly preached. Without a doubt, the life and ministry of James M. Dunn captures the vibrant witness of Baptists in the past and reveals that Baptists do indeed have much to offer for the future of authentic Christian faith.

—Adapted from Aaron D. Weaver,
James M. Dunn and Soul Freedom
(Smyth & Helwys Publishing, 2011)

Soul Freedom and Baptist Identity

Ideas such as soul liberty and soul competency, trumpeted frequently in Baptist history, found a home in the thought, rhetoric, and ministry of James Dunn. During his tenure at the Baptist Joint Committee, Dunn became the public heir of E. Y. Mullins and Baptist leaders before him who insisted that soul freedom was the cornerstone of a faithful Baptist identity. His advocacy for religious liberty and the separation of church and state was especially rooted in his understanding of soul freedom.

While prominent early twentieth century Southern Baptists like Mullins and George W. Truett referred to "soul competency," Dunn used the earlier Baptist language of "soul freedom."[1] Dunn believed that soul freedom was based on a biblical view of people. In the creation account of Adam and Eve (Gen 1:26-27), God called the first humans *imago Dei*, which presupposed freedom. The classic doctrine of soul freedom reveals that people, made by God, can respond to their Creator. "The roots of freedom are deep within the intimate personhood of God," Dunn wrote in the book *Soul Freedom: Baptist Battle Cry* (Smyth & Helwys Publishing, 2000). "All true freedom is in a real sense religious freedom. It is that which replicates the Divine in all of us that makes use *response-able*, responsible and free."

God created and endowed all humankind to be free moral agents. "We are wired up with a chooser and we live with the consequences of those decisions," according to Dunn.[2] "Every freedom, every decision, every deliberate direction taken has certain consequences and invokes some level of [individual] responsibility," he wrote.[3] Freedom and responsibility are indissoluble, and without responsibility, he said, freedom is meaningless, directionless anarchy without accountability.[4] He reasoned that soul freedom and individual responsibility were not invented by government or manufactured by social contract. Rather, all dignity and respect afforded to people comes from God as revealed in Scriptures.[5]

Dunn's view of soul freedom is far reaching and extends well beyond personal morality and personal faith. As the ultimate source of all modern notions of human rights, soul freedom is the cornerstone that precedes and demands religious liberty for all people in the political arena. It is the biblical and theological starting point from which religious liberty naturally follows. "If we all, in some serious way, replicate God, religious liberty is a moral and social inevitability," he wrote.[6]

Genuine faith cannot be coerced by the government. "Unless religion is free, voluntary, personal, intimate and inward, it's not worth anything anyways," Dunn said. Without a truly voluntary faith, individuals may well be kept from an authentic "vital, visceral, life-changing faith."[7]

Dunn's advocacy for an unfettered conscience and uncoerced faith led him to oppose creeds because of their threat to freedom. Like Mullins and other Baptists before him, Dunn noted that creeds were inappropriate prescriptions for what one must believe. He decried creeds as "the necessary requirement to squeeze in and squeak by some theological gate."[8] Confessional statements were not helpful, he said, because they often functioned as creeds, weaponized to ensure doctrinal purity and exclude individuals and groups with differing beliefs. The only confession needed, Dunn emphasized, was the early Christian affirmation that *Jesus Christ is Lord*. "If we have anything remotely resembling a creed, it is the Baptist oral tradition that insists, 'Ain't nobody but Jesus gonna tell me what to believe,'" Dunn preached.[9]

Not surprisingly, Dunn's understanding of soul freedom has received its share of criticism. Critics have accused Dunn as well as Mullins of promoting a radical form of unbounded individualism—faith without authority. Nearly sixty years ago, historian Winthrop Hudson stated that "the practical effect of the stress upon 'soul competency' as the cardinal doctrine of Baptists was to make everyone's hat their own church."[10] Other scholars have followed Hudson's lead, making sweeping claims against the excessive individualism they find in Mullins and Dunn in attempts to chastise Baptists for a poor social ethic or a weak ecclesiology.[11]

Dunn repeatedly refuted critics who claimed that soul freedom led to a hyper-individualistic lone-ranger Christianity. He labeled the dichotomy of individual and community as a false one and contended that the desire for community presupposed voluntary faith. The choice was not one over the other but both together:

> The competence of the individual before God does not demand and in fact precludes Lone Ranger religion. . . . no matter what critics left and right must say, autonomous individualism . . . does not mean that everyone's church is one's own hat. The longing for community and social

Christianity presupposes voluntarism. Without individual autonomy, there can be no authentic community.[12]

Dunn consistently emphasized that Christian experience was always under the authority of Jesus Christ as revealed in the Bible. Experience does not provide extrabiblical or "anything goes" knowledge of God. As Dunn said, "real Baptists still test Scripture by Jesus Christ."[13] Of course, Dunn understood that soul freedom could be abused, but he strongly believed that the freedom inherent in biblically grounded individualism—a voluntary personal relationship with Jesus Christ—was well worth the cost.

James Dunn's writings in this section offer a more in-depth look at his understanding of soul freedom and his vision of Baptist identity. Dunn's articles here reveal the centrality of an unfettered conscience to his theology as well as his understanding of the political implications of an uncoerced faith. Freedom and responsibility go together, he often said. This is one theme found throughout Dunn's writings and speeches.

The Baptist Vision of Religious Liberty

In what is one of his most important written articulations on the subject, James Dunn describes the Baptist vision of religious liberty. This article was published in Proclaiming the Baptist Vision: Religious Liberty, *a book of essays edited by renowned Baptist historian Walter B. Shurden. Dunn's concise overview presents a vision of religious liberty that begins with soul freedom as the "biblical and theological starting point" and ends with church-state separation as the "logical, theological, and political consequence of a faith that springs from soul freedom and extends religious liberty to all."*

> Then God said, "Let us make humankind in our image, according to our likeness; and let them have dominion over the fish of the sea, and over the birds of the air, and over the cattle, and over all the wild animals of the earth, and over every creeping thing that creeps upon the earth."
> So, God created humankind in his image, in the image of God he created them; male and female he created them. (Gen 1:26-27)

Drop a pebble in a pond. Watch the ripples. Concentric circles go out from the center. That spot takes on life. Energy emanates.

That little snapshot symbolizes the Baptist vision of religious liberty. It is a dynamic vision; there is nothing static about it. Baptists see religious liberty as springing from and directly related to the center of the divine-human encounter.

Soul Freedom

Using this pebble-in-the-pond graphic, see the point of impact as the investment of the divine image in all humankind. It is the moment Michelangelo captured with God touching the finger of the first human being. The center circle represents that point of contact.

Genesis 1:26-27 is not a bad place to start. No matter how one reads the Genesis account, it clearly suggests that we mere mortals are moral beings, capable of responding to God. The Adam and Eve story makes no sense at all if an actual response to the Creator was not possible.

Whether one's look at Genesis is the most literal or the most liberal, human beings are able to respond to God. Response-able. Responsible! See where that word came from. If all earthlings are responsible, a certain freedom follows.

That freedom we Baptists call soul freedom. It precedes and goes beyond the Reformation's concept of the priesthood of all believers. Soul freedom is universal. It is the inherent dimension of humanity that invests dignity and worth.

The late F. J. Sheed wrote, "In the Christian view, being a man is itself so vast a thing, that the natural inequalities from one man to the next are a trifle by comparison."[14] Forgive the brother for being born before genderless language, but his point is clear. Maybe we should be reminded by Dorothy L. Sayers's probing book of essays, *Are Women Human?*[15] that being human is "the vast thing."

Soul freedom and the concept of free moral agency from the Baptist point of view finds our volitional capacity written into our being. We are programmed to be choosers. Our software requires it.

The freedom-responsibility aspect of human nature is like a coin; no matter how thin it's sliced it still has both sides. The faces of the free moral agency coin are indissolubly joined. Every freedom, every decision, every deliberate direction taken has certain consequences and invokes some level of responsibility. Every responsibility, every "oughtness," every duty implies some freedom to choose. God did not make puppets, automatons, but persons in the divine image.

Still, in the first small circle, if the pebble dropped in the pond represents the way the Creator meant for us to be, the debates on the divine design have filled libraries, plagued philosophers, and been the excuse for all manner of earthy conflict. The purpose of this modest sally is not to join that battle.

Here one simply argues by assertion that the biblical estimate of humankind is the starting point for understanding religious liberty. If one presupposes creatures made somehow like God—persons, deciders, choosers—then precisely that construction demands freedom.

Every inclusive "whosoever" in the Scripture from Genesis to Revelation suggests not only the personal ability to decide for oneself but a biblical necessity for individual choices. Hear again the closing invitation of Holy Scripture: "The Spirit and the bride say, 'Come.' And let everyone who hears say, 'Come.' And let everyone who is thirsty come. Let anyone *who wishes* take the water of life as a gift" (Rev 22:17, emphasis added).

This assessment of the human condition is a search for the roots of religious liberty. The competence of the individual before God precedes reformation thought because it is rooted, not merely in Scripture, but in the nature and being of God. Made in God's image, we can and must respond. Even not to respond is a response.

God made human beings with a faculty no other can control. The "I" at the center of our being even Almighty God will not trample.

For all who practice an experiential religion, the encounter with Jesus Christ finds the image of God, though marred and effaced, restored. Coming to Christ is the defining moment that ripples out, shapes and changes all of life that follows.

The "new creature" in Christ is touched by the finger of God just as Adam was pictured in Michelangelo's Sistine Chapel. The experiences of the new birth are not simply another event on the cafeteria line of choices but the hinge in our personal history. In coming to God through Christ, we are becoming who we were meant to be. It is precisely "for freedom Christ has set us free" (Gal 5:1).

And so, Baptists understand soul freedom, value it, and are determined to share it with others.

Religious Liberty

The second circle that ripples out is religious liberty. If the center of the ripples represents the way we are made and made over and if the rock hitting the water pictures the soul freedom invested in every last human being replicating God, then religious liberty is in the first order of consequences.

Soul freedom is the biblical and theological starting point and religious liberty naturally follows. If we all, in some serious way, replicate God, religious liberty is a moral and social inevitability.

All Christian missions and evangelism and ethics are predicated upon religious liberty. Without religious liberty are ethical choices meaningful? One could say "yes" to every challenge to "do right," but if saying "no" is not an option what merit are all the yeses?

We invite others to follow Christ with the firm belief that led by God's Spirit they can decide to do so. The whole missionary venture is built upon the assumption (biblically and theologically sound, it seems) that lives can be changed and that folks must freely follow the Lord. We preach that we come to Christ freely or not really. Coercion means hypocrites, not believers.

The Bible mandates faithful proclamation of religious liberty. How can anyone experience God and fail to share that relationship? Even so, the freedom fire that burns in the belly of every Baptist cannot be contained.

We can all say, "I have found the Messiah." And because we can, we must. We understand, in our innards at least, that being made in God's image makes us free and responsible. That understanding, however intuitive and visceral, must also be passed along.

The Golden Rule, no less, makes salespeople of all true Baptists for religious liberty. "In everything, do to others as you would have them do to you" (Matt 7:12). If anyone's religious liberty is denied, everyone's religious liberty is endangered. That's not simply a nice slogan. It is the truth! It describes the reality of any people trying to coexist: some slave, some free. If the powers and principalities can deny or try to deny religious liberty to your neighbor, watch out. You may be next.

It's axiomatic then that Baptists care not simply for their own freedom but for the full freedom of religion for all people. We care even, maybe especially, for those with whom we disagree most. That tests our sincerity.

Historically, it has been true. Roger Williams and John Clarke, Baptist founders in Rhode Island, insisted upon opening the colony to all. Jews and Quakers built houses of worship in Newport when no one else would welcome them. Authentic Baptists to this day see religious liberty as a human right. The best brand of Baptists has a track record of defending human rights through the Baptist World Alliance, the United Nations, and the ballot box in this country with national leaders of courage and insight.

Baptists have also played an important role in political guarantees for religious liberty. The role of such Baptists in the revolutionary/constitutional period like Samuel Stillman, James Manning, and Isaac Backus needs to be retold and retold. They led the struggle to see to it that the United States would have a Bill of Rights. John Leland joined that fight in Virginia. Can one imagine a preacher wearing a label "Baptist" and not knowing and telling often the story of these heroes of our freedom? Is it possible that any Baptist pastor would not do the homework necessary to speak with authority on the Baptist contribution to religious liberty? If so, shame! To walk past a sign that says "Baptist" and not proclaim liberty from the pulpit of a church so tagged constitutes false advertising. To fail to be in touch with the tap roots of religious freedom suggests a certain deadness of the Spirit and the spirit of Baptists.

The flame that burns brightly to "proclaim liberty throughout the land to all its inhabitants" (Lev 25:10) is fueled by knowing the Bible, sharing its message, acting out our faith, and loving God's people. Because we live in a specific time and place, because we are citizens of two kingdoms, and because we must find ways to translate love into justice, a dedication to religious liberty needs hands and feet. The essential corollary of religious liberty, therefore, is the separation of church and state.

Separation of Church and State

As certainly as night follows day, the third circle out from the center in our preaching pond is church-state separation. It is the logical, theological, and political consequence of a faith that springs from soul freedom and extends religious liberty to all. How can that happen? What must be done with government to assure genuine religious freedom for all? How do a people shape the structures of society to secure liberty?

The founders, heavily influenced by Baptists, were not satisfied with the United States Constitution until a Bill of Rights was added. It may be a stretch to find church-state separation as we know it in the Bible as George W. Truett did. But it's certainly compatible with biblical principles.

Truett, longtime pastor of the First Baptist Church of Dallas, Texas, preaching on the East steps of the United States Capitol on May 1920, says:

> To Baptists the New Testament also clearly teaches that Christ's Church is not only a spiritual body but it is also a pure democracy, all its members being equal, a local congregation, and cannot subject itself to any outside control.... In the very nature of the case there must be no union between church and state, because their nature and functions are utterly different. Jesus stated the principle in the two sayings, "My kingdom is not of this

world," and "Render therefore unto Caesar the things which are Caesar's and unto God the things that are God's."

Confusion reigns today around the phrase "separation of church and state." It clearly does not mean separation of God and government. It's not separation of Christians from their citizenship, nor does it mean separation of politics from religion.

Some Baptists fear engagement with the world so much that they would withdraw from contact with the "ungodly." Others have such a triumphal attitude that they think they can use the state to advance God's kingdom. Appropriate distance between the institutions of government and organized religion is to be desired. Separation of church and state has been good for the church and good for the state. Separation is not neat. It's messy, difficult, inconsistent, and it always has been.

Separation is not obsolete. Today more than ever it is important to apply proper tensions between an invasive, intrusive government and religious institutions which are also concerned with all of life. Government often favors religion when it should leave it alone. Churches appeal for state assistance without counting the cost. When government meddles in religion it always has the touch of mud.

Separation is not complete. Martin Marty suggests that the wall of separation has become a "zone." Stephen Carter sees the wall with "many doors in it." They are probably correct. Yet somehow there must remain a distinction, a distance even if the wall is no more than a strand of "barbed wire."

One need simply to look at the relationships of church-state anywhere else in the world to realize the essentiality of church-state separation to religious liberty. With state churches and church-states, freedom vanishes. Even with mild and minimal establishment as in the United Kingdom and Scandinavia, vital religion is watered down. Without the distance between these two institutions that leaves both free, both suffer.

Neither church nor state should be caught in the bear hug of the other. So, perhaps, Truett was right after all: church-state separation may be clearly implied in biblical truth. It certainly flows naturally as a ripple from the impact of soul freedom.

If God made us free and responsible and if God's divine intention is for that liberty to be shared, extended to every soul longing for liberation, then following the biblical design for church and state, both as ordained of God, is the way to go.

Some poet, unknown to me, had it right:

Let Caesar's dues be paid
To Caesar and his throne;
But consciences and souls were made
To be the Lord's alone.

—Reprinted with permission courtesy of Smyth & Helwys Publishing.

No Freedom for the Soul with a Creed

Throughout his ministry, James Dunn stressed that the only acceptable "creed" a Christian should embrace is the living faith exclamation that Jesus is Lord. Dunn makes his popular case against creeds in the article below from the book Stand with Christ: Why Missionaries Can't Sign the 2000 Baptist Faith and Message *(Smyth & Helwys Publishing, 2002). He shared this message countless times in sermons, speeches, and written publications while championing soul freedom. A version of this article first appeared in a book he co-authored with Grady C. Cothen titled* Soul Freedom: Baptist Battle Cry *(Smyth & Helwys Publishing, 2000).*

A creed *prescribes* while a confession of faith *describes* one's approach to religion. A creed is the necessary requirement to squeeze in and squeak by some theological gate.

We Baptists previously have had no catechistic tests for believers. No acceptance of four or four hundred spiritual laws gets one right with God. Neither does swearing allegiance to the 2000 *Baptist Faith and Message*. Repentance and faith, a personal experience of God's grace—not intellectual assent to arguments—saves. It is a spiritual transaction. God's spirit is involved. We have no moral creed.

Even believing and behaving according to code is not in itself redemptive. We "do right" because we *have been saved*, not *to be* saved. We certainly should have no political creed. That is in large measure what produced the first Baptists by that name: a dogged dedication to religious freedom.

Non-creedalism drives some folks mad. Always has. The Apostle Paul had that problem with early Christians in Galatia. He called them stupid, senseless, foolish, idiots (various translations of Galatians 3:1). He reminded them that "it is precisely for freedom that Christ has set you free" (Galatians 5:1)—soul freedom backed up biblically.

Then in Galatians 5:12, he suggested radical surgery for the legalist who could not live without a rulebook religion. Then and now, rationalism reduces religion to rules. Those who clung to the past saw Paul as a no-law man, an antinomian. Their twenty-first-century successors still libel with labels, striking out at those whom they do not understand. A living faith is hard to take. It just literally drives some people crazy.

Creedlessness makes some true believers sad. He said, "I just cannot believe a thing I cannot understand." Poor little fellow.

One's bucket of religion and spirituality is very small if it holds only what one "knows." In the mix of faith and reason, reason has a useful role. It explains or tries to, interprets, sells, and sometimes satisfies. However, if one's capacity for the divine dimension is limited by rational bounds, his or her pail is too small. There are tons of spiritual stuff none of us can get our puny minds around. Whether limited by scientism like some liberals or by rational fundamentalism like some conservatives, the creed-chained character is pitiable.

A binding creed can turn pious people bad. The philosopher Pascal said, "Men never do evil so fully, so happily, as when they do it for conscience's sake."

One need not look at any day's lead news stories to see how hatred, hostility, and violence feed on religious fundamentalism. Other factors—economic, political, and cultural—are involved, but rigid religion makes people as mean as Tasmanian devils out of otherwise decent disciples. Look at the Middle East, the Balkans, India, Northern Ireland, and on and on. Who wants to fight and kill over propositions in the light of the grace God offers?

A living faith not bound by creed makes Baptists glad. It's love not law, faith not fact, persons not propositions, experience with God not expectations of persons at the heart of free and faithful Baptists and all believers of whatever brand. In the blessed absence of a creed, the confession of faith common to Baptists looms large: Jesus Christ is the Lord. That ancient confession is historically potent, theologically eclectic, spiritually significant, religiously accessible, biblically sound, and humanly available. It is enough.

How can a creedless Christianity avoid "I-come-to-the-garden-alone" subjective religion? Doesn't faith without a rational checklist become nothing more than C. S. Lewis's "tickle around the gizzard"? Can a rope of sand bind together believers of the same bent?

Dangers abound. Soul freedom is a risky route. Experiment is close to the essence of experiential Christianity.

Yet the risks are worth taking. The very meaning of "faith" is inextricably entangled in the Baptist brand of belief that insists upon an intimate individual religious commitment. We stay under the umbrella of traditional Christianity. So far, at least, we Baptists have gotten by with this perilous practice of soul freedom with four substantial flying buttresses propping up the churches.

One is a radical Christ-centrism, the Christian doctrine, growing out of the radical monotheism that makes us such soul brothers and sisters with Jewish friends. That high and practical Christology takes seriously the words from 1 Timothy 2:5, "one mediator between God and all humankind." The same noble notion of an immanent and immediate friendship with Jesus sometimes slides into "WWJD"[16] ethical temperature-taking. That's inadequate.

Then, there is, has been, is likely to be a reliance upon the Bible. Even a "liberal Baptist," an oxymoron, insists upon the authority of Scripture and argues that the written record of God's revelation is the "sole rule for faith and practice." The failure to buy the buzz word "inerrancy" hardly makes anyone a Bible-basher.

Another support for the centrality of soul freedom is the insistence on and acceptance of a regenerate church membership. If, indeed, one touts soul freedom for herself, she cannot escape granting it to all other born-again believers. This builds a fellowship of mutual respect, acceptance, and shared pilgrimage. Church members can support, empathize, even admonish and correct one another.

Finally, it must be admitted that one of the safeguards against utter subjectivism on the part of free souls has been the social system, the cultural props, the common-denominator identity that all Christians have in the civil-religion-shaped nation. A culture-wide comfort zone has shielded many believers of all stripes from hard questions and tough decisions about their personal faith. The day in which one could say, "Of course I'm a Christian—I'm an American, aren't I?" is gone.

The pluralism, multiculturalism, and secularism (at its best and at its worst) that we know today requires us to rethink our deepest held beliefs. Soul freedom is certainly one of those beliefs for Baptists.

That soul freedom demands personal interaction and responsibility. Abstract propositions, however true or however close to The Truth, are not enough.

"I know whom I have believed." That's the Scripture (2 Timothy 1:12). Those are the words of the 1883 gospel song by Daniel W. Whittle, not "I know *what* I believe."

J. M. Dawson, first executive of the Baptist Joint Committee, once told me that he and George W. Truett consider themselves "Christian personalists." That terminology seems odd today, but the need for that brand of believer is great.

In fact, one cannot comprehend historic Baptists' passion for religious liberty without catching the intensely personal fever of their faith. It's not so much whether their beliefs are literal or liberal as that they are personal that counts.

The intensely personal nature of biblical faith is a Baptist birthmark. Frank Louis Mauldin has tried to help us catch on in *The Classic Baptist Heritage of Personal Truth* (Providence House Publishers, 1999); "The Truth as It Is in Jesus" is the subtitle. The book contributes significantly to understanding Baptists and our hot-eyed, narrow-minded, loud-mouthed defense of religious liberty and her theological sister, soul freedom.

We have no book quite like this one. It examines and celebrates the biblical and the historic Baptist understanding of personal truth. We have books that explain Baptist faith and practice, others that consider Baptist history, and still more that examine a particular theological or denominational issue. But no other book undertakes the avowed fourfold purpose of (1) identifying and analyzing the distinctive notion of personal truth, (2) demonstrating the existence of a classic Baptist heritage of truth, (3) understanding what it means for Baptists in the classic heritage to equate truth with "the truth that is in Jesus," and (4) making the case that the story of personal truth (along with the stories of faith and freedom) constitutes the soul—the essential core and the common ground—of Baptist identity and integrity.

I heard a propositionalist testify: "I just cannot believe anything that I cannot understand." In this book, Mauldin offers an antidote for that faith-threatening poison. The book and its biblical concept of incarnational truth also save us from the ditches on either side of the Christian way: *sola scriptura* on one side and *sola fide* on the other.

Mauldin documents and demonstrates that Baptists have always majored on experiential religion informed by the "Holy Word of God" and quickened by God's Spirit. The author says it all when he affirms that "Baptists . . . defend the thesis that truth is someone real, not something true." Jesus said, "I am the way, the truth and the life." One who reads this book may discover what a Baptist is.

Baptists are not alone in this dogged focus on personal faith. In 1972, Richard R. Niebuhr probed and provided a theoretical basis for belief, for affection rooted in religious experience. In the afterword of his book *Experiential Religion* he writes, "Human faith is not so much a sum of answers as it is a way of seeing and acting, and books about faith have first of all to describe what faithful men see and believe to be real."

Mauldin brings us one of those "books about faith" which does just that. John P. Newport in his foreword to the book calls it "a unique and important book." Newport acknowledges that Professor Mauldin's "emphasis on the fact that biblical truth is relational is very important."

Walter B. Shurden hits the same note, but denies that Baptist personalism is privatism or "Lone Ranger" religion. "To insist," says Shurden, "that saving faith is personal not impersonal, relational not ritualistic, direct not indirect, private not corporate has never meant for Baptists that the Christian life is a privatized disengagement from either the church or society." Even Walter Rauschenbusch, father of the Social Gospel Movement, gave "experiential religion" as his first reason for being Baptist. Authentic faith requires soul freedom. One who has maneuvered and manipulated to mouth some counterfeit confession not profoundly personal is in danger of losing his immortal soul.

It's *who*, not *what*, we believe that makes us Christian.

—Reprinted with permission courtesy of Smyth & Helwys Publishing.

Called to Be Perpetually Indignant Prophets

James Dunn gave the following address—titled "The Call to be Indignant Prophets"—at New Orleans Baptist Theological Seminary on March 7, 1990. In this address, delivered at an SBC seminary just as Southern Baptist fundamentalists were months away from securing full control over the denomination, Dunn describes soul freedom as "the essence of what it means to be Baptist." He lifts up E. Y. Mullins as a Baptist prophet who gave the Baptist family an "outline of a common minimalist Baptist theology" in his influential book The Axioms of Religion *(1908). Dunn urges Baptists to remain dedicated* to defending religious freedom and to remember the call in Galatians 5:1 to "Stand fast therefore in the liberty wherewith Christ hath made us free."

Jesus would have liked Mexican food, jalapeños, Blue Bell ice cream, and boiling hot chicory coffee. "I know thy works," he said, "that thou art neither cold nor hot: I would thou were cold or hot. So then because thou art lukewarm, and neither cold nor hot, I will spew thee out of my mouth" (Rev 3:15-16).

Moderate may mean merely medium. Temperateness can be tepidity. The worst thing about being called moderate might be that the tag is true. If we moderated the hymnal, we could sing,

"My Jesus, I *like* thee,"
"*Some* to Jesus I surrender,"
"*Appealing* grace,"
"Take my life and let *me* be,"
"How *meaningful* thou art," and
"It is *okay* with my *psyche*."

Baptists have been, at least on one side of the family, a part of the radical reformation, not the reasonable reformation. Our forebears fought for freedom, not toleration. They insisted upon separation of church and state, not cozy cohabitation.

One common characteristic of Baptist saints was their capacity for outrage. Thomas Helwys, Roger Williams, Isaac Backus, John Leland, even the irenic George W. Truett could be righteously indignant.

Our culture values "cool." Emotion for a cause is out. "Controversial" is a dirty word. Look upon the sad soulless shells of former men who must consider the "controversiality quotient" of every utterance before it escapes their lips. Have you ever known a noncontroversial practitioner of religious liberty?

One fears being thought defensive. Yet in the Baptist heritage there are treasures to defend. Could it be that much has been lost for want of fearless defenders of our inheritance?

One does not want to feel guilty or induce guilt. The police manacled and hauled away a man in downtown Chicago a few years ago for doing nothing more than standing on a downtown corner pointing at passersby and saying in stentorian tone, "Guilty." Was it in fact a profound guilt that denied his freedom to preach this universal reality?

Have you noticed that civic righteousness committees have disappeared? So has righteous indignation. One dreads being thought righteous.

Indignation is out of the question. The sense of one's own soul is so diminished that the requisite confidence for indignation has vanished.

Let us pray that we will not be mediocre or medium or moderate.

Ordinary Baptists can be turned into timid doubters by blusterers who have no grasp of the roots of religious liberty. Yet it was a man who saw himself an ordinary Baptist who lined out in lay language the essence of what it means to be Baptist. Edgar Young Mullins gave all Baptists a snapshot of soul freedom in his book *The Axioms of Religion*.

E. Y. Mullins, accepted as a spokesman by Baptists of the North and South, also possessed the perpetual indignation that marks all prophets. It may be that the only quality most of us have in common with the prophets of God through the ages is the ability to get riled. May we harness that trait as holy rage, moral energy even as ordinary mortals.

Perhaps we have forgotten what an ordinary Baptist is. The common attributes are outlined in *The Axioms of Religion*. And because that is who we are and why we are Baptists, we had better not forget them.

Mullins's axioms cohere. His argument is compelling because it is biblically sound, historically accurate, and sociologically useful. In fact, one must at least attempt to glimpse a "Mullins'-eye view" of Baptists to comprehend our present turmoil.

The principles Mullins set out are probably the most user-friendly outline of a common, minimalist Baptist theology. These maxims indisputably describe the Baptist dedication to religious freedom and the separation of church and state.

One reason some people who are called Baptist can behave totally "unbaptistically" is that they have Puritan rather than Baptist roots. One cause of confusion among Baptists over the separation of church and state is the false belief that the distinctively American doctrine came from secular sources rather than theological principles shared widely by disparate Baptists. A malignant civil religion would allow government-prescribed worship in public schools, tax support for parochial schools, federal funding for church nurseries, and the hollow and unfounded claims that this is a "Christian nation." One occasion for this apparent revisionism is the failure to appreciate the importance of religious freedom to missions. All real evangelism is predicated upon the possibility of a free and meaningful acceptance of the gospel message. One comes to Christ freely or not really. The more one is genuinely dedicated to sharing the Christian faith, the more he jealously defends full-orbed freedom.

Mullins, the prophet, hurled a bolt of quintessential Baptist doctrine into both the larger conventions [Northern Baptist Convention and the Southern Baptist Convention] at the beginning of this century. His propositions were warmly and widely accepted. The consensus that emerged kept Baptists from tearing each other apart in the Fundamentalist-Modernist controversy that wrecked many denominations in the first third of the century. The guidelines for being Baptist that he proffered also allowed Baptists to focus on experiential religion, proclamation of the gospel, practical Christianity, mission and ministry because we were not warring over orthodoxy a la Europe. But the point of this message is that *The Axioms of Religion* is descriptive of what is most Baptist about us and that church-state separation is a corollary to that core commitment. The axioms are simply stated:

1. "The *theological* axiom: The holy and loving God has a right to be sovereign."[17] As Bill Leonard says, "God is free; freedom begins with God."[18] All freedom is ultimately religious freedom.

2. "The *religious* axiom":[19] "Every human being is free to come directly to God."[20]

3. "The *ecclesiastical* axiom: All believers have a right to equal privileges in the church."[21]

4. "The *moral* axiom: To be responsible man [sic] must be free."[22]

5. "The *religio-civic* axiom: A free Church in a free State."[23]

6. "The *social axiom*: Love your neighbor as yourself."[24] Personal freedom has communal implications.

The implications of these axioms are inextricably related to the practical, case-specific demands for church-state separation in the trenches. One brings to the political dimension of church-state relations theological presuppositions. These theological underpinnings for church-state policy also reflect on our "baptistness" or, in some instances, our "unbaptistness."

The importance of the individual interpretation of Scripture is a Baptist hallmark. Swedish Baptists were disparagingly called *lazare* (readers). They dared to read the Bible for themselves and so were jailed, hounded, and deported. Some today would impose a crude creedalism. Church and state have jailed Baptists for resisting creeds. "Where the Spirit of the Lord is, there is liberty" (2 Cor 3:17). There are those who would usurp the teaching role of the Holy Spirit.

The priesthood of all believers is a biblical and Reformation doctrine that Baptists give an additional spin, heightening concepts that come with soul freedom and the competency of the individual before God. Yet there are those who are apparently troubled by what they see as the "undermining of pastoral authority," and they appeal for obedience and submission to one's pastor to keep unbridled personal priesthood in check.[25] Thomas Helwys got in trouble for asserting, "The king is a mortall man, and not God therefore hath no power over ye immortall soules of his subjects, to make lawes and ordinances for them, and to set spirituall Lords over them."[26]

We need to remember that the authority of veracity, ringing true, is a significant component in all pastoral leadership, and that "there is one God, and one mediator between God and men, the man Christ Jesus" (1 Tim 2:5). Some would violate, in Truett's phrase, "the Crown Rights of the Son of God" by denying the unique Lordship of Jesus Christ. He alone is go-between and all believers are priests.

Mullins's *ecclesiastical* axiom requires democracy in the local congregation. Baptists traditionally have been faithful to that high ideal; so much so that Martin Marty wrote of the "baptistification" of America. The insistence of Baptists on equal privileges for all church members has clearly had societal and political impact. Yet now there are those who would rather trust an autocracy of "godly men," the term often used. A military metaphor has marched into the meetinghouse. When one hears of a "chain of command" related to a Baptist church, it is, indeed, a misplaced metaphor.

The autonomy of the local church has been the principle recognized in Baptist relationships. Independence and self-governance are as Baptist as the baptistry.

Every congressional testimony given by the Baptist Joint Committee, every amicus brief filed before a court, and every positional document developed by those who respect that autonomy begins with a caveat that "no one speaks for Baptists." Yet some today would engage in the support of candidates or nominees on behalf of Baptists. Some Southern Baptists see resolutions passed by the Convention, if not binding, at least as serious instruction. Various methods are used these days to exert pressure on the local church in decisions that in Baptist theory are left to a specific body of baptized believers to determine for themselves.

In denominational life, the Southern Baptist machinery has historically responded to the clearly expressed wishes of messengers to the Convention. Alas, one seems no longer to be able to count on that. This, too, has church-state implications because our message to the world is muddied, our witness is weakened, and the Southern Baptist Convention is seen by many public servants and national leaders as having a secular political agenda.

The separation of church and state, Mullins's *religio-civic* axiom, has been an important contribution of Baptists to the American scene. From Roger Williams's "livlie experiment" to John Leland's influence on Madison, to George W. Truett's affirmation of religious liberty as "from the first, the trophy of Baptists," we have witnessed to freedom.

We have fallen on a day in which that record is sullied.

Politicians have successfully used their network of churches to promote their personal candidacies. And that was true in 1988 of Baptist preachers in both the Republican and Democratic parties. The very individuals who fought against aid to parochial schools for years are now fighting for aid to parochial preschools. Economic determinism is alive and powerful.

Revisionists in both religion and government would ignore the separation of church and state as an outmoded doctrine. Some would dismiss this safeguard for freedom as un-American.

We have understood and understand today that separation of church and state does not mean separation of God and government, or separation of religion from politics, or separation of Christians from their citizenship. It is, however, a hedge, a guardrail, a guarantee that government will not meddle in the business of religion. It pledges that it is none of the business of government to define the nature and mission of the church. It is a two-way street granting the churches no special favors, taking no tax dollars from everyone to advance the religion of anyone, allowing no church or combination of churches, however powerful, to come between one single soul, however weak, and one's God.

We must remember that the best thing government can do for religion is to leave it alone.

We must continue to protect the religious liberty of those whose beliefs we find offensive. To allow a measure of bizarre religion is a small price to pay for liberty. When the religious freedom of anyone is denied, the religious freedom of everyone is endangered.

The only power that can sustain the dedication to religious liberty, however, is the prophetic vision, the deeply felt awareness that we have a word from the Lord. "Stand fast therefore in the liberty wherewith Christ hath made us free" (Gal 5:1). Our indignation at cloying religiosity that would obscure free choices must be rooted in the freedom God gave us all at the beginning, all of us made in God's image. Our outrage at government intrusions into religious life must be based on a theology of freedom that allows everyone, even our Baptist brothers and sisters, the same liberty we expect for ourselves. God calls us to a way that is cumbersome, frustrating, divisive, and dangerous. God leads us down a path that makes us unsettled and perpetually indignant. But we cannot be Baptists without following in that way. This course calls for courage, not tepidity.

—This address was published in the Spring 1990 issue of The Theological Educator. Reprinted with permission courtesy of New Orleans Baptist Theological Seminary.

Real Baptists

The brief commentary below is an excerpt from a video interview with James Dunn, who was then executive director of the Baptist Joint Committee, at the 1990 Consultation of Concerned Baptists in Atlanta. This meeting was instrumental in birthing the Cooperative Baptist Fellowship. In this interview, Dunn shares about the centrality of "real religious liberty" and church-state separation to the identity of Baptists. He would often emphasize this message of what defined a "real Baptist" throughout the 1990s as moderate and progressive Baptists sought to draw a sharp contrast with the leaders of the Southern Baptist Convention.

Religious liberty is important to Baptists and always has been because it is the social, or the corporate expression, of our most central belief, which is soul freedom. That's the Baptist spin we put on priesthood of all believers— the competence of the individual before God. And, since we insist upon that for ourselves, we believe that we either follow Jesus Christ really or not really.

Ethics and common sense and history demand that we want that same freedom for everybody else. We want that freedom because we believe with all our heart that when anyone's religious liberty is denied, everybody's religious liberty is endangered. And it's important today especially because in our pluralistic society, in our secular world, in our complicated urban life, it is so easy to run roughshod over the minority, to ignore the spiritual dimension of life, to let other concerns that relate to our life together overshadow and completely obscure the freedom of the individual before God. And so it's terribly important that we maintain it.

I'm with this group of like-minded Baptists in Atlanta because I, as well as the majority of people here, am deeply committed and convinced that real Baptists still believe in religious liberty and church-state separation as they always have. The creedalism that says since the majority of us believe *this* and that you have to believe it is the absolute antithesis of what it means to be a Baptist. Baptists have been at their heart and soul dissenters from the very beginning and are still to this day dissenters. This crowd who is meeting here is still as committed to real religious liberty and church-state separation as Baptists have always been, and that's the essence of what it means to be a Baptist.

There are other people who do a better job of evangelism than we do. There are other people who do a better job of stewardship than we do. There are a lot of other people who use as much water as we do to baptize people as we do. But there's no group on the face of the earth by their very identity and history and theological centrism that focus on the freedom of the individual before God in the way that Baptists have. To be a real Baptist is what it's all about as far as I'm concerned and as far as these people are concerned. I wouldn't be anywhere else than here with my friends.

A positive, upbeat affirmation of missions, evangelism and outreach of the gospel, unhindered and untainted by the world, is why these folks are together. They really believe in cooperation. These people affirmed in a vote a few moments ago that they no longer want to be coerced, but they want to cooperate. Cooperative—the word itself implies voluntariness and freedom and spiritual dependence upon the guidance of the Lord. It's not merely a question of human democracy; it's a commitment to be free to do that which we believe God is leading us to do. Baptists have always valued freedom more than uniformity.

Conformity and uniformity are dirty words to a real Baptist.

—Reprinted with permission courtesy of
the Cooperative Baptist Fellowship.

God and Politics

James Dunn delivered the following address at a conference on "Red Letter Christians" at Baylor University's George W. Truett Theological Seminary in Waco, Texas, on September 17, 2008. At the time, he was serving as a professor at the Wake Forest University School of Divinity. In his remarks, Dunn recalls the witness of Baptist leaders of yesteryear such as George W. Truett, John Leland, Walter Rauschenbusch, E. Y. Mullins, J. M. Dawson, and T. B. Maston, all of whom championed a free conscience and a free church in a free state.

What a topic! What a challenge! On our good days we know better than to go there. (We know what Barth meant when he said, "to define God is to deny God.") We are not going to be saying, "God told us to go to war here or the Divine instructed us to drill for oil there." These are absurdities and it's still true that "those who believe absurdities will commit atrocities." Yet, try as we will, we cannot keep "God and politics" out of the same sentence.

George W. Truett, for whom this school is named, set out in righteous rhetoric a theological ground rule: The right to private judgment is the crown jewel of humanity, and for any person or institution to dare to come between the soul and God is a blasphemous impertinence and a defamation of the crown rights of the Son of God.

And so, mindful of those maxims from Barth, Voltaire, and Truett, of blessed memory, we consider gingerly the assignment God and Politics, being careful to avoid impertinences and defamations.

Baptist insights shared by other dissenters who have been blessed or burdened or both by bapistification can illumine any discussion of God and politics. Theological thinking may crack open some political nuts.

Take soul freedom: rooted in the belief that all persons are made in God's image, that human worth and dignity is a derived value. The *imago Dei* passage, Genesis 1:26-27, means at least that we can all respond to God, that all human beings are response-able, responsible—see how we get that word. And, if responsible, free. No matter how thin the coin of creation is sliced, it still has both sides, freedom and responsibility. They go together indissolubly.

That belief in soul freedom has led free churches to believe that everyone and anyone can come to God directly, personally, without filter or formula.

No priest or church or creed or political correctness is needed. Our confession, "Jesus Christ is Lord," is enough.

We are, in that sense at least, red-letter Christians.

We, therefore, cannot conceive of coerced conversion, forced faith, or required religion.

One comes to God freely or not really. That's not simply some weird Baptist doctrine. St. Bernard in his *1128 Treatise Concerning Grace and Free Will* wrote "Take away free will and there remaineth nothing to be saved. . . . Salvation is given by God alone, and it is given only to the free will; even as it cannot be wrought without the consent of the receiver, it cannot be wrought without the grace of the giver." When we transplant that theological thought to the turf of politics, it helps us to understand why it is hard for us as a nation to force democracy on an occupied people— unwilling and unready to accept an ideology, indeed a theology, not their own.

Forcing religion on a people only makes hypocrites. Roger Williams got us started off right in that modality.

A demanded democracy may not be authentic, serve well, or last long.

So then soul freedom describes a faith that is vital because it is voluntary. Bill Moyers calls it a "grown-up faith." Martin Marty's term baptistification "zeros in on the key issue that modernity posed for religion: choice." It's clear that this sort of theological thinking impacts politics.

Then, there's hope: I've been reflecting seriously on a common criticism of many of these best Baptists who have gone before. There's a complaint about many who have made the biggest difference, many who have meant most to me. They have been, it is said, too optimistic. Their theological optimism has skewed their message. Maybe so. I tend to think that they have brought a deep, abiding hope to politics.

John Leland, Walter Rauschenbusch, E. Y. Mullins, J. M. Dawson, T. B. Maston, Jimmy Carter—all mocked, made fun of, looked down upon by a set of "serious" scholars as possessing a hopelessly optimistic theology, ironically because they were hope mongers. Leland exercised great good humor—remember the big cheese. Rauschenbusch was totally invested in the Kingdom of God, present and future.

Mullins was a forward-looking thinker. Maston seasoned his southern fried Social Gospel with a heavy dose of Christian realism. Remember one of his favorite phrases: "abidingly relevant." Martin Luther King had a dream. He sang "We shall overcome." Jimmy Carter still believes in human struggle and conquest. [Political historian] Andrew Bacevich reminds us that if we had heeded Carter's advice we wouldn't be in the mess we are in now.

It's popular never to refer to any of this sort of thinker without reminding hearers/readers how wrong they were in their optimism. They were creatures of their time. "Who isn't?" They have all found some usefulness, some redemptive glimmer, some opportunity to shoehorn the Gospel into the political chaos of their own times.

They have done so not in blind partisanship but in post-partisan idealism.

Dr. Dawson, on whom I wrote my doctoral dissertation, said, "Having attained my majority by the turn of the century, I was infatuated with the optimism of the day and seriously considered Christian Socialism. Then came the Revolution, that ended that sort of talk. Dr. Truett and I considered ourselves Christian Humanists." Dr. Maston and I had many talks about the relative merits of being an independent rather than a party member. He just could not identify with a party. Might have done more good if he had.

The message of HOPE, abstract, biblical, theological, Heaven-sent is clearly not the same as political optimism treated so snidely by the hopeless wretches who know everything but do little.

Gotta have hope. That's about all I have to say about God and politics.

—This address was published in the Winter 2009 issue of *Christian Ethics Today*. Reprinted with permission courtesy of the Christian Ethics Today Foundation.

Notes

1. James M. Dunn (hereafter JMD), *Soul Freedom: Baptist Battle Cry* (Macon GA: Smyth & Helwys Publishing, 2000) 63–65.

2. JMD, "Religious Freedom Award Response," *Journal of Christian Ethics* 5/5 (October 1999).

3. JMD, "The Baptist Vision of Religious Liberty," in *Proclaiming the Baptist Vision: Religious Liberty*, ed. Walter B. Shurden (Macon GA: Smyth & Helwys Publishing, 1997) 32.

4. JMD, "The Christian and the State: A Constructive Task," *Perspectives in Religious Studies* 12/4 (Winter 1985): 23.

5. JMD, *Soul Freedom*, 1.

6. JMD, "The Baptist Vision of Religious Liberty," 33.

7. JMD, "Yes, I am a Baptist," in *Why I Am A Baptist: Reflections on Being Baptist in the 21st Century*, ed. Cecil P. Staton, Jr. (Macon GA: Smyth & Helwys Publishing, 1999) 44.

8. JMD, *Soul Freedom*, 83–84.

9. JMD, "Yes, I am a Baptist," 46.

10. Winthrop S. Hudson, "Shifting Patterns of Church Order in the Twentieth Century," in *Baptist Concepts of the Church* (Philadelphia: Judson Press, 1959) 215.

11. See Charles Marsh, *God's Long Summer* (Princeton: Princeton University Press, 1997) 82–115.

12. JMD, "Yes, I am a Baptist," 46–47.

13. JMD, *Soul Freedom*, 120.

14. Quoted in T. B. Maston, *Christianity and World Issues* (New York: Macmillan, 1957) 38.

15. Dorothy L. Sayers, *Are Women Human?* (Grand Rapids MI: Wm B. Eerdmans, 1971).

16. The acronym WWJD originated in the 1990s "What Would Jesus Do?" movement suggested by Charles Sheldon's novel, *In His Steps: What Would Jesus Do?* first published in 1896.

17. E. Y. Mullins, *The Axioms of Religion* (Philadelphia: American Baptist Publication Society, 1908) 73.

18. Bill J. Leonard, "Varieties of Freedom in the Baptist Experience," *Baptist History and Heritage* 20 (January 1990): 3.

19. Mullins, *Axioms of Religion*, 73.

20. Leonard, "Varieties of Freedom," 3.

21. Mullins, *Axioms of Religion*, 73.

22. Ibid., 74.

23. Ibid.

24. Ibid.

25. See "Resolution No. 5—On the Priesthood of the Believer," in *Annual of the Southern Baptist Convention, 131st session, 143d year, San Antonio, Texas, June 14-16, 1988* (Nashville: Executive Committee, Southern Baptist Convention) 68–70.

26. Thomas Helwys, *The Mistery of Iniquity* (1612; reprint with introduction by H. Wheeler Robinson, London: Baptist Historical Society, 1935).

Chapter 2

Reflections on Being Baptist

The writings included in this section continue to highlight James Dunn's views on soul freedom and Baptist identity. Dunn penned a column titled "Reflections" for the Baptist Joint Committee's newsletter, *Report from the Capital*, ten times per year from 1981–1999. In these columns, Dunn weighed in on a wide variety of current events and issues in Baptist life and American politics. No topics received more attention than freedom and Baptist identity.

Dunn used this platform to challenge readers—which included both supporters and opponents—to embrace and champion soul freedom and religious liberty for all. He urged readers to exercise their God-given freedom and the responsibility that came with it. Freedom and faithfulness were the essence of Baptist identity, and Dunn consistently preached this message through his "Reflections."

To Love, To Act, To Trust

Below is the first column that James Dunn wrote as executive director of the Baptist Joint Committee on Public Affairs. Published in the January 1981 issue of the BJC's newsletter, Report from the Capital, *this article reminds Dunn's readers of the historic Baptist dependence on the Bible. "We take the Bible seriously and place our trust in the God of the Bible," Dunn writes.*

> Four things a man must learn to do,
> If he would make his record true:
> To think without confusion clearly;
> To love one's fellowman, sincerely;
> To act from honest motives, purely;
> To trust in God and heaven securely.

Henry Van Dyke, who wrote these words, was a Presbyterian pastor, poet, writer, and diplomat. As a friend of President Woodrow Wilson, he often applied his personal faith to public causes. We probably remember him best as a hymn writer. He gave us "Joyful, Joyful We Adore Thee," sung to a tune from the fourth movement of Beethoven's Ninth Symphony.

His fourfold charge must have been inspired by the words of Jesus in the Great Commandment, "love the Lord thy God with all thy heart, and with all thy soul, and with all thy mind, and with all thy strength" (Mark 12:30). This commandment for all seasons has remarkable relevance for Baptists right now.

To think without confusion, to love God with one's whole mind, calls for more stewardship of brainpower than most of us muster. One could say many things of this dramatic injunction, but for now it seems that if our minds are in gear, it means at least that we learn something from history.

We need a sense of history. Simply, we ought to have a profound awareness of what has gone before. An appreciation of our roots is often missing. Our quick-fix, fast-learn, instant-coffee culture has, in fact, reduced an entire people to Elton Trueblood's "cut flower civilization."

We Baptists are no exception. The voices of many among us seem to have no awareness of the precious heritage that is ours. Some seem to have forgotten the price that was paid for a free church in a free state.

Beyond a sense of history, it is also imperative that we know the facts of history. We do not live in a spaceship moment with no ties to the past or future. Rather, what's gone before makes us who we are. God has been at work in the lives of his people and it is blasphemy to say that you don't care about history.

Then, we'll apply the lessons of history wisely. If, for instance, we recklessly sow the seeds of religious enthusiasm, insensitive to the consciences of those around us, we will reap the whirlwind of anti-clericalism, division, suspicion, and distrust. So it has always been.

To love one's fellow man, one's neighbor, as himself is the great challenge of Christian social ethics. Fortunately, we do not have to live out the gospel message without help from the past, without biblical principles clearly set out.

To translate the revealed message of God's love into public policy is a massive and sometimes tricky undertaking, but our generation is not the first to try. God's children have been bringing morality to public life for centuries. Christian social ethics is a well-developed discipline, not merely a collection of reactions to news reports.

The underlying and overriding thrust of Christian social concern is in working out God's love in the world. The Bible pleads for a certain solidarity within the human family among all of us made in God's image, all the objects of his love. The Old and New Testaments reveal a special concern for the poor, fatherless, widows. God's word calls us all to be peacemakers interested in "the things that make for peace." The Scripture calls for "justice to roll down as the waters and righteousness as a mighty stream." The biblical revelation demands stewardship on the part of the children of God. We are to be caretakers, not undertakers, of his creation.

Love, for self, others, the creation, is the theme. God's message is consistent, and Christian morality worthy of the name is rooted in and permeated with that love.

To act from honest motives, to love God with all our strength, calls for doing our faith. Faith works. The Christian commitment is not academic, theoretical, or speculative.

As we throw ourselves into the fray, we do so humbly. We will make mistakes. We are free to fail. We are not free to fail to act. Our salvation is by God's grace not a matter of merit, hence we do not always have to win. In fact, in a sinful world we should expect victories by the forces of greed, fear, and hate. We are expected to faithfully act from honest motives, purely.

Finally, to trust in God and heaven securely is the most fundamental appeal of all. Love the Lord thy God with all thy soul. Baptists historically have depended upon the Bible. We take the Bible seriously and place our trust in the God of the Bible. It is that faith that will continue to be the hallmark of the Baptist Joint Committee on Public Affairs.

—James M. Dunn, "Reflections," *Report from the Capital* 36/1 (January 1981): 15. Reprinted with permission courtesy of the Baptist Joint Committee for Religious Liberty.

The Font of Freedom

In this column published in the October 1983 issue of Report from the Capital, *James Dunn argues that "religious freedom is the basic freedom of all . . . because freedom is rooted in the nature and being of God." "The person of God is the font of freedom," he writes, emphasizing that Christians cannot escape from freedom.*

"O you dear idiots of Galatia, who saw Jesus Christ the crucified so plainly, who has been casting a spell over you?"

The literal translation of Galatians 3:1 captures some of the Apostle Paul's intense frustration with church members in what is now central Turkey. The spell they were under was a plague that has recurred often in Christian history. Let's look at it.

The Judaizers were putting law above love. The Christian is under grace not under law. Galatians leaves no doubt. This book is the Christian Declaration of Freedom. Any genuine Christian will be open to the charge of destroying the law. Jesus faced this charge. Stephen faced it. Paul faced it. If law takes the place of love as the basis for Christian ethics, it does so because it is safer; that's the safety of death.

Ever since those misled Galatians, there have been fearful Christians who value security and safety over freedom. Even now some would rather have clear policies, clean answers, and plain guidelines than the burden of having to make choices. Whole herds of Christians prefer an inerrant creed, an infallible church, or a cocksure preacher to freedom of choice.

Those of this mindset long for the good old days. They wish the world was like it used to be. They remember the religion and morality of their childhood as far better than these modern times. Paul faced that tendency with the Galatians. They wanted to continue their Jewish practices and yet accept the grace of God through Jesus Christ. Any time, then or now, that we are locked into looking backward, not free to faith our way forward, clinging to the past instead of trusting in his grace, we are guilty of immoral nostalgia.

The critics of Paul, like some confused believers today, were afraid of pluralism and diversity. They insisted that Gentiles become Jews before being counted Christians, so that spiritual elitism and exclusivity actually became a problem.

Well, you get the point. The careful, cautious element in Galatia put law over love, safety over freedom, authority over liberty, the good old days over the difficult present, the in crowd over reaching out, and ritual over reality. To follow the straight and narrow was okay, but this was ridiculous. To be conservative about change makes sense, but this was extremism.

Paul used his strongest words on these traditionalists. "Stupid Galatians" he called them in Galatians 3:1, and in Galatians 5:12 he suggested that since they were so intent upon following the law with circumcision, they might as well go ahead with mutilation. What sin could prompt such condemnation? They were trying to escape from freedom.

Freedom is fundamentally religious. Religious freedom is the basic freedom of all. That's because freedom is rooted in the nature and being of God. The person of God is the font of freedom. Theology in its strictest sense, the study of God, argues for freedom.

We do not know all that is meant by the Genesis teaching that we are made in the image of God. We do know that the classic doctrine of *imago Dei* reveals much about God and about humankind. At the very least it means that we are able to respond. We are response-able, therefore responsible. If we were not free to make choices, this could not be. The Genesis story makes it clear that God gave man and woman the power to choose. Free moral agency is not a philosophical argument but a universal reality. The personhood of God demands human freedom. We relate to God freely or not really at all. We come to God voluntarily or we stay away.

We know more about the doctrine of anthropology than we admit. I'm speaking of the theological "doctrine of man," not the scientific sociological study. The biblical doctrine of humankind makes it plain that we are innately free. We understand that in our innards.

Every year around Christmas, the baby dolls of the year appear in the stores everywhere. There must always be some new feature, some gimmick to sell them. A few years back the hot item was a baby that talked. Pull a cord on its back and it would say, "I love you, I love you." Even before the mechanism broke, the children in our extended family got tired of playing with it and threw it aside. Even three- and four-year-olds knew that the words were mechanical and, therefore, meaningless. "I love you" coming from a dumb doll sounded like words but was only noise.

But let a little Dennis the Menace, a ragged-jeaned, dirty-faced, scuffed-shoed, runny-nosed young'un grab you around the legs and hug your neck, look into your eyes with his eyes of innocence and say, "I love you," and it can melt a heart of stone.

We understand instinctively that unless one has the power to say "no," then his "yes" is meaningless. Unless one can refuse, then her acceptance is hollow. We know this inwardly because that is the way God made us. We are programmed for freedom. We're wired up as persons with a choice. Unless our chooser is allowed to function, we are less than the persons God made us to be.

The Bible teaching about sin takes into account this free moral agency that can be tainted, perverted, and used wrongly. We cannot be forced in matters of the will. Being human means being free.

The biblical doctrine of salvation is indissolubly, inextricably tangled with the other great doctrines. That is why we as Baptists want no state-written, government-prescribed prayer in the public schools. We want no tax dollars for our churches or our schools. The best thing government can do for religion is to leave it alone.

Force, even minimal or subtle force, does not mix with freedom. Religious experience must be free to be genuine. Any religious decision that's not free is useless or worse. We come to Jesus Christ freely in love, drawn by his grace. We live the Christian life because-we-have-been-saved not in an in-order-to-be-saved morality. It's grace not law, Christ not creed, persons not propositions that take precedence in the Christian life. We can't escape from freedom. It is for freedom that Christ has set us free.

—James M. Dunn, "Reflections," *Report from the Capital* 38/9 (October 1983): 15. Reprinted with permission courtesy of the Baptist Joint Committee for Religious Liberty.

Soul Freedom and Sola Scriptura

In this April 1985 column, James Dunn warns against those who would pit soul freedom and sola scriptura *against one another, noting that Baptists have historically insisted on a balance between the two. This pointed commentary came as the "Battle for the Bible" was raging and dividing the Southern Baptist Convention. "Baptists on our good days throughout history," Dunn emphasizes, "have insisted upon an affirmation of the authority of Scripture that has been broader than proposition . . . a guide for living rather than a term for arguing."*

Soul freedom sits serenely by the side of the soul authority of Scripture as expressions of the Baptist basis for faith. The two watchwords may seem contradictory on casual reading.

When either spiritual slogan—soul freedom or *sola scriptura*—is made absolute, they are pitted against each other. Can they coexist creatively?

First, Baptists at our best have insisted upon balance between authority and experience, the objective and the subjective, the outer and inner. We have been such radical monotheists that we have refused to see the Bible as a paper pope. With dogged determinism regularly misunderstood and made fun of, we insist upon approaching the living God as ultimate and immediate authority.

There's room for a little variety of expression in a Baptist pattern for authority. For us the last word comes *either* (1) from the Bible as made alive, explained, applied, and tested by the work of the Holy Spirit *or* (2) from the living Lord as we come to know God through the Scriptures, as we are informed and kept on the track by the revelation of God's Word. Speaking of tracks, it takes both external and internal perceptions of religious liberty to keep us from being derailed.

Then, our understanding of the Bible calls for action. The Scriptures are not to be held, defended, argued, fought over, or analyzed so much as accepted and acted upon. We are taught from earliest childhood to be doers of the word and not hearers only. Dietrich Bonhoeffer, who acted on his faith until it cost his life, commented on the only appropriate response to God's word: "The hearer of the word who is not at the same time the doer of the word thus inevitably falls victim to self-deception (Jas. 1:22). Believing himself to know and to possess the word of God, he has, in fact, already lost it again, because he imagines that a man can possess the word of God for a single instant otherwise than in doing it."

Bonhoeffer went further to suggest that one could not be faithful to Scripture while preoccupied with debate *about* it:

> The irreconcilable opposite of action is judgement . . . 'if thou judge the law, thou art not a doer of the law, but a judge' (Jas. 4:11). There are two possible attitudes to the law: judgement and action. The two are mutually exclusive. The man who judges envisages the law as a criterion which he applies to others, and he envisages himself as being responsible for the execution of the law. He forgets that there is only one lawgiver and judge 'who is able to save and to destroy' (Jas. 4:12). If a man employs his knowledge of the law in accusing or condemning his brother, then in truth he accuses and condemns the law itself, for he mistrusts it and doubts that it possesses the power of the living word of God to establish itself and to take effect itself.

A smug arrogance mars the mien of those who presume to sit in critical judgment on the word of God. What a lofty perch, what a remarkable vantage point one assumes in dogmatically telling other believers what must be said of Scripture without having yet practiced it.

Finally, Baptists on our good days throughout history have insisted upon an affirmation of the authority of Scripture that has been broader than proposition, more holistic than rationalistic, a guide for living rather than a term for arguing. This Baptist is unwilling to play today's silly word games in evangelical circles over who believes the Bible most. The spirit-led, time-tested confessions of the past seem to say it better.

One clings to the traditional Baptist view of Scripture as the sole rule for faith and practice not because it says less but because it says more, not because it is a lower, less demanding claim for biblical authority but because it is higher and life-encompassing.

The Philadelphia Baptist Association, the first Baptist association in America formed in 1707, got around to adopting a confessional statement in 1742. It said, "The Holy Scripture is the only sufficient, certain, and infallible rule of all-saving knowledge, faith and obedience." Good enough, that takes in how one lives as well as what one believes.

That confession was good enough for Baptists north and south. It was accepted by associations in Virginia, Rhode Island, South Carolina, Kentucky, and Tennessee. Far earlier, 1611, Thomas Helwys had held simply that the Scriptures were to be reverently used "as conteyning the Holie Word of God, which onlie is our direction in all things whatsoever." Is that inclusive enough?

More recently, Southern Baptists reflected earlier confessions in the introduction to a 1963 statement saying the Bible is the "sole authority for faith and practice," thus touching orthopraxy as well as orthodoxy. Could it be that one reason for the popularity of the expression has been anxiety about creedalism?

Baptists have always known and been nervous about the tension between Scripture as sole authority and precious soul freedom. Evidence of this concern that individuals interpret Scripture freely is seen in Article XXI of the *Philadelphia Confession*:

> God alone is Lord of the conscience, and hath left it free from the doctrines and commandments of men which are in anything contrary to his word, or not contained in it. So that to believe such doctrines, or obey such commands out of conscience is to betray true liberty of conscience; and the requiring of an implicit faith, and absolute and blind obedience, is to destroy liberty of conscience and reason also.

Baptists live out their biblical faith in soul freedom.

—James M. Dunn, "Reflections," *Report from the Capital* 40/4 (April 1985): 15. Reprinted with permission courtesy of the Baptist Joint Committee for Religious Liberty.

Separation as the Best Guarantee for Religious Freedom

With appeals to Baptist theology and ethics, James Dunn emphasizes the biblical foundations of church-state separation and offers an argument for why Baptists should hold firm to this historic distinctive in his November/December 1991 column. "Believing in the separation of church and state doesn't make one a Baptist, but it is hard to believe that one could be a Baptist and not cling tenaciously to that baptistic doctrine." This statement—which Dunn would invoke frequently over the years—revealed the centrality of church-state separation to Dunn's personal theology and perspective on Baptist identity.

Where in the Bible is the separation of church and state taught? The question is asked. Sometimes the questioner is earnest and urgent. For those of us who take the Bible seriously, it is not a bad question.

Brooks Hays, with his gentle humor, would comment, "As Jesus said, and he was right . . . ." Well, as Jesus said, "Render therefore unto Caesar the things which are Caesar's; and unto God the things that are God's" (Matthew 22:21). That's a start. Jesus plainly spoke of a difference between what is God's and what is government's.

Then there is no one proof text in the Bible on which to hang the Jeffersonian metaphor, "a wall of separation between church and state." There are, however, biblical principles, theological presuppositions, historical examples, and pointed stories that form a firm foundation for keeping these two institutions distinct.

The biblical record leaves no doubt that all people are moral creatures. All human beings are response-able, responsible, and free. All three great religions of The Book (Judaism, Christianity, and Islam) affirm the doctrine of *imago Dei*, the idea that humankind somehow replicates God (Genesis 1:26, 27). Whatever else that means, it requires that moral nature. Persons decide. Our "chooser" is close to our essential core.

Adam and Eve could want, wish, and will. Every wonderful "whosoever will" in Scripture—from the capacity to choose at creation (Genesis 1) to the invitation in Revelation 22:17—"Whosoever will, let him take the water of life freely"—cries out for soul freedom.

That soul freedom marks the mystery of humanity: "a little lower than the angels" (Psalm 8:5), yet "there is none good, but one, God" (Mark 10:18). We are able to soar but apt to sink, capable of freedom but inclined to oppress.

Scripture also portrays us all as social beings. Our decisions and deeds have social consequences. That condition, individuals entangled in the lives of others, demands religious liberty. Joshua put it straightly to the children of Israel: "Choose you this day whom ye will serve; . . . but as for me and my house, we will serve the LORD." (Josh 24:15). Jesus loved the rich young ruler but let him go away (Mark 10:17-22). The master did not zap, tackle, or trip him.

The appeal of Jesus requires decision. "Whosoever *will come* after me, *let* him *deny* himself, and *take up* his cross and follow me" (Mark 8:34). That personal commitment cannot be made by anyone else. This is no proxy religion. Nor are there any filters, emanations, or intermediaries. There is one mediator between God and all humankind, that one is Jesus (1 Timothy 2:5). Christians from the early church subscribed to the simple affirmation "Jesus is Lord." That puts followers of Jesus on an equal footing. The "law of liberty" further binds all believers in love for one another, extends unto the "least of these" (Matthew 25:40).

The spiritual estimate of humankind shared by Jews and Christians sees us all as political animals. The Bible tells the stories of kings and generals, prophets and priests, good and bad government. The early church saw government *per se* as good, ordained by God (Romans 13) but potentially as an instrument of evil (Revelation 13).

When one examines the record of civil disobedience, heroic martyrdom, faithful witness, it is clear that churches closest to Jesus' day were not followers of a watered-down civil religion. No muddle-headed merger of God and country confused the church at first. They said with Peter, "We ought to obey God rather than men" (Acts 5:29). They understood that the ways of government were not the ways of God. "Not by might, nor by power, but by my spirit, saith the LORD of hosts" (Zechariah 4:6). Those first-century Christians were too busy running *from* the Roman Senate to consider running *for* it, but they did know the difference between church and state.

Baptists hold to the separation of church and state as the best guarantee for religious freedom.

Our *theology* demands it. Faith is appropriated personally; God's grace is experienced individually; one comes to Jesus Christ freely or not really; everyone must be free from the state's coercive powers in matters of religion.

Our *ethics* require it. If we do unto others as we want them to do unto us, if we believe that God loves the whole world, if we accept the image of God in every fellow human being, if we love our neighbor as we love ourselves, all people are entitled to real religious liberty.

Our *experience* commends it. The American experiment in church-state separation was in significant measure initiated by Baptists. Roger Williams, John Clarke, Isaac Backus, Samuel Stillman, John Leland, and others advanced this innovative relationship.

State religions are bad in principle. One can see the dangers and corruptions of ties between church and state in Latin America, Ireland, and Iran. One can see the chaos and violence that attends state-supported religion in Lebanon, Sri Lanka, and Nepal. One can see the debilitating absence of conviction and vitality that accompanies an established church in England, Spain, and Sweden.

Yet, in 1991, different dominant religions are actually pressing for recognition as the official national "church" in India, Poland, and Romania. We warn against the tyrannies inherent in such an arrangement. We affirm the spiritual value of the separation of church and state.

Believing in the separation of church and state doesn't make one a Baptist. But it is hard to believe that one could be a Baptist and not cling tenaciously to that baptistic doctrine. How else do we protect and defend those seminal beliefs in freedom of conscience, the priesthood of all believers, the right of private interpretation of Scripture, real religious liberty for all believers, as well as those who refuse to believe, a free church in a free state?

Without those protections, how else can we ensure the integrity of authentic evangelism, a prophetic witness, and an unhindered mission to share the whole gospel with whole people in the whole world?

A church in such a close partnership with government that one cannot tell when worship leaves off and patriotism begins has slipped into idolatry. Without a healthy distance, the prophetic vision is blurred, the witness is muffled, and the gospel compromised.

Finally, when the church's mission is tinted, tainted, or tailored by the state, she has ceased to be the bride of Christ and fallen into an incestuous bed of cultural captivity.

Why is a sin-sick society so deaf to the good news? One reason is clear. Too many Christians have been willing to let public institutions do too much of the church's job. The church has the marvelous assignment: "O Zion, haste thy mission high fulfilling; To tell to all the world that God is light; That he who made all nations is not willing; One soul should perish, lost in shades of night. Publish glad tidings; Tidings of peace; Tidings of Jesus; Redemption and release."[1]

> —James M. Dunn, "Reflections," *Report from the Capital* 46/12 (November/December 1991): 15. Reprinted with permission courtesy of the Baptist Joint Committee for Religious Liberty.

Distinctly Baptist

In this April 1994 column, Dunn takes on critics who contend that a creedless Baptist has no confession of faith. "We say with the early church: Jesus Christ is Lord," Dunn writes, adding that "being Baptist means respect"—agreeing to disagree and being honest about differences. Dunn offered this inclusive approach as Southern Baptist fundamentalists continued their pursuit for theological conformity and purity at the state and local levels after securing control of the national convention in 1990.

Being "distinctly Baptist" is a tall order . . . so few folks are. And we fuss so much about what that means.

The only creed for Baptists is: "Ain't nobody going to tell me what to believe."

The use of lowercase for baptist, a concept originating with Howard Moody, is not meant to diminish our great historical tradition, but rather as a reminder of the fact that baptists are individuals, and wherever two or three are gathered, there is a congregation of baptists. There is not a Baptist Church, regional or national, no Baptist Faith, no Baptist Worship that is codified or normative for all baptist people.

We suffer from semi-baptists today who would make creeds for us of what they believe and think we should. Some invoke a moral creed. It really just has two test poles—abortion and homosexuality. Some blatantly make a creed of secular politics. I was interviewed for the *700 Club* in January and the reporter asked, "Is it possible for one to be a Democrat and a Christian?"

The absence of a creed, however, does not mean that we have no confession of faith. We say with the early church: Jesus Christ is Lord.

We join the Reformation watchword: *sola fide*.[2]

In fact, our skittishness about creeds makes more important our confessions and more personal and more focused our faith.

One of the loudest fundamentalists in the current unpleasantness in Southern Baptist life testified publicly, "I learned at Princeton that I just cannot believe what I cannot understand." Poor fellow. Where does that leave one, when the just live by faith? Little "b" baptists cry *sola fide* like Texans yell, "Remember the Alamo."

The absence of a creed does not mean the lack of coherent content to our belief. One can identify baptist principles that logically stick together.

When Martin Marty speaks of "the baptisification of America," most religionists know what he means . . . and lament it. But like it or not, one can know if he or she has been baptistified.

> If soul freedom is important,
> if the priesthood of all believers is more than a slogan,
> if one insists on interpreting the Bible for himself,
> if one defends the right of each person to come to the Bible and led by the Holy Spirit to seek its truth,
> if one believes that she must accept Jesus Christ personally, freely, or not really,
> if the church functions as a democracy,
> if in the fellowship of churches each one is autonomous,
> if there is no pope, presbyter, president, or pastor to rule over you,
> if no mortal has the power to suppress, curtail, rule out or reign over the will of the congregation . . .

then you have probably been baptistified.

These consistent freedom forces form an orderly pattern. Being baptist also means respect, affirmation, and honest honoring of differences. After all, if folks are free, they may not all agree with us. They have a right to be wrong.

So we insist not on toleration for those outside our particular perspective but on freedom. Roger Williams called toleration a weasel word, implying human concession, while freedom is gift of God. Little "b" baptists, even the ones who were Deists, and Anglicans and Methodists have fought for real religious liberty. Of course, we insist on freedom *from* religion for those who choose it. If one cannot say "no," her "yes" is meaningless.

Religious freedom and its essential corollary, the separation of church and state, are still part of the baptist non-creedal bundle of beliefs.

Back in 1905, E. Y. Mullins in *The Axioms of Religion* set out the non-binding, non-creedal content of a little "b" baptist.

—James M. Dunn, "Reflections," *Report from the Capital* (19 April 1994): 3. Reprinted with permission courtesy of the Baptist Joint Committee for Religious Liberty.

Equal Privileges: A Hallmark of Baptists

In his May 1994 column, James Dunn reflects on the "revolutionary doctrine" that all Christians are entitled to equal access within the church. He questions how a church could carry the name "Baptist" and discriminate based on gender, age, race, and other factors. "More invidious and common perhaps is the de facto *denial of full membership because of some selective system of sin-sizing," he writes.*

Three years prior to this column, the Cooperative Baptist Fellowship had formed and become Dunn's new "denominational home," embracing an egalitarian approach of affirming the callings of women and men alike to pastoral ministry. This stood in stark contrast to the Southern Baptist Convention, which sought to exclude women from denominational life and the pulpit. Dunn's pointing to "sin-sizing" was a certain reference to the heightening conversation in Baptist life about homosexuality. Just two years earlier, the SBC had voted to disfellowship two North Carolina churches for their welcoming and affirming stance toward gays and lesbians.

Quintessential democracy. The starting gun for sustainable human rights. A laboratory for soul freedom. The baseline for church polity and politics. A consistent corollary for the competence of the individual before God. A Baptist distinctive or hang-up or cantankerousness.

One or all of those phrases fit the affirmation that "all believers have a right to equal privileges in the church." It is elemental: religious liberty starts at home. It is a revolutionary doctrine. It's an idea to which most freechurch adherents pay lip service. Edgar Young Mullins spelled it out in a lecture before the American Baptist Publication Society in 1905.

The notion, like all ideals, is far from being realized. Some churches bearing the name "Baptist" withhold equal privileges on the basis of gender, age, race, or some other external factor. More invidious and common perhaps is the *de facto* denial of full membership privileges because of some selective system of sin-sizing. A sin of certain assessed magnitude can cut off equal access.

Human fallibility skews the democratic ideal. Orthodoxy is my doxy. Heterodoxy is your doxy. Tradition, cultural norms, and Sunday school theology weigh heavily in determining the dispensation of "equal privileges."

The Baptist biblical vision has not encompassed a doctrine of sinless perfection. Therefore, whether one takes the Bible seriously, sees it as authoritative, or deems it inerrant, there is an instant catalog of perversions, transgressions, and fallings short.

The New Testament, for instance, has more to say about sinful misuse of wealth than about heaven and hell combined. One of every ten verses in the New Testament deals with greed or hunger or poverty and an appropriate response. Count 'em! The sins identified or implied in the biblical record offer a formidable challenge to any advocate of church purity and evenhanded ecclesiastical discipline.

So go back to the principle: all believers have a right to equal privileges in the church.

The same regard for Scripture protects one from believing that equality of privilege refers to an equality of spiritual and mental capacities. Nor does this rule of thumb diminish appreciation for diversity of gifts and differences of calling.

The right of direct access to God makes the church a family. Brothers and sisters with a common allegiance to Jesus Christ do not take equality before God lightly or as an excuse for self-centered individualism.

The tangible reality of a fellowship of believers in real time with actual flesh-and-blood concerns bound by love serves as a powerful deterrence to cowboy Christianity. The principle of equal privileges in the church tends to curtail, not create Lone Ranger religion. At least, that is the way it ought to work. Powerful paradox: the lordship of Christ and the autonomy of the individual soul. "Jesus Christ is Lord" was the first confession of the church. As Mullins wrote, "The first and finest expression of Christ's lordship over the individual believer is the gift of autonomy." Paradox? Mystery? Yes.

Dependence on the work of the Holy Spirit serves as the supreme safeguard. Christ said that he must go away in order for the Holy Spirit to come. Thus, according to Christian doctrine, he exchanged his presence for his omnipresence.

As Baptists have practiced the rights of all believers, all papacies, episcopacies, diaconates, or ruling pastors are like commissions to control the sunshine. Shocking are *ad hoc* power plays in which a few individuals conspire to act for the church. Creeds and church legislation are unbiblical barriers between the believer and one's Lord.

Nothing so violates the basic nature of a Baptist church as the assumption of power by a few. The prerogative of congregational control is rooted deep in the theology of individual access to God and the polity of every believer having equal privileges in the church.

Semi-baptists have always tried their hand at creeds. There is a human hunger for uniformity and a universal temptation to conformity. A need for comfort levels causes folks who know better to go along to get along. Confrontation and contention are avoided at all costs.

Creedmakers find full employment in 1994, pushing and enforcing their moral creed with just two test poles—abortion and homosexuality. Others blatantly make a creed of secular politics. I was interviewed for the "700 Club" in January and asked, "Is it possible to be a Democrat and a Christian?"

Mullins commented on creeds: "Creeds are useful as interpretations of Scripture at any particular period but as soon as they become binding they become divisive. Laws of any kind—those which affect the faith or the life—inevitably lead to mischief in the church."

Hence, a voluntary association of believers unites for the purposes of worship and watchcare, for witness and work, for mission and ministry, for education and edification. In that sort of gathering, democracy alone accords with the nature of God's kingdom. No other polity than democracy leaves the soul free.

Martin Luther admitted that the real church and the real authority is in the local congregation. But in characteristic Martin Luther candor, he said that the "wild Germans" were not ready for congregationalism.

We proceed to affirm freedom, assuming that church members have been "tamed" by the Spirit of God. The working principle that all believers are directly answerable to Christ is dangerous, explosive, open to abuse. One can be certain that it will be misinterpreted and misused.

Yet the introduction of indirect authority, creedal filters, mediation, and intermediaries possesses greater danger. That danger is the failure to see Jesus Christ as sole authority.

For Baptists to be faithful to our own best insights, for Baptists to continue to champion religious liberty, for Baptists to be Baptists, we must practice freedom in our churches. We are guilty of high hypocrisy; we are full-fledged phonies if we talk freedom of religion and act less than freely at church. Democracy and vital religion share this ennobled view of individual freedom. All believers have a right to equal privileges in the church.

The late Brooks Hays liked to say, "Never dilute the oil of anecdote with the vinegar of fact." A story comes from the church that was his for many years, the Calvary Baptist Church in Washington, D.C. Whether wonderful anecdote or factual report, it bears repeating. When Chief Justice Charles Evans Hughes walked the aisle of the church to present himself for membership, a Chinese washerwoman from the neighborhood, Chinatown, came seeking membership at the same time. It has long been said that the pastor commented, "The ground is wondrously level at the foot of the cross."

So it is. So all believers have a right to equal privileges in the church.

—James M. Dunn, "Reflections," *Report from the Capital* (3 May 1994): 1–2. Reprinted with permission courtesy of the Baptist Joint Committee for Religious Liberty.

Helwys's Demand for Religious Freedom for All Troubles Some

James Dunn shares about the legacy of Thomas Helwys and his famed appeal for universal religious liberty in this column published in the August 1998 issue of Report from the Capital.

Who was the first Baptist? Some think it was John the Baptist. But seriously, how far back can one go with the distinctly Baptist family tree?

Personally, I do not want to be more than a distant cousin to some of the sects mentioned in J. M. Carroll's booklet, *The Trail of Blood.* Much can be made of Baptist kinship with Anabaptists. My nominee for the first Baptist who resembles the present breed of that label is Thomas Helwys (1575–1616).

We are profoundly indebted to Mercer University Press for bringing within reach of ordinary mortals *A Short Declaration of the Mystery of Iniquity* by Thomas Helwys. Richard Groves has edited and introduced this brief book.

He has rescued this class from unintelligible and antiquated punctuation and spellings and made available a text accessible to modern readers.

Helwys, along with John Smyth, identified first with Puritans. Later he joined Separatists and then Anabaptists but after that established the first Baptist church. In *The Mystery of Iniquity*, he sets out, for the first time in English, the notion of liberty of conscience as a stack pole theological concept, church-state separation as a basic belief.

Barry White sees Helwys distancing himself and a little band of believers from their Anabaptist brothers and sisters. Helwys, like Baptists today, used a modern English translation of Scripture, gave power to all church members, saw civil government as ordained by God, allowed civil servants to be members of the church, practiced believer's baptism, and eliminated infant baptism. Thomas Helwys could probably join the Baptist church in your town.

He founded in 1612 the first Baptist church on English soil. It was the little book, however, that got him in trouble. Mere toleration was the liberal idea regarding religious freedom, as it is yet in much of the world.

Helwys called for "universal religious liberty—freedom of conscience for all." "Let them be heretics, Turks, Jews or whatsoever, it appertains not to the earthly power to punish them in the least measure."

Helwys's Baptist qualifications include his bundle of beliefs that are seen as a distinctly Baptist configuration:

1. believer's baptism;
2. congregational church government;
3. the right of individual interpretation of Scripture;
4. universal religious liberty; and
5. separation of church and state.

His demand for religious freedom for all humankind—made in God's image—troubled some Christians then and troubles some now.

His understanding of the church and of sin, his high view of Scripture, his estimate of humankind, his theology in the strictest sense of the word make him a candidate for Baptist No. 1.

Thomas Helwys put passionate commitment behind his beliefs. He would certainly have trouble with Baptists who claim the name and defame the same.

In the context of his time, he crafted a confession of faith that collected key concepts still Baptist. His emphasis upon a religion that was distinct from the state, his juxtapositions with tangible alternatives, gave shape to being Baptist. Other expressions of Christianity had multiple authorities. With Helwys, Scripture ruled. Some had external religiosity. Helwys held high inner devotion. There were those who could accept some measure of coercion in religion. For Helwys, faith had to be voluntary to be vital.

This little book may well be the defining Baptist document. In fact, one key phrase fixed Helwys's fate. He wrote, "The king is a mortal man and not God, therefore, hath no power over ye immortal souls of his subjects, to make laws and ordinances for them and to set spiritual Lords over them . . . ."

That king, the same King James whose name is in the front of your Bible, had that first Baptist jailed and killed. Church-state separation dearly bought.

—James M. Dunn, "Reflections," *Report from the Capital* (4 August 1998): 3. Reprinted with permission courtesy of the Baptist Joint Committee for Religious Liberty.

Soul Freedom Nothing but a New Name for a Profound Word: Faith

In 2000, James Dunn penned this classic column following his retirement from the Baptist Joint Committee. With his typical flair, Dunn champions soul freedom. Echoing George Truett, he highlights the historic Baptist commitment to this "crown jewel of humanity"—the right of private judgment. "When anyone's religious freedom is denied, everyone's religious freedom is endangered," Dunn writes. This would be one of Dunn's final columns published in the BJC's newsletter, Report from the Capital.

Baptists in the news cause Baptists and non-Baptists to ask, what is a "Baptist," anyway?

In 1908, E. Y. Mullins set out "the doctrine of soul's competency in religion under God as the distinctive historical significance of Baptists." What I'm calling "soul freedom" is the capacity to deal directly with God, nothing but a new name for a profound word: faith. That's what marks a Baptist.

Karl Barth got in the act visiting with Louie D. Newton in 1958. He said, "How I thank God for Mullins. . . . Mullins gave the world a mighty phrase—the competency of the soul." Soul freedom feeds the *heart hunger* found in millions of persons seeking immediacy in religion.

Yet the business section of *The New York Times*, June 15, 2000, ran an article by Virginia Postrel on the Southern Baptist declaration "that the Bible bars women from serving as pastors." Ms. Postrel is the author of *The*

Future and Its Enemies, an apt label for some Baptists. Even the death-rattle defiance of propositionally propped-up fundamentalism against women pastors is, in an odd way, evidence of the universal heart hunger for soul freedom.

Baptists have historically held that religious liberty and all human rights are rooted in the recognition of soul liberty. When anyone's religious freedom is denied, everyone's religious freedom is endangered.

The Baptist basic, soul freedom, describes authentic religion as:

1. Personal—Human personality is the only adequate medium for the self-revelation of a personal God. Frank Louis Maudlin sums it up: "Truth is greater than truths. It is not about something. For truth is reality and reality is someone: It is the person of the Living God and of Jesus Christ come near."

2. Social—The competence of the individual before God does not slight Christianity. Without individual autonomy, there can be no authentic community. Soul freedom spawns a striving for social justice. The very idea that each human being is made in the image of God invests in every single individual such transcendent worth that any difference between this one and that fades into nothingness by comparison.

3. Experiential—We more often act our way into believing than believe our way into acting.

4. Voluntary—As Glenn Hinson writes, "To be authentic and responsible, faith must be free. Obedience to God must be voluntary, or it is not obedience." Voluntary religion, in Baptist eyes, is the only valid religion.

5. Pluralistic—Pluralism does not mean moral relativism. One keeps values and identity living amongst other values that one can neither destroy nor approve. Bill Moyers on his "Genesis" television series said, "Differences between faiths are real, not to be papered over for nicety's sake, but people with deep, intractable differences can teach and learn from each other. We grasp what Emerson meant when he said, 'We measure all religions by their civilizing power.'"

6. Androgynous—Real Baptists do not believe that any mortal can tell God whom he may call to ministry. Bill J. Leonard anticipated the awful end of authentic baptistness. The first Southern Baptist Convention defended slavery, yet "even the most rabid . . . fundamentalist must admit that slavery is not a divinely ordained practice. Yet, here we go again." Now a practical misogyny is "God's will" for one breed of Baptists speaking for God. Leonard went on, "To his everlasting credit, Paul sowed the seeds of

our maturity, perhaps without realizing the full implication of his vision. In Galatians 3:28 he wrote: '. . . there is neither male nor female; for you are all one in Christ Jesus.'"

George W. Truett was right in a speech on the East Steps of the U.S. Capitol, May 16, 1920: "The right to private judgment is the crown jewel of humanity, and for any person or institution to dare to come between the soul and God is a blasphemous impertinence and a defamation of the crown rights of the son of God."

> —James M. Dunn, "Reflections," *Report from the Capital* (25 July 2000): 3. Reprinted with permission courtesy of the Baptist Joint Committee for Religious Liberty.

Notes

1. Mary Ann Thomson, "O Zion, Haste," TIDINGS, 1868, hymnary.org/text/o_zion_haste_thy_mission_high_fulfilling.

2. Latin phrase meaning "by faith alone."

Church-State Philosophy

For James Dunn, the separation of church and state was the logical theological and political consequence of an unfettered conscience and uncoerced faith. Biblical principles, theological presuppositions, and historical examples lay the firm foundation that demands church-state separation, according to Dunn. Since the state is incompetent to judge spiritual matters, he thought the conscience must be wholly free from the state's coercive powers in matters of faith and religion.

The Christian ethic also requires church-state separation. "If we do unto others as we want them to do unto us, if we believe that God loves the whole world, if we accept the image of God in every human being, if we love our neighbors as ourselves, all people are entitled to real religious liberty," Dunn said. He would frequently invoke Baptist history in his writings and speeches, pointing to the witness of Baptist leaders such as Roger Williams, John Clarke, Isaac Backus, and John Leland to make his point that the Baptist heritage commends church-state separation.[1]

Dunn's church-state philosophy was grounded in a principle of neutrality that promoted fairness and equality—a principle that can be traced back to the political thought of Roger Williams. This Baptist separationism was not a "strict separation" that is often accused of anti-clericalism, anti-Catholicism, and hostility toward religion. Instead, Dunn's separationist perspective demanded a robust reading of the First Amendment's Free Exercise Clause and an interpretation of the Establishment Clause that required government to be strictly neutral toward religion.

Dunn reacted fiercely against critics who attacked Thomas Jefferson's metaphor of "a wall of separation of church and state." "Some of us believe that it is a metaphor rooted in good theology—render unto Caesar what is Caesar's, unto God what is God's; that it has proved patently useful as the guarantor of liberty; that while it is not absolute, it is not obsolete and that it should be treated as a distinctive aspect of the American experiment," he wrote. Dunn questioned whether anyone could possibly value soul freedom without seeing the dire need for church-state separation.[2] "If American history makes any eloquent appeal, it is for the separation of church and state," he maintained.[3]

The separation of church and state is rarely neat and is never absolute, according to Dunn. As a no-aid separationist, he rejected all legislative efforts to fund or aid religion. Due to America's thriving pluralistic society, he believed that government-funded religion was not possible or desirable even if a minority of the Founding Fathers like Patrick Henry envisioned such a relationship. "Persons of conscience of all religious and non-religious hues insist that it is impossible to attain an idyllic state of governmental fairness with aid and benefits for all religions," he said, observing that "when the government claims to aid all religions, it never fails to play favorites." Strict neutrality, not benignity, is the proper role for government in relation to religion, he said.[4]

The separation of church and state should not be equated with the separation of religion from politics. This was a truth that Dunn frequently espoused for nearly fifty years. In a pluralistic democracy, he fully understood that religion and politics will mix, must mix, and should mix. He often declared that "mixing politics and religion is inevitable but merging church and state is inexcusable." While it was no simple plan for the right mix of politics and religion, Dunn viewed the principle of church-state separation as an attempt to write into public policy "the notion that there is no place for coercion in the choice, exercise, or perpetuation of religion." "Separation of church and state means at least that Church and State have different reasons for being, diverse functions, separate sources of funding, distinctive methods and strategies and identities."[5]

While noting that separation of church and state does not define Baptist theology, Dunn said that it is "a logical, inextricable, inevitable corollary of religious liberty . . . it is the plug which if pulled out of our machine, the motor dies [and] we go no more."[6] He often stressed that "it is hard to believe that one could be a Baptist and not cling tenaciously to that baptistic doctrine."[7]

The writings that follow further articulate Dunn's church-state philosophy, a perspective that is distinctly Baptist and rooted in deeply held theological commitments to an unfettered conscience before God and an uncoerced faith that puts itself to action in the political arena on behalf of justice, mercy, and the common good.

The final two selections in this section—a speech and an article—offer an overview of many of the specific church-state challenges that Dunn confronted during his tenure at the BJC from 1981–1999. While the issues have evolved some over the years, many of the same church-state concerns still exist and remain relevant.

Religion and Politics: A Proper Mix

Five years into his tenure as executive director of the Baptist Joint Committee on Public Affairs, James Dunn published an academic articulation of his church-state philosophy in Perspectives in the Studies of Religion, *the respected journal of the National Association of Baptist Professors of Religion. This article, titled "Religion and Politics: A Proper Mix," was based on a keynote address Dunn gave two years earlier in October 1984 at the annual gathering of an organization for evangelical historians called the Conference on Faith and History. That address was titled "The Christian as Political Activist."*

In this article, Dunn warns that the Religious Right aims to destroy a traditional understanding of how church and state should relate to one another, emphasizing that the mixing of politics and religion is inevitable (and necessary), but the merging of church and state is inexcusable. To support his call for political engagement, Dunn appeals to the biblical themes of freedom, responsibility, and love for neighbor, citing passages such as Luke 12:14: "For unto whomsoever much is given, of him shall much be required." He draws from history to make the case against actions and policies that undermine church-state separation, invoking the words of "Father of the Constitution" James Madison, Roger Williams, and John Leland.

A pernicious plot endangers the delicate balance between church and state in the American experiment.

The difficulty with the Religious Right extremists who are now receiving so much attention is not that they are wrongly active but that they are actively wrong. The political activism of Christians is not the problem. Rather, rampant apathy and invincible ignorance constitute the greatest challenges.

We are seeing in the United States today a deliberate attempt to collapse the distinction between mixing politics and religion (which is inevitable) and merging church and state (which is inexcusable). There is hard evidence of a willful contempt for the First Amendment.

The bill of particulars includes

1. The attempt to pass an amendment to the United States Constitution allowing government-prescribed prayer in public schools. State-approved religious exercises would pervert authentic religion.

2. The push for tuition tax credits that would divert public funds to private and parochial schools. Such a regressive, elitist educational policy,

an approach so dangerous to the public schools, would also assure government intrusion into private and parochial schools.

3. The clamor for court stripping which came within six votes of succeeding in the U.S. Senate. It seems unthinkable that anyone would encourage robbing the Supreme Court and other federal courts of jurisdiction over civil and religious liberties.

4. The threat of a constitutional convention for the first time in two centuries. Only two more states are needed to call such a convention which, if it exceeded its call, might wreak havoc with the Bill of Rights.

5. The appointment of an ambassador from the United States to the Roman Catholic Church. Kenneth W. Dam of the State Department exposed the serious First Amendment violation when he was asked in a U.S. House hearing why we should have an Ambassador to the Holy See. He said, "It would allow the United States to influence the political positions of the Roman Catholic Church."

We are seeing an unprecedented revisionism regarding the American tradition of church-state separation. This trend threatens religious liberty.

Inevitable Mixing

From the believer's perspective, there is no other choice. Not to take a stand in the political context is to support the status quo. To accept things as they are is to indicate either that one is satisfied with present policies, that the situation is hopeless, or that his religion has nothing relevant to say.

To fail to alarm another morally assures that one will remain morally asleep himself. There is no neutral ground in a vital, changing democratic society. To "stay out of politics" or to assume a smugly superior pose as an independent above it all is itself an alignment with the forces of evil, a cheap cop-out.

Withdrawal from the world is a time-tested denial of religious realism, an evasion of ethical responsibility. Biblical truth must be fleshed out, incarnate. That means translating whatever one perceives to be revealed truth into contemporary terms, seeking proximate solutions with policies and candidates.

The Bible also teaches that every blessing carries piggyback a matching responsibility, "For unto whomsoever much is given, of him shall much be required" (Luke 12:48). Freedom to participate in a democracy demands responsible citizenship.

Again, the biblical understanding of love involves far more than sentiment. Caring for one's neighbor in concrete terms requires engagement with the political process because politics affects so vastly every nook and cranny of life.

From the legal angle, as well, it is assumed that religion will affect politics. Recent Supreme Court rulings have recognized that "churches as much as secular bodies and private citizens" may participate in political debate.[8]

Justice William Douglas, an advocate of church-state separation, insisted that "We are a religious people, whose institutions presuppose a Supreme Being."

Even more recently, Justice Brennan agreed. In concurring that ministers should not be banned from public office he wrote, "Government may not as a goal promote 'safe-thinking' with respect to religion and fence out those from political participation, such as ministers, whom it regards as overinvolved in religion."[9]

The record is clear. The courts have repeatedly held that the churches and other religious organizations are expected, even welcomed participants in the political arena. Religiously active people will not check their most deeply held beliefs at the door as they enter that arena. Rather, with all the risks involved, the demands of conscience informed by religion will be constitutionally brought to bear on public policy decisions.

From the broader social viewpoint, as well, religion has influenced and will continue to influence political choices. Harvey Cox insists, "Politics without a vision of the common good . . . is reduced to the art of brokerage between power interests." Cox recognizes the difficulties of involvement by many diverse religious groups in a highly complex governing process, but he does not give up on mixing religion and politics because as he says, "1. Our politics needs it. 2. Our faith requires it. 3. Our people want it."[10]

Dean M. Kelley, astute champion of religious freedom, predicts that "the churches are going to go on meddling with the social, political, and economic systems that affect the lives of human beings until hunger, war, vice, injustice, poverty, sickness, and suffering are eliminated."[11]

There is no doubt that mixing politics and religion is inevitable. The very nature of a society that holds in tension religious pluralism and a democratic political process guarantees that the mix is inevitable and inevitably explosive.

There are no guarantees that mixing religion and politics will be easy, constructive, or peaceful. Indeed, there is no direct route from the Bible to the ballot box. Even the dogmatist Carl Henry admits that one cannot leap from "individual spiritual rebirth to assuredly authentic and predictable public policy consequences"; rather, that "equally devout individuals may disagree over the best program for achieving common goals."[12]

The formulas for admixture of these two basic ingredients of society are many. It is all the more remarkable, therefore, that for 200 years religionists and politicians have stayed within bounds as much as they have. A certain mutual respect and fair play have held sway much of the time.

The United States Catholic Conference stakes out the church's role in the political order as including "education regarding the teachings of the church . . . analysis of issues; measuring public policy against Gospel values; participating . . . in the debate over public policy; and speaking out with courage, skill and concern on public issues involving human rights and social justice."[13]

Since mixing politics and religion is inevitable to a degree, Lewis B. Smedes suggests a rule of thumb for measuring that degree: "Do not trade off a dear liberty for a small morality." With John C. Murray, we should probably be content to get a small amount of personal morality converted into civil law.[14]

Alas, there is not a neat recipe that spells out the proper mix of politics and religion. There's the rub. The religious demands upon political decisions ought always to be tested by the highest public good, limited by the bounds of reason and persuasion, and expressed with the humble awareness that one just might be mistaken.

Inexcusable Merging

Both mixing politics and religion and keeping church and state separate presuppose a condition that is not: an informed citizenry. The fanaticism of the Religious Right springs from a soil of ignorance for which religious and political leaders must accept some responsibility.

"Seventy-seven percent of Americans polled in 1980 said they didn't know what is included in the First Amendment."[15] How can Americans hope to safeguard religious liberty without any understanding of the constitutional safeguards? We must understand the basic meaning of church-state separation.

Justice Hugo Black wrote for the Supreme Court in 1947, "The 'establishment of religion' clause means at least this: neither a state nor the federal government . . . can pass laws which aid one religion, aid all religions, or prefer one religion over another."[16]

The historical revisionists are bothered by Justice Black, but they must come to terms with Mr. Madison's parallel persuasion if they continue citing "the Founding Fathers." Paul J. Weber in Notre Dame's *Review of Politics*, April 1982, makes it clear that Madison favored separation of church and state and utterly opposed state establishment of any religion as well as a national religion. "Along with Jefferson, he urged the idea that government did not depend on a structural or supportive relationship with religion for legitimacy or good order. 'While Madison did not deny that sound religion is necessary to civil government, he flatly denied that establishment is.'"[17]

Mixing politics and religion is inevitable, but merging church and state is inexcusable. "Establishment has three components: coercion, disabilities (for those not established), and privilege. More, Madison trusted in the power of religion to thrive if left to its own resources, which is precisely the notion pro-school prayer and pro-establishment (of theism) people want to depart from."[18]

It is fair to tag as rewriters-of-history those who would have government-licensed religion, aid to church schools, or an ambassador to a church. Even nonpreferential favoring of religion in general violates the rights of nonbelievers as does any governmental recognition of religion. "In Madison's view, government must stay out of religious matters; it cannot give legal support to religion as a privileged category, even if that support be only financial or honorary, laudatory, or commendatory, since these are discriminatory. Religion, in short, must be totally disestablished if the religion of each citizen is to be given equal protection."[19]

When Harry Truman tried to appoint an ambassador to the Pope in 1950, William Warren Sweet's letter of protest reflected the same insistence upon no establishment. "All of our freedoms constitute one bundle, and if one is destroyed the whole bundle is destroyed. To give special consideration to one church, as a national policy, would undoubtedly produce a chain of events of serious import."[20]

Even when mixing religion and politics, one honors the spirit of separation. When Ted Kennedy spoke to the Liberty Baptist College on October 3, 1983, he set out a pragmatic position: mix but do not merge. "In drawing the line between imposed will and essential witness, we keep church and state separate—and at the same time, we recognize that the city of God should speak to the civic duties of men and women."[21] In distinguishing between mixing politics and religion and church-state separation, Senator Kennedy set out four tests: "respect the integrity of religion itself," "respect the independent judgments of conscience," "respect the integrity of public debate," and "respect the motives of those who exercise their right to disagree."[22]

If American history makes any eloquent appeal, it is for the separation of church and state. Roger Williams insisted, "It is impossible for any man or for all men to maintain their Christianity by the sword, and to maintain thereby a true Christianity." John Leland echoed his Baptist forebear: "Experience has informed us that the fondness of magistrates to foster Christianity has done it more harm than all the persecutions ever did."

Church-state separation is an attempt to write into public policy the notion that there is no place for coercion in the choice, exercise, or perpetuation of religion. Separation of church and state means at least that church and state have different reasons for being, diverse functions, separate sources of funding, distinctive methods and strategies and identities.

The merger of a sort of fuzzy Judeo-Christian consensus with patriotic Americanism has produced a civil religion that constitutes a challenge to church-state separation. This idolatrous religion depends upon patriotic fervor to be its Holy Spirit, Adam Smith its prophet, and television and movie actors to be its priests and missionaries. It has a bumper sticker for a creed: "America Love it or Leave it."

Billy Graham recognizes the danger to authentic religion posed by this media-fed monster. He says, "To tie the Gospel to any political system, secular program, or society is wrong and will only serve to divert the Gospel. The Gospel transcends the goals and methods of any political system or any society, however good it may be."[23] If only Dr. Graham and all of us would identify consistently and denounce unequivocally the counterfeit claims of civil religion.

It is not easy to keep clear this distinction. Those who attempt to maintain the tension suffer the two-handedness that Harry Truman despised. He said he "hated those two-handed fellars who were always saying 'on the one hand, but on the other hand.'"

One of the burdens of active citizenship in our modern, complex democracy is the burden of ambivalence. Honesty and awareness leave one stuck with difficult choices. Only the oversimplified positions of extremists, Left and Right, allow freedom from agony. Perhaps this pain is what the Preacher had in mind: "The more you know, the more you suffer: the more you understand, the more you ache" (Eccl 1:18).

"Where does one draw the line between mixing politics and religion and merging church and state?" It is a popular question, often asked simply to shut off debate. The challenge works as a cut-off valve because there is no simple, easy, short answer.

The question implies a neat worldview in which everything is black or white, good or bad. This either-or mentality is not the exclusive disease of religious and political fundamentalists. In fact, dualism infects American life. It insists upon every issue being divided from top to bottom by a vertical line with a right side and a wrong side.

Rather, a horizontal line with opposing views, differing ways of looking at things, or balancing considerations at either end is probably a more useful model. In many of the polarities, paradoxes, contradictions, or competing goods that complicate the church-state debate, one draws the line and then travels it, or draws the line and discovers that traveling the line is fraught with creative tension.

Often there is tension between the religion clauses of the First Amendment. Equal access legislation passed the summer of 1974 affirms the right of student-led, secondary school groups to meet for religious purposes with the same freedom that secular groups meet. The "no establishment of religion" and the "free exercise" guarantees are held in delicate balance.

Look at the ongoing debate among Roman Catholics over the implied dichotomy between personal morality and public policy. Governor Cuomo and Representative Ferraro insist that one should not enact into law his personal moral code, and the Bishops point out that one cannot divorce deeply held personal beliefs from views on public issues. Both sides are correct, to a degree. Consider the obligation of a president of the United States to use the "bully pulpit" for moral leadership and the oath taken to defend the Constitution. These duties sometimes conflict. Contrast: President Richard M. Nixon promised a Roman Catholic Bishop that he would "find a way around the Constitution" to provide aid for parochial schools. President John F. Kennedy promised Houston pastors that he "would not look with favor upon a President working to subvert the First Amendment's guarantees of religious liberty."

Think of the profound pressures to maintain enough consensus to govern, enough unity to conduct foreign policy, enough dedication to common values for a frame of reference to allow discussion and debate and at the same time the conflicting and equally profound dedication of Americans to diversity, to pluralism, and to the basic freedoms written into the Bill of Rights.

Listen to voices from one side warning about secular humanism being an established non-religion and those from another side warning about repressive fundamentalism. Both deserve to be heard. Fear of modernity, the desire to revive a day that never was with values it never possessed is an immoral nostalgia. All humanism is not secular and all secularity is not evil. On the other hand, some political "realists" despise any reference to moral and spiritual convictions, depend upon unaided reason, and insist that self-interest is the only standard by which to measure foreign policy. These are real secular humanists who do threaten humane values and America's leadership role.

Hear the cliché that the state "cannot legislate morals." Some draw a line that would rule out any attempt to regulate personal behavior. Yet, in some sense, all legislation deals ultimately with morality, good and bad, right and wrong. Once again, the reasonable response must be to a degree, to a degree.

Recognize that personal attributes shaped largely by one's faith enter the seesaw act. Conviction and a measure of certainty are necessary to enter the political process. Timid politicians lose. Yet the political world needs humility as well as conviction, and God's children have reason to help supply both. Don Shriver cites Oliver Cromwell who "said to two contentious groups of Scotsmen, 'I beseech you, by the mercies of Christ, think that you may be wrong!' Judge Learned Hand is often invoked when he said, 'The Spirit of Liberty is the spirit that is not too sure it is right.'"[24]

Face another continuum. On one hand, it is held that only individual citizens should be involved in politics with the churches educating, motivating, moralizing but never becoming involved corporately and, on the other hand, that churches not only may but must act on their stewardship as prophetic witnesses. For the individualistic approach, there are Christian but nonecclesiastical corporate entities from the Moral Majority to Bread for the World providing citizenship outlets. Those insisting upon a corporate witness plead that for the church or synagogue to remain silent given its charter, its identity, its profession of faith, is involvement on the side of negative forces. Not to decide is itself a decision.

Dean Kelley pleads for those who disagree with the electronic preachers to refute them in the democratic marketplace of ideas, not to try to silence them. This is the most rudimentary lesson of civil liberties.

Other continua are to be taken into account in dealing with the questions of how much mixing is too much and where is the line that sets off church from state. A few of the more obvious involve motive, biblical warrant, understanding, entanglement with government, and the methods used in advancing one's views. Each of these considerations involves a whole range of questions of degree.

For example, is the motive for one's political involvement self-interest or the public good? Of course, this test alone is too subjective to be reliable and every engagement is found somewhere along the line from mean selfishness to utter altruism. Political parties, public servants, and specific policies must also be subjected to this kind of examination. For instance, the eminent historian Henry Steele Commager says that the present administration is the "least compassionate administration in the whole of American history." Whether one agrees with his assessment is not the issue. The point is that such an evaluation is proper and necessary. It answers one of those "to the degree" questions.

To what degree do forays into public policy find biblical warrant, spiritual sanction, and historical precedent? Is the attempt to influence government based on principles of stewardship, compassion, justice, human rights, the pursuit of peace, and concern for the hungry?

At what level of understanding and education do those operate who would mix politics and religion? Certainly, all citizens cannot become technical experts and policy specialists. Yet we can do our homework and refuse to follow anyone blindly.

To what extent does the policy, practice, or proposed legislation that is the subject of consideration entangle government with religion, merge church and state? A healthy distance, an institutional integrity, is one of the relative factors to be taken into account.

Where on the scale from coercion to persuasion does the political activism fall? It is not likely to be totally pure at either end of the line. Edward M. Kennedy cautioned his audience at Liberty Baptist College that persons of deep religious faith "may be tempted to misuse government in order to impose a value which they cannot persuade others to accept."[25]

The tensions, tugs, conflicts, and contradictions between polar concepts could be multiplied. Sometimes both of the poles are useful, proper, and essential in determining right and wrong as with the classic interplay between love and law, freedom and fixity, experience and authority. At other times both extremes are to be rejected and the appropriate balance found somewhere in the middle.

The deliberate attempts to collapse the distinction between mixing politics and religion and merging church and state will fail if persons of good will who believe in religion and care about democracy will act. Niebuhr's words are relevant: "Man's capacity for justice makes democracy possible, but man's inclination to injustice makes democracy necessary."[26] The same can be said of the precious doctrine of religious liberty which makes church-state separation and political involvement necessary. A proper mix is Christian virtue.

> —This article appeared in the summer 1986 issue of
> *Perspectives in Religious Studies* 13/2, pages 151–60,
> and is reprinted with permission.

Church and State: Friends or Enemies?

In the commentary below, James Dunn offers an abbreviated and popularized articulation of his philosophy of church-state relations and political engagement. He urges individuals not to stay out of politics while also warning against efforts to coerce the consciences of citizens through policies and political actions that threaten church-state separation. This article was featured in the August 1988 issue of The Student, *a magazine for college students published by the Sunday School Board of the Southern Baptist Convention.*

A pernicious plot endangers the delicate balance of church and state in the American experiment.

Extremists who receive so much attention are not wrongly active but actively wrong. The most disturbing factor in the religio-political scene is not rhetoric but policy proposals.

There is a deliberate attempt to collapse the distinction between mixing politics and religion (which is inevitable) and merging church and state (which is inexcusable). Hard evidence of a willful contempt for the First Amendment includes:

1. The attempt to pass an amendment to the Constitution allowing government-prescribed prayer in public schools.

2. The push for tuition tax credits which would divert public funds to private and parochial schools.

3. The clamor for court stripping, which came within six votes of succeeding in the U.S. Senate.

4. The threat of a constitutional convention for the first time in two centuries.

5. The appointment of an ambassador to the Roman Catholic Church. This trend threatens religious liberty.

Mixing Politics and Religion: Inevitable

For the believer, there is no other choice. To accept things as they are is to indicate either that one is satisfied with present policies, that the situation is hopeless, or that the gospel has nothing relevant to say.

To "stay out of politics" or assume a smugly superior pose as an "independent-above-it-all" is itself an alignment with the forces of evil, a cheap cop-out.

Withdrawal from the world is a time-tested denial of religious realism, an evasion of ethical responsibility. Biblical truth must be fleshed out, incarnate.

The Bible also teaches that every blessing carries piggyback a responsibility, " . . . For unto whomsoever much is given, of him shall much be required . . . " (Luke 12:48). Freedom to participate in a democracy calls for activism.

Caring for one's neighbor in concrete Christian terms requires engagement with the political process because politics affects every nook and cranny of life.

From the legal angle, as well, it is assumed that religion affects politics. Supreme Court rulings have recognized that "churches as much as secular bodies and private citizens" may participate in political debate.[27]

In concurring that ministers should not be banned from public office, Justice Brennan wrote, "Government may not as a goal promote 'safethinking' with respect to religion and fence out those from political participation, such as ministers . . . ."[28]

The record is clear. The courts have held that the churches are expected, even welcome, participants in the political arena. Religiously active people will not check their most deeply held beliefs at the door as they enter that arena.

Dean M. Kelley predicts that "the churches are going to go on meddling with the social, political, and economic systems that affect the lives of human beings until hunger, war, vice, injustice, poverty, sickness and suffering are eliminated."[29]

Alas, there is no neat recipe for the proper mix of politics and religion. There's the rub.

Merging Church and State: Inexcusable

Both mixing politics and religion and keeping church and state separate presuppose a condition which is not: an informed citizenry. Fanaticism springs from a soil of ignorance for which religious and political leaders must accept some responsibility.

"Seventy-seven percent of Americans polled in 1980 said they didn't know what is included in the First Amendment."[30] How can Americans hope to safeguard religious liberty without any understanding of the Constitution?

Justice Hugo Black wrote for the Supreme Court in 1947, "The 'establishment of religion' clause means at least this: Neither a state nor the federal government . . . can pass laws which aid one religion, aid all religions, or prefer one religion over another."[31]

If American history makes any eloquent appeal, it is for the separation of church and state. John Leland echoed his Baptist forefathers, saying, "Experience has informed us that the fondness of magistrates to foster Christianity has done it more harm than all the persecutions ever did."

Church-state separation attempts to write into public policy the notion of no coercion in the choice, exercise, or perpetuation of religion. Separation of church and state means at least that church and state have different reasons for being, functions, sources of funding, methods, strategies, and identities.

Billy Graham recognizes the danger to authentic religion posed by merging church and state. He says, "To tie the Gospel to any political system, secular program, or society is wrong and will only serve to divert the Gospel. The Gospel transcends the goals and methods of any political system or any society, however good it may be."[32]

The deliberate attempts to collapse the distinction between mixing politics and religion and merging church and state will fail if persons of goodwill who care about religion and believe in democracy will act. Niebuhr's words are relevant: "Man's capacity for justice makes democracy possible, but man's inclination to injustice makes democracy necessary."[33] The same can be said of the precious doctrine of religious liberty which makes church-state separation necessary.

—Reprinted with permission courtesy of
Lifeway Christian Resources.

Standing for Religious Freedom

Religious freedom is rooted in the nature of God, and being made in the image of God, human beings enjoy both responsibility and freedom, including the responsibility to stand for religious freedom. This is one of the messages James Dunn had for Texas Baptists in the following column published in 1994.

> Humpty Dumpty sat on a wall,
> Humpty Dumpty had a great fall,
> And all the king's horses,
> And all the king's men,
> Couldn't put Humpty together again.

That's my text. Or, if you prefer Scripture, as I do, to Mother Goose, let's go with Philippians 3:13-14: "Forgetting those things which are behind, and reaching forth unto those things which are before, I press toward the mark for the prize of the high calling of God in Christ Jesus."

There has been a seismic upheaval in Baptist life. In the midst of it, Texas Baptists have doggedly determined to remain Baptists. With fresh attention to local churches and lay leadership, with a reaffirmation of the state convention, with creative channeling of resources through the Cooperative Baptist Fellowship, Texas Baptists are staying committed.

I invoke Humpty to describe the national Baptist crash because the coup has cut the taproot, pulled the rug out from under the Baptist furniture, denied the distinctive that makes us Baptist.

Our very Baptist brand name, our basic ingredient—freedom of religion—has been tinkered with. Even real, Training Union-trained Baptists have forgotten that freedom is what is Godlike about us. Freedom is the goal, the good, the intent of God's work for us in Christ Jesus. "It is precisely for freedom that Christ has set us free" (Galatians 5:1).

In that spirit of freedom, we find the method, the modality for relating to the world, the church, and each other. "Where the Spirit of the Lord is, there is freedom" (2 Corinthians 3:17). The way of freedom has always been God's method. "Not by might, nor by power, but by my spirit, saith the LORD" (Zechariah 4:6). Every moral issue requires free moral agency.

Our freedom is rooted not in the Constitution of the United States, nor the Bill of Rights, nor history. It is not rooted in a church, a creed, a belief, a book, not even the Bible. Our freedom is rooted in the very nature of God.

Being made in the image of God, we are able to respond to God. We are response-able, responsible, and free. Responsibility and freedom are inseparable, God's purpose for us, the most Godlike thing about us. And it is the plan of the Creator that we be free creatures in our knowing, our choosing, our loving, our being.

That essential freedom is not debatable, not optional, nonnegotiable. Fundamentalists have not caught on to that yet.

All that we are and do is vitally connected to the way God made us. Missions and evangelism are predicated upon religious freedom. We depend on the possibility—the necessity—of a free and Spirit-led response to the gospel. We all follow Jesus freely or not really.

We have no creed. Oh, well, we do have an oral tradition that takes on the force of an unwritten creed. You hear it especially in Texas Baptist churches. It goes, "Ain't nobody going to tell me what to believe."

We come to one another as priests all. The priesthood of all believers rules out ruling pastors. In fact, the term "ruling pastor" is an oxymoron—ruler, no pastor; pastor, no ruler. And one who thinks he's a ruling pastor is an ordinary moron!

We come to each church as a democracy and to a fellowship of autonomous churches. Someone visiting the First Baptist Church of Washington, D.C., asked how we could belong to the SBC and the American Baptist Churches. The answer, in good Baptist ecclesiology, was "We don't belong to them; they belong to us."

We value religious freedom so highly because we cannot by definition be Baptists without it. Baptists from the first affirmed church-state separation.

Smyth said, "the magistrate is not by virtue of his office to meddle with religion or matters of conscience." Helwys said "the king is a mortal man and not God, therefore hath no power over ye immortal souls." Helwys, incidentally, was put to death for that belief by the very King James whose name is on your Bible.

E. Y. Mullins set out the freedom connection in his *The Axioms of Religion*:

- God is free—the theological axiom.
- All souls have an equal right to direct access to God—the religious axiom.
- All believers have a right to equal privileges in the church—the church axiom.

- To be responsible, one must be free—the moral axiom.
- A free church in a free state—the religio-civic axiom.
- Love your neighbor as yourself—the social axiom.

Freedom of religion and its corollary, the separation of church and state, has been the trademark, the hallmark, the birthmark of Baptists.

It just irritates the "dickens" out of fundamentalists for us to focus on freedom. I suspect that's not because they are concerned for our eternal souls as apostate antinomians, but because they need a creed.

The fundamentalist mindset fears freedom because faith is risky and freedom is a burden. The creedalist despises diversity because one cannot trust anyone who doesn't think as he does.

But ours is an experiential faith, lively and liberated. Our churches are non-creedal and connected only by choice. We want this same freedom for others, however bizarre their beliefs, so we demand that the state keep out of the religion business.

When anyone's religious freedom is denied, everyone's religious freedom is endangered. Religious freedom defines who we are, how we work, what we value, even why we witness.

The climate today is hostile to both the separation of church and state and the free exercise of religion. Both religious clauses of the First Amendment are at risk.

The prime threat to religious liberty comes from the Supreme Court itself. The Chief Justice (William Rehnquist) has written that "the wall of separation between church and state is a metaphor based on bad history; a metaphor which has proved useless as a guide to judging. It should be frankly and explicitly abandoned."

Worse, he went on to contend that the evils aimed at in the First Amendment were only the establishment of a national church and preferential aid for one religion over others. His subsequent opinions have reflected his persistence in error.

Justice Antonin Scalia gutted free exercise when he wrote it is "a legal luxury we can no longer afford" and proceeded to dump the long-standing balancing test that allowed government to intrude in religion only when there is a "compelling state interest."

Since then, more than four dozen reported cases have been decided in the light of Scalia's new test, and religion regularly loses. Churches have been excluded from desired and convenient zoning districts and "house churches" have been banned.

Prisoners have been denied the right to attend Chuck Colson's Prison Fellowship Outreach meetings. Orthodox Jews and Hmongs have been forced to submit the bodies of family members to autopsies without extenuating circumstances. A New York Landmarking Commission dictated to a church how it could use its building.

But the entire religious community has come together in a coalition led by Buzz Thomas of the Baptist Joint Committee. We are now waiting for the Senate to act on the Religious Freedom Restoration Act (S.578) which the House of Representatives passed without dissent May 11.

Pandering religious entrepreneurs also challenge religious freedom. Mr. Bakker is in jail. Mr. Moon has served time. Mr. Falwell just paid a $50,000 fine for using tax-free religious broadcasting as a front for partisan political activities.

One of the most dangerous distortions of religious freedom comes from Pat Robertson and his highly partisan so-called Christian Coalition. He built a television empire with tax-deductible gifts under the cover of tax exemption then put it on the market and amassed vast wealth for himself and his family.

For Jesus' sake, indeed!

But one does not have to look at the Court or the television evangelists to find enemies of religious freedom and its guarantor, church-state separation. From up in Aledo, Texas, comes David Barton's slick but inaccurate videotape, "America's Godly Heritage." It is a hot item in many churches; I hope not in yours.

Soul freedom, religious liberty, and church-state separation are like three concentric circles. At the center in the smallest circle burns the fire of the biblical, theological doctrine of soul freedom with which we began, made, somehow, in God's image, intended to be free and responsible.

The next ring outward, religious liberty, is the moral and social consequences of voluntary faith and personal conversion. If we claim that freedom for ourselves, we must defend it for others too: loving our neighbors as ourselves, doing unto others as we'd have them do to us.

Finally, the outer circle is the separation of church and state, the constitutional principle that serves as a fence, a guardrail, a wall protecting individual religious freedom.

It may be true, as Martin Marty suggests, that we no longer have Thomas Jefferson's high and impregnable wall; at best we may have only a "zone of separation." But we must maintain some distinction between the institutions of government and religion.

We must keep up the fence, even if it is just a strand of barbed wire. If you do not favor the separation of church and state, you might want to move to Beirut or Belfast or Bosnia.

Separation of church and state does not mean separation of God from government, or Christians from their citizenship, or even religion from politics. It does mean, however, that religion doesn't run the state government, does not define, control, promote, or inhibit religion.

It is precisely for freedom Christ has set you free. It is not to provide a heavenly hellfire escape, or peace of mind, or to help us integrate our personalities or actualize ourselves. It is not even to "glorify God and enjoy Him forever."

For freedom, in freedom, we were created to be incarnate, fleshed-out role models of God's love and grace. We are free and responsible, caring for the liberty, sharing with others the spiritual freedom one can know in Jesus Christ.

But as long as some so-called Baptists persist in the Galatian heresy—attempting to escape from freedom—old Humpty has had a great fall and we can't put that sucker together again.

But whatever they do, free and faithful Baptists will not only survive. We shall overcome.

—Reprinted with permission courtesy of Bill Jones and Texas Baptists Committed.

Religious Liberty and Church/State Separation Go Hand in Hand

Throughout his tenure (and even before) at the Baptist Joint Committee, James Dunn pressed the important point that religious liberty and church-state separation are twin concepts. He often described soul freedom/religious liberty/ church-state separation as three concentric circles. In this chapter from the book titled Defining Baptist Convictions: Guidelines for the Twenty-First Century *(1996), Dunn continues this emphasis, drawing from examples in Baptist history such as Roger Williams, John Leland, and George W. Truett.*

Soul freedom is the fire that burns in the innards of every true Baptist. From Thomas Helwys's insistence that "the king is not the Lord of the conscience" to this day, the identifying mark of the breed called Baptist is that dogged determination to be free.

No proof text is needed because the passion for freedom is rooted in the person and nature of God in whose image all humankind is created. Before any constitution, any social contract, even before the biblical revelation lies the way in which we were all made—responsible to God and free to respond (and take the consequences).

If that is the biblical and theological principle driving religious liberty, then the ethical, moral, and social implications of that transforming idea demand the same freedom for every other human being. If we do love our neighbors as ourselves, if we do unto others as we want them to do to us, if, indeed, what's sauce for the goose is sauce for the gander, we want religious liberty for everyone.

Another's religious liberty denied is everyone's religious liberty endangered. Firmly rooted in biblical belief and the ethical demands coming directly from those convictions, Baptists have stood for separation of church and state since we were first labeled "Baptists."

The same King James whose name is in the front of your Bible is the one who ordered the death of Thomas Helwys, the first Baptist pastor in England. Helwys's crime was simple: the king was not his spiritual master. Government, however good, could not be God.

One does not go to the Bible for instruction as if it were a political science textbook. Yet the Bible speaks to the relation of religion to political life. Baptists who slight the distinctive of church-state separation deny their birthright.

Some today cannot see that clear biblical teachings inform one's estimate of humankind, sin, righteousness, and redemption. Biblical doctrine fuels and empowers believers to seek spiritual liberation for all. The Bible has shaped our best insights and noblest traditions as "people of the Book." The universal freedom of religious conscience is taught in the Bible.

If you are interested in examining this contention in detail, see "Separation No Myth: Religious Liberty's Biblical and Theological Bases" in the summer 1994 issue of the *Southwestern Journal of Theology*. Scholar Jim Spivey sets out simply the biblical basis for church-state separation.

Happily, however, one does not have to depend upon Bible verses alone to persuade for the institutional separation of religion and government. Logic, history, compassionate common sense, prudence, and political realism also make the case.

Separation of church and state does not mean the separation of God from government. No thinking modern would allow that sort of division between the sacred and the secular. The God whom we love and serve seeks out every nook and cranny of life.

Separation does not require the separation of religion from politics. In fact, many of the most dedicated advocates of church-state separateness have been at the same time prophets to the powers that be, serious social critics, champions of peace and justice.

Roger Williams fought for the Native Americans and became their hero and mentor. John Leland took on every injustice in sight and set an impossibly high standard on political activism by preachers. Walter Rauschenbusch, who had a Baptist appreciation for separation of church and state, is known as the "father of the Social Gospel."

No. One does not need to separate religious fervor from political action. If anything, the opposite is true.

Nor does separation of church and state mean separation of Christians from their citizenship. Christian citizens will be more involved, not less, if for no other reason than to see that no religious faction forces its views on the state and that the state remembers that it has no rule over the conscience.

It is dangerous for churches or any other religious institutions to be caught in the bear hug of the state—smothering. It is equally as bad if a church bear squeezes the body politic. The great Baptist leader Gardner Taylor reminded us that separation of church and state is essential if for no other reason than that people of faith "need a little swinging room." These two institutions must act on, speak to, listen to, and learn from each other.

W. A. Criswell, a well-known Baptist, was seen on national television saying that "the separation of church and state is a figment of the imagination of some infidel." How sad. How wrong.

It has become popular to say that "the separation of church and state is found in the constitution of the U.S.S.R., not in the U.S. Constitution." While it is true that the precise words do not appear in the Constitution, the concept is clearly there.

The word "Trinity" does not appear in the New Testament. That does not deny the triune God. The phrase "separation of church and state" does not appear in the Constitution; it is nonetheless a reality of American government. The separation of church and state is a reality rooted in reality.

The two institutions have different purposes. The church is to bring people to God, advance the Kingdom of Heaven, glorify God, edify the saints, and do God's work in the world. Put it in your own words. Jesus taught, "My kingdom is not of this world."

The purpose of government, at least in this land, is to "provide for the common defense and promote the general welfare." The state encompasses all citizens and is accountable to all, believer and unbeliever alike.

The two aspects of our lives have different constituencies. Citizenship in this nation is not the same as identification with a church or any other kind of religious entity.

If one is born in Denmark, he or she is zap! a Lutheran. Being born in Iran suggests Muslim identity. But Baptists and other free-church folk expect one to be born again before becoming part of the church. We believe in a regenerate church membership. Even those without such strict standards know that church and state have different constituencies. There is no such thing as a "Christian Nation." Only persons, not nations, can be Christians.

The two, church and state, have different findings, different bases of support. The church is supported with tithes and offerings. Religion requires voluntary support. That is a big difference. Try not paying your taxes if you doubt the distinction.

The two loyalties engage different methods to accomplish their goals. The state may use force. Coercion is not only acceptable by the state; it is a necessity. The Bible teaches about the use of force by the state in Romans 13.

The church, on the other hand, relies upon persuasion. The prophet cried out, "Not by might or by power, but by my Spirit, saith the Lord."

Roger Williams warned that the use of force might make a nation of hypocrites but would not produce one Christian. And so, voluntary religion has served both church and state well in this country.

The "lively experiment" envisioned by Roger Williams has worked. With the separation of church and state, this nation has the greatest freedom of religion, the least religious conflict, the largest number of people in church/synagogue/temple/mosque every week, the highest percentage of voluntary religious participants, the most missionaries and people-helpers sent out to other countries, and the best record of giving for religious causes of any nation on the face of the earth—all in the name of religion.

The recognition of the reality-rooted distinctions between church and state appeals to the best in people. To be free to decide for oneself in matters of conscience is essential. It evokes our essence, made in God's image. To exercise one's own volition is integral to our nature as spiritual beings. It integrates our physical, mental, and spiritual natures. To individually invest one's life in causes beyond oneself is basic to the way we are all wired or programmed, to use a current word picture. The baseline of our being requires freedom. It is the way we have been since Adam and Eve.

We must respond freely to be responsible. That is true even if—especially if—we make the wrong choices. Everyone has the right to be wrong. It is none of the business of government to control thoughts and minds. It is beyond the capacity of government to control hearts and spirits. And so we rejoice in the separation of church and state as a corporate recognition of that reality. The awareness of the real differences between church and state also accepts the awesome awfulness of the worst in human beings. We saw the bloodshed and horrors of the Crusades and the Inquisition in the name of Jesus. We know what happened in Hitler's Germany when the churches lost their voice and the state dominated every aspect of life.

But one need not look back to see what takes place in Lebanon where religious movements have become mere parties to the warfare that continues. See how religious struggle for control of the government mechanism has dehumanized Northern Ireland. Look at Bosnia and see the religion-fueled hatred that sustains the push for ethnic cleansing. Do not forget that much killing has been done in the name of Jesus or Islam.

A biblically shaped view of how human beings actually behave directed the presuppositions of those who gave us the Bill of Rights. James Madison, who was trained at what later became Princeton, had a sober assessment of the human capacity for evil. He wanted to build in checks and balances to moderate the harm men could do. For him it was "men."

John Leland, Virginia Baptist preacher and powerful influence on Madison, made the conclusion clear: "Sad experience, the best teacher, has taught us that the fondness of magistrates to foster Christianity has done it more harm than all the persecution ever did."

In such sentiment was found the groundswell of support for church-state separation. The founders knew firsthand the devilment done in the name of God. They had seen the religious wars in Europe, the persecution unto death perpetrated in the theocracy of Massachusetts, and the imprisonments of Baptists for preaching the gospel in Virginia. A happy coalition of enlightenment thought and evangelical belief came together to give the United States a rule of law with documents, the Constitution and the Bill of Rights, to guarantee the continuance of church-state separation.

George W. Truett and many others have insisted that the greatest contribution of the United States to the science of government is the lively experiment in the separation of church and state. Thank heavens we do not have the rule of thumb that prevailed in Europe: "*Cuius regio, eius religio*—whose the rule, his the religion." Nor do we observe the rule of the majority in matters spiritual.

Rather, the rule of law guarantees against the tyranny of the mood of the majority at any moment. The protections afforded in the Bill of Rights are not up for majority vote.

The Bill of Rights is counter-majoritarian. Justice Hugo Black was asked what the words "no law" mean in the first phrase of the Bill of Rights. He replied, "They mean two things: 'no' and 'law.'" That plain. That safe for all God's children. Congress shall make no law respecting an establishment of religion.

Justice Robert Jackson wrote, "If there is a fixed star in our constitutional constellation, it is that no official, high or petty, can describe what shall be orthodox in politics, nationalism, religion, or other matters of opinion, or force citizens to confess by word or act their faith therein."

Herschel H. Hobbs, Baptist wiseman, wrote, "Religious liberty entails the separation of church and state, a principle declared by Jesus [himself] (Matt. 22:21)"—(*The Baptist Messenger*, 16 March 1995).

Daunting is the challenge to conserve and defend the distinctive marking on the beast called Baptist that insists upon separation of church and state. The popular mood of the country is much like that of Henry Ford, who said, "History is bunk." With little or no knowledge of our roots, it is difficult to understand our plight. There is a greedy, selfish secession of the successful from social responsibility. This, too, makes for blurring of the lines drawn by principle in the past. Political opportunists join the ignorant and the elitist in a unified disregard for religious liberty and its essential corollary, the separation of church and state.

What shall we do?

1. Study history, the Constitution, the Bill of Rights. Know how we got the documents of democracy and why. If we do not understand why we have these safeguards for freedom, we are not likely to defend them.

2. Engage others in study. Evangelistically, promote the examination of our heritage of religious freedom. There is a wealth of good materials available from the American Baptist Churches, Americans United for the Separation of Church and State, and the Baptist Joint Committee.

3. Encourage the celebration of religious freedom in civic and community settings. Many opportunities leap out at you in ministerial alliances, in civic groups like Lions, Rotary, and Optimist clubs, and in Masonic settings. Masons are especially dedicated to religious freedom.

4. Subscribe to *The Journal of Church and State*, the magazine *Church and State*, and the fortnightly newsletter *Report from the Capital*. Together, these keep you informed of developments in this realm.

5. Read newspapers and news magazines, and watch responsible television analysis to stay abreast of current developments.

6. Participate in the political process. That means more than voting. It means taking part in precinct politics and writing letters asking candidates their positions on church-state issues.

7. Warn everyone you know about those television entrepreneurs of religion, radio talk shows, and blatantly political coalitions that deny the separation of church and state, promote a brand of civil religion, and cling to narrow tests on issues that would diminish everyone's religious freedom.

8. Practice your own religious freedom by freely and gladly joining those of like mind and spirit in the worship of God, the practice of faith, and the compassionate caring modeled for us all by Jesus Christ.

It is precisely for freedom that Christ has set you free. The separation of church and state is a necessary safeguard.

—This article appeared as a chapter in the book *Defining Baptist Convictions: Guidelines for the Twenty-First Century*, edited by Charles W. Deweese (Franklin TN: Providence House Publishers, 1996). Reprinted with permission.

Freedom's Roots: Back to the Bill of Rights' Beginning

In this chapter from the book The Trophy of Baptists: Words to Celebrate Religious Liberty *(Smyth & Helwys Publishing, 2003), edited by J. Brent Walker, James Dunn's successor at the Baptist Joint Committee, Dunn discusses the origins of the First Amendment in the U.S. Constitution and the contributions of Baptist leader John Leland in ensuring that guarantees for religious liberty were included in the Bill of Rights.*

Religious liberty and its constitutional guardrail, the separation of church and state, are in big trouble today. Just listen to what they are saying (and doing) in Washington:

• Justice Antonin Scalia and four Supreme Court cohorts demolished the tried and true requirement that government demonstrate a "compelling interest" before it can fiddle with our religious practice. He called this invaluable safeguard a "luxury" that we can no longer afford as a society.

• The Chief Justice of the United States, William Rehnquist, believes that Mr. Jefferson's protective wall of separation between church and state is a "metaphor based on bad history" which should be "frankly and explicitly abandoned."

• The Solicitor General of the United States, Kenneth W. Starr, has asked the Court to overturn decades of legal precedent requiring government to adopt a posture of neutrality toward religion. His misconceived interpretation of the First Amendment would allow the states and federal government to engage in religious exercises so long as they do not coerce anyone to participate or threaten to set up a national church.

• President George W. Bush has recently called for "choice in education" as a fix for our ailing public schools—a sanitized foil thinly wrapping the decades-old attempt to get tax dollars into religious schools.

• This past fall, Congress (debunking religious liberty is not a partisan practice) limited the tax deductibility of donations to churches and other nonprofit organizations, thus inviting by example fiscally strapped local taxing authorities all over the country to prey on church coffers.

How ironic it is for religious liberty to be under severe attack at precisely the moment when we should be celebrating its fruition—the 200th anniversary of the ratification of the Bill of Rights! This incredible ignorance on the part of our policymakers about our heritage and the true meaning of the Bill of Rights provides a propitious but sad occasion to look back over the last two centuries.

Look back not for arcane argument about "original intent." Look back not for academic nitpicking. Look back to learn the lessons we never learned or to be reminded of the truths we have forgotten. Look back to put the origins of the Bill of Rights in context, to gain perspective, to capture the essence so that when mixed with current conflict one will hear not simply the words but also the music.

Word pictures, snapshots, of four key figures in the Bill of Rights family tree hopefully will humanize the history. The roles of these chosen forebears fall along a continuum from lofty principle to low-down politics, from abstract to concrete. Chopping the continuum of contributions by Roger Williams, Thomas Jefferson, James Madison, and John Leland into arbitrary, speech-sized divisions is but one design for getting back to the Bill of Rights' beginning. Special attention is here given to the first freedoms and the first words of the First Amendment, which begins the Bill of Rights. Those words are simply "Congress shall make no law respecting an establishment of religion, or prohibiting the free exercise thereof." The words "no law," as Justice Hugo Black liked to say, mean plainly "no law," favorable or unfavorable.

Roger Williams fathered philosophically the American experiment in freedom of religion. Some of his London friends thought him "divinely mad." He shaped his colony of Rhode Island into the home of the otherwise minded. Some detractors preferred to call it "Rogue's Island" or "that sewer" or "the licentious republic."

It was a far cry from socializing with royalty as he had in London to barren New England. He was a graduate of Pembroke College, Cambridge, Charterhouse scholar from 1623 to 1629. Running interference for him had been the leading legal scholar of the day, Sir Edward Coke. Williams's famous friends and classy connections included John Milton and Oliver Cromwell. Now it had come to this: cast out into the bitter winter, "the howling wilderness," as he wrote, "not knowing what bread or bed did mean" for fourteen weeks.

This was part of the price Roger Williams paid for insisting upon freedom and not mere toleration as the standard for the treatment of religion. He despised toleration as the measure of the majority religion's relationship with dissenters. Williams understood that toleration is a human concession, but liberty is a gift of God. Government has no right to enforce religious uniformity or to collect taxes for support of the clergy. Indeed, Williams prefigured the freedom of religion guaranteed in the First Amendment.

Perry Miller places Williams at the fount of freedom: "Now as all the world knows, this Separatist [Williams] figures in history as the pioneer of religious freedom, even of democracy." And in a later work the Harvard scholar Miller praises Williams as a "prophet of religious liberty" who has molded the American character. "For the subsequent history of what became the United States, Roger Williams possesses one indubitable importance, that he stands at the beginning of it."

Oscar S. Straus, a Jewish scholar, wrote of Williams, "He was not the first to discover the principles of religious liberty, but he was the first to proclaim them in all their plenitude, and to found and build up a political community with those principles as the basis of its organization."

This practicing philosopher of freedom, Roger Williams, is nominated as one of the four founders most responsible for the First Amendment. He is disproportionately important because he first challenged the old-world patterns of toleration, theocracy, church states, and state churches. He was banished, ostracized, ridiculed, and thought to have windmills in his head. He died poor and rejected, nothing much to show for his labors . . . except the American experiment of religious liberty and the most vital churches in the world. As Charles Kuralt says, "Today they've put him on a pedestal. The figure atop the capitol dome is called the Independent Man. He can see the whole state [of Rhode Island] from up there, the first state to be disrespectful and disreputable and free."

Thomas Jefferson initiated intellectually the chain of legislation that led to the First Amendment and through agitation for it to the Bill of Rights. He was proud of the "Virginia Statute for Religious Freedom." Getting it passed was, he said, "the severest contest in which I have ever been engaged."

Patrick Henry, popular orator, had opposed the statute and pushed a contrary bill that would have established general assessments for the churches. Jefferson was in France and responded to letters from James Madison, who was leading the fight for Jefferson's proposed separation of church and state. Madison wrote, fearful that all was lost. Mr. Henry's taxation of all citizens to support the churches had passed two readings and seemed certain to become law on passage of third reading. "What shall we do?" he asked Jefferson. Jefferson replied, "What we have to do, I think devotedly to pray for his [Henry's] death."

As it worked out, Madison wrote the brilliant "A Memorial and Remonstrance Against Religious Assessments"; Mr. Henry was elected governor—a post that did not have veto power; George Mason lobbied his peers; Baptists, Presbyterians, and others produced petitions with hundreds of names; the Virginia Statute for Religious Freedom passed on January 1786; and Governor Patrick Henry, with no veto, signed into law on January 19, 1786, the bill he had fought.

The importance of this one bill cannot be overestimated. Harvard historian Bernard Bailyn called the statute "the most important document in American history, bar none." The Virginia Statute was the "model for the guarantee of religious liberty incorporated in the U.S. Bill of Rights." What did this often-forgotten law do for generations following?

It protected the right to say "no" to all religion. One does have freedom *from* religion as well as freedom *for* religion in this country, no matter what powerful presidents and popular preachers may say. Without the freedom to say "no," all one's "yeses" are meaningless.

It denied tax support to the churches. As Jefferson said, "to compel a man to furnish contributions of money for the propagation of opinions which he disbelieves is sinful and tyrannical."

It set out separation of church and state, later memorialized by Jefferson's metaphorical "wall" in an 1802 letter to the Danbury Connecticut Baptist Association.

It guaranteed the free exercise of religion, not mere toleration or a condescending concession.

This Jeffersonian view of religious liberty and church-state separation found its way into the Bill of Rights. The revised standard version of the First Amendment as mentioned in the beginning of this article holds that it simply (1) rules out favoritism among religious groups and (2) prohibits an official State church, but endorses God-in-general and supports generic religion.

But the Supreme Court, history, and common sense consistently contend that the Establishment Clause embraces much broader—Jeffersonian if you will—restraints on government than these simple prohibitions.

The record of the Senate debates over approval of the First Amendment eloquently refutes all claims that a sort of preferential establishment was all the amendment intended to prohibit. As paraphrased from Stokes and Pfeffer's *Church and State in the United States*, the debate reveals the recommended alterations to the First Amendment.

In 1789, on the first day of debate, the Senate acted in the following ways:

1. A motion was made to strike out the words "religion, or prohibiting the free exercise thereof," and insert "one religious sect or society in preference to others." This motion was DEFEATED.

2. A second motion was made to strike out the amendment altogether. This motion was DEFEATED.

3. A motion was made to adopt the following instead of the words we have: "Congress shall not make any law infringing the rights of conscience, or establishing any religious sect or society." This motion was DEFEATED.

4. A fourth motion was made to amend the amendment to read "Congress shall make no law establishing any particular denomination of religion in preference to another, or prohibiting the free exercise thereof, nor shall the rights of conscience be infringed." This motion was DEFEATED.

It is clear that what the founders of this Republic had in mind in this specific regard is not the aid-to-all-religions view of the revisionists. It was offered to them and they "decisively rejected it." Justice Harry Blackmun knows his history. He recently wrote, "We operate in the belief—almost the conviction—that in the United States there is a wall between religion and the State. Jefferson's influence is very strong."

May it ever be.

James Madison was "the most important Founder institutionally speaking," as William Lee Miller argues, and Sam Rabinove agrees. In our expansive tradition of religious liberty, one should not minimize Madison's philosophical and intellectual gifts. For all of Roger Williams's philosophical and practical precedents and all of Thomas Jefferson's brilliant accomplishments, yet it was little Mr. Madison who institutionalized religious liberty.

To all appearances, Madison was an unlikely candidate for greatness. He was by his own description sickly, frail, timid, and self-conscious. He had other liabilities among the rough-hewn frontiersmen of his day. He was small, five feet four inches tall, never weighing much over 100 pounds. One contemporary called him "little and ordinary." Another said he was "no bigger than a snowflake." He was wealthy. His father owned 4,000 acres of land. He was brainy and bookish. He was never a fighter. Though made a "Colonel," his only duty was on the parade ground. Nowadays on campus he would be a "nerd," in the media the quintessential "wimp." Yet, what a man!

James Madison saw the need for a strong central government and worked to "enable the government to control the governed, and in the next place, oblige it to control itself." He had learned well a sober, realistic estimate of humankind from his teacher Witherspoon at Presbyterian pre-Princeton New Jersey College. "All men having power ought to be distrusted to a certain degree." So today the checks and balances exist, given to us by the "Father of the Constitution."

Behind the scenes he plotted and schemed, cut deals, engaged in every sort of chicanery to get General Washington to the Constitutional Convention, and then kept the only substantial record of the proceedings that brought forth the Constitution. Only after he died, when his widow, Dolly, sold his notes of the convention debates, did the nation become aware of his influence. One must agree with Fred Barbash when he says, "It is fair to say that the Constitution would not have come about without him."

Many persons even today fail to appreciate Madison's role as author of the Bill of Rights. Since he had wavered in support for such a bill, some people fail to see that once he was convinced that the ratifying conventions made a bill of rights the condition for ratification, he changed his tune. Madison pledged to work for such a bill. He was true to his word. He kept his promises. As William R. Estep says,

> Those who had staked their hopes on Madison's integrity and commitment to freedom of religion were not disappointed. On June 7, 1789, Madison, considering himself bound in honor and in duty, submitted the first version of the no-establishment clause of an amendment that after ratification became the First Amendment in the Bill of Rights.

He never needed to be converted to the cause of religious freedom. In fact, he became a "patriot" at the age of twenty-two, specifically because of his passion for religious liberty. According to Merrill Peterson, "The cause of religious freedom became Madison's passport to Revolution." The Virginia squire had considered the ministry and law as career options but found his vocation in the American Revolution.

Finally, John Leland symbolizes the sort of founder who provided politically for the Bill of Rights, especially the First Amendment. A Roger Williams philosophy, a Jeffersonian rationale, and a Madisonian structure would have all been useless without popular support. Bailyn says that the revivalists supplied the troops for the Bill of Rights. History supports this.

Thomas J. Curry gives credit to Leland, the least well known of these four founders. "Until Leland," Curry writes, "no religious thinker matched the thought on Church and State of Roger Williams of the previous century."

In his critical role, Leland brought together in his own life and work the converging streams that made the lively experiment of religious freedom possible. Both rationalism and pietism, according to Mead, "were but obverse sides of a single movement which gathered enough power and momentum during the eighteenth century to sweep in religious freedom and the separation of church and state over the opposition of traditional orthodoxy in the churches."

The merging lines of dissent made possible, rather virtually demanded, the hitherto unheard-of departure from the earlier concepts of the way religion regulates society. From the Constantinian symbiosis and the sacral society that came from it, until this American impertinence, all the philosophical presuppositions, structures of religion and government, and awful bloodlettings had taken place in the bedroom of the incestuous marriage of church and state, a damnable union.

The final attraction that had brought the two together was the appeal to have the support of the flesh for the battles of the Lord. Theodosius the Great had issued decrees for the church that finalized the union begun by Constantine.

The Holy Roman Empire had with its two-swords concept propped up the ill-fated marriage that brought forth the progeny of crusades and inquisition. The Protestant Reformation brought timid reformulation of the relationship but dared not consider divorce. It took the combined and collective strength of the rationalists and the radical religionists to produce in the context of the American Revolution the religious freedom guarantees of the Constitution and the First Amendment. This was a new thing on the Earth. It was, as many have suggested, the only distinctive contribution of the American Revolution.

Estep traces convincingly the converging lines of dissent in his *Revolution within the Revolution*. He lists as champions of the uncoerced conscience under the rubric "rationalists" such thinkers as Marsilius de Padua (1325), Castellio (1555), John Locke, Voltaire, David Hume, Rousseau, and, finally, Jefferson and Madison. Estep's honor roll of religious radicals includes Balthasar Hubmaier (1524), Menno Simons (1539), John Smyth, Thomas Helwys, Leonard Busher, Roger Williams, John Clarke, Isaac Backus, and, finally, Leland. They all shared the dangerous doctrine that Christ alone is Lord.

The peculiar individualism that sprang up on this continent was the product of these two strong streams of thought. It is curious that so many scholars have somehow been able to ignore one-sidedly the partnership.

On one hand, the Religious Right has seen only the evangelical contribution. The fervor of the "enthusiasts," especially in colonial Virginia, was critical to shaping America's way in church-state relations. This is especially true since they were the most politically active and numerically significant segment of the citizenry.

On the other hand, admirers of the enlightened have acted as if the third-grade social studies text offered adequate and sufficient explanation of the roots of civil and religious liberties by attributing them solely to the work of Jefferson and Madison. Either partial perspective is in error. Many of today's church-state conflicts might be diminished with a more complete understanding of the beginnings of church-state separation.

No one more than Leland captures the color and people power of those who demanded guarantees for religious liberty and civil rights. He was a giant of a man, on the road, among the folks. The big red-haired preacher was stumping southwestern Virginia denouncing state support for religion. On one occasion, an Anglican clergyman challenged him, saying, "The minister should get tax support so he will not have such a hard time preparing his sermons." Leland said, "I can expound the scriptures without any special preparation." "Let's see if you can," replied the clergyman. "What . . . would you do with Numbers 22:21, 'And Balaam . . . saddled his ass'?"

Leland gave the setting and proceeded, "(1) Balaam, as a false prophet represents a state-hired clergy. (2) The saddle represents the enormous tax burden of their salaries. (3) The dumb ass represents the people who bear such a tax burden." Leland's humor and logic prevailed. Leland argued effectively, "Experience has informed us that the fondness of magistrates to foster Christianity has done it more harm than all the persecutions ever did."

The Enlightenment leaders teamed up with the frontier preachers of liberating religion. Together they brought about the first nation on the face of the Earth with real religious freedom, full religious freedom for all, even those who are not religious.

It was Leland and hundreds like him who turned the tide for religious freedom and even the Bill of Rights. J. Bradley Creed in his 1986 dissertation on Leland summarizes his contribution as the political engineer of the First Amendment:

> While his doctrine of the human conscience was an essential contribution to the debate over church-state issues, he did not break much new ground in terms of political theory. His genius lay in his ability to take the insights of leading political figures and make them intelligible to the common man. At party meetings and in Fourth of July speeches, he effectively mixed the basic tenets of liberal democracy with strong doses of common-sense pragmatism and pietistic fervency. John Leland and the Separate Baptists of Virginia cannot be given sole credit for the ratification of the Federal Constitution, but their role was essential. They acted as a bridge between the more landed politicians and the general populace which clamored for greater protection of individual freedoms.

Warren E. Burger, former Chief Justice of the United States, is correct in his recounting of history regarding the Bill of Rights. The delegates who met Philadelphia had decided not to have a bill of rights. "But," as Burger reminds, "when the Constitution went to the states for ratification, there was popular demand for additional individual liberties."

The Constitution just squeaked by in three key states' ratifying conventions. In each instance, it was clear that the people were demanding a bill of rights. In Massachusetts and Virginia, it became the condition for ratification without which there would have been no constitution. The final vote in Massachusetts was 187-168 in favor of ratification: a ten-vote shift would've defeated it. Champions of a bill of rights Samuel Stillman and Isaac Backus led the motley mix of twenty-five Baptists and other separatists who agreed to vote for ratification if they were promised a bill of rights.

In Virginia, it was 89 to 79. The deal was clear and unmistakable. Votes to ratify depended upon pledges to support a bill of rights. It was the people who wanted and got the Bill of Rights. The folk on the frontier, in their fear of an oppressive state and corrupt church, demanded protection from both. As Senator Sam J. Ervin Jr. said, "When religion controls government, political liberty dies; and when government controls religion, religious liberty perishes."

Some religionists today see the First Amendment as a one-way street designed only to protect religion from the state. These revisers hold that the Bill of Rights restricts and limits only government. While they may have the letter of the law on their side, the spirit of religious liberty and its corollary the separation of church and state are much broader.

Edwin M. Yoder Jr. would agree with Madison in his theological pessimism regarding religionists. He writes, "Ours is a world in which hot-eyed people are on the prowl, seeking to thrust their creeds into your space and mine. If they had their way, would America escape the fate of Persia [or Iraq], Lebanon or Ireland? Optimists obviously believe that Americans are immune to the pitfalls of spiritual pride that have ripped those societies apart. I'd as soon not run the risk."

Hence, we have, "Congress shall make no law respecting an establishment of religion or prohibiting the free exercise thereof."

—Reprinted with permission courtesy of
Smyth & Helwys Publishing.

Pluralism: Another Word for Freedom

The following article appeared in the 1998 book The Role of Religion in Politics and Society, *edited by Harold Heie, A. James Rudin, and Marvin Wilson and published by the Center for Christian Studies of Gordon College in Wenham, Massachusetts. The article was written for a diverse audience of Christians and other people of faith. Dunn comments on threats to pluralism (e.g., triumphalism and ethical relativism) and misguided approaches to dealing with pluralism (e.g., civil religion). "When confronting pluralism," he writes, "we are all called to accept people who understand their beliefs, work together for the common good as we understand it."*

> In the past half-century, American society has become noisily and notoriously pluralistic. This has made Roger Williams more relevant, for he had strong opinions about what government should do about religious pluralism: leave it alone. Turks, Jews, infidels, papists: leave them alone.[34]

These eloquent words of Edwin Gaustad offer a working characterization of pluralism. This specific Christian perspective is one shared by Franklin Littell in his pioneering study, *From State Church to Pluralism*. Littell concludes, "The situation of religious voluntarism and pluralism in which the American Protestants now find themselves, understood historically, is a positive good—both theologically and politically."[35]

The challenges to the sort of pluralism spoken of by Gaustad and Littell are many and varied. On the other hand, the popular acceptance of the reality of pluralism, as Robert Booth Fowler puts it, is "the greatest challenge for the New Christian Right."[36]

The traditional threats to pluralism are clear. One is triumphalism. This spirit is not academic. I speak from experience. I grew up in a Baptist church in which we were taught to be soul winners. To be a witness to the power of God is not enough. To share our faith lovingly and to depend upon the Holy Spirit to convict of sin and righteousness was not adequate. We had to "draw the net" and we were taught how to do just that. Many, if not most, conservative Christians today have a better understanding of evangelism, but militant, manipulative "outreach programs" are alive and well.

Pardon, if you can, further confession. For a dozen years I directed the social justice programs of the 2.2 million-member Baptist General Convention of Texas. With our 5,500 churches scattered through every legislative district of the state, we had to be good stewards of influence. We learned on the state level what many evangelical Christians are only belatedly understanding on the national scene. Since we could not deny the existence of power, we could not but be good stewards of it.

We led crusades that stopped the legalization of gambling in 1968, 1974, and 1978. We made a difference in juvenile justice, prison reform, welfare, pornography, and drug laws—heady stuff! We, of course, had to write about it—*Politics: A Guidebook for Christians* was the result. Imagine my chagrin when 15 years later I picked up *Newsweek* to see Jerry Falwell pictured holding up a copy of it suggesting to all the world where he had learned politics. Pitfalls to avoid as seen from the pit.

Sometimes the triumphalism is so theologically parochial, so evangelistically fueled, and so ethically insensitive that outsiders cannot even imagine its depth and pervasiveness. Excellent illustrations are current attempts to comprehend the antisemitism of pro-Israel evangelicals. Of course, it's possible, maybe even necessary, to tout the nation Israel without loving Jews, caring about religious freedom, or respecting their history or beliefs. For takeover-minded fundamentalists, Jews are but pawns for narrow eschatology and/or prospects for evangelism—hardly candidates for an "I-Thou" relationship.

Less offensive than the "We are #1" attitude but still troubling is the promotion of tolerance as the mother's milk of pluralism. Both Christians and Jews fall into this trap. It's easy to do. Toleration is certainly better than intolerance.

Yet Roger Williams had something when he saw toleration as a "weasel word." It implies a superior and an inferior party, the tolerator and the tolerated. It is a concession of men. Freedom is the gift of God. Pluralism is on shaky ground if it rests on mere toleration.

Theologism, the religious parallel to scientism, is a misplaced faith in propositions and sincerely held theological beliefs marketed as the necessary pillars for public policy. Carl F. H. Henry frequently reminds us that "there is no direct route from the Bible to the ballot box."[37] In a way, the phenomenon of which I speak is nothing more than a sort of sophisticated, soft-shelled triumphalism. The notion that the better trained, more theoretical evangelical has a corner on a just and redemptive approach to politics may offer only a difference in degree and not a difference in kind from those who are more overtly theocratic. In fact, timid theocrats may be more dangerous to the voluntarism at the heart of the American experiment than the noisier kind. They are not as easy to spot.

The foundation for freedom that we call pluralism is not without burdens, Brunner's "awful burden of freedom." Princeton professor Clifford Geertz says that "thanks to the deprovincialization of the world, we're going to be in each others' faces more."[38]

We are already experiencing that syndrome in the tide of multiculturalism that "has raised the consciousness of the academic community, even as it has also raised the contentiousness within that community."[39]

The danger of ethical relativism is frequently linked to pluralism. In fact, the word "pluralism" is used pejoratively by many evangelicals, often as a code word for the absence of absolutes.

The anthropologist Geertz says it well, though in a different context:

> Understanding what people think doesn't mean you have to think the same thing. You don't just say "whatever you do is fine," just saying "it's their culture" doesn't legitimize everything. . . . I hold democratic values, but I have to recognize that a lot of other people don't hold them. So, it doesn't help much to say, "This is the truth." That doesn't mean I don't believe anything.[40]

Geertz argues that the task is to find a way to keep one's values and identity while living with others' values—values you can neither destroy nor approve.

Still another approach to dealing with pluralism in the political context is the adoption of a lowest common denominator sort of civil religion. The religion of the national political conventions sweeps over us like a warm bath. It neuters religion and prostitutes politics. Many see God as the national mascot.

The oft-cited example of our civil religion at its worst is the appeal by President Eisenhower: "Our form of government has no sense unless it is founded in a deeply felt religious faith, and I don't care what it is."[41]

In 1973, Senator Mark Hatfield, whose conscience keeps getting him in trouble, shook up a national prayer breakfast with this comment:

> If we as leaders appeal to the god of civil religion, our faith is in a small and exclusive deity, a loyal spiritual advisor to power and prestige, a defender of only the American nation, the object of a national folk religion devoid of moral content. But if we pray to the biblical God of justice and righteousness, we fall under God's judgement for calling upon His name, but failing to obey His commands.[42]

So perils there be plenty in pluralism. What shall we do?

Harry Truman used to say that he hated those "two-handed fellows, who were always saying 'on the one hand, but on the other hand.'" Sociologists have given the concept the acronym "otohbotoh." Alas, it cannot be avoided. In fact, an approach employing a frank acceptance of the tensions between the contradictory and the complementary may help maintain integrity and retain humility.

When it comes to Christian citizenship and political participation, there is a need to strike a balance between opposites or counterparts of a common theme: conservatism and liberalism, civil obedience and disobedience, order and justice, local and state responsibilities, national and international commitments, and the relationship between church and state. Both parts of the dyad should always be kept under consideration. Conciliation rather than conflict should be the goal. Since tension is inevitable, every effort should be made to make it creative tension. Compromise and accommodation may even lead to or be real reconciliation.

A few illustrations of this sanctified ambivalence come to mind: the tugs between the individual and the institutional aspects of life, the challenge to patience between instant and incremental tactics, and resolution between the tendencies to emphasize the idealistic or the incarnational assaults on a social problem.

Individually, we understand that the pluralism protected by the separation of church and state enhances rather than diminishes personal freedom. Separation of church and state does not mean separation of the believer from citizenship, or separation of God from government, or even separation of politics from religion. The principle does have, however, something significant to do with shaping the proper role of religion in American politics.

When institutions are involved, the separation of church and state is the law of the land, a reality that has been good for religion and good for government. No matter what some latter-day revisionists may say, this distinctive contribution of America to the science of governing is alive and well. Church and state have different constituencies, different purposes, different sources of funding and different methods.

Instant resolution of all problems beckons. Bill Moyers says that the digital clock is a metaphor for American life: we see nothing before or after the present moment. Faithlessness in the power of the truth they proclaim seems to mark the rush to legislate or even amend the United States Constitution on the part of many of the political preachers. They certainly have no corner on that impatience but incrementalism seems wise when we consider tinkering seriously with fundamental freedoms, especially the first freedom.

Sober judgment is advised before we allow government to institute any taxes for religion, tests for theology, or laws for prayer. A critical evaluation suggests that political panderers and well-intentioned moralists may be moving in that direction.

John Leland, Baptist evangelist on the Virginia frontier, said, "Experience . . . has informed us, that the fondness of magistrates to foster Christianity has done it more harm than all the persecutions ever did."[43]

Theologies and theories not rooted in a realistic assessment of the human condition do more harm than good as well. Too often the churches suffer the bankruptcy of disembodied idealism. This is as true of gung-ho political activists as of the monkish mystics who practice a strategy of withdrawal.

Reinhold Niebuhr tried to warn of this limit of liberalism in *Moral Man and Immoral Society*, and behold some of us acted as if he had no glimmer of the truth and others are even yet behaving as if he had told the whole truth.

The alternative to sterile head trips, whether secular or sacred, liberal or conservative, Reformed or Anabaptist, is not "realism." What's that? Rather, the balancing factor to our loftiest political pies-in-the-sky may be a fully fleshed-out attack. An incarnational idealism should call out the best in all people of faith.

Christians facing pluralism need to remember that the church is a divine-human institution. That is not settling for a lower view of our corporate expression of faith. The truth to be told is in tune with our highest aspiration—to be like Jesus, of whom it is said in Philippians 2:7, he "emptied himself, taking the form of a slave being born in human likeness . . . humbled himself and became obedient to the point of death." How can one argue with that sort of self-giving? What intellectual display can begin to match sacrificial caring for people?

When confronting pluralism, we are all called to accept people who understand their beliefs, work together for the common good as we understand it. The best thing government can do for religion is to leave it alone. The best thing we can all do for church and state is to keep them separate so that neither is caught in the bear hug of the other.

The American way of pluralism has worked well. The nation has the greatest freedom of religion, the least religious conflict, the largest number of people in church/synagogue/temple/mosque every week, the highest percentage of voluntary religious participants, the most missionaries and people-helpers sent out to other countries, and the best record of giving in the name of religion of any nation on the face of the earth.

As Senator Kennedy said at Jerry Falwell's Liberty University in 1983, "The foundation of our pluralism is that government will never determine which religion is right, and religion will not put its imprimatur on some politicians while damning others because of their political views."[44]

—Reprinted with permission courtesy of Gordon College.

Church and State: The Separation of Powers

James Dunn delivered the address below at the annual seminar of the Christian Life Commission of the Southern Baptist Convention on March 24, 1981. This presentation came just three months into Dunn's tenure as executive director of the Baptist Joint Committee. He reminds the gathering of Southern Baptist ethicists and denominational leaders that the separation of church and state "has never meant the separation of Christians from their citizenship or the separation of God from government." Political engagement is the "ethical corollary of the theological doctrine of incarnation," and active involvement in politics is the duty of both "churches and church people," he says.

As he regularly did in his public speeches and written works, Dunn concludes with a call to action urging his Baptist brethren to be advocates for religious liberty and church-state separation. "We dare not betray by our apathy and inaction the blood-bought liberty that is our Baptist heritage," he says.

Two hundred years after John Leland was arguing for church-state separation, we're still at it.

Leland was a rambunctious fellow who had made a mark in his corner of Virginia. He ultimately influenced James Madison and was a major contributor to the First Amendment.

One of my favorite Leland stories: He met head on in public with a clergyman who had challenged Leland's attacks on the established church. The Anglican said, "The minister should get tax support so that he'll not have such a hard time preparing his sermons." Leland responded, "I can expound the scriptures without any special preparation." The high churchman called his bluff and said, "Very well then, what would you do with Numbers 22:21, which reads, 'And Balaam . . . saddled his ass'?" Leland gave the setting and said, "The passage clearly has three points: (1) Balaam, as a false prophet, represents the state-hired clergy. (2) The saddle represents the enormous tax burden of the salaries of these tax-paid preachers, and finally, (3) the dumb ass represents the people who would bear such a burden."

I'll not press the analogy of his illustration. Almost exactly 200 years from that event we sit down together and discuss the role of the church and the state. I would suggest that there are four pivotal issues that we face just now:

1. The Definition of Church-State Separation
2. The Place of Religion in Education
3. The Intrusion of Government in Church Affairs, and
4. The Changing Role of the State

The Definition of Church-State Separation

First, we need to hammer away at our understanding of the relationship of church and state. Within the past year a great deal of foolishness has filled the papers and pulpits with exchanges about church and state. Some brethren labeled "Baptist" have been severely criticized for violating the sacred Baptist principle of separation when they became actively, if belatedly, involved in social and political issues.

Now, there are some serious criticisms of the theology, ethics, and methodology of the so-called "New Religious Right." But, for the most part, one cannot fault their call for Christian citizens to be active in the political process.

We need to rethink what we believe about, first, the relationship of Christians to the world and, then, the relationship of religion and politics. These two broader questions will determine the way in which we view church-state questions.

It is as if we were dealing with a three-layered cake with the bottom layer of "Christians and the world," upon it the layer of "religion and politics," and finally, much smaller in scope than the other two, the level of church-state relations.

Our Baptist record of relating Christians to the world, a basic question of Christian social ethics, is not a consistent or appealing story.

In short outline, the doctrine of *imago Dei*, the idea that all persons are made in the image of God, has profound implications for all three layers of that symbolic cake. F. J. Sheed says, "The concept that all persons are made in the image of God is an idea of such transcendent importance that any difference between this person and that fades into nothingness by comparison." If we believe that every person replicates God, we will relate to the peoples of the world differently from the "average citizen" who knows only undifferentiated masses, nationally tagged populations, or pawns of economic systems.

The doctrine of the incarnation also powerfully affects the notion of the Christian's relationship to the world. Our favorite verse says, "God so loved the world . . . ." In taking on flesh, Jesus Christ ennobled all humankind. Yet much of our religion is nervously nationalistic and limiting to loving the world only as we feel required to by the missionary challenge.

I need not stay long at a theological dig with you; but it is clear that when we are true to the high calling of God in Christ Jesus, we care passionately about the world around us. Our compassion is rooted in a sense of solidarity with all mankind. We know that we all suffer the same fragmented human condition and that Jesus came to bear it with us, and to give us hope.

There is a deep sense in which we are one with all sinners. *Nihil a me humanae alienum puto.* "Nothing human is alien to me." G. K. Chesterton said, "We are all in a small boat on a stormy sea and we owe each other a terribly loyalty."

Out of this sense of responsibility for the world about him, Brunner advised us to maintain a Christian posture in the world: Bible in one hand, newspaper in the other. I fear that a good many Baptists have made a choice and read one or the other but not both.

One of the real reasons for the confusion that exists in Baptist life about church-state relations is massive, unmitigated, pervasive, and unyielding ignorance. Not stupidity—ignorance, in the strictest definition of the word.

Will Rogers said, "We're all ignorant but just about different things." Well, there are lots of different things about which we are all ignorant.

As a whole, we don't even do as well as Will Rogers. He said, "All I know is what I read in the papers." A quick test of any Sunday evening church crowd would reveal that we don't even read the papers. Take the "prayer in schools" issue. Never have so many, who knew so little, continued to say so much, so long.

Do you know about poor Bill Clark? He was up for confirmation before the U.S. Senate a few weeks ago. He's now the number-two man at the State Department. (He has since become the head of the National

Security Council.) They asked him if he would name the Prime Minister of South Africa; he couldn't. Zimbabwe? He couldn't. They asked him to describe the struggle going on in the British Labor Party. He couldn't. The Dutch papers labeled him: Nitwit. A little harsh, perhaps, but there's really no excuse for any of us not doing our basic homework about the world in which we live. Do you remember the ugly American? There's an uglier Christian American. He is the one who does not know about or care about the world around him. Arrogant ignorance is insufferable, not knowing and not knowing that we don't know.

On a Baptist campus a few years ago I stayed in a dorm in which the guys bragged that there was not a daily newspaper because they were "into Jesus." I suspect that we'd all be a little relieved not to have to take the current events test of "My Weekly Reader." Compare and contrast Mugabe and Mobuto. What are the various theories of economic development operative in third world countries? Distinguish between Mali and Malawi. The point I want to make is simple. We do not love the world as we claim to. The irrefutable proof lies in our failure to be global citizens, Christians who know the world.

Anti-intellectualism in American life has crept over into church life and multiplied. There's a certain parochialism among us that's inexcusable.

I know a good many of you and you know me, so I am aware of the danger in this sort of meddling. Let Elton Trueblood say it: "Mediocrity is sin and heresy."

The Christian who denies the social dimension of the gospel is putting a premium on ignorance, resting on an immoral nostalgia for things once learned, and modeling mediocrity.

The word of God is quick and powerful and effective; it is so in context, and that context is the world not just the inner life.

We need to rewrite the song: "Turn your eyes upon Jesus, and the things of earth will grow strangely *clear* in the light of His Glory and Grace." We've sung the "dim" heresy of the song and acted it out in our "dim" witness.

Enough about Christians and the world. Yet I am convinced that we can't even begin dealing with church-state relations apart from a right understanding of how Christians relate to all human institutions.

Then we have to look at religion and politics because this is often confused with the church-state question. The separation of church and state has never meant the separation of Christians from their citizenship or the separation of God from government.

Hitler held: "We claim this earth, let the church have the hereafter." We tend to agree instead with William Temple who said, "Since we cannot deny the existence of [the church's] power, we must simply be good stewards of that power."

For years, we've been pleading for involvement—the ethical corollary of the theological doctrine of incarnation. There is a big task before us in describing and displaying how the churches are involved in politics.

It's clear that the church is at its best when it is teaching, motivating, evaluating, and holding up ideals. But in a democracy, a more specific engagement with public policymaking is unavoidable by churches and church people.

Fortunately, we're not expected to provide a specific prescription for every ill. Yet from the beginning the church has been involved in politics.

First, then, we have a great deal of educating to do on defining appropriately the role of church and state. Our lack of broad-based constituency who understand the difference between separation of church and state and separation of religion and politics has left our people vulnerable to the ego-driven electronic churchmen who manipulate for money the basically uninformed and drifting members of our churches.

All one has to do to identify that egomania is listen critically to their appeals to themselves, their feelings, their experiences as their highest authority (no matter what they say about the Bible). Count the uses of the first person singular pronoun to sense their vision for America. Without any sign of understanding Christian ethics, they would impose by force of law their own brand of morality. They really want a theocracy, not a democracy. It's clear that each one of them wants to be Theo.

So, without a view of Christians and the world that's rooted in the Bible, theology, history, and Christian ethics, one cannot hope to understand the interplay of religion and politics; and without understanding of religion and politics, there's not much hope for a workable definition of church-state separation.

The Place of Religion in Education

The second pivotal issue we face is the place of religion in education. It is a serious question and not to be taken lightly. The public schools are in real trouble in some of our large cities, though they are far healthier, and more effective, at least outside the central cities, than their harping critics admit.

The focus of attention right now seems to be on the place of religion in the public schools . . . specifically prayer in schools. In the history of this nation, the Supreme Court has handed down five decisions regarding religion in the public schools. It is the last three of these that catch all the attention today.

Engel v. Vitale: school-sponsored prayer is unconstitutional; *Abington School District v. Schempp*: Bible reading and the Lord's prayer are unconstitutional in the classroom; and the November 17, 1980, decision which said that a school district may not be required to post the Ten Commandments in the classroom.

Because such heat has been generated over these decisions with so little light, let's look for a moment at the "school prayer" cluster. It is my view that Baptists should be grateful for these decisions as temporal, legal safeguards for church-state separation. Church is itself a fence or a hedge about religious liberty.

1. First, we should be honest about the issue. The battle is not "to put prayer back in the schools." That's offensive to theology—it's as if we had the power to dump the Heavenly Father in a wheelbarrow and cart Him around—but it's also offensive to common sense. It is state-sanctioned prayer these people are really seeking. For the state to allow prayer implies that it has the power to disallow prayer. We cannot accept that. Prayer has not been forbidden. When it comes to laws and amendments to "return religion to the schools," there's a simple rule of thumb: If something's not broke, don't fix it.

2. Then, there's a serious theological issue for Baptists regarding the nature of prayer. Genuine prayer can't be permitted or prevented. Hollow ritual is meaningless and not real prayer. All religion to be real has to be freely, voluntarily entered. Hear these simple arguments, though I've discovered that those whose minds are made up won't listen, you might stumble upon one undecided.

A. Christians cannot fully join non-Christians in their prayers, and, so, non-Christians should not be expected to enter Christian worship. (It could well keep them from ever actually becoming Christian.)

B. School prayers would either be effective, in which case they'd constitute indoctrination and be therefore unfair, or they would be ineffective, in which case they'd constitute dilution. We've always seen the benefits of mechanical prayer as minimal.

3. Next, there is a very practical consideration regarding implementation. Most would agree that in the classroom there should be no compulsion to conformity, no coercion of conscience. Yet which one of you wants to tell a little 8-year-old girl that she may stand aside, leave the room and not participate, marking her as the one that doesn't believe in the God of the class? Who among us would want to be the teacher to tell an 11-year-old boy: "Well, if you don't want to leave the room, you may play like you're praying"? It's bad religion and bad law; there is no way to apply fairly school prayers in a pluralistic society.

4. *Finally, there's a historic argument against school prayers.* Look at the other nations of the world where church and state are wed and prayers are said in school. Would this ritual really make the difference some claim? It hasn't brought churchgoing to England; peace to Northern Ireland; vital faith to Spain; clean newsstand to Denmark; morality to Sweden; or common decency to Iran.

No, the claims that everything went wrong because prayer was thrown out of school are patent poppycock.

Unless every individual is free to say "no," then his "yes" is nothing, and that applies even to children. A plastic doll that says "I love you" when you pull a string means nothing, but a Dennis the Menace child, strong willed, rebellious with a mind of his own can say "I love you" and melt a heart of stone.

George W. Truett on the steps of the United States Capitol said, "If by lifting one finger I could cause a man to become a Christian against his will, I would not." That's the spirit that understands that schools aren't in the business of prayer. Shouldn't be. The best thing government can do for religion is leave it alone.

The other side of the religion/education coin involves the use of public money for private and parochial education. The particular threat just now is labeled "tuition tax credits." The various plans would allow a tax credit on one's income tax for a set amount if it were spent for education at a private or church-related school. It's just as much a tax expenditure decision by the Congress as if a line item were added to the budget. Not a deduction, a credit—taxes not paid by the individual involved and therefore to be paid by the rest of us who claim no such credit.

What's wrong with tuition tax credits? They are

1. *Discriminatory*—help for those who need it least. The really poor do not have the $500 to $1,000 required to qualify for this one additional form of welfare for the rich.

2. *Inflationary*—offering a new initiative in federal spending with uncontrollable cost escalation. A Father Bredeweg of the National Catholic Education Association testified for tuition tax credits in the last Congress because "it would enable us to increase tuition." Even Al Senske, the Department of Education's secretary for nonpublic education and a strong supporter of such a plan, lamented that "federal budget considerations and our total economy rule it out at this point." A new entitlement program would represent another ongoing drain on the treasury.

3. *Unconstitutional*—because, in fact, almost 80 percent of the funds would wind up in the parochial schools of one denomination. The Supreme Court in *Nyquist* (1973) ruled out tax credits on constitutional grounds. Excessive entanglement with religion is unavoidable.

4. *Undemocratic*—because they would encourage and subsidize segregated academies at worst and sorry, substandard schools at best. The taxpayer would have no say over the way that part of his tax dollar is spent: taxation without representation. At present, taxpayers can follow their education dollar through the thousands of freely elected school boards. The school board can be forced into premature retirement. Tuition tax credit dollars are beyond the voter's control.

5. *Divisive*—because they would mandate competition and infighting for the public dollar. Private and parochial schoolmen would be rooting like little pigs at the trough of tax money.

6. *Dishonest*—because it would use the parent as the conduit for tax dollars to flow into schools where otherwise they could not go constitutionally, a subterfuge, an attempt to do indirectly what is directly illegal.

7. *Illogical*—in convoluted reasoning unworthy of the United States Senate, Senators Moynihan and Packwood argue that because parents have the right to send their children to private and parochial schools, the taxpayer must help them do it.

8. *Destructive*—of the public schools, allowing the nonpublic schools to skim off the best and leave the difficult, more expensive-to-educate children with the public systems. The issue is nothing less than the future of the public schools. We'd be paying a premium with tax dollars withdrawing children from the public schools.

Discriminatory, inflationary, unconstitutional, undemocratic, divisive, illogical, dishonest, destructive . . . other than that, tuition tax credits are okay!

The Intrusion of Government in Church Affairs

For a third pivotal issue in church-state relations one would have to cluster loosely labeled "government intrusion in church affairs." In 1980, many of us in this room spent hours, some of us days, working on two specific aspects of the phenomenon: ERISA and the Overseas Earned Income tax exclusion for missionaries. Had these two government goofs not been corrected, literally millions of dollars given through our churches would have been needlessly, unfairly, and, I'm convinced, unconstitutionally diverted from the purposes for which they were given.

The Employees Retirement Income Security Act (ERISA) would have demanded a burdensome and costly division of our annuity work, a tangle of government red tape when one moved from a denominational missions job to a local church or vice versa, and a blatant supervisory invasion of our pension plan by the Internal Revenue Service. Incidentally, the cluster of corrections required in ERISA legislation has not been completed and we must respond to Dr. Darold Morgan's leadership to finish the job.

The income tax placed on our missionaries in developing countries would have cost the Foreign Mission Board at least $1 million annually and, thereby, penalized missions advance that much. However, if it were fair, legal, and constitutional, we would simply have had to pay it. All three of the tests mentioned above were at least open to debate. Is it fair for not-for-profit workers going into serving vocations in developing countries to have to pay taxes both in the sending country and the host country? Is it consistent with our national policy and with complex tax laws, credits, and incentives for those who are engaged in charity with the hungry to be penalized? Is it honoring the free exercise of religion to exact a burden not even placed on some entrepreneurial ventures in the same under-developed nations? December 24, 1980, President Carter signed into law the exclusion, giving relief.

We'd probably better remain alert, however, because other evidences of intrusion demand and may be more serious in the long haul than these two just mentioned. In fact, when you look at the time, money, and effort that it took to correct these two federal foul-ups, prospects for the future are not bright.

William P. Thompson, stated clerk of the United Presbyterian Church, has said it well:

> A pervasive pattern of governmental activities at all levels constitutes a serious threat to the free exercise of religion. We must protest vigorously

the growing tendency by government to distinguish between "churches" on the one hand and the agencies, institutions, and programs created by churches in the exercise of their faith on the other. The protection of the Constitution should extend to both. We must oppose the progressively narrower definition of religion appearing in regulatory, legislative, and judicial decisions. This tendency, if unchecked, would restrict the shield of the First Amendment to a shrinking sphere of religious activity . . . private, sacerdotal, and liturgical aspects. . . . The similarity of these developments to the restraints imposed by totalitarian regimes of the right and left, as they have ruthlessly privatized religion, should give us pause.

What are the manifestations of this trend?

1. Lobby disclosure legislation that would make church groups accountable to the federal government for its witness in public affairs. Such monitoring is unacceptable for prophetic religion in a free society. We attempt to influence legislation as an integral aspect of our faith.

2. Tax exemption of the churches allows the IRS to apply its self-devised, sometimes secret, inconsistent, "substantiality" tests to church organizations bearing public witness. Churches and other not-for-profit organizations may speak up only so long as the IRS in its wisdom is convinced they have not spend a "substantial" portion of their budget attempting to influence legislation.

3. The "integrated auxiliary" question: requiring filing annual informational returns (Form 990). In this issue, the IRS arrogated unto itself the highly questionable role of determining what is and what is not "religious." (A word of caution: All church-related agencies which do not qualify as integrated auxiliaries need to file Form 990 but clearly mark it Under Protest. The failure of any agency to file would enable IRS to pick the weakest delinquent and bring suit against it. If IRS won that case regulations would be legally established for all agencies.)

4. Unemployment taxes and parochial schools: at issue is the government's authority to define the nature and mission of the church.

5. The IRS and Enrollment of Parochial Schools—controlling admission policies of church schools, ignoring the membership patterns of the churches themselves.

6. The EEOC and church schools have the government attempting to control employment practices in schools dedicated to the training of ministers, even at the seminary level where no tax dollars are involved.

(Federal District Judge Eldon Mahon, January 23, 1980, ruled in favor of Southwestern Baptist Theological Seminary.)

7. Investigation and evaluation of the "cults." We Baptists were considered a cult not long ago.

8. The National Labor Relations Board has determined to take jurisdiction of labor-management relations in Catholic schools.

9. The Worldwide Church of God has been placed in receivership by a California court claiming civil jurisdiction over its exercise of religion.

10. Several cases have the courts involved with church splits in which presbyterial or episcopal church government systems are threatened by the government imposing congregational polity on the local church by judicial fiat.

11. Responsibility of the parent religious group for contacts and liabilities of subsidiaries—the Pacific Homes Corporation of the United Methodist Church.

12. Solicitation in public places by the Hare Krishnas and the Seventh Day Adventists.

13. Disclosure of income by religious groups.

14. Conflict of employment schedules with religious beliefs.

The Changing Role of the State

A fourth pivotal issue that merits consideration is far broader and more over-arching than the sort of particulars just mentioned. Ultimately, this last issue may be the most significant. It involves the changing role of the State in regulating the lives of its citizens. Some of the very persons pleading and working for less government are contradictorily pushing for laws that, to be enforced, would push close to the 1984 portrayed by George Orwell.

William Buckley suggested on a recent program that the teaching of the Bible in the public schools shouldn't pose any problem. "It should be taught as an allegory. That would satisfy any intelligent, informed citizen." Old smarty pants Buckley doesn't understand the problem.

If the so-called Human Life Amendment to the United States Constitution were passed and consistently enforced, we'd have government in the doctors' offices and the bedrooms. To insist that personhood commences with conception has implications that even ardent anti-abortionists may not have considered. The IUD would be unconstitutional. Taking a morning-after pill would be murder. Each miscarriage would have to be federally examined. Every "D&C" would bring the obstetrician-gynecologist under the scrutiny of constitutional law.

Disturbing to me are the thousands of therapeutic abortions received by children to 15 years of age that would be stopped; all are victims of rape or incest—few promptly reported, none legal under the sort of laws proposed by hardline anti-abortionists. With them a one-hour-old zygote or a one-week-old embryo is the same as a fetus or the same as the life of a mother. One specific brand of theology would be written into the Constitution of the United States if the Human Life Amendment people had their way. It is a church/state issue when the sex ethic of one theology is pushed as the law of the land.

A good many attempts to regulate the lives of private citizens sound more like Calvin's Geneva than the United States of America.

Eighty-three amendments to the United States Constitution are currently under consideration. Some of them would alter the First Amendment. Others would call a new Constitutional Convention, opening "Pandora's box" to the whim of public sentiment at the particular second.

It is at least illustrative of the danger to note how last year's ardent advocates of the balanced budget—the subject of one of the constitutional amendments proposed—were suddenly this year's reasonable promoters of an increased debt limit. It was "necessary," "practical," and "our turn now." What will happen if the fickle winds of political popularity begin to misshape the Constitution?

We face a situation in the nation in which we must decide if we want to start writing into the Constitution whatever the majority of the moment may demand. We must determine if we are willing to allow the State to regulate in a way that we have no escape even in the Courts. We have to judge if we are ready to abandon the rights and guarantees given us in the Constitution and Bill of Rights.

Baptists have stood for religious liberty, rooted in soul freedom based on our voluntary approach to matters spiritual. Now is no time to turn back.

We dare not panic and succumb to the loud voices that would drown out dissent.

We dare not allow the apparent public tide of security seekers to run roughshod over freedom.

We dare not betray by our apathy and inaction the blood-bought liberty that is our Baptist heritage.

—James M. Dunn Papers, MS 632, Z. Smith Reynolds Library
Special Collections and Archives,
Wake Forest University, Winston-Salem NC.

A Threatened Heritage

James Dunn penned the following article for the July 1994 issue of The Whitsitt Journal, *the publication of the William H. Whitsitt Baptist Heritage Society. In this article, Dunn outlines what he believed to be the most important threats to religious freedom in the mid-1990s. Most notable (and controversial) of these was his description of the Catholic Church as "still represent[ing] a challenge to wholehearted religious liberty."*

Religious freedom is under threat. Like Jews in the entrance hall of the Holocaust and semi-baptists in the late great Southern Baptist Convention, those most in danger do not always see the threat. So there is some usefulness in naming the demons.

It has become socially unacceptable to call names and identify enemies. Political correctness left, right, and middle rules it out. Yet, as Bill Moyers says, "The virulent extremism that infects the Southern Baptist Convention is highly contagious."

Here are six specific challenges to our heritage of religious freedom. There is an overlap of allegiance among constituents and practitioners. Some good folk who know better may some days be snookered into softheaded sympathy with these shysters. But religious freedom is at risk and now is the time to sound the alarm.

Revisionism

Rewriting history is a growth industry. Revisionists seem to have convinced a significant slice of the populace that the separation of church and state is a latter-day innovation. Chief Justice William Rehnquist in his dissent in the *Wallace v. Jaffree* case wrote, "The 'wall of separation between church and state' is a metaphor based on bad history, a metaphor which has proved useless as a guide to judging. It should be frankly and explicitly abandoned" (*Wallace v. Jaffree*, 472 U.S. 38 107 (1985), Rehnquist, J., dissenting).

At least four times in that dissent, he states or alludes to his limited version of the scope of the First Amendment. "The evil to be aimed at,"

Rehnquist wrote, was "the establishment of a national church, and perhaps the preference of one religious sect over another."

The utter wrongheadedness of Rehnquist was never more eloquently refuted than in Justice David Souter's concurring opinion in the *Lee v. Weisman* case (112 S. Ct. 2649 [1992]). Souter wrote, "Forty-five years ago, this Court announced a basic principle of constitutional law from which it has not strayed: the Establishment Clause forbids not only state practices that 'aid one religion over another,' but also those that 'aid all religion.'"

Justice Souter went on for 23 pages in an elemental history lesson. The founders clearly intended separation of church and state. Government in this country is meant to be neutral regarding religion.

David Barton has released a videotape titled "America's Godly Heritage" in which he argues that America is a "Christian Nation," legally and historically. He also asserts that, through our dedication to the principle of church-state separation, we have systematically ruled religion out of the public arena, particularly the public school system. This is not a new argument, but Barton is especially slick in his presentation. His well-oiled rapid-fire sentences have just enough ring of truth to make him credible to a large number of people. However, the presentation is laced with exaggerations, half-truths, and misstatements of fact, and his citation of supporting research is scant at best and often nonexistent.

Roman Catholicism

You may squirm at my listing the Roman Catholic Church as a threat to religious freedom. I understand. Some great champions of social justice like Robert Drinan are exceptions. Yet no informed observer of the political scene can honestly ignore the millions of dollars being spent right now to get public monies for parochial schools. No fair-minded scholar can overlook the revelations in a splendid new book, *A New Rite: Conservative Catholic Organizations and Their Allies* by Steve Askin. No careful student of the Roman Catholic Church can deny the impact of Catholic social policy on domestic and political ethics.

It has been the popular opinion of the Catholic hierarchy in the United States that "the separation of church and state" is a "shibboleth of doctrinaire secularism."

Citizens for Educational Excellence led by Robert Simons and many other groups are active agents for the Roman Catholic political agenda. Anyone at all interested should see Askin's excellent book.

Franklin H. Littell in an address March 25, 1994, pointed out that

> today Christendom has the most reactionary Roman Catholic leader since Giovanni Ferretti (Pius IX, 1846–1878). During his formative years under communist dictatorship, Korol Wojityla (John Paul II) learned to close up carefully—to go through the house at the end of every day, checking from cellar to attic to be sure windows are closed and barred. His encyclicals, including the latest (*Veritatis Splendor*), express again the unreformed and the unreconstructed reduction of the Christian way of life to the level of obedience to Roman administration and submission to a theological triumphalism expressed in propositonal format.

Dr. Littell's distinguished record needs no defense. His scholarship and ecumenical objectivity stand.

Unfortunately, Pope John XXIII and Vatican II notwithstanding, the Roman Catholic Church on the whole still represents a challenge to wholehearted religious liberty.

Politicization

The forces listed above all tend to feed a mentality that reduces the faith of our forebears to a political perspective. Sometimes, as in April this year, we learn of an overt attempt to do just that.

A small group of well-off, white, male, right-wing Republicans produced an ambitious document called *Evangelicals and Catholics Together: The Christian Mission in the Third Millennium*.

One begins to catch on when their reasons for existence are spelled out. Among their purposes are "legal protection for the unborn," "parental choice in education," battling "anti-religious bigotry in entertainment media," and "upholding vibrant market economies."

Don't be fooled by those who conflate political agendas with "God talk."

One of the serious threats to the *moral authority* of the religious community is the shortsightedness of those who sacrifice the permanent on the altar of the temporary.

One of the most serious threats to the *political process* is the politicization of religion.

One of the most serious threats to *civility in society* is the medieval use and abuse of religion as weapon in polemical politics.

Evangelicals, many of whom are intimately suspicious of creedalism, are going to reject any working moral creed when they consider seriously the implications. Most experiential Christians, born-again believers, just cannot buy a two-point test of their Christianity: Do we all agree on abortion and homosexuality? The Christian faith is more, as important as those may be.

The political creed is almost as obvious in the *Evangelicals and Catholics Together* document. Lurking just beneath the surface is the question asked so often by Pat Robertson, "Is it possible to be a Democrat and a Christian?"

Beyond that, the very peaceful pursuit of politics is pushed beyond possibility by those who want to make every political objective cause for a holy crusade. We have already seen the killing, the chaos, the human hurt promoted by crusaders against all who disagree with their moralistic agenda. The sad results of religion being locked into political molds have been seen in Beirut, Belfast, and Bosnia. It is a very human thing to do. It has happened all through history. Anyone who thinks it cannot happen here is weak in theology and wanting in history. Germany had a heavier dose of religion and more learnin' per square head than any nation up to the rise of Hitler. Yet we know what happened there.

Commodification

"Commodification"—that six-syllable word is the subject of a new book, *Selling God: American Religion in the Marketplace of Culture*. R. Laurence Moore, a history professor at Cornell University, traces the history of religion peddling in the United States.

Churches are reaching new heights (or pits) of matching market research with consumer wishes. The megachurch, the super church so interested in "meeting the needs" of metropolis, builds in the bowling lanes, drops any doctrines that might offend, and downplays the Baptist tradition. After all, religious liberty does include even freedom *from* religion.

The bland leading the bland have no time for history and little interest in denominational distinctives. I am in two or three churches a week and I am routinely informed that "most of our people know nothing about being a Baptist."

There is a common-denominator religious exercise that consists of a few "little praise songs," a lot of promotion for church activities, and a sweet sermon, sometimes moving, often helpful, occasionally even biblical but never explicit about the heritage of our faith. Culture-bound pop religion is a threat to religious freedom. What is the antidote to these poisons?

Three Modest Suggestions

Recapture the Baptist genius of experiential religion. Capitalize on Baptist distinctives growing out of that vital faith. Do our homework—*Every Baptist a Baptist.*

Curious that it took a Jewish literary critic at Yale, Harold Bloom, to spotlight for the nation Baptists' seminal American theologian. Bloom's book *The American Religion* finally accords E. Y. Mullins the place due to him. Bloom rightly sees Baptists as "the largest of all our Protestant faiths, and the most experiential."

Bloom writes,

> Edgar Young Mullins I would nominate as the Calvin or Luther or Wesley of the Southern Baptists, but only in the belated American sense, because Mullins was not the founder of the Southern Baptists but their re-founder, the definer of their creedless faith. An endlessly subtle and original religious thinker, Mullins is the most neglected of major American theologians. Pragmatically he is more important than Jonathan Edwards, Horace Bushnell and the Niebuhrs because Mullins reformulated (perhaps even first formulated) the faith of a major American denomination.

Our only creed is "ain't nobody gonna tell me what to believe." But our dependence upon the Bible, our dominating belief in the Lordship of Jesus Christ, our understanding of the work of the Holy Spirit place us squarely in the camp of born-again Christianity. The absence of a creed does not mean that we have no confession of faith. We say with the early church: Jesus Christ is Lord. We share the Reformation watchword: *sola fide.*

The absence of a creed does not diminish the intensity of our commitment. Baptist history reveals that our forebears have been passionately dedicated to doctrine. The absence of a creed does not deny all coherent content to our beliefs, which leads to the second suggestion: magnify Baptist distinctives.

If soul freedom is important, if the priesthood of all believers is more than a slogan, if one insists on interpreting the Bible for one's self; if one defends the right of each person to come to the Bible and led by the Holy Spirit to seek its truth, if one believes that she must accept Jesus Christ personally, freely, or not really; if the church functions as a democracy; if in the fellowship of churches each is autonomous; if there is no pope, presbyter, president, or pastor to rule over you; if no mortal has the power to suppress, curtail, rule out, or reign over the will of the congregation, you have probably been baptistified.

Every Baptist a Baptist

These consistent freedom forces form an orderly pattern. Being Baptist also means respect, affirmation, and honest honoring of differences. After all, if folks are free they may not all agree with us. Everyone has a right to be wrong. So we insist not on toleration for those outside our particular perspective but for freedom. Roger Williams called toleration a weasel word; it implies human concession, while freedom is a gift of God. Little "b" baptists, even those with other tags, have fought for real religious liberty.

None other than our own Walter B. Shurden has contributed significantly to recapturing Baptist distinctives. His 1993 book, *The Baptist Identity*, is popular among real Baptists wherever they are found. Real Baptists are hungry to explore identity questions. It may be the teachable moment.

We need to dedicate ourselves now to a new motto: *Every Baptist a Baptist*. It will take hard work. We might never have seen the necessity short of the present unpleasantness. Creativity, imagination, courageous leadership, gutsy outspokenness are needed.

If we keep alive the Baptist vision of religious freedom, we will read and study and sell and push Estep, Cothen, Shurden, Leonard, Bloom, and Mullins. We will give through the Cooperative Baptist Fellowship and peddle *Baptists Today* and recommend Smyth and Helwys. We will stick with the Baptist Joint Committee and say good words for the Baptist Theological Seminary at Richmond and Truett Seminary and other expressions of theological education with integrity. We will seize the day as a wonderful opportunity to reclaim the Baptist focus on freedom.

I am not suggesting that the Southern Baptist Convention as such can be recaptured. It is over.

We are like those folks you see on television news after a tornado has blown it all away. We are like the survivors of Sarajevo, like the Jews being hauled away in *Schindler's List*, some of them denying to the last minute that such horrors could happen. Of course, it's not the same. But the differences are in degree not in kind of inhumanity.

Maybe we will do our homework and grow informed members able to make intelligent decisions. Maybe laypeople will assume leadership, churches will exercise autonomy, theological education will find a fresh start, and we will all recapture the voice once ours and the message, "it is precisely for freedom that Christ has set you free."

—Reprinted with permission.

Notes

1. JMD, *Soul Freedom: Baptist Battle Cry* (Macon GA: Smyth & Helwys Publishing, 2000) 44–45.

2. Ibid., 47.

3. JMD, foreword to Mark Whitten's *The Myth of Christian America: What You Need to Know About the Separation of Church and State* (Macon GA: Smyth & Helwys Publishing, 1999) v.

4. JMD, "Neutrality and the Establishment Clause," in *Equal Separation: Understanding the Religion Clauses of the First Amendment*, ed. Paul J. Weber (New York: Greenwood Press, 1990) 55–63.

5. JMD, "Religion and Politics: A Proper Mix," *Perspectives in Religious Studies* 13/2 (Summer 1986): 155–56.

6. JMD, "Religious Freedom Award Response," *Journal of Christian Ethics* 5/5 (October 1999).

7. JMD, *Soul Freedom*, 46.

8. *Walz v. Tax Commission*, 397 U.S. 664 (1970).

9. *McDaniel v. Paty*, 435 U.S. 618 (1978).

10. Harvey Cox, "Our Politics Needs Religion," *The Washington Post*, 2 September 1983, D8.

11. Dean M. Kelley, "Meddling in Politics," *Liberty* 79/4 (July-August 1984): 13.

12. Carl Henry, "Evangelicals Out of the Closet, But Going Nowhere?" *Christianity Today*, 4 January 1980, p. 2.

13. USCC Administrative Board, "Political Responsibility: Choices for the '80s," 22 March 1984, p. 1.

14. Lewis B. Smedes, "Cleaning up the Nation: Nine Theses on Politics and Morality," *The Reformed Journal*, June 1980, p. 13.

15. Elizabeth Kester, "Celebrations: Understanding Liberty, Justice and Equality," *The Washington Post*, 4 July 1984.

16. *Everson v. Board of Education*, 330 U.S. 1 (1947).

17. Paul J. Weber as quoted in *Context*, 1 July 1982, 2.

18. Ibid.

19. Ibid.

20. James L. Ash, Jr., *Protestantism and the American University: An Intellectual Biography of William Warren Sweet* (Dallas: Southern Methodist University Press, 1982) 128.

21. Edward M. Kennedy, "Tolerance and Truth in America," (Liberty Baptist College, 3 October 1983).

22. Ibid.

23. Billy Graham, "Why Lausanne?" *Christianity Today*, 13 September 1974, p. 4.

24. Donald W. Shriver, "What's Wrong with Born-Again Politics," *The Christianity Century* 97/32 (22 October 1980): 1002.

25. Kennedy, "Tolerance and Truth."

26. Reinhold Niebuhr, foreword to *The Children of Light and the Children of Darkness*, 1944.

27. *Walz*, 397 U.S. 664 (1970).

28. *McDaniel*, 435 U.S. 618 (1978).

29. Kelley, "Meddling in Politics," 13.

30. Kester, "Celebrations."

31. *Everson*, 330 U.S. 1 (1947).

32. Graham, "Why Lausanne?" 4.

33. Niebuhr, *The Children of Light*.

34. Edwin S. Gaustad, *Liberty of Conscience* (Grand Rapids MI: William B. Eerdmans, 1991) 219.

35. Franklin H. Littell, *From State Church to Pluralism* (New York: The Macmillan Company, 1962) 200.

36. David Cantor, *The Religious Right: The Assault on Tolerance and Pluralism in America* (New York: Anti-Defamation League, 1994) 68.

37. Carl F. H. Henry, "Evangelicals Out of the Closet, But Going Nowhere?" *Christianity Today* (4 January 1980): 21.

38. Quoted in David Berreby, "Clifford Geertz," *New York Times Magazine* (9 April 1995): 46.

39. Edwin S. Gaustad, "Barbarians and Memory," *Journal of Church and State* 37/1 (Winter 1995): 9.

40. Quoted in Berreby, "Clifford Geertz," 47.

41. *New York Times*, 23 December 1952, 16.

42. Quoted in Edwin S. Gaustad, "Religious Liberty: Baptists and Some Fine Distinctions," *American Baptist Quarterly* 6/4 (December 1987): 244.

43. In L. F. Greene, ed., *The Writings of the Late Elder John Leland* (New York: G.W. Wood, 1845; reprint, New York: Arno Press, 1970) 278.

44. Kennedy, "Tolerance and Truth."

School Prayer

School prayer was an issue that received significant attention from James Dunn during his tenure at both the Texas Baptist Christian Life Commission and the Baptist Joint Committee on Public Affairs. Many Americans—especially in the Bible Belt—were deeply disturbed by two prayer-related decisions of the U.S. Supreme Court in the early 1960s. In *Engel v. Vitale* (1962), the Supreme Court barred government-prescribed prayer in public schools, and *Abington v. Schempp* and *Murray v. Curlett* (1963) declared as unconstitutional the practice of requiring public schoolchildren to read the Bible and recite the Lord's Prayer. Critics of these decisions frequently charged that the Supreme Court had kicked God out of public schools. Over the years, this accusation evolved into a widely accepted myth.

In 1971, a major national push was made to reverse these decisions with an amendment to the U.S. Constitution. Before the "Nondenominational Prayer Amendment" was narrowly defeated in the U.S. House of Representatives, Dunn and the Texas CLC voiced strong opposition, emphasizing that "no government has the right to determine either the place or the content of prayer."[1]

A decade later there was another significant nationwide push for a constitutional amendment on prayer. President Ronald Reagan announced on May 7, 1982, his intent to propose to Congress an amendment to allow school-sponsored prayer in public schools. Reagan's proposal was seen as a gesture to Religious Right leaders like Jerry Falwell. For Falwell, Reagan's prayer amendment was a step toward effectively reversing the Court's controversial decisions.

Dunn immediately condemned Reagan's proposal and did so on the front page of *The Washington Post*. "It is despicable demagoguery for the President to play petty politics with prayer," Dunn told the newspaper. "He knows that the Supreme Court never banned prayer in schools. It can't. Real prayer is always free." Dunn accused the President of being "deliberately dishonest" by joining ranks with religious leaders whom he believed had misinterpreted the Supreme Court's rulings on prayer and Bible reading in public schools. Reagan knew better, retorted Dunn. "He knows that the court in those prayer rulings affirmed and encouraged studies about religion in public school classrooms. What the court has done is protect religious liberty."[2]

Dunn stressed that mandatory or supervised prayer is antithetical to the Baptist tradition. He believed that Reagan's prayer amendment would permit government-sponsored prayer. "You hear it called 'putting God in schools,'" Dunn said. "It is as if the Divine could be dumped into a wheelbarrow and carted out. The charge that everything went wrong because they threw prayer out of schools is patent poppycock."[3] He argued that "to make public prayer a political football is to deny the meaning of prayer." Pointing out that some politicians continuously refer to the misnomer that God has been expelled from the classroom, Dunn declared, "The God whom I worship and serve has a perfect attendance record, never absent or even tardy."[4]

Several months after publicly lambasting President Reagan, Dunn stepped into a firestorm at the contentious 1982 meeting of the Southern Baptist Convention. Prior to his report to the convention in New Orleans, a messenger made a motion to censure Dunn for his remarks regarding the President. However, this didn't cause Dunn to soften his criticisms. He warned the 6,000 Southern Baptist messengers that Reagan's prayer amendment would uproot the First Amendment, radically alter the Bill of Rights, and put the government in the business of making decisions about religion. The amendment, he said, would "give sanction to Buddhist prayers in Hawaii, Mormon prayers in Utah, and Muslim prayers in the Bronx," and it would "run roughshod over the consciences of the weak, young and numbered." In contrast to authentic prayer, Reagan's amendment would reduce prayer to the "lowest common denominator" and "possibly inoculate school children against authentic religious experience," Dunn said.[5]

Despite Dunn's warnings, a majority of the messengers voted to adopt a resolution in support of Reagan's amendment. This vote made the SBC the only major denomination in the U.S. to endorse the amendment. While the fundamentalist leaders of the SBC championed the resolution, Dunn lamented it as an "incredible contradiction of our Baptist heritage."[6] When SBC leaders defended the resolution on the grounds that government would not regulate the prayers, Dunn pointed to a White House document stating that communities would have the power and freedom to select and compose the prayers used in public school classrooms. It would later be revealed that an aide to President Reagan, Morton Blackwell, had worked with Religious Right leader Ed McAteer to advise SBC Resolution

Committee chairman Norris Sydnor, and a rumor was circulated that a White House staffer had written the SBC prayer resolution.

Nearly two years later, Reagan's prayer amendment received a vote. However, while a majority in the Republican-controlled Senate affirmed the amendment, it fell eleven votes short of the required two-thirds needed. This debate over school prayer would set the stage for future fights between the BJC and SBC, leading to the two groups formally severing ties in 1990. The selected columns in this section feature Dunn's commentary on the issue of school prayer and were written in the context of this debate over Reagan's prayer amendment.[7]

Prayer Amendment: Unneeded, Unwanted, and Unworkable

This column appeared in the July 1982 issue of the BJC's newsletter, Report from the Capital, *in response to President Ronald Reagan's proposed prayer amendment. Dunn accuses President Reagan of "joining the ultra-fundamentalists" and declares that Reagan had "forsaken conservatism regarding the Constitution" and was "playing politics with prayer."*

Working for nine brands of Baptists is never dull. It reminds me of the prospective employer who told the young applicant: "We'll have no 'yes' men around here. I cannot tolerate a nay sayer. There's no room for an equivocator. What do you think?"

I'll not equivocate. Mr. Reagan has submitted his prayer amendment. It's unneeded, unwanted, and unworkable.

Unneeded—What kind of conservative would uproot the First Amendment, changing the Bill of Rights for the first time since its adoption in 1791? Robert W. Kastenmeier, a member of the House Judiciary Committee, says it's "an attempt to alter the historic interpretation of a key feature of the Bill of Rights."

Most of us believe that the Constitution should be amended only under the most extreme circumstances. Odd, isn't it, how many of the very people using that argument against the Equal Rights Amendment suddenly see wisdom in radically altering the First Amendment?

Unwanted—Most major religious bodies have seen the folly of this meddling in religion. Why? Why? Could it be that someone is playing politics with prayer? It's no use to say, "what harm can come from prayer in schools?" Ask the parents of dead children in Northern Ireland what harm can come from politicized prayer in schools.

Dr. J. M. Price, dean of religious education in Southern Baptist life, used to say, "We are as responsible for those whose (religious) experiences we bungle as we are for those we never reach at all." Don't tell me there is no harm.

Of course, there have been some overreactions on the part of educators to the present limitations. I heard of one muddleheaded principal who patrolled the lunchroom yelling at students who silently bowed their head to say a blessing. Stupid!

Why, pray tell, does anyone think there wouldn't be excesses if the so-called "prayer amendment" would pass? We'd have more evangelistic trap services in school assemblies, and courses in Christian doctrine would spring up in the flavor of the local majority. Don't tell me there's no harm.

Unworkable—One conservative columnist has suggested, "It's odd to see the same people who don't want sex education, because that isn't the proper role of the public schools, inviting the same secularized educators they distrust to supervise religious observances." Why? Why? Maybe playing politics with prayer?

Practically every constitutional authority to comment has opposed the ill-conceived amendment. That includes the present Solicitor General of the United States, Rex E. Lee. When he was dean of the Brigham Young University Law School, shortly before joining the Reagan administration, he asked in one of his books on constitutional law, "What does the Government gain by requiring or authorizing school prayer in the public schools? In most cases, the recital is a sterile exercise, a group exercise totally lacking in individuality, spontaneity, or real expression of conviction. To the extent that any students pay attention to the words, some will believe them, some will find them irrelevant, and to some they will be positively offensive." Why? Why? Perhaps, playing politics with prayer?

Leo Pfeffer tells about the little boy who, after having to repeat the 23rd Psalm, wanted to know, "who is the good Mrs. Murphy" who will follow him the rest of his days. Seems he'd misunderstood "goodness and mercy."

We at the Baptist Joint Committee on Public Affairs know we don't have all the answers. You can make several possible responses.

1. You can tell the Committee we didn't say what we've said. You can tell the Conventions, Boards, and Conferences they were wrong, and you can reverse the direction we've headed since E. Y. Mullins, George W. Truett, J. M. Dawson, Louie Newton, C. Emmanuel Carlson. (It's not logical but it's parliamentarily possible.)

2. You can call on every Christian school child in America to pray at home and church and even to have a pray-in at school before every exam and at all other testing times. (It would do more good than compelled ritual.)

3. You can give us some practical, constructive advice about how to maintain creative tension toward a healthy separation of church and state. We're still in the business of guarding religious liberty and there are plenty of places that government is meddling in church life.

4. You can help us educate the educators in the positive ways that religion can and should be studied in the public schools. (It was Justice Tom Clark who said in 1963, "It certainly may be said that the Bible is worthy of study for its literary and historic qualities. Nothing we have said here indicates that such study of the Bible or of religion, when presented objectively as part of a secular program of education, may not be effected consistent with the First Amendment.")

5. You can tell us how you'd handle group prayer where the teacher is a cult member and now set free to do her weird thing, or where the majority are active proselytizers, or where you have one emotional upheaval after another. (It's unfair to force little children to act as defense lawyers to defend their religious liberty.)

In a party rally two days before the Rose Garden announcement of the amendment to get government into daily devotionals, the President of the United States suggested that campaign workers use the prayer issue in the 1982 campaign (*Washington Post*, 5 May 1982). Joining the ultra-fundamentalists in this, the President has deserted principles he claims to love dearly. He has forsaken conservatism regarding the Constitution, strict construction in interpreting it, and the goal of freedom from government intrusion. Why? Why? Possibly playing politics with prayer?

Playing politics with prayer is a sin. This is not a silly grin, dirty tricks issue. Liberty should never be taken lightly. This strikes at the root of the freedom tree; once cut down, it cannot be brought back to life.

It's time for a response from all who care. Stay true. Hold fast. Pray free. Speak up. Do right. We don't need a government prayer permit. Say so!

> —James M. Dunn, "Reflections," *Report from the Capital* 37/7 (July 1982): 15–16. Reprinted with permission courtesy of the Baptist Joint Committee for Religious Liberty.

Secularization, Trivialization, Collectivization

Several months after his first column lambasting President Reagan over his proposed prayer amendment, Dunn penned a second column denouncing efforts to return government-sponsored prayer back to public school classrooms. This column was featured in the November 1982 issue of the BJC's newsletter, Report from the Capital. *Dunn accuses his conservative foes of promoting secularization, which is what he claims would be the result of government-sponsored prayer in public schools.*

Words carry a peculiar freight, trigger a reaction in specific settings. The "school prayer" debate involves some odd words, four to seven syllables long.

Consider *secularization*: simply to transfer from ecclesiastical to civil use. More precisely, to make secular: "that which is of or relating to the worldly or temporal as distinguished from the spiritual or eternal."

Secularization is exactly what would happen to prayer if some folks had their way. The most intimate and inner expression in religion would be drafted, conscripted, and dragged from its rightful setting where it is tenderly taught and spiritually shared. Prayer would be put into uniform and forced to do civil duty, to tote the values of the common culture, to bear the burdens of pop religion.

Prayer, as in "school prayer," is a component of civil religion. It is of necessity watered down. Whether prescribed by some level of authority like the teacher on the beat or the spontaneous outbursts of self-anointed spiritually superior students, it's watered-down worship. There is something cheap about making prayer come under civil service, used to "quiet the kids down."

Isn't it ironic that folks who quake at the danger of secular humanism are the very ones pushing for prayer in the public schools, an ultimate secularization?

Consider *trivialization*. We live on several planes, but they intersect and intertwine. One cannot and should not attempt an arbitrary division between the sacred and the secular. Christians accept Jesus Christ as the Lord of all life.

Yet it is possible to put down, make light of, reduce to ridicule The Holy. Abraham Heschel, a great man of faith, spent his life attending awe as the ultimate emotion. Louis Cobb said, "The bump of reverence on the American head is a dent."

Great hunks of humanity in this country see nothing wrong with "using" prayer. If we who have been given our lives to Him Who Was and Is and Ever Shall Be mean what we say and sing on Sunday, we will resist trivialization.

At seminary, we had a yell for the intramural football team: "Yea black! yea gray! Seminary, Seminary! Let us pray!" Irreverent? Certainly!

However, it was as dangerously irreverent and threatening to the spiritually sensitive as the move to allow government to get into religious observance. It seems that the Religious Right would like to name God the National Mascot. Trivialization!

Next, think about *reductionism*. For some, school prayer may not be tainted by this term. If, for you, prayer is nothing but ritual, mechanical observance, surface activity that has little if anything to do with heart-felt religion, it doesn't matter. If prayer is repeating rote phrases without engaging the mind, who cares what goes on in school.

If so-called school prayers are effective, compelling, and meaningful, then they constitute indoctrination, evangelization, and they have no part in the patterns of public school life.

On the other hand, if prayer is weak-kneed and wishy-washy, a poor imitation of the real thing, then it constitutes a threat to authentic religion, contradicting what is being taught at home and church or synagogue. School "praying" can work like a flu shot. An inoculation of diluted deism can make some children immune, or at least resistant, to real religion.

Mr. Justice Stevens was correct in calling school prayers "compelled ritual." That's reductionism.

Now look at *revisionism*. Rewriting history is a growth industry of the fundamentalists who have recently come alive to their civic duties. It takes the place of study and research. It portrays Colonial America as a Christian nation. In fact, less than 20% of those people had any church connection. It portrays the Founding Fathers as great men of the Faith. In fact, some were bounders, others deists, all sons of the Enlightenment. It minimizes the dedication of the framers of the Constitution to Jefferson's "wall of separation" between church and state.

In evaluating recent history, advocates of religious exercise in the public classroom moan that all our present ills stem from "putting God out of the schools" (as if the Heavenly One could be carted about). In fact, school prayers have been faithfully and widely practiced in other countries and they haven't brought idealistic Islam to Iran, churchgoing to England, religious toleration to Belgium, sexual morality to Sweden, freedom of thought to Spain, or peace to Northern Ireland. They pray in schools there.

Collectivization is another real danger in our world. We don't need homogenized culture and religion in this country any more than it is needed in communist lands. Part of our strength lies in our pluralism and diversity. If we had prayers in public settings, they could be Buddhist in Hawaii, Mormon in Utah, Baptist in Mississippi, Roman Catholic in New Mexico, and Black Muslim in Harlem.

On the other hand, someone has suggested that public school prayer to be fair would have to be addressed "to whom it may concern."

Lowest-common-denominator religion is not worth much to anyone. Emil Brunner criticized collectivism, saying that it makes up society "like briquets of so many pulverized individuals." Moves to approve school prayers are steps toward collectivization.

One more word: *authoritarianism.* The dictionary says it is "of, relating to, or favoring a principle of often blind submission to authority as opposed to individual freedom."

Most of the folks for "returning prayer to the schools" have never thought about how such a practice fosters authoritarianism. It does so even and especially with the dedicated and caring teachers of small children. Most often these teachers do not want that role. They'd reject it if they could. Many, if not most of them, understand that for prayer to be real it has to be free. They're not interested in "favoring a principle of blind submission," particularly when it comes to religion. Most Americans are not opposed to individual freedom. We hate authoritarianism.

Explain these words to your Congressman, will you? The Supreme Court was right to reject government meddling in religion and efforts to legalize school prayers.

—James M. Dunn, "Reflections,"
Report from the Capital 37/4 (November 1982): 15.
Reprinted with permission courtesy of
the Baptist Joint Committee for Religious Liberty.

Voluntary Prayer or Required Ritual?

The issue of government-sponsored prayer in public schools (or "voluntary prayer" as supporters called it) would be resurrected repeatedly throughout the 1980s and into the 1990s. When the issue resurfaced in 1989, Dunn again took to the pages of Report from the Capital *to define "voluntary prayer." Here, he emphasizes that "formal institutionally sanctioned prayer" and prayer with a "captive audience" is not voluntary.*

Eliminate and do away with redundancy!

We should expect more than we do of members of the U.S. Congress in regard to their use of our mother tongue.

One Mr. Dannemeyer of California has successfully tacked an amendment on legislation funding vocational education which would promote/permit/require (?) "voluntary prayer."

The amendment reads, "No funds shall be made available under applicable program in this Act to any state or local educational agency which has a policy of denying or which effectively prevents participation in prayer in public schools by individuals on a voluntary basis." But then in debate on the matter, May 9, 1989, the Congressman said, "there is no effort on my part as the author of this amendment to mandate that we have voluntary prayer." Good for him. We don't need mandated voluntary prayer.

For public schools to get into the business of religion, the catch phrase is "voluntary prayer."

There are only two problems with that. What is generally under debate is neither voluntary nor prayer.

Any sort of oral, spoken, group-attended, formal, institutionally sanctioned prayer in the public school classroom is not voluntary. It is not voluntary because the hearers are there under mandatory school attendance laws. A captive audience of children has trouble making genuinely voluntary responses. Responses are ordered and structured in the classroom. At least to some degree, I hope. If prayer is "used" as a disciplinary device (Alright, boys and girls, shut up and pray!), it's hardly voluntary or prayer.

Mr. Justice Stevens, speaking to the American Bar Association in 1982, tagged government-prescribed religious exercises "required ritual." He was right. The objective sought so sincerely by some is not voluntary.

That settles it. If it's not voluntary, it's not prayer. If it is voluntary, no one under heaven can prevent it.

Public schools *can* teach much *about* prayer/s. No child should get far in public education without knowing that Americans pray in many different ways. Some believe that they must kneel for prayer, humble and sincere. Some make the sign of the cross. Others must pray aloud with lifted hands. Others bow their heads and close their eyes. Still others must face a certain direction. Some earnest pray-ers prefer a physical aid or symbol to assist their prayers. Some do not believe they can pray in the presence of others.

School children everywhere can be taught that prayer is related to one's own religion and that each of us should honor and respect the right of others to practice their faith freely without being made to conform to someone else's prayer. Those of tender age and receptive conscience should certainly not be made to feel odd or different if their family's treasured beliefs do not fit the majority practice. Nor should children be nudged or intimidated to enter into any sort of religious exercise at all in the public school setting.

Further, one of the most important things that public schools can teach about prayer is that the state cannot prevent it or permit it. There is more to life than that which falls under government's umbrella. Vital to the American experience is the experiment that keeps church and state separate enough that neither can dominate the other.

What is it then that those who insist upon public school religion really want? Many of them, like me, are from a regenerate church tradition and believe that faith must be personal. One follows Jesus Christ freely or not really. One prays from the heart or doesn't really pray.

What would be gained by some watered-down exercise that might offend as many as it helps? Most thoughtful promoters of oral prayers in public institutions recognize that the form, context, and actual practice would vary widely.

Many problems, some real, some imagined, do exist and fuel the push for public school religion.

One is ignorance of what is constitutional and what is not. Members of Congress in this Year of our Lord 1989 are still standing on the floor of the U.S. House of Representatives interpreting "the decision of the U.S.

Supreme Court in 1962 (as) saying that we no longer would have voluntary prayer in public schools." Wrong!

Another problem is exaggerated response to the Court decisions of the 1960s in fear and misunderstanding. That response comes from teachers, principals, administrators, and school boards. Much work needs to be done to clarify and keep the delicate balance between no establishment of religion and the free exercise thereof. Stories are told about a teacher who forbade a child to bow his head and silently say a table grace in the school lunchroom. Persons of goodwill and common sense should find out if such stories are true. If so, the teacher should be corrected.

A third aspect of the problem that allows well-meaning but misled people to push for state-sanctioned prayers is the public focus on what cannot be done.

A disturbed pastor called me from a small town in Louisiana and described how a church of another denomination was taking all the public school children whose parents gave their consent into a church building for religious education two hours each week. It didn't seem right to him. The more we talked, the more evident it became that the church was probably properly engaged in a released-time program. Churches everywhere have the facilities, the people, and the opportunity to do more than a few minutes of teaching religion. My only counsel to this brother and others like him is "Go thou and do likewise." But that takes work.

Another option for significant involvement with the public schools is through volunteers helping in the regular school day or providing directed activities, a study hall, tutoring after the school day. Latch-key kids find a safe, healthy place to hang out if churches are willing to open their doors. But that requires some creativity and planning.

Groups of students in secondary schools may gather before or after the school day for voluntary religious activities if the school permits any limited open forum for other sorts of clubs. The "equal access" legislation of Sen. Mark Hatfield and Rep. Don Bonker simply guarantees religious clubs the same free speech that other groups enjoy. But that demands some initiative on the part of students.

Voluntary required prayer for individual groups who are freely mandatorily assembled is not the answer or the question.

The bill that bears Mr. Dannemeyer's amendment goes now to the Senate. Maybe they have a dictionary.

—James M. Dunn, "Reflections," *Report from the Capital* 44/7 (July–August 1989): 15. Reprinted with permission courtesy of the Baptist Joint Committee for Religious Liberty.

Notes

1. "1971 Report of the Christian Life Commission," in *Annual of the Baptist General Convention of Texas* (Dallas TX: BGCT, 1971).

2. Herbert H. Denton and Marjorie Hyer, "Reagan to Ask Hill for Prayer Amendment," *The Washington Post*, 7 May 1982, A1.

3. JMD, quoted in Larry Chesser, "Establishing Religious Beliefs a Threat to Liberty," *Report from the Capital* 36/10 (November–December 1981): 16.

4. JMD, "Reflections," *Report from the Capital* 38/3 (March 1983): 15.

5. "SBC Backs Prayer," *Biblical Recorder*, 26 June 1982, 2–3.

6. Ibid.

7. Martin Tolchin, "Amendment Drive on School Prayer Loses Senate Vote," *New York Times*, 21 March 1984, A2–3.

Tuition Tax Credits and Vouchers

Tuition tax credits and vouchers were two recurring church-state issues that James Dunn addressed and vigorously opposed throughout his ministry. Battles over parochial aid were common in the Texas legislature when Dunn directed the Texas Baptist Christian Life Commission from 1968–1980. He was involved in numerous efforts to oppose legislative attempts to fund private and parochial elementary and secondary schools. In response to well-financed and highly organized attempts by Catholic lobbyists to secure state aid for Catholic schools, he helped to establish the Citizen's Association for Public Schools to counter these efforts at the Texas state capitol in Austin.

Dunn argued that parochial aid would violate each citizen's right to the free exercise of religion by compelling others to support religious institutions not of their choosing. "To force a citizen to support a school of a religious group in which he does not believe is to violate his religious conscience," Dunn said in the CLC's 1971 annual report. "The Gospel is to be supported voluntarily not through government coercion."[1]

He also led the CLC to fight tuition tax credit proposals benefiting parents who sent their children to sectarian schools. In 1972, Dunn described a tuition tax credit proposal that was making its way through the Ways and Means Committee of the U.S. House of Representatives as a "perversion of the basic purpose for taxation and a serious threat to religious liberty." Dunn called the plan "a blatant attempt to make millions of middle Americans pay the bills for private and parochial schools operated by the wealthy."[2] Six years later, he was still speaking out against tuition tax credits, calling such proposals "one of the most serious attacks on church-state separation in our generation." Dunn argued that tuition tax credits would serve as a means of re-segregating the public school system in the South.[3]

From 1977–1978, more than 100 tuition tax credit bills were introduced in Congress. In August 1978, President Jimmy Carter led the successful opposition to a legislative amendment in the U.S. Senate that would have granted federal tuition tax credits for parents with children in private/parochial schools. Dunn backed the president in this endeavor, but Carter's opposition to tuition tax credits would be used against him by Ronald Reagan during the 1980 presidential campaign. However, newly elected President Reagan's own efforts in early 1982 to pass tuition tax credit legislation were unsuccessful thanks in part to the efforts of Dunn and the Baptist Joint Committee.[4]

During the 1990s, Dunn and the BJC spent much energy fighting legislative efforts to use tax dollars to fund private and parochial education. In 1991, under the banner of "School Choice," President George H. W. Bush proposed educational reforms to grant federal vouchers for parents to send their children to public, private, and parochial schools. Dunn described this effort as just another "scheme"—like the tuition tax credit proposals of the 1980s—to divert tax dollars to church-related schools.[5] That same year, Dunn led the BJC to adopt a statement detailing their opposition to vouchers:

> This attempt to do indirectly (through vouchers) what cannot be done directly (by direct grants) is constitutionally suspect, bad public policy and a disingenuous political tactic. . . . Parental choice through vouchers is no substitute for our responsibility to make all schools "schools of choice" in a constitutionally permissible way.[6]

In his monthly column, Dunn explained to his readers that "Defending voucher plans as indirect aid to religious institutions rather than direct support for sectarian schools is a distinction without a difference." This short quote gets to the heart of Dunn's no-aid separationist philosophy. Government aid to religious institutions whether direct or indirect was unacceptable. Public money was to be used only for public purposes, and, in his view, religious education was not compatible with a definition of "public purpose."[7]

Voucher proposals were rejected by the U.S. Senate in early 1992.[8] Several months later, President George H. W. Bush unveiled a similar plan while campaigning for reelection. Dunn described the new plan as an "election-year stunt."[9] This voucher proposal named the G.I. Bill for Children died in Congress when President Bush's bid for reelection failed. Unfortunately for voucher proponents, President Bill Clinton supported a different type of "school choice" that limited parental choice to public schools.[10]

During the second term of the Clinton Administration, voucher legislation passed for the first time in both the U.S. House of Representatives and the U.S. Senate. The Senate approved a voucher bill in 1997 and the House passed a voucher measure on April 30, 1998. This voucher program would have provided "opportunity scholarships" to 2,000 low-income students in the District of Columbia. However, three weeks after the legislation passed in the House, President Clinton vetoed the D.C. vouchers bill as promised. No attempt to override the voucher veto was made by the Republican-controlled Congress.[11]

Dunn continued to assail "voucher schemes" on a regular basis in his monthly column. He insisted that vouchers were unconstitutional because public funds subsidizing private religious education had the effect of advancing religion in violation of the First Amendment. Beyond church-state concerns, Dunn was most worried about the effects of voucher programs on public schools. In these debates about vouchers, Dunn believed that nothing short of the future of public education was at stake. The "Reflections" columns in this section from the BJC's newsletter, *Report from the Capital*, highlight Dunn's consistent opposition to tuition tax credit and voucher proposals.

Tuition Tax Credit Pottage

James Dunn spoke out against a bipartisan tuition tax credit plan in the July 1981 issue of Report from the Capital. *Dunn's use of the phrase "public money for public purposes" captures his philosophy toward education funding.*

"Public money for public purposes" is not a bad motto. The failure to meet that test of public policy is the greatest fault with tuition tax credit plans now before the United States Congress.

Delegates to the National Catholic Education Association meeting in New York in late April were read a telegram from President Reagan that said, "This administration will support tuition tax credits for private education" (*RNS*, 24 April 1981). More than a dozen tax credit plans have been introduced in Congress, most allowing a taxpayer credit on his income tax for a certain amount of his private or parochial tuition costs.

The best-known 1981 version of the recurring bad idea is the one introduced by Senators Daniel P. Moynihan (D-NY) and Robert Packwood (R-OR). It would return to the taxpayer by means of a tax credit 50 percent of his tuition up to $250 for starters.

What's wrong with this approach to education aid?

1. First, it's *unconstitutional*. As Senator Ernest F. Hollings says, "in 1973 the U.S. Supreme Court's *Nyquist* decision reaffirmed the position of our Founding Fathers by striking down a New York State tuition tax credit plan because it violated the First Amendment's establishment clause" (*Washington Post*, 14 March 1981).

No one can escape the conclusion that public funds benefit the sponsoring church. The net result is that the taxpayer is forced to subsidize religion, and overwhelmingly one brand of religion at that. Thomas Jefferson wrote, "To compel a man to furnish contributions of money for the propagation of opinions which he disbelieves is sinful and tyrannical."

Senator Moynihan does not deny that the constitutional problems exist, but with an attitude beneath the responsibility of the U.S. Senate says, "pass the suspect legislation, let the courts decide."

2. Then, it's *regressive*. It would offer aid to the people who need it least. The poor who do not want their children in available church schools or who cannot afford them, even by supplementing the tax aid, must fall back on public schools. Many parents do not have enough income to benefit from a tax credit. The half of the population with more modest incomes would be left out in the cold.

The Reverend Paul Schetelick, co-pastor of Blessed Sacrament Parish in Newark, says, "We can fool ourselves and say we are serving the poorest of the poor, but people on welfare can't afford our schools" (*New York Times*, 24 April 1981). Sharing this view is Dr. James S. Coleman, author of a new report praising parochial schools. He "fears that tuition tax credits would mostly aid wealthier families, who pay substantial income taxes, and do little or nothing for disadvantaged minority students" (RNS, 24 April 1981).

The result of such welfare for the well-off would be free choice for those with money and compulsory miseducation for the rest.

3. Next, it's *expensive*. Estimates vary from $4 billion to $6 billion annual costs, depending upon the exact plan passed, the extent of private and parochial school benefit. A tax credit is labeled a "tax expenditure" and is just as much a cost to taxpayers as any other budget line item. Odd, isn't it, that at a time of slashing federal aid to education some senators are pushing for this sort of spending. As Senator Everett Dirksen once said, "You spend a billion here and billion there and before long you're talking about real money."

4. Further, it's *inflationary*. Such an incentive from federal policy would make for a wild escalation in the cost of private education. A Father Bredeveg of the National Catholic Education Association testified for tuition tax credits before the last Congress, indicating that "it would enable us to increase tuition."

Moynihan admits that tax credits might lead to higher tuition. *The New York Times* predicts that the "cost of this uncontrollable entitlement could rise spectacularly" (10 March 1981).

5. Also, it's *unfair*. The larger rather than the smaller church schools would be favored. The parochial systems already in place would have a distinct advantage. There is even a regional warp for the Northeast quarter of the country. Six of the seven cities with the largest percentage of school children in church schools are Cleveland, Chicago, Milwaukee, Philadelphia, New York, and Boston.

To appeal for fairness because "parents and private and parochial school children pay both taxes and tuition" is to advance an odd principal of tax equity. The elderly, singles, and couples without children support public services in general and don't whimper for tax credits to evade supporting public education.

6. Beyond that, it's *divisive*. This sort of state support for church schools would arouse the competitive worst in church folks. They'd be rooting for tax credit advantage like an overlarge brood of hungry piglets. The fellow who doesn't think Christian leaders would come to that needs to reexamine his understanding of original sin.

Americans are already sharply divided on the issue. A Gallup-*Newsweek* poll (March 1981) reveals that 34% favor an income tax credit, 52% oppose it, and 14% are undecided. Legislative flim-flam that codifies the will of a vocal and pushy minority never makes for tranquility.

The divisiveness would cut far deeper in the social fabric than competition between church schools. Some of the troubles in Northern Ireland today stem from the school systems which have prevented children from mingling and knowing one another.

7. Again, it's *destructive* of the public schools. The future of public education is at stake. A government subsidy would place a bounty on the head of school children for their withdrawal from the public schools. Joseph A. Califano, Jr., former Secretary of Health, Education, and Welfare, described tuition tax credits as a "devastating blow to public school education in this country," a proposal that "stands the American tradition of public education on its head" (*Dallas Times Herald*, 27 February 1978).

Carl Rowan fears that if such a scheme were made law, "The public school system will become a crippled outpost for children of families so poor that, even with tuition tax credits, they can't send their children to private schools" (*Dallas Morning News*, March 1978).

8. Still, it's *undemocratic*. There would be a sort of taxation without representation if tax credit maneuvering prevailed. The decisions regarding private and parochial schools would be made beyond the reach or influence of the taxpayer. Public schools have their problems responding to the 16,000 local school boards. But, that's democracy at work.

9. Penultimately, it's *dishonest*. To use the parents' tax credit for a conduit to get tax monies into private and parochial schools is a tad shady. The constitutional tests have made it clear that it's not right to try to do something indirectly that is directly forbidden. Such a subterfuge is unworthy of the U.S. Congress.

10. Finally, it's *intrusive*. Government regulations would inevitably and legitimately follow an alternative school system in which the public had such a vested interest. Thomas A. Shannon, executive director of the National School Boards Association, contends that, "without strict regulation, there would be no way to prevent the subsidies provided through tax credits from helping schools that endorsed values of communists, the Ku Klux Klan or other groups" (*New York Times*, 23 April 1981). Andrew Greely, noted Catholic sociologist, and others oppose tuition tax credits because of increased government control of parochial schools.

One of the great strengths of private and parochial education is found in the freedom from government intervention. It would be sad to see that freedom swapped for a mess of tax credit pottage.

President John F. Kennedy understood the perils of public support for private and church-related schools. He said on September 15, 1960, "I believe in America where the separation of church and state is absolute… where no church or church school is granted any public funds or political preference."

Government's duty is to leave private schools alone.

> —James M. Dunn, "Reflections," *Report from the Capital* 36/7 (July 1981): 14–15. Reprinted with permission courtesy of the Baptist Joint Committee for Religious Liberty.

Forswear Funnymentalism (and Vouchers)

Vouchers were a hot topic of discussion in James Dunn's Report from the Capital *columns throughout the 1990s. In this June 1991 commentary, Dunn takes aim at the various rationales offered to justify using tax dollars to aid religious educational institutions.*

Funny mental tricks are needed to justify taking public money for nonpublic purposes. Yet there are those who are making the mind leaps and doing the ethical contortions necessary for such stunts.

"Choice" schemes attempt to launder public funds by passing them through parents' pockets in the form of vouchers. Defending voucher plans as indirect aid to religious institutions rather than direct support for sectarian schools is a distinction without a difference.

It is a well-established principle of law that one cannot do through the back door what could not be done through the front. Educational vouchers are a blatant attempt to do exactly that. If it is unconstitutional for public schoolteachers to teach secular subjects in parochial schools, as the Supreme Court has ruled, then the use of public monies to pay parochial school teachers is even more offensive to the Constitution.

As Justice William O. Douglas wrote, concurring in *Abington v. Schempp*, "[It] is the use to which public funds are put and not to whom they are provided that is controlling.... What may not be done directly may not be done indirectly lest the Establishment Clause become a mockery." Justice Jackson wrote in comments on *Everson v. Board of Education*, "The prohibition against establishment of religion cannot be circumvented by a subsidy, bonus, or reimbursement of expense to individuals for receiving religious instruction."

Church-related schools hardly have a reason to exist without providing religious instruction and indoctrination. Even if it is not precisely the religious dimensions of the institutions that are supported, no fast book work by accountants, no shifting the government money from one pocket to another to maintain the fiction that no taxes teach religion, will keep the ethical slate clean for church schools indirectly receiving federal funds. Religious school folks of all stripes were shocked when the *Grove City* decision demonstrated that regulation of church schools results even when financial aid is received indirectly in the form of student assistance such as Pell Grants or vouchers.

How in the world, then, when vouchers promise a morass of governmental regulations that many "choice" supporters oppose, can any reasonably well-informed church leader indirectly invite "regs" and guidelines? Why would anyone who pays even token tribute to separation of church and state welcome this false advertising in educational reform? "Choice" indeed! It's more a matter of chance.

One shouldn't have to dignify with debate such ploys for political advantage, but one must. If one learned nothing else from the 1980s, surely it is now clear that slick slogans by the media masters can, in fact, alter the political landscape and thrust the entire nation into unchartered territory. Recent history demonstrates that Congress, the courts, and the citizenry seem to think that the First Amendment can be set aside by majority vote. The majoritarian motto seems to be "You can fool most of the people all of the time and that's enough."

Why, then? Why would tolerably well-educated, religiously inoculated, politically aware persons who should know better sound a timid note in opposition to any so-called "choice" plan?

Three reasons come to mind:

Bad faith. One must not rule out a certain devious stripe. It runs through all humankind . . . total depravity, original sin, ontological limits, human frailty, and all that. One need not impute motives. The opposite is the case. Despite the yuppie decade, godly greed, holy war, and sanctified selfishness are still oxymorons. Subscribers to those socially sanctioned secular modes are suspect in the churches, synagogues, and temples of this land.

Supporters of schemes to direct money, energy, and attention to vouchers veiled as choice probably didn't sit down and say to themselves, "I think I'll be hypocritical, inconsistent, and flip-floppy." The result is the same as if they had. Just a few years ago, for instance, Baptist leaders were virtually unanimous in opposition to all diversions of tax money to sectarian causes. Now many of those very same people are on the bandwagon for a proposal masquerading as choice.

What is different? Does one oppose parochial schools until one has parochial schools? An ethic shaped by economics? Does one accept the party line of an ultra-conservative political agenda which openly advocates destruction of the public schools? An ethic for private school parents? Does one in the protesting mainstream of religious life do an about face and accept the push for aid to parochial schools he has protested all those years? An ethic flexible enough to be dissenting then, established religion now?

Care, great care, should be exercised in evaluations of this sort. "Judge not" the Scripture enjoins. Yet one also reads "by their fruits ye shall know them." A little "fruit inspection" is called for.

Again, why this surge of support for a plan bearing the misleading word choice?

Some have *an anecdotal understanding of public policy* rooted in bad history. Yes, there were founders who wanted non-preferential aid to all religion. They were the ones who lost the battle 200 years ago. The ones who won wanted more specific, explicit, binding constitutional language: "Congress shall make no law respecting an establishment of religion." The proponents of government-guided funding of church-run schools fail to see that public policy in this country is rightly built on the presupposition that religious institutions must generate their own support without any sort of propping up by the state.

Over and over in the last 30 years the electorates in state after state have overwhelmingly rejected every plan for promoting nonpublic schools at the expense of the common school. The most recent such victory for public education was in Oregon in November 1990.

Finally, one must conclude that some big backers of educational revisionism simply have a *truncated theology*. Desperately eager to be biblical, they do not take sin seriously or socially enough. Understanding the need for personal salvation, they somehow miss the nexus between theology and public policy.

Sinful, social beings that we are, we need separation of church and state to protect church from state, state from church, and to protect us all from each other.

When it comes to forsaking the common school, too much is at stake; don't defect from tried and true, constitutional common sense, safeguards for liberty. Forswear funnymentalism.

> —James M. Dunn, "Reflections," *Report from the Capital* (June 1991): 15. Reprinted with permission courtesy of the Baptist Joint Committee for Religious Liberty.

Public Money for Public Purposes

In this May 1994 column, Dunn continues to emphasize his "public money for public purposes" motto. In typical fashion, he uses alliteration to press his point that voucher schemes and school choice proposals are bad for both church-state separation and public education.

Public money for public purposes, right? Sounds simple, doesn't it? Yet situationalists are always ready to set aside principle.

Government has no business in the religion business. Yet some are so eager to get tax dollars that they are willing to sell their souls for a message of public money pottage.

Quite apart from the letter of the law, anyone responsible for a religious institution should remember that "he who pays the fiddler calls the tune." The very qualities for which a church-related school is brought into being can be bartered away for bucks.

All over America, voucher schemes and so-called "choice" programs are being advanced that would provide, directly or indirectly, public funding for parochial schools.

What is wrong with these plans? They bear several common characteristics.

Unconstitutional

No one can escape the conclusion that public funds benefit the sponsoring church, thereby advancing religion. The taxpayer is forced to subsidize someone's religion. Thomas Jefferson wrote, "to compel a man to furnish contributions of money for the propagation of opinions which he disbelieves is sinful and tyrannical."

Undemocratic

The "choice" rests with the private and parochial schools that can turn away slow learners, discipline problems, whomever they will. Though all taxpayers would bear the burden of taxation, they would not elect the leaders of religious schools or choose the teachers or set the policies: taxation without representation.

Unfair

Most of the parochial schools in this land belong to one denomination with systems already in place. This constitutes an unfair advantage. There is even a regional bias for the Northeastern quarter of the country. There is a *de facto* unfairness about national voucher schemes.

Regressive

No plan has yet been set forth that would favor the folks who need it most. The Rev. Paul Schetelick, co-pastor of the Blessed Sacrament Parish in Newark, says, "We can fool ourselves and say we are serving the poorest of the poor, but people on welfare can't afford our schools." A voucher scheme for parental choice for those with money offers compulsory miseducation for most: welfare for the well-off.

Expensive

A decade of debate over the deficit and the national debt has made Americans entitlement conscious. Why in the name of heaven would we institute yet another inflationary, escalating entitlement?

Divisive

State support for church schools arouses the competitive worst in regions, religions, educational philosophies, sects, cults, and the emerging "teach-for-profit" entrepreneurs. Some advocate a sort of Adam Smith, shoe salesman competition as an education cure-all. We'd have competition all right, but its greedy dark side would likely obscure any benefits. Kids are not commodities.

Destructive of the Public Schools

The future of public education is at stake. A government subsidy would place a bounty on the head of school children for their withdrawal from the public schools. Labor Secretary Robert Reich has warned about "the secession of the successful from social responsibility." School bond issues are being defeated. School budgets are being cut. Some public school systems have actually been abolished. Any plan providing public money for private and church schools stands the American tradition of public education on its head.

President John F. Kennedy said, "I believe in an America where the separation of church and state is absolute . . . where no church or church school is granted any public funds or political preference."

It's still better that way.

> —James M. Dunn, "Reflections," *Report from the Capital* (17 May 1994): 3. Reprinted with permission courtesy of the Baptist Joint Committee for Religious Liberty.

School Choice: Wrongheaded Reform of Public Education

James Dunn shares additional reasons why school choice is "wrongheaded reform" of public education in an article published in the June 1996 issue of Christian Ethics Today. *He declares he could not "vouch for vouchers," explaining how destructive these schemes are to public schools and a healthy relationship between church and state.*

School choice is the right name for a wrongheaded reform of public education. It is the private schools with the choice . . . they decide whether to accept a child or not.

I cannot vouch for vouchers. Such schemes are at least:

UNPREDICTABLE—running the risk of funding even Nazi, Ku Klux Klan ventures, or worse;

UNFAIR—giving social sanction to schools that can reject the discipline problem, the deficient learner, the disabled, while public schools serve all children;

UNCONSTITUTIONAL—violating the no establishment clause since the courts have made it clear that it is illegal to do something indirectly that is directly forbidden, like laundering funds for faith-based schools by filtering them through parents;

UNWORTHY—blessing the secession of the successful from their social responsibility by providing welfare for the well-off (Nothing could be much more regressive.);

UNTHRIFTY—starting a new federal spending program with a multi-billion dollar expenditure, highlighting the hypocrisy of precisely the politicians who are so concerned over the deficit;

UNDEMOCRATIC—exempting elitist schools from public control, beyond the reach of the voter, unaccountable to the local electorate;

UNJUST—devising a discriminatory *de facto* windfall for the larger in-place parochial system, which belongs to one church;

UNETHICAL—destroying the public school system by siphoning off money, skimming strong students, draining parent power from public education, leaving two separate and unequal systems: private and pauper;

UNPRINCIPLED—subscribing to an odd principle of equity: "Since I've decided to send my child to a special school, you-all taxpayers must subsidize me."

UNCALLED-FOR—ignoring voters who have turned down 16 of 17 tuition tax credit or voucher plans in state referenda and the 60 percent to 30 percent rejection of vouchers by the American people (Peter D. Hart survey, 1995);

UNECONOMICAL—inventing a new escalatory entitlement while slashing federal aid to public education from a high of 9 percent of the budget in 1949 to a proposed 1.4 percent next year;

UNSUCCESSFUL—playing like the Wisconsin experiment[12] is a winner, though it has failed economically, educationally, and politically;

UNSYMPATHETIC TO FREEDOM—inviting the inevitable government entanglement with regulations and guidelines that always follow public monies (He who pays the fiddler still calls the tune.);

UNWORKABLE—recognizing that there has not yet been a plan proposed that would cover tuition and transportation for the poorest children;

UNTRUTHFUL—shifting money from one pocket to another to claim that public funds would not benefit the sponsoring church or advance sectarian purposes; tad shady, eh?;

UNSUSTAINABLE—raising false hopes among poor people who will never with any such scheme be able to send their children to exclusive schools;

UN-AMERICAN—establishing a new sort of taxation without representation on the controlling boards of publicly funded private schools;

UNFAITHFUL—failing the biblical call for believers to be salt and light in the world, witnesses in the public square;

UN-CHRISTIAN—accusing those of us who don't want our tax dollars to bankroll private causes of discriminating against Christians. Shame!

Other than all that, vouchers might be OK.

—Reprinted with permission courtesy of the Christian Ethics Today Foundation.

Notes

1. "1971 Report of the Christian Life Commission," *Annual of the Baptist General Convention of Texas* (Dallas TX: BGCT, 1971).

2. "Baptist Hits Tax Credit for Private Schools," *Dallas Morning News*, 9 October 1972, p. 22.

3. "1978 Report of the Christian Life Commission," *Annual of the Baptist General Convention of Texas* (Dallas TX: BGCT, 1978).

4. Lawrence J. McAndrews, "Late and Never: Ronald Reagan and Tuition Tax Credits," *Journal of Church and State* 42/3 (Summer 2000): 467–83.

5. "Private School Aid Plan Draws Prompt Criticism," *Report from the Capital* 46/5 (May 1991): 8–9.

6. "House Panel Oks Voucher System," *Report from the Capital* 46/10 (November–December 1991): 8–9.

7. "Same Song, Another Verse: Congress Again Rejecting Parochial School Aid," *Report from the Capital* 47/4 (April 1992): 4. See also JMD, "Reflections," *Report from the Capital* 46/6 (June 1991): 15.

8. "Senate Rejects Parochiaid Proposals," *Report from the Capital* 47/2 (February 1992): 6. Dunn declared, "The votes in the Senate are significant."

9. "Bush Team Unveils 'New' Voucher Plan," *Report from the Capital* 47/7 (July–August 1992): 8.

10. Pam Parry, "Congress Rejects Parochial Aid—Again," *Report from the Capital* 47/8 (September 1992): 4.

11. "Congress OKs D.C. Vouchers; Veto Expected from President," *Report from the Capital* 53/9 (5 May 1998): 1.

12. In 1990, the city of Milwaukee began the country's first voucher program where families below a certain income level could send their children to the public or private nonsectarian K–12 school of their choice, with tuition paid by the state. In 1995, religious "sectarian" schools were included in the voucher program, sparking lawsuits over the program's constitutionality.

Chapter 6

RFRA, Equal Access, and Faith-based Initiative

The year 1990 was a momentous one for church-state relations. On April 17, 1990, the U.S. Supreme Court dropped a "constitutional bombshell" that, according to James Dunn, "gutted the Free Exercise Clause of the First Amendment" with its decision in *Oregon Employment Division v. Smith*. This case concerned the denial of unemployment benefits to two Native Americans, Alfred L. Smith and Galen W. Black, who had been fired from a drug rehabilitation organization for using peyote, an illegal substance, in a religious ceremony. For the first time in an unemployment compensation case, the Supreme Court sided against the religious believer and for the state.

Writing for the majority, Justice Antonin Scalia held that government would no longer be required to demonstrate a "compelling state interest" to justify burdening the free exercise rights of its citizens. "If prohibiting the exercise of religion . . . is . . . merely the incidental effect of a generally applicable and otherwise valid provision, the First Amendment has not been offended," Scalia wrote. He reasoned that Oregon's law prohibiting certain drugs—peyote among them—was a "law of general applicability"; it applied to everyone, not just members of the Native-American Church. As a result, the Free Exercise Clause could no longer be used as a defense against such laws.[1]

For three decades, the Supreme Court had used the "compelling interest test" established in *Sherbert v. Verner* (1963) to decide free exercise cases. After the *Smith* decision, the burden was no longer on the state to demonstrate an important reason or "compelling interest" to interfere with religious freedom. Many scholars and advocates were outraged by the Court's ruling, especially Dunn, who described Scalia's opinion as "an outburst of judicial activism unworthy of a conservative judge." He wrote that Scalia "gutted the Free Exercise Clause from the First Amendment" and "cavalierly set aside the need for a 'compelling state interest' before government can restrict the free exercise of religion."[2]

Outrage was wide and deep in both the religious and academic communities. Dunn and BJC General Counsel Oliver "Buzz" Thomas helped bring together an extremely diverse coalition of religious and civil liberties groups to lobby for a legislative remedy. Named the Coalition for the Free Exercise of Religion, this BJC-led coalition included liberals and conservatives, Christians and secularists, Jews and Muslims, Hindus and Sikhs, from People for the American Way to Concerned Women for America.[3]

The remedy—named the Religious Freedom Restoration Act (RFRA)—was introduced in the U.S. House of Representatives on July 26, 1990. Co-authored by Thomas, RFRA was designed to prevent the federal and state governments from substantially burdening a person's free exercise rights unless the burden furthered a compelling interest and was the least restrictive means of furthering that interest. Dunn believed that by reaffirming the compelling state interest test, RFRA would restore the religious liberty that the Supreme Court, in *Smith*, had stripped away.[4]

Initially, RFRA met some stiff resistance from the U.S. Conference of Catholic Bishops. The Bishops worried that RFRA would create a new statutory right to abortion. With the eventual inclusion of additional language to assuage their concerns, the legislation was able to move forward and RFRA was unanimously approved by the House of Representatives, passed in the Senate 97-3, and signed into law by President Clinton on November 16, 1993. This was a resounding victory for religious organizations and a significant accomplishment for the BJC, which played a pivotal role in brokering a compromise and putting pressure on lawmakers from 1990–1993.[5]

Less than two months prior to the introduction of RFRA, the U.S. Supreme Court ruled in favor of equal access legislation allowing secondary school students to gather in student-led prayer and Bible study groups before and after school hours on public school property within certain reasonable limits. After helping to defeat President Reagan's prayer amendment in 1982, Dunn began to search for legislation to strengthen the religious liberty of children and teenagers in public schools. He also aimed to alleviate the concerns of parents who mistakenly believed the Supreme Court had banned God and prayer from school with earlier decisions that found state-sponsored prayer (1962) and school-sponsored Bible readings (1963) in public schools to be unconstitutional violations of church-state separation.

Dunn worked with his longtime friend Mark Hatfield, a Republican senator from Oregon, to introduce legislation ensuring that secular and religious non-school-sponsored student groups would be granted equal access to any limited open forum created in a public school when its students met on their own initiative for religious discussion and prayer and without any official encouragement or sponsorship. Under this legislation, a limited open forum would exist when a public school allowed non-curriculum-related secular student groups and clubs to use school facilities during non-instructional time for their meetings and other activities. Consequently, the existence of a limited open forum would require public schools to allow religious clubs the same use of its facilities.[6]

Testifying in support of equal access legislation in the House of Representatives, Dunn stated that the legislation would aid school officials "in making difficult decisions about the proper role of religion in the public school classroom" and would relieve some of the pressure on Congress to pass a constitutional amendment on school prayer. Equal access legislation was needed to restore "basic fairness" to the public schools, Dunn said.[7] After nearly two years of hearings, lobbying, and negotiations, the Equal Access Act passed the Senate (88-11) and the House (337-77). President Reagan signed the Equal Access Act into law on August 11, 1984. Dunn and the BJC were lauded for their role in helping to birth and ensure passage of this legislation.[8]

With these two significant legislative accomplishments, Dunn and the BJC would also find much success defeating various voucher proposals and other legislation that, in their view, would weaken religious freedom protections and undermine church-state separation. But Dunn would face an uphill battle and ultimately a losing one in "Charitable Choice"—the name given to a section of the Welfare Reform Act of 1996.

The brainchild of Senator John Ashcroft, a Republican from Missouri, Charitable Choice authorized states to contract, using federal funds, with houses of worship and other faith-based organizations to administer and deliver welfare-related social services. The purpose of Charitable Choice was to allow faith-based organizations, including churches, to compete with private secular social service providers for federal aid. According to the legislative provisions, neither the federal government nor states receiving federal welfare funds were permitted to exclude any organization from consideration due to its "religious character."[9]

Dunn spoke out against Charitable Choice, emphasizing the damage it would do to religious liberty via intrusive government regulation and diminishment of the prophetic role of faith groups in critiquing the state. In his last months as BJC executive director, Dunn took aim at Vice President

Al Gore, a personal friend, who had voiced support for Charitable Choice (letter included in this section).

Dunn continued to be an aggressive opponent of Charitable Choice, which became known as the "Faith-Based Initiative," even in "retirement." In a 2003 column, he would blast President George W. Bush's "Faith-Based Initiative" as "profoundly wrong-headed," warning again that federal funding of religious ministries would violate the First Amendment, divide faith groups who would be forced to compete with one another, and result in excessive entanglement between church and state.[10]

The columns in this section were published in the BJC's monthly newsletter, *Report from the Capital*, and featured a selection of Dunn's comments on the Religious Freedom Restoration Act, Equal Access Act, and Charitable Choice. Additional columns highlight the connectedness between religious liberty and freedom of the press; threats from "revisionists" to church-state separation; and reflections on church-state philosophy, political engagement, and a theology for public policy.

Render therefore unto Caesar

In this Report from the Capital *column, which came in September 1990 just months following the Supreme Court's landmark* Oregon v. Smith *ruling, Dunn discusses the application of Jesus' call in Matthew 22:21 to "Render therefore unto Caesar" to modern religious freedom issues.*

The words of Jesus, "Render therefore unto Caesar the things which are Caesar's; and unto God the things that are God's" (Matthew 22:21), have abiding relevance.

Through Christian history, that charge of Jesus has been taken seriously. It has meant at least that (1) there is a difference between the moral ruler and divine Providence, (2) that followers of Jesus can tell the difference, and (3) that one has some duty in both earthly and heavenly directions.

Elaborate "two kingdom" theories have been constructed. Doctrinal systems have been accommodated to medieval political reality. Sharp, unrelenting dualism has justified a chasm between the sacred and the secular.

In the American context, the biblical teaching has taken on a more practical, tangible shape. It has undergirded the concept of the separation of church and state. On May 16, 1920, from the east steps of the U.S. Capitol, George W. Truett quoted the Matthew verse and said, "That utterance of Jesus . . . is one of the most revolutionary and history-making utterances that ever fell from those lips divine. That utterance, once for all, marked the divorcement of church and state. It marked a new era for the creeds and deeds of men. It was the sunrise gun of a new day."

While the principle of separation is suggested, the practical consequences are far from clear. What is Caesar's? What is God's? How does one tell the difference? What is involved in "rendering" to each realm its due?

No neat, simple system offers answers. Most Americans, certainly those in the free churches, reject the complicated casuistries of medieval theologies, both Catholic and Protestant. Nor has secular society found any consistent juridical formula that fixes once and for all the boundary between church and state.

It is a struggle. It's never settled once and for all. It is an important dimension of everyday ethics.

One resolves church-state conflicts only for the time being. We settle these massive issues of what belongs to God and what belongs to country one small issue at a time and only provisionally at that. Let's face it, we must learn to live with that tension. At best, we can make it a creative tension, an instructive conflict resolution, a redemptive experience.

Or, to put it another way, determining where to put the wall of separation between church and state is a delicate balancing act. The most mundane political decisions that believers make involve the divine-human nature of the church, the divine-human dimensions of the Bible, the divine-human tugs at the individual's heart.

Then, with concrete examples, let us apply the principle of creative tension and ask which things are Caesar's?

Child-care legislation since March 1990 awaits action in a House-Senate conference committee. The tension between competing goods is abundantly present in this proposed legislation. Yet a large portion of the $27 billion to be spent over the next 5 years would go into church-related daycare programs.

As citizens we should not want tax dollars to support the programs of religious institutions. It matters not if the government funds would not go *directly* for religious instruction. As public monies flow into sectarian operations, the money is simply shifted from one pocket to the other to insure federal aid for the religious institution. It's merely a matter of bookkeeping. The freedom essential to witness is compromised with the acceptance of the public's money.

It is none of Caesar's business to fund the child-care ministries of the churches.

Then, on April 17, 1990, in the case of *Employment Division v. Smith*, the United States Supreme Court tinkered with the delicate mechanism that protects the free exercise of religion in this nation, the First Amendment. Supreme Court Justice Antonin Scalia in a stroke of judicial activism discarded the traditional test by which the Supreme Court has decided whether it may meddle in religion. He declared religious liberty a "legal luxury."

For decades, the Court has insisted upon a high threshold in the wall of separation—the state must have a "compelling state interest" before it can set aside a religious liberty.

Already, the BJC, along with a diverse coalition of other religious groups, is spearheading support for the Religious Freedom Restoration Act of 1990 (HR 5377). This bill reaffirms the compelling state interest test and restores the religious liberty that the Court, in *Smith*, took away.

It is none of Caesar's business to make a rule restricting the free exercise of religion without grave cause.

On June 3, 1990, the United States Supreme Court found Equal Access legislation to be constitutional. This 8-1 decision allows secondary school students to gather in student-led prayer and Bible study groups before and after school hours on public school property within certain reasonable limits.

The decision authored by Justice O'Connor restored a proper balance between the separation of church and state and the constitutional guarantees of free speech and free exercise of religion.

The Baptist Joint Committee with a number of other religious organizations is committed to seeing to it that this important decision is fairly interpreted and implemented.

It is none of Caesar's business to rule out student religious gatherings when the free expression of ideas is otherwise permitted.

One may see the "no establishment" and "free exercise" clauses of the First Amendment as held in creative tension. "Congress shall make no law respecting an establishment of religion *or* prohibiting the free exercise thereof." Because the Bill of Rights is a vital, living document and because the institutions of this pluralistic nation are in such constant flux, no rigid rule of thumb about which things are Caesar's will work for long.

That does not deny the validity of the principle. In fact, if anything, the wisdom and usefulness of the biblical teaching is reinforced as each generation must apply it to its own test cases.

—James M. Dunn, "Reflections," *Report from the Capital* (September 1990): 15. Reprinted with permission courtesy of the Baptist Joint Committee for Religious Liberty.

Dear Mr. Vice President: Say It Ain't So

Below is an open letter James Dunn penned to U.S. Vice-President Al Gore following his decision to support "Charitable Choice" legislation to allow taxpayer dollars to fund faith-based ministries. This letter appeared in the June 1999 edition of the BJC's newsletter, Report from the Capital.

Dear Mr. Vice President:
I know you. I like you. You mean well. But this time, as we say in Tennessee and Texas, "you've ripped your britches." Your speech in Atlanta, May 24, bugs me.

The very idea: buying into Sen. Ashcroft's so-called "Charitable Choice" scheme—allowing government dollars for church ministries.

Right off the bat, I resent and reject your suggested **false alternatives** of "hollow secularism or right-wing religion." Millions of Americans have a profoundly religious shared vision that is neither secular nor right-wing.

It's faith that is vital precisely because it is voluntary. It's people-serving programs that work because they are faith-based, not fund-based. When government "helps" religion it always has the touch of mud. It unfailingly hurts religion.

You've set up false choices like the straw men of a debater. These odious opposites, we too reject.

But it's not a "dead-end debate" that keeps alive the separation of church and state. It is, rather, the dynamic dialogue that's been going on ever since little Mr. Madison defeated the popular Patrick Henry over this very issue.

Then, there's the matter of **false promises**. The notion that public funds will not "alter the religious character" of faith-based programs requires a leap of faith that even Kierkegaard couldn't make.

You're right, faith-based organizations (already governmentalized as FBOs) do show special promise because they are free and faithful—words you and I know well as Baptists. With tax monies, however, come reporting, monitoring, regulation, oversight, inhibition, entanglement, and boxing in.

That's not evil. It's just human. It's inevitable. It's necessary. We all want to know where our tax dollars go. We want a say in how they are spent. We yell about it. We think we can do better. And when the differences of religious opinion fuel the fights, the battles get deafening and damaging indeed.

In fact, there's a hubris in not accepting the lessons of history and living with the humility called for by our humanity. Look at Ireland, Indonesia, India, the Balkans. Who do we think we are? We have a perfectly good plan, but we are not perfectly good people. False promises: part of politics, but you can do better.

Finally, there's evidence of **false premises:**

That government-generated money would "help" organizations begun and sustained to "lead persons to a saving relationship with Jesus Christ." We don't call that proselytizing.

The Christian Women's Job Corps, which you are right to cite, has touched thousands of lives in the Welfare to Work process. But the exciting program of the Woman's Missionary Union, Southern Baptist Convention, has not taken one penny of government "partnership," precisely because they want to call the shots in their own ministry.

That the legal distinction between "religiously affiliated" (organizations that can take tax dollars) and "pervasively sectarian" (organizations that can't) will not work. Who says? Maybe we've not worked hard enough at understanding, interpreting, and applying that well-accepted distinction. Let's give it a try before we abandon it for something far riskier.

That Americans are afraid to make the connection between spirituality and politics. We're not. Every political debate is saturated with believers battling. Every institution of society has a theological tenor. Every crisis calls forth religious response. We simply say, "Uncle Sam, don't meddle with my church."

Religious freedom and church-state separation are a package deal.

Tinkering with the delicate balance of faith-based ministries could easily destroy the very distinctives that are the secret of their success.

Mr. Vice President, don't buy this "Charitable Choice" stuff; it's the wrong way to do right.

It's not too late to patch your pants. Tell us more, quick, please.

James

—James M. Dunn, "Reflections," *Report from the Capital* (1 June 1999): 15. Reprinted with permission courtesy of the Baptist Joint Committee for Religious Liberty.

Siamese Twins: Freedom of Religion and Freedom of the Press

Religious freedom and freedom of the press are inextricable. That is James Dunn's message in this February 1984 column in Report from the Capital. *"These two most precious of rights come from common roots, flourish in the same environment, and are threatened by the same enemies," Dunn writes.*

They live together like Siamese twins: freedom of religion and freedom of the press, inextricable. Religious liberty and freedom of the press stand or fall together.

The First Amendment of the United States Constitution casts together the freedoms that have come to define what Americans mean by the word "freedom." It makes sense. An honest dedication to the American way in civil and religious liberty is a piece of whole cloth. When it comes to caring about freedom of the press and freedom of religion, if either concern is genuine the other is implied.

These two most precious of rights come from common roots, flourish in the same environment, and are threatened by the same enemies.

There's something shockingly inconsistent about a caterwauling evangelist invoking the censorship of the righteous Right but insisting that freedom of religion gives him guaranteed immunity. As bad or worse is the hypocrisy of a cynical, secular newsman who would defend freedom of the press to his last ballpoint but betrays nothing of the spirit of liberty in his dealings with religion. Why are some reporters so hostile to religion and some churchmen so paranoid about the press?

Preachers of a vital, full-throated religion dare not tolerate repression of expression. On the other hand, principled practitioners of journalism cannot honestly insist on the people's right to know and carelessly ignore threats to religious liberty and church-state separation.

The idea of a free conscience underlies each of the personal freedoms set out in the First Amendment. Without it the freedoms of religion, speech, press, assembly, and redress are reduced to words on paper.

It was the fiercely held view of the founders that the conscience must be unfettered that gives the First Amendment substance. Such an idea was grounded in natural law, the rights of which were considered beyond the legitimate bounds of government and government officials. Freedom of conscience was thus considered "unalienable," as were the other fundamental rights that flow from it.

When it comes to the founders, they were sons of the enlightenment and children of the covenant. They held strongly to a subjective concept of free conscience and objective truth as real and within the reach of ordinary mortals. These two truth peddlers—the religionist proclaiming the Truth revealed and the reporter revealing all of the truth he can discover—have more in common than they realize.

In an interesting way the First Amendment to the U.S. Constitution catches the strands of both Renaissance and Reformation and braids them together. Here the individualism of the Reformation and the optimism of the Renaissance are entwined; here the "faith alone" of the Reformation and the "faith in reason" of the Renaissance are codified.

If freedom of religion offers the profound theological base for the American experiment, freedom of the press proves that we mean business. For government to meddle with either is to endanger both. For lovers of liberty to fail to defend either freedom belies a failure to understand freedom of conscience, soul liberty. Freedom of the press and freedom of religion are indissoluble.

We live in a day when those at the highest levels of government seem to fear truth-telling. They try to restrict the truth-tellers or ridicule them as being guilty of "leaks." They limit the right of the people to know and invoke prior censorship to keep the facts about their deeds from some future generation. They restrain the press. A heavy-handed government, whether exercising censorship on writers or prescribing religion for the public schools, is the enemy of freedom.

A seventeenth century, politically active Baptist divine had all this together. He understood the interrelatedness of freedom of the press and freedom of religion. He wrote "as good almost kill a man as kill a good book; who kills a man kills a reasonable creature, God's image; but he who destroys a good book, kills reason itself, kills the image of God, as it were in the eye."

If the First Amendment pulls together some golden threads from both enlightenment and reformation, this member of Cromwell's cabinet embodied in his person the best of both. He presupposed, Augustinianly, that all truth is from God and so he was not afraid of truth. Responding to an act of Parliament passed in 1643 requiring all books and pamphlets to be licensed before publication, he was willing to risk truth to the open market of ideas. "And though all the winds of doctrine were let loose to play upon the earth, so Truth be in the field, we do injuriously by licensing and prohibiting to misdoubt her strength. Let her and Falsehood grapple; who ever knew Truth put to the worse, in a free and open encounter?"

In November 1644, John Milton published *Areopagitica*, his most famous plea for free speech and a free press, deeply rooted in his understanding of religious freedom. "For who knows not that Truth is strong next to the Almighty; She needs no policies, nor stratagems, nor licensings to make her victorious, those are the shifts and the defences that error uses against her power. Give her room and do not bind her."

The peculiar presuppositions of the Founding Fathers followed them to lump together freedom of religion and freedom of the press. They never doubted that conscience is free nor that truth is real.

—James M. Dunn, "Reflections," *Report from the Capital* 39/2 (February 1984): 15. Reprinted with permission courtesy of the Baptist Joint Committee for Religious Liberty.

Downright Silliness of Church-State Revisionism

James Dunn challenges the "revisionist" view of church-state relations embraced and espoused by the Reagan Administration in this October 1985 column. In doing so, he appeals to the legacy of the Founding Fathers, the majority of whom favored the separation of church and state.

Whatever happened to the First Amendment? One conservative think-tanker, Walter Berns, advocates "a program of assistance on a non-discriminatory basis, across the board, to all churches, all religions, all sects." Justice Rehnquist delivered a veritable tirade in his dissent on the *Jaffree* case in which the Supreme Court ruled out government-managed moments for silent prayer in Alabama schools. He says, "The evil aimed at" by the First Amendment was "the establishment of a national church, and perhaps the preference of one religious sect over another."

Attorney General Meese laments the Supreme Court's "hostility" to religion. Education Secretary William Bennett would establish a yet unspelled-out Judeo-Christian value system for public schools. He does not bother to reconcile the sometimes-conflicting axioms of his hyphenated lowest-common-denominator religion. True believers all, they often labor brilliantly to rewrite history.

Their revised standard version of the First Amendment holds that it simply rules out favoritism among religious groups and prohibits an official State Church but endorses God-in-general and allows impartial government aid for churches.

The Supreme Court, however, consistently holds that the Establishment Clause embraces much broader restraints on government than these simple prohibitions. That the men mentioned above believe the Court's decisions do not square with the intentions of the founders is irrelevant.

What does one say of this new interpretation of the religion clauses? The revised, limited version (1) was not intended by the founders; (2) is not possible now even if it had been intended; (3) is not desirable even if it were possible.

1. A civil religion was not intended by the founders. The "Founders" were sharply divided. Madison, Jefferson, and George Mason stood against Patrick Henry in the passage of the Virginia Statute of Religious Liberty (1786). When Henry held up passage of the bill, Jefferson wrote Madison from France, "What we have to do, I think, is devoutly pray for his death." That's sharp division. Rehnquist in his *Jaffree* dissent pettily points out that Jefferson was in France at the later date when the Bill of Rights was under consideration. Is it possible to imagine the gathering that gave us the First Amendment without the hovering presence of Jefferson?

Madison in pleading for Virginia's ratification of the new Constitution said, "There is not a shadow of right in the general government to intermeddle with religion," a view consistent with his earlier comment on the statute when he wrote Jefferson that the bill had "extinguished forever the ambitious hope of making laws for the human mind." Madison's logic requires a separation of church and state well beyond an injunction against the establishment of a national church.

That plea of Madison is relevant today: "Who does not see that the same authority which can establish Christianity, in exclusion of all other

Religions, may establish with the same ease any particular sect of Christians, in exclusion of all other Sects?"

The founders were divided but the majority favored the separation of church and state.

It is strange indeed that Justice Rehnquist should appeal to the Northwest Ordinance of 1787 and the tax-supported religion aimed at the Indians as arguments for his accommodationist views. There is no more shameful chapter in American history than our attempts to merge the military and missionary urges in dealing with the first Americans. Native Americans suffered much from government's attempts to blend force with faith.

2. Impartial aid to all religions is not possible now even if it had been intended. The impartiality required for any sort of juggling between religions and anti-religions and nonreligions is beyond mortal capacity. The objectivity demanded, the above-it-allness would put one a shelf above God. The sort of dispassionate evenhandedness called for is unheard of in either politics or religion. Put these lively disciplines together and it is ludicrous to think of an established government policy of balanced support for all religions.

Beyond that theological argument stands the empirical challenge of over 3,000 religions in the United States entitled to equal footing. Try describing them, understanding them, identifying with them and their aspirations.

Support for religion from the state is not possible even if some founders envisioned it. Free churches tend to want to stay free. Persons of conscience of all religious and nonreligious hues, by abstaining from involvement with government, skew the equation and make it impossible to attain that idyllic state of governmental fairness toward all religions.

3. Government-blessed religion is not desirable even if it were possible. History cites horrible examples of government trying to use religion for its own ends, or the dominant regional religion ruling the roost to the great distortion of justice, persecution of minorities, and religion-spawned hatreds and prejudices. Jews, Baptists, and Quakers have been protesting church-state entanglement from those days to these.

When the state gets into the missionary business, it fouls things up. When government claims to aid all religions, it never fails to play favorites. When government tries to find an agreeable level of religious involvement, it winds up advancing a generic, all-purpose God.

It is a mistake to assume that the Free Exercise Clause is pro-religion and the no-establishment clause hostile to religion. The two clauses do contradict each other if pushed to extremes, but taken together both religion clauses of the First Amendment provide the bulwark for religious liberty.

Religious liberty is not a gift of the state. Government has the touch of mud in matters religious. Strict neutrality, not benignity, is the proper role for government in regard to religion.

Government is neutral not supportive of religion, so citizens are not forced to support religious practices and opinions they oppose, so government is not evaluating or supervising religious institutions, so the state is not engendering divisiveness and religious warfare.

The revisionist view that would turn away from separation of church and state is downright silly.

—James M. Dunn, "Reflections," *Report from the Capital* (October 1985): 15. Reprinted with permission courtesy of the Baptist Joint Committee for Religious Liberty.

A Theology for Public Policy

In this September 1988 column, James Dunn urges the development of a theology for public policy rooted in a commitment to soul freedom and experiential religion. "The principle of separation of church and state, however, does not consign believers to privatistic religion, nor does this cherished Baptist doctrine separate God and government," Dunn writes.

The words of Jesus in Matthew 22:15-22 help put in perspective the Christian's duty to the state. Here, discipleship and citizenship are stated as intersecting values, the state having legitimate claims on the lives of Christians and Christians a responsibility to the state.

These claims are justified by the divine order of things. Yet the duties owed to the state and God are not the same. The difference is a matter of God's intent. And the different responsibilities to God and government must be determined anew by Christians in every time and circumstance.

Because the church is a divine-human institution, because the Christian life is a divine-human experience, and because the Bible is a divine-human book and our only rule for faith and practice, we must continue to decide what is Caesar's and what is God's. The Bible, as interpreted by the Holy Spirit, tests what seems to us to be God's leading.

The sanctified intellects given to us by God, the fellowship of believers within which we seek to know God's will, the positive and helpful structures of society, home, church and school—all are practical aids in service for the greatest good, protection for the weak and disadvantaged, restraint of evil, and reward of virtue.

When all is said and done in the competition between church and state, we must depend upon God's word to engage us in creative tension, to enable us to learn and grow, and to sustain us in the inevitable misunderstandings, ostracisms, and sufferings that occur when confronting the principalities and powers of this world as faithful followers.

With an emphasis upon soul freedom, experiential religion, and the priesthood of all Christians, free church people must develop a theology for public policy. It will demand expansion at times, evaluation by biblical norms, and interpretation by informed disciples in every culture, economy, and political dispensation.

Augustine said, "Christ died for me as much as if I were the only one for whom he had to die." This notion of dignity and worth of the individual is the bedrock foundation of Christian citizenship. This respect of personhood puts people ahead of politics and profits. This doctrine of democracy deals a blow to elitism and racism and economic theories that posture as help for the common person by strengthening the wealthy and powerful: trickle-down righteousness.

We may not know all the right answers, but under God we're bound to try to ask the right questions. As Christians saved by grace not works, we are free to fail, but we're not free to fail to act. The least a theology for public policy can do is affirm persons, call for justice, insist upon freedom, teach stewardship, act on faith, and pursue the heavenly vision.

The Judeo-Christian Ethic has fostered a public policy that is positive, is forward looking, and has an explicit faith in the future. How different has our history been from the defensive, self-serving, escapist mentality of those who see public institutions doomed.

A responsible public policy informed by religious values pursues the heavenly vision, as in Augustine's *City of God*, whose "alabaster cities gleam undimmed by human tears," or in Martin Luther King's dream: "I have a dream that my four little children will one day live in a nation where they will be judged not by the color of their skin but by the content of their character."

The minimum requirement of Christian citizens in any form of government is to hold faithfully to one's own convictions of New Testament goals for the human family. Every policy of government should be measured by those goals. To the degree that it is possible even in the most repressive regime, the implications of clear teachings from God's word should be shared within the family of faith, taught to one's children, and handed down from generation to generation. The deepest held insights of our faith about the common life should be a matter of public witness.

How do we respond to that call in this country with our insistence upon the separation of church and state? In the inevitable mix of politics and piety, the appropriate distance between church and state is often diminished. When candidates for the presidency of the United States use the church collection plates for campaign funds, as one Baptist preacher-candidate advised, or proclaim their pursuit of the high office a spiritual crusade to bring an absent God back to government, as an ex-Baptist preacher does, both stomp on the spirit of church-state separation.

Still, from the believer's perspective, politics and religion must be mixed. Not to take a political stand is to endorse the *status quo*. To fail to sound the moral alarm when necessary suggests that one may be morally asleep. To stay out of politics or to assume a smugly superior pose as an "above-it-all independent" is itself an alignment with the tide of evil, a cheap cop-out. Withdrawal from the world denies biblical realism.

Our law assumes that religion will affect politics. Supreme Court rulings recognize that "churches as much as secular bodies and private citizens" may participate in political debate. Justice William O. Douglas, an advocate of church-state separation, insisted that "we are a religious people, whose institutions presuppose a Supreme Being."

More recently, Justice William Brennan, arguing that ministers should not be banned from public office, wrote, "Government may not as a goal promote 'safe-thinking' with respect to religion and fence out those from political participation, such as ministers, whom it regards as overinvolved in religion." Religiously active people are not compelled to check their most deeply held beliefs at the door as they enter the arena of public involvement.

Mixing politics with religion is inevitably explosive, carrying no guarantees that it will be easy, constructive, or peaceful. Indeed, there is no direct route from the Bible to the ballot box. Carl F. H. Henry admits that one cannot leap from "individual spiritual rebirth to assuredly authentic and predictable public policy consequences . . . ."

The principle of separation of church and state, however, does not consign believers to privatistic religion, nor does this cherished Baptist doctrine separate God and government.

We are given no neat recipe for the admixture of politics and religion. There's the rub. Moreover, as Christians we are challenged to translate biblical truth into contemporary political terms. This can be done only after we, ourselves, have been transformed by that Truth. Believers must not fail in this awesome responsibility because no one else in society is as well equipped to fulfill this most prophetic role.

—James M. Dunn, "Reflections," *Report from the Capital* 43/8 (September 1988): 15. Reprinted with permission courtesy of the Baptist Joint Committee for Religious Liberty.

"Separation" Not a Bad Word

James Dunn reminds his readers of the historic Baptist commitment to keeping church and state separate while being politically engaged and "attacking social evil." "There's a disingenuousness in claiming that Christians cop out of their political responsibility by hiding behind the wall of church-state separation," Dunn writes in the January 1991 issue of Report from the Capital.

There is a silliness going around. It's not new. Patrick Henry suffered from it for a spell and then almost recovered.

Henry, in opposing Virginia's proposed Statute for Religious Freedom, suggested that public decency depends upon government support for religion. He, like some notable religious figures today, thought that society could be made more moral by a certain coziness of church and state. Happily, John Leland, James Madison, George Mason, and Thomas Jefferson prevailed and disestablishment became the American way. Leland lamented, "sad experience has taught us that the fondness of magistrates to foster religion has done it more harm than all the persecutions ever did."

The current silliness doesn't stop at supporting that organized religion must have a certain favored status; it assumes that an evil conspiracy is preventing a persuasive proclamation of the gospel in the public square. No one that I know of, not the most dedicated separationists, not even the organized advocates of neutrality, is denying full and free expression of the Christian message in the marketplace. In fact, some of the most purely secularist people are among the first to defend the full religious expression.

Baptists certainly have never been intimidated by or timid about attacking social evil. We and our forebears have fought demon rum, dirty books, drugs, gambling, and prostitution. Baptist ancestors struggled for social justice, peace, and world order. Towering figures in the application of the gospel to the political process have been Baptist preachers, Walter Rauschenbusch and Martin Luther King, Jr., among them. We forget sometimes that George W. Truett in 1919 led a march up Constitution Avenue to the steps of the U.S. Capitol. There, in a famous speech, he pled for the ratification of the League of Nations. In prophetic wisdom, he said that to fail to support President Woodrow Wilson's visionary plan for peace would be a "gravely immoral act." The U.S. Senate, led by Henry Cabot Lodge, Sr., committed that "gravely immoral" deed. The League of Nations never amounted to much. One need only recall WWII to appreciate Truett's insight.

These same public men, prophets to the political system, believed in and practiced the separation of church and state as an essential corollary for religious freedom. They knew that separation of church and state did not mean separation of God and government, or separation of Christians from their citizenship, or separation of religion from politics.

No, there's a disingenuousness in claiming that Christians cop out of their political responsibility by hiding behind the wall of church-state separation. Laziness—maybe, cowardice—surely, ignorance—often can all contribute to the evasion of good citizenship. Most of us know in our innermost depths that we have no excuse for avoiding political engagement. We surely cannot use church-state separation to dodge our duty. It is a straw man set to be knocked down to argue that Baptists use "separation" as an excuse for non-involvement.

In fact, the clear separation of church and state provides the distance from which the church can speak prophetically to the state. The distinction between the institutions of government and religion is a peculiarly American arrangement that has been good for both church and state. As Garry Wills reminds us in his new book, *Under God* (Simon and Schuster), "The success of the Madisonian ideal has vindicated Madison's maxim that 'religion flourishes in greater purity without (rather) than with the aid of government.'" Wills goes on to say, "America has remained deeply religious while taking ever more seriously the idea of separation. It is false to think that recent court decisions have made religion less important or effective in America, or even in our politics."

Further, the possibility of an effective impact upon the formation of public policy requires space between the believer and the object of one's prophetic witness, the structures which one would affect. Wills again: "If

Madison is any guide, our churches are not, even now, too separated from political support. They should be freer still, which would make them more powerful and, paradoxically, more political. That is one of the American paradoxes we can be most proud of—that our churches have influence because they are independent of the government."

"Separation" is not a bad word. It's a Baptist word, a constitutional concept, an American idea. It seems clear that there must be another agenda driving the present attempts at the revision of history. Could it be that the current reevaluation of the principle of separation is fueled by an institutional greed for government goodies? Could it be that some see that they must reinterpret historic insistence upon disestablishment before they can fund religious programs with public monies? These tactics are not succeeding.

Tax credits and vouchers for church-related schools and preschools have not fared well at the polls. Such public funding for private and parochial institutions was rejected in November by Oregon voters. So now, we hear of the schemes to take tax dollars for religious entities referred to under the innocuous banner of "choice." The all-American value of "competition" is appealed to as a way of diverting everyone's tax trust into someone's parochial program. Could it be that the reassessment of church-state separation is related to these pragmatics?

Surely some *real* reason drives those who seem compelled to challenge the American experiment of church-state separation. There are tensions. The delicate balance of "no establishment" of religion with the "free exercise" of self-sustaining sects of every sort is a formula for chaos. Yet the experiment is worthy of constituting. It's the chaos of liberty.

Garry Wills in *Under God*, subtitled "Religion and American Politics," concludes with this eloquent assessment: "No other government in history had launched itself without the help of officially recognized gods and their state-connected ministers. It is no wonder that, in so novel an undertaking, it should have taken awhile to sift the dangers and the blessings of the new arrangement, to learn how to best live with it, to complete the logic of its workings. We are still grappling with its meaning for us." May it ever be so.

Maybe the compulsion to revise the standard of church-state separation is a serious threat to religious freedom and more than a silliness.

Maybe we'd better be busy explaining why it's necessary to maintain the separation of church and state.

But for certain, as Baptists we must recognize the urgency of upholding the Baptist Joint Committee—a cooperative endeavor of ten national

Baptist bodies in the United States—at the forefront in support for the separation of church and state, that most vital link to and guarantor of religious liberty for all Americans.

> —James M. Dunn, "Reflections," *Report from the Capital* (January 1991): 15. Reprinted with permission courtesy of the Baptist Joint Committee for Religious Liberty.

How to Mix Religion and Politics

In this July 1994 column, James Dunn offers a concise articulation of his philosophy of political engagement—a call to practice a free and faithful politics. "Christians should be involved in politics, but with Christian goals, methods, attitudes, and preparation," Dunn writes.

The separation of church and state does not require separation of religion from politics.

Every authentic act of worship is pregnant with political possibilities. Every true theological belief has public policy implications. Every ethical outgrowth of religious experience makes demands on stewardship of influence in a democracy.

In fact, part of the reason for a clear-cut distinction between religious and political institutions is to allow the church to speak to the state prophetically. Religion rightly resists the totalitarian and theocratic tendencies of government. Organized religion dare not allow herself to be held in a bear hug by politics. People of faith need swinging room to act on principalities and powers.

Yep, religion and politics *do* mix. Have to!

Yet, *how* does the mixing it up take place? There's the rub.

We learn by negative example. One sees how *not* to relate religion and politics in the Falwell model. The only word accurate in the name of the Rev. Jerry Falwell's "Old Time Gospel Hour" is the word "hour." If some poor lost soul should tune in hoping to hear a word of amazing grace, she would go away hungry. It is political propaganda, little if any gospel.

A few years ago, Jerry Falwell was pictured in *Newsweek* holding up a copy of *Politics: A Guidebook for Christians*, edited by yours truly. Alas, for any part I may have had in energizing and engaging Mr. Falwell in politics I repent.

Yes, *Christians should be in politics up to their gills* ...

But not in a politics of personal destruction. The spirit of engagement, the attitude, the tone of voice are important where a person of faith practices politics. A measure of humility, honesty, and helpfulness and honor for the person, the process, and the office are essential marks of any Christian critic of a public official. Conducting an overt hate campaign against the president of the United States is out of bounds. Falwell's "Circle of Power" video implies that President Clinton is complicit in murder. As E. J. Dionne Jr. says, "Falwell is apparently willing to spread sleaze but not to take responsibility for it." The scandal entrepreneurs offer no evidence for any of their accusations.

But not in a politics that makes political doctrine a test of faith. Rep. Vic Fazio takes a stab at defining this problem, saying no one "should have a corner on defining religion and politics in the same breath." That phrase focuses on human fallibility, always an appropriate exercise. Carl F. H. Henry has held for years that there is no direct route from the Bible to the ballot box.

One apologist for the Religious Right insists that these religious extremists simply stand where "most Americans stood 30 years ago." He may be right. Maybe that's the problem.

It is dangerous to elevate political platforms to the level of biblical ethics.

But not in a politics of irresponsibility. The moment that a religious figure crosses the line between biblical exposition, interpretation, and application and plunges into the political fray, he should expect at that very moment to be open to criticism. If any religiously motivated citizen cannot stand the heat of rigorous examination of his motivations, proposals, and arguments, perhaps he or she should stay out of the kitchen. It is downright silly to hear these folks, who are themselves so ready to libel by label, howling "anti-Christian bigotry."

But not in a politics of balkanization. We have rejected the European model of "Christian parties." And for good reason. Examine the way they work in Italy or Germany. Look at religion-driven politics in Northern Ireland.

No, there is certain failure of faith by those who would do by political power what they have despaired of being done by the power of God. The Divine Spirit alone can bring about much that Christians seek and only by the free and faithful followers whom heaven desires.

Christians should be involved in politics, but with Christian goals, methods, attitudes . . . and preparation. We should do our homework, speak out in a Christian tone of voice, and be prepared to live with the consequences of joining the debate.

>—James M. Dunn, "Reflections," *Report from the Capital* (12 July 1994): 3. Reprinted with permission courtesy of the Baptist Joint Committee for Religious Liberty.

Notes

1. Ronald Flowers, *That Godless Court? Supreme Court Decisions on Church-State Relationships* (Louisville KY: Westminster John Knox Press, 2007) 42–43. See also *Employment Division, Department of Human Resources of Oregon v. Smith*, 494 U.S. 872 (1990).

2. JMD, "Reflections," *Report from the Capital* 47/1 (January 1992): 15. See also "Reflections," *Report from the Capital* 48/2 (February 1993): 15.

3. "RFRA Attracts Broad Support," *Report from the Capital* 47/1 (January 1992): 8.

4. JMD, "Reflections," *Report from the Capital* 45/8 (September 1990): 15.

5. Ron Fournier, "Clinton Signs Freedom of Worship Law," Associated Press, 16 November 1993.

6. Dan Martin, "Committee Supports Equal Access Bill; Affirms Opposition to School Prayer," *Report from the Capital* 39/4 (April 1984): 5.

7. JMD, quoted in Larry Chesser, "Dunn: Restore 'Fairness,'" *Baptist Standard*, 4 April 1984.

8. Flowers, *That Godless Court?* 120–21; Bob Terry, "Editorial," *Word & Way*, 2 August 1984, p. 7.

9. Lewis D. Solomon, *In God We Trust? Faith-based Organizations and the Quest to Solve America's Social Ills* (Lanham MD: Lexington Books, 2003).

10. JMD, "No Faith Based On Your Initiatives, Mr. Bush," TomPaine.com, 5 May 2004 (JMD's original source; website no longer exists).

Chapter 7

Congressional Testimony

James Dunn was invited to give testimony before state legislatures and U.S. congressional committees as an expert on church-state issues. Filing amicus briefs and providing testimony were and remain an important aspect of the work of the Baptist Joint Committee.

This section includes two notable examples of such testimony. The first came at the outset of Dunn's time at the BJC when he was given the opportunity to voice his opposition to the selection of an ambassador to the Vatican before the Foreign Relations Committee of the U.S. Senate on February 2, 1984. Throughout its history, the BJC had taken a consistent stand against efforts by the White House to send a U.S. envoy or ambassador to the Vatican. In 1983, the BJC under Dunn adopted a statement reaffirming its opposition to diplomatic relations.

As President Reagan was preparing to nominate an ambassador to the Vatican, Dunn penned a public letter urging the president to "support church-state separation and oppose the establishment of diplomatic relations with the Vatican." "Establishing a diplomatic post with any church tramples the Establishment Clause of the First Amendment to the Constitution by showing preference to one religious faith over another," Dunn said. "For the Administration to pretend that the naming of an ambassador to a church has nothing to do with religion is a ludicrous leap of logic smacking of Orwell's *1984*."[1]

This was also an issue that had historically united Southern Baptists. When President Reagan moved to establish full diplomatic relations with the Vatican, every living former president of the Southern Baptist Convention (sixteen total) signed a letter of protest. The Executive Committee of the SBC and eleven Southern Baptist state conventions also registered their opposition.[2]

Reagan's nomination was described as intending to improve communications with the Vatican at a time when Pope John Paul II was becoming more involved in international affairs. His nominee, William Wilson, was not a surprise. Wilson was a California real estate developer who was a longtime friend of Reagan and had served as the President's personal representative to the Vatican since 1981. During the previous year, Congress had quietly repealed a nineteenth century prohibition of diplomatic relations with the Vatican.[3]

In the view of Dunn and other Baptist leaders, the Vatican was primarily a church headquarters rather than a sovereign state, and, therefore, sending an ambassador to a "church headquarters" was an inappropriate conferral of favor on a particular religion. For the State Department to seek a relationship allowing the U.S. to influence the political positions of the Holy See reflected "an arrogant and blatantly volatile posture" and "is contrary to everything we mean by separation of church and state," Dunn charged. He told the *New York Times* that Reagan's action was "a dumb, bungling move by an Administration that doesn't seem to understand the first lesson about church-state relations."[4]

The second testimony in this section came in 2001, two years into Dunn's "retirement" while he was serving as a professor at Wake Forest University School of Divinity. In a confirmation hearing before the U.S. Senate Committee on the Judiciary, Dunn shared his opposition to the nomination of former Senator John Ashcroft to be Attorney General of the United States under the new administration of President George W. Bush. Ashcroft had helped include a provision called "Charitable Choice" in the Welfare Reform Act of 1996, which authorized states to distribute federal funds to houses of worship and other faith-based organization for the purposes of providing social services.

As noted in the previous section, Dunn was vehemently opposed to "Charitable Choice" as he believed it to be a violation of church-state separation that would certainly change the religious character of faith-based ministries via intrusive government regulation. He warned that Charitable Choice would cultivate religious division as faith groups compete with one another for federal funds. Dunn's testimony in these two instances—seventeen years apart—offers a glimpse at his public advocacy before Congress to protect religious freedom and raise awareness about church-state concerns that might not have been popular but were nevertheless vitally important.

Testimony on the Nomination of William Wilson to Be Ambassador to the Holy See

James Dunn offered the following testimony on February 2, 1984, opposing the nomination of any ambassador to the Vatican before the Foreign Relations Committee of the U.S. Senate.

I am James M. Dunn, Executive Director of the Baptist Joint Committee on Public Affairs. It is composed of representatives from eight national cooperating Baptist conventions and conferences in the United States. These groups have a current membership of nearly 30 million.

The Baptist Joint Committee seeks to give corporate and visible expression to the voluntariness of religious faith, the free exercise of religion, the interdependence of religious liberty with all human rights, and the relevance of Christian concerns to the life of the nation. Because of the congregational autonomy of individual Baptist churches, we do not purport to speak for all Baptists.

No living mortal can appropriately, adequately, honestly, and constitutionally serve as ambassador of the United States of America to the Roman Catholic Church. I come today not to comment on the abilities and propriety of the particular nominee, rather to insist that the appointment of any official ambassador from this nation to the Holy See is wrong.

Baptist bodies see such a diplomatic move as a clear violation of the principle of church-state separation. Separation of church and state does not mean separation of God from government, separation of religion from politics, or separation of religious persons from civic duties. In the American tradition, it has clearly meant the institutional integrity of both church and state, a strict prohibition of the state's advancing or inhibiting any church or all the churches, a total ban on the meddling of the state in the affairs of the church, a refusal to tolerate favored status for any one church or group of churches or special privileges being afforded to the church.

This American principle of church-state separation, at the very least, forbids the entanglement of church and state in precisely the fashion proposed by sending an ambassador of our government to the Roman Catholic Church. The Senate of the United States has behaved in a manner unworthy of its sacred trust in its hurry to appoint an ambassador to the Pope. Without debate, discussion, hearings, or a record vote, the ban on representation to the Holy See was set aside. With less than a week's notice, these hearings were announced. Dozens of other individuals, major faith groups, and organizations concerned with religious liberty deserve to be heard. What is the hurry?

A confirmation hearing is not a proper forum for serious examination of constitutional and public policy questions. The democratic process has been circumvented. We ask this Committee to compensate for past congressional failure to secure input by scheduling other hearings at a later date and delaying the Committee's vote on confirmation until the more substantive issues have been aired.

It has been suggested that United States foreign policy would be set forward and that some intelligence network would become available to our nation by establishing such a formal relationship. If any credence at all is to be given to these suggestions, they pinpoint precisely what we oppose. This entangling alliance would be the occasion for practical problems for all those engaged in the far-flung missionary venture in developing countries. Because of anti-American, anti-religious, and anti-democratic sentiments in many countries, missionaries would actually become symbols of American interests. Should the United States Senate follow this unwise course, it would offer an occasion for misunderstanding, an invitation to chaos and confusion, and would place a burdensome albatross upon every American who represents religion overseas.

The rest of the world has seen the unique role of church-state relations in the United States as a safeguard for freedom and a model for the relationship of religion and government. We cannot avoid this global spotlight so long as we are the world's most powerful nation, so long as we present freedom, so long as we are a beacon light of religious liberty. This pattern has been good for the church and good for the state. The Establishment Clause has been well litigated and the established precedents are clear. Perhaps the simplest statement was made by the Court in *Everson v. Board of Education*, 330 U.S. 1, 15-16 (1947):

> The "establishment of religion" clause of the First Amendment means at least this: Neither a state nor the Federal Government can . . . pass laws which aid one religion, aid all religions, or prefer one religion over another. . . . No tax in any amount, large or small, can be levied to support any religious activities or institutions, whatever they may be called, or whatever form they may adopt to teach or practice religion. Neither a state nor the Federal Government can, openly or secretly, participate in the affairs of any religious organizations or groups and vice versa.

Finally, I would like to respond in a sentence or two to each of the major arguments which has been made in favor of establishing full diplomatic relations with the Holy See.

1. The Holy See may be distinguished from the Roman Catholic Church. This is nonsense. Archbishop Eugenio Cardinale says the Holy See is "the supreme organ of the Church universal in its contacts with other members of the international community."

2. In appointing an ambassador to deal with Pope John Paul II, we are honoring a true man of God and a dedicated opponent of communism. We agree. We feel that this Pope is an outstanding leader and hope that he has many more years of service. Is the suggestion that, following the selection of the next Pope, the United States will reappraise its commitment based on the personality of the individual selected?

3. One hundred and six states now have relations with the Holy See at the ambassadorial level. "Everybody is doing it!" is an argument that never persuaded my mother and probably not yours either. President Reagan, on November 4, 1983, said, "One hundred nations in the United Nations have not agreed with us on just about everything that's come before them where we're involved, and it didn't upset my breakfast, at all." The important point, however, is that the United States alone has a First Amendment which forbids this action.

4. This action will give the Pope more political leverage in his quest for peace and his struggle against communism. Is this not the same Pope who directed his priests and nuns to avoid political involvement?

5. Opposition to full diplomatic relations with the Holy See is an expression of anti-Catholic bigotry. This may be true in some instances, but it is untrue and unfair to paint all opponents with the same brush. The main thrust of our opposition is support for a clear separation of church and state. We would object to the appointment of an ambassador to the Archbishop of Canterbury, who heads a worldwide Anglican Church, or to the World Council of Churches with their vast network of cooperating churches. The principle is the same in all cases: both church and state function better when they are effectively separated from each other.

In conclusion, we again request that the Committee on Foreign Relations postpone action on this nomination until after the Congress has had ample time for hearings and debate on this important matter.

—James M. Dunn Papers, MS 632, Z. Smith Reynolds Library
Special Collections and Archives, Wake Forest University,
Winston-Salem NC, USA.

Testimony on the Nomination of John Ashcroft to Be Attorney General of the United States

James Dunn offered the following testimony on January 19, 2001, before the U.S. Senate Committee on the Judiciary.

James Dunn: I appreciate the opportunity to present testimony before this distinguished committee and respectfully announce at the outset that I'm opposed to the confirmation of Senator John Ashcroft to be Attorney General. I testify for myself because I'm not representing Wake Forest University, but I now teach at the Divinity School of Wake Forest University.

From my perspective, the long history of Senator Ashcroft's identification with and approval of the political agenda of right-wing extremism in this country convinces me that he's unqualified and unreliable for such a serious trust. I speak primarily of one of his most notable initiatives, the so-called Charitable Choice legislation. A full-frontal assault on the First Amendment mars Senator Ashcroft's career. He has favored government-prescribed religious exercise in the public schools, posting some version of the Ten Commandments, thereby secularizing sacred Scripture, and paying public monies for private and parochial schools. These outrageous initiatives, they pale compared to one being considered to contribute to Charitable Choice schemes.

Senator Hatch has rightly and rigorously insists, and I quote, "Those charged with enforcing the law must demonstrate the proper understanding of that law." That's the point at which I contend that Senator Ashcroft has amply demonstrated that he does not understand the First Freedom, "Congress shall make no law respecting an establishment of religion."

He's come down against settled law that he speaks of frequently, case law, and the American way in church-state relations. It seems that he just doesn't get it. That's the kindest and most generous interpretation of his opposition to church-state separation. Either he has a blind spot, a lapse, or he's one of those who would willfully and intentionally destroy the doctrine of church-state separation that we've known in this country.

He was also party to an incredible abuse of the Free Exercise Clause, keeping Missouri the only state in the nation to exempt church-sponsored daycare centers from fire, health, and safety regulations. One state-exempt center in St. Louis was found to have 100 children with two adults caring for them. Dog pounds in that state have more state supervision than church-based childcare.

When government advances religion in any way, it inevitably becomes involved in religious practice. Charitable Choice, so called, allows and, perhaps, compels state governments to provide taxpayer-funded social services through pervasively sectarian institutions. My doctoral studies and 35 years of serving Baptist and social justice agencies give me a heightened appreciation of the separation of church and state as an essential protection for both vital and voluntary religion.

As the principal architect of Charitable Choice legislation, Senator Ashcroft tacked it onto Welfare Reform [legislation] in a last-minute vote in August of 1996. I and many others have been challenging the constitutionality of this legislation because we believe that the dumping of tax dollars on faith-based programs is dangerous. We cannot afford to abandon the separation of church and state. It's the greatest contribution of the United States to the science of government. We cannot deny that the American way in church-state relations, which involves a separation of the institutions of religion from the institutions of government, has been good for both the church and the state. It's clear that religious liberty's essential corollary is the separation of church and state. When anyone's religious freedom is denied, everyone's religious freedom is at risk. Having one's tax dollars taken by government coercion and turned over to pervasively sectarian outfits to do good threatens everyone's civil and religious liberties.

Some truisms are true. He who pays the fiddler calls the tune. There is no religion-related regime that I know of that wants the rules and regulations or even the reporting that goes with government-handled money. It's clear that most ministries sell their souls for a mess of politics—tainted pottage the very day that they embark on the course of government gimmes. One cannot assume that tax dollars will not change the nature, even the freedom and effectiveness, of faith-based programs. It requires a leap of faith that even Kierkegaard couldn't muster to think that the source of funds will not shape to some degree the programs that those funds pay for.

Practical partnerships between government and religion abound already, but most Americans have absolutely no idea how significantly charitable choice schemes would and are changing current law, or worse, eviscerating religion's vitality by developing a dependence upon tax money for church-based programs. Such plans permit exactly what the Supreme Court repeatedly has prohibited, the use of government money to finance religious activities. They offer an invitation to federally funded proselytizing with a legal license thrown in to boot.

I'm acutely aware of the traditions of this august body and generally appreciative of the high degree of mutual respect and forbearance exhibited by senators in their interaction with one another. That's precisely what concerns me because I see the possibility that the United States Senate could sacrifice religious liberty, civil rights, civil liberties on the altar of senatorial civility. I pray that you'll not do that, and I appeal to you not to confirm Senator John Ashcroft as Attorney General.

Senator Patrick Leahy (Democrat, Vermont): Thank you, Professor Dunn. I know from your bio, you served as a pastor and a campus minister, and a college teacher, served on the Baptist Joint Committee, and so on. I was struck by something you said in your testimony, something about the childcare centers. I'm a parent, as many on this panel, and blessed to be now a grandparent. I've always thought when a child . . . usually about the most vulnerable of our society are our children, and we should do everything possible to protect them. We don't ask what religion they are or anything else. We just make sure they're protected whether they're going to school, or they're going to a childcare center or anything else. Can you elaborate on just what the situation was you were talking about?

James Dunn: Yes sir.

Senator Leahy: I think the one thing that will unite every one of us on this committee is we want our children protected.

James Dunn: Yes sir. For a number of years, there have been attempts to bring childcare centers in Missouri under the fire, safety, and health regulations that apply to non-church-related childcare centers. Senator Ashcroft has consistently opposed that and continued to insist, as long as he had an influence in that realm, that church-related childcare daycare centers were exempt from those state-imposed rules and regulations for fire, safety, and health protection.

Senator Leahy: What are some of these fire and safety things? What are we talking about?

James Dunn: Crowding, overcrowding in the facility, number of children that would relate to each adult, the ratio between children cared for and the adults, the fire protection facilities that are required in other public facilities even though they are in church . . .

Senator Leahy: Fire escapes and things like that.

James Dunn: Fire escapes, and doors, and windows, and so on. I'm not completely at sea over this issue because for 10 years when I was the Director of the Christian Life Commission in Texas, Lester Roloff and Corpus Christi fought the state regulations for fire, health, and safety that were proposed in Texas and finally passed after a survey was done. Only 3 of over 600 church-related daycare centers opposed those protections. I was outraged when I learned that the Missouri law had exempted church-related daycare centers, which account for a great number of daycare centers, from the laws that protect children in regard to fire safety and health regulations, food preparation, all that sort of thing.

Senator Leahy: Am I mistaking your position to say if a child is going to be in a childcare center, they should have the same level of protection wherever they are?

James Dunn: Absolutely.

Senator Leahy: Their religion makes no difference.

James Dunn: Absolutely.

Senator Leahy: It's a child. A child is a child is a child.

James Dunn: That's right.

Senator Mike DeWine (Republican, Ohio): Professor Dunn, to summarize your testimony, I take it that you're vehemently opposed to Charitable Choice.

James Dunn: Yes.

Senator DeWine: You disagree with Senator Ashcroft on the issue, correct?

James Dunn: Profoundly so.

Senator DeWine: Yes or no, yes or no, summary?

James Dunn: Yeah, I disagree with him on Charitable Choice.

Senator DeWine: You disagree with him. Thank you.

Senator Leahy: Did you want to elaborate?

James Dunn: Yeah, I'd like to add one short paragraph, two sentences. I'm absolutely convinced—

Senator DeWine: I think I understand your testimony. I just want to make sure. My only point is that's your testimony. That's your summary of your testimony. We appreciate it for that fact. You're welcome to elaborate, but that's my summary of your testimony.

James Dunn: Thank you.

Senator DeWine: It's a legitimate public policy debate that we can have.

James Dunn: Yeah. My point is simply on Charitable Choice that we've not had a legitimate public policy debate in either the House or the Senate on the issue of Charitable Choice. With all due respect, I would like to suggest or challenge the members of the House and the Senate to do their homework about the very dangerous issue of dumping tax dollars into pervasively sectarian institutions. We've debated vouchers and other issues, but I don't think we've yet begun to debate the Charitable Choice issue, and I hope you'll do your homework with some of the things that need to be done on Charitable Choice.

Senator DeWine: Professor, I appreciate it. It's a legitimate public policy debate. Thank you.

James Dunn: I hope we have it. I don't think we've had it yet.

> —James M. Dunn Papers, MS 632, Z. Smith Reynolds Library Special Collections and Archives, Wake Forest University, Winston-Salem, NC

Notes

1. JMD, quoted in Larry Chesser, "Vatican Request 'On Hold,'" *Baptist Standard*, 11 January 1984, p. 4. See also Kenneth A. Briggs, "Church Groups Denounce Reagan Move," *The New York Times*, 11 January 1984, A4.

2. "All Former SBC Presidents Oppose U.S.-Vatican Move," *Biblical Recorder*, 11 February 1984, p. 5.

3. Steve Weisman, "U.S. and Vatican Restore Full Ties after 117 Years," *The New York Times*, 11 January 1984.

4. JMD, quoted in Chesser, "Bid to Influence Vatican Draws Criticism from Dunn," 5.

Christian Ethics

During his teenage years, James Dunn received an introduction to social ethics from his pastor, Woodrow ("Woody") Wilson Phelps. Phelps was pastor of Evans Avenue Baptist Church in Fort Worth and a doctoral student at Southwestern Baptist Theological Seminary. At Southwestern, Phelps studied under Thomas Buford Maston, who is regarded as the preeminent shaper of Christian ethics and Christian social concern among Southern Baptists in the twentieth century. Maston was responsible for helping to make Christian ethics a field of academic inquiry in the Southern Baptist Convention. He was a pioneer in many areas, particularly race relations, where he was an unflinching proponent of racial equality through both desegregation and integration. Dunn would later follow in Phelps's footsteps and pursue a doctorate in ethics under Maston. The esteemed Southern Baptist ethicist had a profound influence on Dunn before, during, and after his studies at Southwestern with his emphasis on "applied Christianity."

Dunn came to realize under Maston's tutelage that ethics could not be divorced from evangelism nor evangelism from social concern. Personal redemption and social concern belonged together. This notion, novel for many Southern Baptists, would serve as a guiding principle throughout his life. While much of Dunn's ministry was focused on public advocacy and political engagement in his roles as director of the Texas Baptist Christian Life Commission (1968–1980) and executive director of the Baptist Joint Committee on Public Affairs (1981–1999), Dunn had a considerable writing and teaching ministry focused on Christian ethics.

The three selected texts in this section—an academic journal article, a Sunday school lesson, and a public address—reflect Dunn's lifelong commitment to teaching and preaching about the importance of Christian social ethics to Southern Baptists. He did so with a style that did not shy away from calling out his denomination for urging an inadequate ethic of political engagement short on specifics. "We have acted too often as if it didn't matter what Christians voted for, so long as they voted," Dunn says in his address. "We have preached political involvement as if it were an end in itself." A biblical ethic "does not have to be vague and toothless," he noted. "A biblical ethic will offer enough substance and direction in political decisions to get us into trouble."

Ethical Emphases in Galatians

During his ministry, James Dunn contributed several articles to academic journals focused on theology and ethics. The following article appeared in the Fall 1972 issue of the Southwestern Journal of Theology, *the journal of his alma mater, Southwestern Baptist Theological Seminary. Dunn highlights the ethical emphases of the Apostle Paul's Epistle to the Galatians, characterizing the ethic of the Galatians as being "non-systematic, practical, and profoundly religious"—a characterization that also captures Dunn's own approach to faithful politics or what his mentor, T. B. Maston, called "applied Christianity."*

How can one isolate the ethical elements in Galatians? The book maps the theological ground of Christian ethics. The writer saw morality and religion as one.

The love of God issues in love for fellowman. The Cross of Jesus Christ marks the source of Christian ethics. The Holy Spirit bears ethical fruit in the lives of believers.

The whole book of Galatians is in a sense an ethical treatise. It establishes a because-we-have-been-saved rather than an in-order-to-be-saved morality.

Galatians puts law in its place. It presupposes freedom, accountability, and responsibility, thereby allowing ethics, demanding morality.

Traditional approaches that see the ethical content in Galatians beginning only with Galatians 5:1 or 5:13 are not valid. The theological ethic or the ethical theology of the Apostle Paul will not yield to that sort of vivisection.

The vital truth of Galatians is that Christ sets us free. This living theology always finds ethical expression. A truly Christian ethic cannot be torn from its dynamic source.

First, examine the ethical implications of some theological concepts in Galatians. It seems clear that Paul had no use for any theology that did not work out in everyday life.

Theology of the Galatians Ethic

Paul wrote to combat Judaizers who were misleading Galatian Christians about the importance of law. The distorted view of law which Paul fought was ethical error as well as theological heresy.

This sort of legalism keeps cropping up in Christianity. It is an easy type of morality for the unthinking mind. It meets the need that some people have for specific commands.

Carl F. H. Henry insists that "Fundamentalism in practice requires the believer to abstain from certain 'social evils' in order to be acceptable with God. . . . Christian ethics thereby becomes an index of legalistic 'don'ts,'"[1] and in part a means of salvation. With Paul, the issue was clear: either the law, or Christ, not both.

The law may serve some useful function (3:10, 3:24), but it is not the basis of Christian religion or ethics. The believer is not to be under that yoke (5:1). He is called unto liberty (5:13).

The law approach is an alternative to grace (1:6), a dead option (2:19). The Christian is not under law (4:5, 5:18, 6:15).

The child of God "stands in relation to the Law no longer as a servant but as a free man. He still respects it as a declaration of the will of God. But this declaration expresses as a demand what in his new creaturehood has now become the object of love and willing fulfillment."[2]

Christians are free from the law (2:16). They look to Christ for salvation and for strength and direction for living.

If, then, it is Christ and not keeping the law that makes man right with God, what is the relationship between the Cross and Christian ethics? Galatians 2:20 speaks of this vital connection.

Every generation endures its own "I-am-nothing" heretics. They interpret mechanically the phrase "yet not I, but Christ liveth in me" (2:20). James S. Stewart in the classic *A Man in Christ* answers them.

> Paul deliberately guards against the possible pantheistic interpretation by reasserting the religious attitude where "Thou" and "I" stand over against each other. Clearly Paul's view is that the man whom Christ begins to possess does not thereby cease to be himself . . . . Christian experience does not depersonalize men and reduce them to a monotonous uniformity: it heightens every individual power they have.[3]

Believers do not have all their moral questions answered, but they are in the right Light, in the proper perspective for viewing themselves and the world of moral claims and possibilities. The follower of Christ has a radically new self-image. He sees his physical life and all life in time qualified by the existence of eternity. "He is a new man, no longer struggling to keep a code of law, but rather expressing in grateful abandon the life of Christ in him."[4]

The faith (2:16, 2:20) which is the way to God's grace is not a cheap evasion of moral responsibility. Rather, it "works by love" (5:6).

It is clear that for Paul faith and love are really inseparable. William Barclay points out that in Galatians 5:6 Paul "speaks of faith working through love, or, as it perhaps may be better translated, faith energized, set in action, by love. . . . Love must be based on faith."[5]

The atonement, then, and the faith of the Christian in the saving work of Christ are literally the lifeblood of an authentic Christian ethic. The cross reconciles God and man and brings them into full moral accord.

The power that brings new life is the Holy Spirit. The effective work of the Holy Spirit helps and prods Christians to ethical conduct (4:6, 5:5, 16, 17, 18, 22, 25).

The Holy Spirit does not eliminate the need for decision making, remove the necessity for human effort, or erase all conflict and struggle in the Christian life (5:17).

He does, however, offer confidence and assurance in the new relationship that exists with God. "The believer . . . knows that his acceptance with God is not conditioned upon his own moral successes or failures, but that he has been incorporated into the family of God on the basis of Christ's sacrifice."[6]

Further, the work of the Holy Spirit as seen in Galatians was not so much sudden raptures, ecstatic, or emotional experiences as the inward rule of life known by the fruit He produces. A man's conduct becomes an index of his possession or non-possession of the Holy Spirit.

Even so, the Holy Spirit does not annihilate the old self. A man is saved as he is "enabled to bring the only self which he has, with its limitations and its possibilities, into participation in the redemptive power which Christ incarnates."[7]

Another theological emphasis of Galatians with ethical implications is the central theme of the book: freedom. Without freedom there cannot be an authentic ethic. Unless man is in some sense free to choose and is responsible for his actions, his life has really no ethical value.

Beyond this, a principle of conduct is morally binding upon me only if I can regard it as law which I have accepted for myself. Paul saw this sort of freedom as a reality for Christians.

This full freedom is derived from God. It "is not a function of the self, but a function of a relationship—a relationship to God. Freedom, says Paul, rests in a heavenly and not an earthly citizenship"[8] (4:26-28).

Paul called men to come to a kind of freedom that is realized only as one is subject to Christ (6:2). He referred to certain moral laws of the universe (6:7) which when obeyed bring a higher freedom, a freedom in bondage.

Nature of the Galatians Ethic

Paul's authority for the ethical teachings he offers in Galatians is clear. He saw himself as holding an apostolic commission (1:1), "one sent," an ambassador. He saw his message as divinely revealed (1:11-12) and not dependent upon tradition. He exercised his authority with specific instructions (5:2).

One finds various incentives for ethical conduct in Galatians. Paul appeals to the example of Christ (3:27), the certainty of punishment or reward (5:21, 6:7-10), common sense (3:2-3), and the love for neighbor (5:14).

The ethic of Galatians might be characterized as being non-systematic, practical, and profoundly religious. Paul knew the evils of his day (1:4, 2:15). The moral teachings of Paul in this book are designed to meet specific needs but are not trapped in the times.

The goal of Paul's ethic was to do the will of God. This obedience was the true continuation of the covenant ethic set out in the Old Testament (4:28).

The ethic revealed in Galatians is one ready for battle. Paul's stress upon the passive virtues should never be understood as weakness. His passivity of soul never affected his moral energy.

When Peter suffered an attack of cold feet regarding relations with Gentile Christians, Paul boldly corrected him (2:11-14). The ethical posture set out in Galatians does not involve yielding to extremists. It does not fail to see hypocrisy clearly and identify it courageously. Paul had an ethic for controversy which demanded public remonstrance for public errors.

Paul did not like the suggestion that he was only telling men what they wanted to hear (1:10). The force of his convictions did not allow the Apostle to be a fence-sitter. The ethic of the writer of Galatians demanded that he tell the truth even at a price. That dogged determination to say what needed to be said to combat evil lent weight to the moral authority of his teaching. He possessed a certain authority of veracity.

He was true to this moral duty even when it led him to unpopular and unpleasant bluntness (4:16). The Apostle, caught up in the heat of controversy, may have gone beyond the call of duty when in bitter sarcasm he wished that his opponents would go beyond circumcision to castration (5:12). No one could accuse Paul of timidly fighting for moral principle.

The ethic for controversy indicated in Galatians seems harmonious with the view of Martin Marty expressed in *Religion and Social Conflict.*

> If you do not specify and confront real issues, what you do will surely obscure them.
>
> If you do not alarm anyone morally, you will yourself remain morally asleep.
>
> If you do not embody controversy, what you say will be an acceptance of the drift to the coming human hell.

It is interesting that immediately after the most biting expression in the epistle, Paul's suggestion of Judaizer self-mutilation (5:12), comes the setting out of the basic ethic of the book (5:13-14), love. In fact, commentators have most often seen Galatians 5:13 as the first verse of the "ethical section."

Such a chopping of the epistle into theological and ethical parts does violence to Paul's indissoluble union of religion and morality that was his Hebrew heritage. This division also tends to reduce ethics to rules of conduct and to slight the more profound ethical emphases mentioned above: the rejection of legalism, the ethical dynamic of the Cross, the Holy Spirit's ethical function, and the moral essential of freedom. Yet it is clear that in Galatians 5:13–6:10 one finds explicit moral teachings. Understanding the passage depends upon recognizing the love mentioned in Galatians 5:13-14 as the basic principle, the integrating factor in the ethical content of the book.

Basic Principle of the Galatians Ethic

Galatians holds the most eloquent denunciation of a religion of law. Then Paul appears to about-face and plead for the fulfilling of all the law (5:14). All that the law as an expression of God's will actually demands is love rightly understood.

It is not easy, however, correctly to understand the full ethical import of agape in Galatians 5:6, 13, 14, and 22. The following insights may be helpful.

This love is a measure of one's religion. Once again religion and ethics merge. One expresses his love for God toward his neighbor, made in the image of God. The conservative theologian Carl F. H. Henry comments on Galatians 5:14, "A lack of neighbor-love becomes a lack of love for God."[9] Further, in real life it is a phony distinction to separate faith from agape. They go together (5:6). Georgia Harkness offers an analysis of the relationship. "It appears that *pistis* (faith) is very intimately connected with love and it is 'faith working through love' (Gal. 5:6) that sums up the Christian's moral obligation."[10]

The love spoken of is also a test for ethics. Gardner states it well. "Agape directed toward the neighbor is, for Paul, the central ethical principle; and, indeed, without it no action—not even the most severe form of self-sacrifice—is fully ethical in quality" (1 Cor. 13:3).[11] Others see Paul actually putting love in the place held by the *summum bonum* in other ethical systems.

"That which is good" can hardly be other than a synonym for love. All other commandments were so thoroughly subordinated to the commandment of love that he could say that whoever had fulfilled this commandment stood in the moral scale as if he had fulfilled the whole law (5:14).[12]

Luther rightly saw that this ideal offers a continuing challenge since no one can say that he has fulfilled this commandment. "It sounds short and easy, but show me the man who can teach, learn, and do this commandment perfectly."[13] Yet part of the marvelous ambivalence of this ethical principle lies in the fact that while the realization of agape is inexhaustible it is not an esoteric ethic beyond the reach of every man. Again, Luther labels it practical and attainable, at least to some degree.

> If you want to know how you ought to love your neighbor, ask yourself how much you love yourself. If you were to get into trouble or danger, you would be glad to have the love and help of all men. You do not need any book of instructions to teach you how to love your neighbor.[14]

This center of Pauline ethics, love, extends to all men, even enemies. So long as one is human, he is to be the object of Christian love. On the other hand, there is a special mutual responsibility for all believers for each other (6:1-2).

The distinctiveness of the basic ethical principle in Galatians lies largely in the absolute impossibility of separating faith from love, religion from morality, the Cross from conduct, and the Holy Spirit from ethical behavior. In this regard Christian ethics are unlike the pagan moralities of Paul's day and the philosophical ethics systems of this day.

Alexander describes this unique ethic.

> The ideal and the motive are one. The highest good is at once aim and incentive. The love of God experienced in Christ is the deepest motive to Christian morality just because it is held forth as the chief good. Love in Christ's eyes is the supreme motive. As we ourselves receive all our good gifts from God, so the giving of them in our turn is the very law of our lives.[15]

This view, it seems, makes more sense and is more consistent with the ethical emphasis of Galatians and the New Testament than Joseph Fletcher's treatment of Galatians 5:14. The unitary understanding of religious experience and ethical motivation, the objective work of Christ and its subjective appropriation, the Holy Spirit's indwelling and outworking, would rule out the substitution of the word "justice" for "agape" as Fletcher suggests.

> Every time we think "love" we should say "justice." For justice has not been hopelessly sentimentalized or romanticized, or individualized. Not only is it Christian love but, as communication, it says it. It says what the biblical agape means. If we are to have one ethical logion, as Paul put it in Gal. 5:14, then let it be justice.[16]

Fletcher hardly has the solution. Another of the new moralists, John A. T. Robinson, was closer to the view of this article in his comments on Galatians 5:14. He says, "The deeper one's concern for persons, the more effectively one wants to see love buttressed by law," but he also contends that "if law usurps the place of love because it is safer, that safety is the safety of death."[17]

The law of love as a basic ethical principle is, indeed, dangerous. It demands faith. But in Christ duty and desire can become one. The ethical ideal ceases to be an abstraction and takes on life, the basic ethic of love, incarnate.

Personal Dimensions of the Galatians Ethic

A mark of Paul's ethical teachings is his concrete, well-defined treatment of vices. Paul does not hesitate to be negative. In the epistles Paul uses at least 42 different terms for vices. Most of them are listed in Galatians (5:19-21). They are easily spotted in the lives of others but not seen so clearly in one's own life. This is true, no doubt, because, as Barclay puts it,

> . . . Every one of them is a perversion of something which is in itself good. Immorality, impurity, licentiousness are perversions of the sexual instinct which is in itself a lovely thing and part of love. Idolatry is a perversion of worship, and was begun as an aid to worship. Sorcery is a perversion of the use of healing drugs in medicine. Envy, jealousy and strife are perversions of that noble ambition and desire to do well which can be a spur to greatness. Enmity and anger are a perversion of that righteous indignation without which the passion for goodness cannot exist. Dissension and the party spirit are a perversion of the devotion to principle which can produce the martyr. Drunkenness and carousing are the perversion of the happy joy of social fellowship.[18]

The myriad modern translations and commentaries on this passage open vast opportunities for ethical analysis. In this particular instance it seems that a simple chart would be useful, listing the moral faults named in Galatians with an attempt to contemporize.

1. an occasion to the flesh (5:13)—license, self-indulgence
2. adultery (5:19-21)—loose sexually, whoredom, unchastity
3. fornication—prostitution, sexual intercourse outside of marriage
4. uncleanness—filthiness, pus covered, polluted personality
5. lasciviousness—indecency, unrestrained living it up
6. idolatry—status seeking, anything taking God's place
7. witchcraft—encouraging demon activity, drug abuse, sorcery
8. hatred—hostility, the precise opposite of agape
9. variance—strife, discord
10. emulations—jealousy
11. wrath—temper fits, explosion of emotion
12. strife—selfishness, a petty, little spirit
13. seditions—dissension, hassling
14. heresies—special interest groups, childish cliques
15. envyings—grief at someone else's good, ill will

16. murders—killing
17. drunkenness—drinking excesses, satiated, loaded
18. revelings—horsing around, wild parties
19. desirous of vain glory (5:26)—arrogant, popularity seeking
20. provoking of another (5:26)—competitive
21. think himself something (6:3)—conceit, bigheaded

The distinctiveness of the Christian ethic is seen in many ways in the "Fruit of the Spirit" passage (5:22-25). One sees again the unitary nature of the Christian experience. The nine traits listed describe a single pattern of personality, not random characteristics. The inner, vital tone of Christian ethics is also clear as contrasted with a merit system that is attained by dint of diligent effort. Barclay always says it appealingly:

> The plain fact is that this Christian love is the fruit of the Spirit; it is something which is quite impossible without the dynamic of Jesus Christ. That is why it is futile to talk about the world accepting the ethics of the Sermon on the Mount and of Christian love. The plain truth is that the world cannot accept them; only the Spirit-filled, Christ-devoted Christian can.[19]

One sees in the fruit figure of speech (5:22-23) the inevitable flow of virtues from the Christian life, the capacity for bearing seed and producing more fruit, the necessity of a continuing union with the source of life, and the absence of a counterproductive obsession with one's own morality.

Agape love is listed first because the others evolve from it. It is an unconquerable good will which seeks the highest good for the other man no matter how he has hurt you. This involves an act of will as much as emotions. One sees snapshot illustrations of this virtue at work in other passages (5:13, 14, 26; 6:1, 2, 10).

Joy is second only to love. Other ethical systems do not include this concept. Joy is a distinctively Christian moral quality.

Peace is the last of the first triad of virtues which all refer to inner qualities. "Its meaning here is probably the same as in Rom. 5:1, 'tranquility of mind' (based on the consciousness of right relation to God)."[20]

Longsuffering combines the word for steadfastness and the refusal to yield under pressure with the word for slowness to anger toward those whose actions were calculated to annoy. One really demonstrates longsuffering only in his relationship with those whom he could "give what is coming to them." Agape is the secret of longsuffering. "Love suffers long" (1 Cor. 13:4).

Gentleness may be better translated kindness. The Christian is humble in his self-estimate, kind in his dealings with others. The great beauty of this virtue lies in the Christian's passing on to others the way in which God has treated him.

Goodness is the practical outworking of kindness. It is a Good Samaritan readiness to serve. The man who possesses this virtue is the "good ole boy" who always lends a helping hand.

Faith means also faithfulness and the terms cannot be separated. It refers especially to one's relations with his fellow men and describes the faithful faith that works (James 2:17-18).

Meekness may be better understood as freedom from rudeness or harshness. The Greeks saw it as the golden mean between undue resentment or touchiness on one hand and groveling submission on the other. The man with this quality is as little concerned with his personal rights as a humble man is with his own great worth. Galatians 6:1 illustrates precisely this virtue. This ethical trait allows a knowledge of good and evil that is not censorious. It permits, in Bonhoeffer's words, "a judgment of reconciliation and not of disunion, a judgment by not judging, a judgment which is the act of reconciling."[21]

Temperance is the responsible self-discipline that recognizes and responds personally to the moral order of the universe (6:7-8). Far from encouraging a dependence upon some sort of automatic, overpowering spiritual force that makes a man good in spite of himself, the Galatian ethic calls for deliberate effort, hard work, and the kind of self-mastery that involves sacrifice (5:24). One who has this quality engages in an athletic type of moral training (1 Cor. 9:25-27) and is master of himself to be fit to serve others. Persistence is another attribute of this virtue. Sticktoitivity is fruit of the Spirit (5:1, 6:9).

Social Implications of the Galatian Ethic

Paul knew that man cannot make it alone. Even his strong call for individual freedom was tempered by love (5:13). The best safeguard against letting liberty degenerate into license is continuous service to one another. The Christian does not live to himself but in context. There is no such thing as an isolated Christian.

Paul was no wandering street preacher. He brought the disciples into organized communities. A Christian would have a tough time in the blackness of paganism as a loner.

Even the vices set out in Galatians 5:19-21 require one with whom, or against whom, the sinner may sin, and the oneness within the Christian fellowship was so pervasive and strong that even gross moral failure did not destroy it (6:1).

This solidarity which bound believers together was possible because the Holy Spirit actually lives in the Christian and makes him one with every other believer. This constitutes the starting point of new humanity (6:15). Each moral teaching and practice was tested by its effect upon the brother (5:13). If it met the test, it did, indeed, "fulfill the law of Christ" (6:2). This oneness has broader social implications, however, since Christians are "to work for the renewal of the life of society on all levels—in politics, social welfare, education, industry, commerce, in short, wherever we are involved or can be involved."[22]

Galatians 3:28 is a thunderbolt reminder that man, made in God's image, redeemed by the blood of Christ, has infinite worth and dignity. There can no longer be distinctions and barriers between man and man. In Christ, contempt and feelings of superiority and lack of forbearance are unthinkable and strike a deathblow at the heart of any Christian fellowship in which they arise.

Attitudes toward the poor are related to this concept. Paul was anxious to help those in need (2:10). He would have been shocked at the hatred for welfare recipients in the lives of some Christ-claimers today. Luther soundly corrected those who said, "If salvation is not a matter of doing, why should we do anything for the poor?" The reformer, with Pauline zeal for those in poverty, said,

> In this crude manner they turn the liberty of the spirit into wantonness and licentiousness. We want them to know, however, that if they use their lives and possessions after their own pleasure, if they do not help the poor, if they cheat their fellow-men in business and snatch and scrape by hook and by crook everything they can lay their hands on, we want to tell them that they are not free, no matter how much they think they are, but they are the dirty slaves of the devil, and are seven times worse than they ever were as the slaves of the Pope.[23]

Slavery could not live in the atmosphere of Galatians 3:28. This verse has been rightly called the charter for the abolition of slavery.

Political life has felt the impact of the ethical thrust of Galatians. People have cherished political freedom when they have known the true spirit of freedom (5:1). Democracy can only endure where there is genuine concern for others (6:1), awareness of the human family's solidarity (3:28), and authentic freedom (5:1). Ernest F. Scott goes so far as to say that "every movement that makes for a national or social freedom may justly claim the support of religion. If this is refused, religion is false to itself, for it exists for the very purpose of making men free."[24]

Racial problems today are no worse than the hot hostilities that divided the racial and cultural groups of Paul's time. In fact, Jewish attitudes reflected in the Old Testament were thoroughly racist and narrowly nationalistic. For Christians considering matters of fellowship in a church, those distinctions are nonexistent (3:28). Howard Colson rephrases Galatians 3:28 for today when he says,

> If the world is ever to see a demonstration of Christ's power to recreate a new humanity out of all peoples, no believer can afford to shut out anyone from Christian fellowship because of cultural, social, racial, or national backgrounds. To do so is a violation of the Gospel as Christ gave it and as Paul understood it.[25]

The German theologian Jurgen Moltmann commented on Galatians 3:28 in a passage quoted in *The Radical Bible*.

> By undermining and demolishing all barriers—whether of religion, race, education, or class—the community of Christians proves that it is the community of Christ. This could indeed become the new identifying mark of the Church in our world, that is composed, not of equal and likeminded men, but of dissimilar men, indeed even of former enemies. This would mean, on the other hand, that national churches, class churches, and race churches are false churches of Christ and already heretical as a result of their concrete structure.[26]

And Finally

Paul gave a central place to morality. The ethical emphases of Galatians cannot be ripped from its total fabric. They are, rather, integral and interwoven in the basic message of the book. God's relation to men is redemptive in purpose. Man's relation to God comes through a vital union with Jesus Christ and from that union there is fruit.

> —Reprinted with permission courtesy of
> Southwestern Baptist Theological Seminary

The Ethical Teachings of Jesus: Sunday School Lesson

In the following Sunday school lesson, James Dunn teaches about the ethical commands of Jesus and emphasizes the inseparable relation between theology and ethics in Jesus' teachings. This would be a recurring theme throughout Dunn's ministry as he would often—in his speeches, sermons, and writings—similarly note that religion and politics were inseparable. For Dunn, love was central to the ethic of Jesus, and from that emphasis came an urgent call to service in the world.

Biblical Foundations for Study and Application: Matthew 12:50; John 4:34; 8:29; 14:31; Ephesians 5:2; Hebrews 12:2-3; 1 Peter 2:21-25

John 1:17 indicates that even Moses gave only law to humanity while Jesus brought "grace and truth." Jesus' contribution was due to his own uniqueness: "The Word was made flesh, and dwelt among us . . . full of grace and truth" (John 1:14). The incarnation is the basis for the uniqueness of Jesus' teachings. Since "God was in Christ, reconciling the world unto himself" (2 Cor. 5:19), Jesus taught with a note of authority (Mark 1:22).

Jesus and His Teachings

E. Stanley Jones caught the connection between the uniqueness of the person of Jesus and the distinctiveness of his teachings.

> We are not primarily what the Moslems call *Ahlekitab*—"the People of the Book"—we are primarily "the People of the Person." It is not said in the Book, "The Word became printer's ink," but it is said, "The Word became flesh." Had the Word become printer's ink, we should have followed. Instead our code is a character. We follow a living mind instead of a fixed letter. Therefore, our goal is a flying goal—always ahead of us, inexhaustible. We believe that in Christ we have discovered an ultimate.[27]

Not only did God take on human form in Jesus Christ, but that which he would teach was made flesh. Here is the answer to the uniqueness of Jesus' teachings. Jesus said: "I am . . . the truth" (John 14:6). He was the living embodiment of truth. He was what he taught. Whatever the subject, he incarnated it and taught from the overflow of his own life.

The disciples could never feel that Jesus was teaching anything vague or abstract. It was all being made concrete and personal before their eyes.

If one accepts the incarnation as fact and the Scriptures as authoritative, Jesus is the ideal of Christian ethics. Followers of Jesus, then, find their moral example in him. He claimed for himself obedience to the Father's will (Matt. 12:50; John 4:34; 8:29; 14:31).

The men who wrote the New Testament unanimously pointed to Jesus as the moral ideal (Eph. 5:2; Heb. 12:2-3; 1 Pet. 2:21-25). Jesus' life harmonized perfectly with his ethical ideals.

Jesus and His Commands

In what specific ways are the ethical teachings of Jesus different from those of other great men? How are his moral guidelines superior? Henlee H. Barnette listed nine distinctives of Jesus' ethic.[28]

1. Jesus gave new emphasis to the inseparable *relation between theology and ethics*. His was a thoroughly religious ethic. And the moral teachings of Jesus found root in his relationship to God (Matt. 5:48). For Jesus, religion without ethics was unthinkable. Ethics without religion is impossible (Jas. 2:17).

2. *The power to realize the ideal* is another mark of the Jesus ethic. Barnette called it the "energy which comes from faith in God." Jesus' ethical teachings were not theoretical abstractions but were practical and workable. The ethics of Jesus are rooted in religion and are alive (John 15:5).

3. It follows, then, that the ethical teachings of Jesus are *for redeemed persons*, made new by the power of the Holy Spirit (John 3:3).

4. Jesus' ethic possessed *a new inwardness* (Matt. 5:21-30). The commands of Jesus were written upon the hearts of early Christians. He brought a new intensity which precluded man's living on the surface.

5. The *value of the individual* was elevated in the ethic of Jesus. He repeatedly demonstrated his estimate of the worth of one person. Jesus saw each individual as an object of his unconditional love and concern.

6. A *positiveness* missing in other religions marked the morality of Jesus. He had no use for a goodness of "no-no's." The Christian ethic takes the initiative (Matt. 5:23-25; 7:12). It is positive.

7. *Love was given new meaning and centrality* in the ethic of Jesus. This love cannot be fully appreciated apart from an understanding of the life and mission of Jesus (Rom. 5:8). Jesus intensified the nature (John 13:34) and extended the reach (Matt. 5:44) of love. The love that Jesus taught is unique, unconditional, and selfless.

8. Growing out of this emphasis on love, Jesus' ethic contained a *new and distinctive concept of service* (Mark 9:35; Luke 22:27). Jesus elevated the ideal of service. The combination of humility and service, illustrated by the washing of the feet of the disciples, was a unique expression of his teachings.

9. The final and highest distinctive of the ethical teachings of Jesus rests in *his own*. This concept, already discussed, is the seal of uniqueness to the ethical teachings of Jesus. What he taught, he was.

Living the Commands of Jesus

A serious study of history affirms the uniqueness of Jesus' ethical teachings. The impact of his early followers upon the world is difficult to refute. The practical results of the ethical teachings of Jesus are not to be ignored. They practiced purity of life, deemed child-life sacred, scorned lying and slander, turned from rapacity and greed, bore no false witness, coveted no man's property, valued persons more than things, sought no revenge, cared for widows and orphans, were prepared to die for their faith, accepted the slave, protected women, stood by one another.

The historical evidences for the uniqueness of Jesus' teachings have been recognized by unlikely disciples. The results of Jesus' ethical teachings are a matter of historical record. Honest history reveals that hospitals, orphanages, care for the elderly, humane treatment of the insane, prison reform, respect for womanhood, and most mercy institutions are the direct result of Jesus' teachings.

No ethical teacher in history has exercised a comparable influence on the life and thought of mankind.

If the impact of Jesus' ethics is so widespread, why does the man on the street fail to see it? J. B. Phillips insisted that men have not honestly given the teachings of Jesus a fair chance in the marketplace of ideas.

It is not, I repeat, that the thinkers, the writers and the leaders of popular thought, in whatever media, have for the most part studied Christianity and rejected it as unhistoric, impractical and outdated. It is simply that they have not studied it at all! I believe their attitude of almost total ignorance to be quite indefensible. In my own experience, I find it perfectly extraordinary that men and women of unusual ability in their respective spheres have rarely taken the trouble to give their adult attention to such a unique way of life as that proposed by Jesus Christ.[29]

The unbeliever is in an awkward position. He asserts by his unbelief that most of the good in his world is built upon man's capacity to believe what he regards as a lie: "that God was in Christ." He enjoys countless benefits won for humanity in the name of him whom he denies.

Training Plans

1. What makes the teaching of Jesus unique? After the group has spent time discussing this, place the following outline on the chalkboard or on newsprint.
   - The nature of Jesus
   - Jesus' relationship to the Father
   - Jesus' mission
   - Key teachings of Jesus
   - Illustrations of the kind of life Jesus lived
   - Results of Jesus' life and teachings

Assign each of the six points to different members. With the help of the session content, select Scripture passages that illustrate each point. Share findings.

2. What other support can be found for the uniqueness of Jesus' teachings other than scriptural? List your findings on a chalkboard or on newsprint. To assist the group in discussion suggest
   - Historical movements
   - Institutions
   - Cultural influences
   - Personal experiences

Ask members to share personal experiences of trying to put the commands of Jesus into action.

3. Ask the group to evaluate the following statement: No other person in all of history has contributed as much to the ethical improvement of man as has Jesus.

>—James M. Dunn Papers, MS 632, Z. Smith Reynolds Library Special Collections and Archives, Wake Forest University, Winston-Salem NC, USA.

Southern Baptists and Christian Ethics

James Dunn delivered the following address at the 1976 annual meeting of the Christian Life Commission of the Southern Baptist Convention in Nashville, Tennessee. He was then serving as director of the Texas Baptist Christian Life Commission. In his remarks, Dunn calls on Southern Baptists to "take a fresh look at Scripture and reinterpret it for our day" so that the church may "rediscover its biblical identity." A person's lived witness rather than a person's doctrine "is the best test of faithfulness to Scripture," he said, emphasizing the inseparable nature of the call to faith, discipleship, and soul freedom.

Dunn also makes important comments about women in ministry, noting that "women actually believe that the concept [of the priesthood of the believer] includes them"—a pointed reference to the Southern Baptist Convention's exclusion of women from ordained ministry. He said women leave the SBC for other denominations "not because they are less Christian" but because "they are more Christian than we are prepared for them to be."

It is a new day for Southern Baptists in this country. More people know about us than ever before. People know more about us than ever before. There are more of us for people to know about than ever before.

Our very bigness saddles us with a fresh responsibility that is frightening. Beyond our sheer size, changes that have taken place among us and about us give us an ethical charge to keep.

One mark of that new day for Christian ethics is a new acceptance of the ethical aspect of our religion. Once the Southern Baptists who worked at applied Christianity and social concern had to fight for recognition of their message as valid. Now it seems at times that we are being accepted to death. If anything, we stand in greater danger today of being taken for granted than crucified. Oh, there are flashbacks to the good ole days when we deserve our paranoia, when everyone really *is* out to get us. But, most of the time, the brothers and sisters who are our best friends are a bit bored with our persecution complex. Most Southern Baptist leaders now know that trying to decide between ethics and evangelism is like trying to decide whether to breathe out or breathe in.

Among us, then, we ethics-types had better admit that we are seen by many of our brethren as part of the establishment. There may be more liabilities than blessings in that account.

About us change is rapid. Even the immediate future is utterly unpredictable. The opinions and attitudes of Christians are confused and in flux. This unpredictability makes it practically impossible to project the responses to a position statement or program or piece of literature.

We can't assay "how it will fly in Peoria" or Waco. That may be a real blessing. We might as well go ahead and be bold. The situation in which we find ourselves today imposes a new freedom. Our conventional wisdom, measured responses, careful courage, and neat euphemisms may be more dangerous than candor and forthrightness.

A recent article by Ken Briggs in the *New York Times* indicated that the social concerns of American denominations have become more global and less national. American Christians are more outward looking and less preoccupied with themselves. Southern Baptists reflect that trend to some degree. We have discovered, I hope, that world hunger may be as important as determining whether students will be allowed to dance at Carson-Newman College.

It appears that Southern Baptists have also joined the human race in being more interested in the future than in the past. The defense of Baptist traditions and formulas that worked once upon a time is no longer a part of our program assignment. We can look forward rather than backward. The energy, ecological, and food crises demand a forward-looking posture. Our understanding of God's involvement in the world allows progress, a vital approach. Economist Robert Heilbroner suggests that we're all asking, "What has posterity ever done for me?" Happy Hubert H. Humphrey at the height of wisdom pointed out that "the future is before us." It took a while, but we *do* accept that.

We could ramble on about the new day or debate the nature of its newness; but enough of that. What constitutes the current challenge to Southern Baptist ethics? Do we have a "born-again" ethic that meets the challenge?

It seems to me that the challenge to Christian ethics (Southern Baptist style) is threefold. First, we must try to make honest our protestations that the Bible is our rule for faith and practice. Then, we need to see if we can derive some ethical corollaries from whatever basic Baptist belief holds us together. Finally, it appears that we should examine the ways in which we work out practically our social ethic.

The biblical nature of our ethic needs to be reemphasized and reinterpreted. T. B. Maston constantly reminds us of the importance of keeping a solidly biblical ethic. The high priority of teaching, writing, and speaking on biblical ethics cannot be overdone. To lay a biblical basis for Christian ethics is a job that will not stay done. It has to be repeated over and over. Just as each generation has to rewrite its theology, so the relationship of biblical principles to social issues has to be reestablished again and again.

It is not hollow lip service that Baptists offer the Bible. We honestly do see it as authoritative and many among us are willing to flock to almost anyone who will offer a string of answers from the Bible. Look at Bill Gothard's family ethic success, Bill Bright's evangelism, John Conlan's call to Christian citizenship, and Hal Lindsey's explanation of last things. It apparently doesn't matter to many folks that they are buying a mutilated interpretation of the Bible.

The four movements mentioned above have several common weaknesses. They are loosely liberal because they cavalierly refuse to take the *whole* Bible seriously. They are at the same time cheaply conservative because they pander to the lowest common denominator for safely popular folk religion. They all offer "answers"; "solutions" that are so simple that they are downright dishonest. They prey on the ignorance of good folks who are hungry for a word from the Lord.

Though these extra-church, quasi-Christian movements have great faults, we are no less to blame if by default we permit Baptists to find biblical instruction only with the hucksters. The very success of these operations is, at least partially, an indictment of our ineffectiveness. The appeal of these salesmen lies in large measure in uncritical acceptance of biblical authority. The time is right for Baptists who say that they believe the Bible to act like it.

We also need to take a fresh look at Scripture and reinterpret it for our day. The church just might rediscover its biblical identity.

It is dangerous to accept certain biblical premises: that faith works; that love issues in service; that Jesus is Lord; that servanthood is the Christian way; that the Kingdom of God is primary; that the cross-life is for disciples.

It's not far to an ethic which makes radical demands if one begins with a conservative view of the Bible as "the sole rule for . . . practice."

One's life rather than one's doctrine is the best test of faithfulness to Scripture. The call to faith and to discipleship are the same and cannot be separated.

Those who go back to biblical roots for their ethic and take it seriously are disturbingly radical. Jim Wallis in his *Agenda for Biblical People* (Harper & Row, 1976) offers a perspective that is difficult to challenge. He reminds modern Christians that in the early church,

> To say that Jesus is Lord was to register a public protest and declare that Caesar was not Lord. It was to make a political as well as a theological affirmation. Proper worship, in this context, had deep political consequences as it would in our context if worship were properly understood. (76)

Few of us would fuss with the proposition that "a proper understanding of the biblical witness in human affairs has deep political consequences." Yet, when it comes to making specific application of the biblical ethic to particular political issues, it is not easy to be brave enough to challenge the system that buys our big cars.

For instance, it is difficult to sanctify avarice. In the light of a biblical ethic clearly on the side of the poor and oppressed, how can one justify a "trickle down" economic theory? The Scriptures are uncompromising in their demand for economic justice.

If we keep claiming to be biblical, we're going to have to stop our soft-headed approval of the economic *status quo*. We cannot call a marketplace Christian that is fueled by greed. We can explain how it came to be. We can rationalize our acceptance of it among alternatives. We can defend it pragmatically. We can accommodate to it. We can understand and sympathize with those who are trapped in it. But we cannot honestly call it Christian.

It seems to me that the needed biblical ethic must possess enough specificity to challenge particular political positions. One reason that we are experiencing a resurgence of right-wing extremism is that Christians of all sorts and stripes do not understand that their basic ethical beliefs have clear and concrete political implications. And so, they are suckers for anyone quoting Scripture.

We have acted too often as if it didn't matter what Christians voted for, so long as they voted. We have preached political involvement as if it were an end in itself. At the risk of being clear enough that you'll understand what I mean, here are some specific illustrations.

If love and justice mean anything, they take on political interpretations.
If forgiveness has any substance, it has something to do with amnesty.
If nonviolence and a nonretaliatory spirit smack of the Sermon on the Mount, they also relate to gun control.
If Jesus does take the form of the "other" as an exploited class, then he cares more about persons than profits.
If the Bible evidences concern for economic justice, then jobs for everyone is a high priority.

Baptist leaders in the past have not failed to be specific. It is difficult for me to imagine John Leland tinkering with the First Amendment to the Constitution. It is hard for me to conceive of Martin Luther King, Jr. supporting a blanket prohibition of busing to achieve racial balance. It is impossible for me to see any compassionate pastor ruling out all therapeutic abortion.

The point is simply that a biblical ethic does not have to be vague and toothless. A biblical ethic will offer enough substance and direction in political decisions to get us into trouble. It does matter what we believe if, as Wallis puts it, one wants "to be rooted in Christ and judge one's life and social environment in light of the reality of the Kingdom of God." It is not easy to be radically Christian because, "It is to continually scrutinize all social and political 'givens' and to challenge all that conflicts with obedience to Christ."

A retirement of biblical ethics is one of the challenges of the new day for Southern Baptists. The need is apparent. The time is right.

If Baptists have a distinctive doctrinal contribution, it must be our belief in soul freedom or the competence of the individual before God. It is a doctrine much displayed and much distorted. Blind individualism, selfish irresponsibility, destructive divisiveness, and a wishy-washy anything-goes attitude have all been unfairly attributed to the Baptist belief in individual responsibility before God.

Soul freedom is a distinctive Baptist belief and it does offer certain challenges to a contemporary ethic. I think we need an update of E. Y. Mullins's *The Axioms of Religion*. In this outstanding book, the author pursued some doctrinal and ecclesiological corollaries of the belief in soul freedom. I certainly haven't thought through this at great length and don't claim any systematic approach to the task, but some ethical implications are also clear.

If we really believed in soul freedom, our denomination would offer a far greater place of service to laypersons. Soul freedom is a universal Christian quality. One of the great challenges to Southern Baptists in this new day comes at the point of a drastic upgrading of the place of laymen and laywomen in the denomination. We are far more clergy-dominated than most denominations that admit they have clergy.

I believe that there are many more laypersons than pastors among Southern Baptists with a keen social conscience and a willingness to give leadership on social issues. They continually appeal for meaningful involvement. They search for practical, specific opportunities for ministry. They ask for concrete instructions on how to be effective citizens, better parents, Christian employees. They hunger for more than we are giving them. Many of them have taken seriously the priesthood of the believer doctrine. Women actually believe that the concept includes them. When we fail to respond, many of the brightest and the best drop out or go to another denomination. They leave us not because they are less Christian, rather, because they are more Christian than we are prepared for them to be.

If we really believed in soul freedom, our approach to ethics would be far more action oriented. Soul freedom allows great liberty for one whose relationship is directly with God. A deep belief in the priesthood of the believer lets one launch out on faith in spite of controversy, opposition, and certain defeat. Conscience by consensus is hardly Baptist. We are free to fail. We are not free to fail to act.

Education and clarification of the issues is high on the agenda of those who deal with social problems. Study and analysis must never be seen as an end. "Ha, we understand that better." Speaking to the issues and studying them are not substitutes for engagement in the task of social change (though many who study issues think they have actually done something). Besides, the best learning takes place in the laboratory of action.

Ours is a working ethic, not a philosophical discipline. Ours is a person-centered faith-ethic, not a study topic. We Southern Baptists are accused rightly of cowardice when we don't back up our beliefs with action. We can't preach and teach folks into effective discipleship without showing them the way. We are not going to fulfill the program assignments of our various Christian Life Commissions until we demonstrate *how* to those who engage in social problems of the day.

Education without action doesn't teach. Action without education is not worth doing.

If we really believed in soul freedom, we would be far more ecumenical in spirit and in practice. Soul freedom extends to all who trust Jesus Christ as Savior and focuses upon a relationship with God far more compelling than any denominational loyalty. Soul freedom makes soul brothers and sisters of all who know Him. The hymn reads, "Who serves my Father as a son is surely kin to me."

Brooks Hays likes to say, "As Jesus said, and He was right . . . ." Well as the beloved Brooks Hays said in a speech to the Southern Baptist Historical Commission, and he was right, "We should be willing to use such phrases as 'Christian unity' and 'the ecumenical spirit.'"

But more than simply using such phrases, we can see new cooperation developing in this new day. And the fastest way to realize that new brotherhood is by working side by side in common causes of Christian service.

If we really believed in soul freedom, we would be far more engaged in a Christian ethic that is all encompassing in the basic meaning of the word "ecumenical." Soul freedom implies that the death of Jesus for me "as if I were the only one for whom He had to die" alters my relationship to every other person. G. K. Chesterton said, "We are all in the same boat in a stormy sea, and we owe each other a terrible loyalty."

We will begin to see the structures and systems of a society more from the vantage point of the victim. We will realize the ethic of Jesus Christ only as we identify with those who suffer as He did.

As Jim Wallis puts it,

> Only a white society can regard racism as merely a social problem. Only the affluent can view poverty simply as an economic question. Only a war-making nation can understand its destructive policies as just a political issue. Biblically, human suffering is a deeply spiritual issue and an urgent moral concern of the people of God regardless of the way the world may label and categorize its various "problems."

The Baptist understanding of soul freedom or the competence of the individual before God has timely ethical implications. At our best, we might bring insightful progress to a social ethic for this new day.

However dedicated we may be to biblical ethics and however sound our working theology, practical problems remain. The application of the gospel to all of life faces multiple challenges in this new day.

Southern Baptists have had difficulty reconciling the tension between social and personal ethics. Two individuals that I know about symbolize it.

The first one was a fellow seminary student of mine. He was tuned in to our era. He was alert, sensitive, alive to the great moral issues of the day. He was in touch with the problems of race relations, war, poverty, hunger. He understood something of international affairs. In fact, he was not just a talker; he was a doer. He's been a part of the answer to these problems on the foreign missions field.

He was home on furlough and sat in front of me at Southwestern Baptist Theological Seminary. I was quite impressed with him. That's the reason I remember something else about him. On every test he sat there and cheated. Even cheated on the Ten Commandments.

I remember another guy. I didn't know him. I heard about him on the radio one afternoon. He was an upright citizen, a good, moral man. He didn't drink, curse, smoke, chew, or any of those things. He was one of the community leaders, an outstanding citizen.

That afternoon I winced when NBC weekend news reported that this Baptist deacon—solid citizen, moral man—had wrapped a bullwhip around the face of one of his Baptist deacon brothers trying to cross the Edmund G. Pettus Bridge in Selma.

The reconciliation of these dimensions of the Christian ethic may be one of the easier problems. The same love for persons—made in God's image, bought with the blood of Jesus Christ—motivates personal morality and social concern.

One cannot choose between personal ethics and social concern. If either is genuine the other is implied. The more authentic one's personal morality, the more extensively he wants to engage in Christian social action. The more genuine one's social ethic, the more deeply he is committed to living a personally moral life before God.

We must give some real care and attention to maintain both emphases. Our more fundamentalistic and traditional brethren disdain "the Social Gospel." Our more liberated friends look down on "petty morality." These labels tend to minimize mutually important aspects of Christian ethics. Other tensions, however, cause even greater problems.

Many matters of social concern are sharply divisive. "Liberal" and "conservative" are labels for libel. Moral questions tend to become objects of great emotional heat and little light. Issues tend to polarize and politicize people into sharply divided camps.

More often than not these polarizations make it more difficult to find the truth. When one insists that "this is a clear-cut, black-and-white, 'yes' or 'no' issue," it often means that he doesn't understand the problem.

The issue of Vietnam so divided the American people. Now busing, abortion, school prayers, marijuana, and a dozen other issues tempt people to join one side or the other of a destructive, irrational debate.

A Southern Baptist ethic in this new day must include better ways to help Christians deal with controversy. Even though Christianity officially conquered Gnosticism in the fourth century, Southern Baptists along with most of the other people in our culture continue to believe in the duality of opposites. Gnosticism divided the cosmos into the forces of Light and Dark, Good and Evil, the Spiritual and Material.

Many of the problems we face come from thinking, feeling, speaking, and acting that has been conditioned by this outmoded duality. The duality of the gnostic heresy was officially rejected by the early church, but it still plagues us.

Though our new day is one of the many paradoxes, we try to deal with it as the ancient Manicheans did. In doing this we often get impaled on both horns of our dilemma.

We fail to recognize that two conflicting viewpoints may be contrary without being contradictory. We often assume a false dualism. Sidney Harris offers a well-known illustration of this:

> Both we and the Russians assume that we have contradictory systems and that if one is proved "right" the other is proved "wrong," or vice versa. In actuality, no such contradiction exists: we have contrary systems, or polarities, and it is entirely possible that some third system, combining the better elements of each, might be superior to either Communism or Capitalism. The reason we get so confused on this question is that Dictatorship and Democracy are true contradictories; you can have one or the other but not a combination of both.... Communism and Capitalism are polarities, or contraries, while Dictatorship and Democracy are genuine opposites, or dualities. (*The Authentic Person*, Argus Communications, 25–26)

Harris goes on to make some other useful distinctions. His working definitions may be helpful in overcoming either-or thinking. He suggests that "a duality is fundamentally a contradiction that cannot be brought into alliance with its opposite."

One cannot have peace while having only a "small war," or be a "little pregnant" or be "nearly a virgin."

Harris then uses freedom and security to illustrate polarity over against duality. The feeling of security gives us freedom. The ideas of freedom and security complement one another in a kind of creative tension. In a just social order, polarities of freedom and security are kept in balance. There is enough freedom to reward exceptional enterprise but also enough security to give people free and rational choices.

On a personal level many of our constituency still talk about the Flesh and the Spirit as if they were opposites. A "holistic" view of persons doesn't allow for that division. Even Love and Hate, once seen as dualities, may be polarities.

Harris suggests that maintaining the tension between seeming "opposites" is the chief way to cope with most of our dilemmas in the modern world. "And this is just the hardest attitude imaginable for a race of beings conditioned for a millennia to swing to one opposite or the other" (39).

To adopt a creative tension of Christian social ethics is not a cop-out, not an acceptance of "holy neutral" on social problems or the pursuit of the golden mean. It is not an attempt to take a safe middle-of-the-road position. That's usually just tepidity and timidity. To grasp a paradox and hold it in tension requires courage and wisdom.

For a moral man to live in immoral society requires a social strategy. The maintenance of creative tension is an attempt to reconcile the biblical ideals with the realities of life. This approach is, it seems to me, consistent with the transformation ethic of the New Testament.

Southern Baptists have an opportunity to contribute significantly to the understanding of Christian social ethics. We must think well, be true to the Bible, love people, dare to act, and work hard. "Unto whomsoever much is given, of him shall be much required."

—James M. Dunn Papers, MS 632, Z. Smith Reynolds Library
Special Collections and Archives, Wake Forest University,
Winston-Salem NC, USA.

Notes

1. Carl F. H. Henry, *Christian Personal Ethics* (Grand Rapids MI: Wm. B. Eerdmans Publishing Co., 1957) 420.

2. Helmut Thielicke, *Theological Ethics*, Foundations, vol. 1, ed. William H. Lazarreth (Philadelphia: Fortress Press, 1966) 136.

3. James S. Stewart, *A Man in Christ* (New York: Harper & Bros. Publishers, n.d.) 167.

4. L. Harold DeWolf, *Galatians: A Letter for Today* (Grand Rapids: William B. Eerdmans Publishing Company, 1971), 45.

5. William Barclay, *Flesh and Spirit* (London: SCM Press, Ltd., 1962) 70.

6. Henry, *Christian Personal Ethics*, 381.

7. E. Clinton Gardner, *Biblical Faith and Social Ethics* (New York: Harper & Row, Publishers, 1960) 156–57.

8. Robert T. Osborn, *Freedom in Modern Theology* (Philadelphia: Westminster Press, 1967) 14.

9. Henry, *Christian Personal Ethics*, 431.

10. Georgia Harkness, *Christian Ethics* (New York: Abingdon Press, 1957) 71.

11. Gardner, *Biblical Faith*, 88.

12. Morton Scott Enslin, *The Ethics of Paul* (New York: Abingdon Press, 1957) 241.

13. Martin Luther, *A Commentary on St. Paul's Epistle to the Galatians*, trans. Theodore Graebner (Grand Rapids MI: Zondervan Publishing House, n.d.) 217.

14. Ibid., 218.

15. Archibald B. D. Alexander, *The Ethics of St. Paul* (Glasgow: James Maclehose and Sons, 1910) 157.

16. Joseph Fletcher, *Moral Responsibility: Situation Ethics at Work* (Philadelphia: Westminster Press, 1967) 57.

17. John A. T. Robinson, *Christian Morals Today* (Philadelphia: Westminster Press, 1964) 26.

18. Barclay, *Flesh and Spirit*, 39.

19. Ibid., 66.

20. Ernest DeWitt Burton, *A Critical and Exegetical Commentary on the Epistle to the Galatians*, The International Critical Commentary, 44 vols. (New York: Charles Scribner's Sons, 1920) 314.

21. Dietrich Bonhoeffer, *Ethics*, trans. Neville Horton Smith, ed. Eberhard Bethge (London: SCM Press, Ltd., 1960) 157.

22. William Neil, *The Letter of Paul to the Galatians*, The Cambridge Bible Commentary of the New English Bible (London: Cambridge University Press, 1967) 86.

23. Luther, *St. Paul's Epistle to the Galatians*, 215.

24. Ernest F. Scott, *Man and Society in the New Testament* (New York: Charles Scribner's Sons, 1946) 253.

25. Howard P. Colson and Robert Dean, *Galatians: Freedom through Christ* (Nashville: Convention Press, 1972) 65.

26. Jurgen Moltmann, quoted in Hellmut Haug and Jurgen Rump, eds., *The Radical Bible*, trans. Erike J. Papp (Maryknoll NY: Orbis Books, 1972) 114.

27. E. Stanley Jones, *The Christ of the American Road* (Nashville: Abingdon-Cokesbury Press, 1944) 20.

28. Henlee H. Barnette, *Introducing Christian Ethics* (Nashville: Broadman Press, 1961) 44–46.

29. J. B. Phillips, *God Our Contemporary* (New York: The Macmillan Co., 1960) 50–51.

Chapter 9

Christian Advocacy

During his fourteen years at the CLC (twelve as director), James Dunn urged Texas Baptists to accept their responsibility to be advocates in the public square, participating in the political process as Christian citizens. Promoting a political engagement ethic motivated by Jesus' call to love others (Great Commandment) and grounded in a commitment to soul freedom, Dunn preached that the Bible calls every Christian to responsible citizenship. Baptists were to be "lobbyists," according to Dunn, who emphasized that "biblical theology clearly calls Christians to political action, to attempts to influence legislation, to lobbying." Democracy depends on the participation of citizens, and to be a good Christian in a democracy was to be a good lobbyist, Dunn noted. Choosing to stay out of politics was a "cheap cop-out" (see "Lobbying Isn't a Dirty Word").

In calling others to be advocates and exercise their "Christian citizenship," Dunn reminded his listeners and readers that God requires Christians to do justice and love mercy (Micah 6:8). Christians should use the Bible responsibly in political debates and avoid the tactics of the Religious Right such as invoking Scripture selectively to justify a narrow, partisan political agenda and judging a public servant's Christian faithfulness on the basis of a single issue.

Dunn was a loud and effective advocate on behalf of many pressing issues in the Lone Star State during his tenure at the Texas CLC. He advocated on behalf of juvenile justice reform, immigration reform, and environmental regulations before the Texas legislature. He also fought efforts to legalize gambling and further the interests of the alcohol industry. A tireless supporter of public education, Dunn championed the need for comprehensive sex education and bilingual education. Most notably, he did not shy away from controversial issues such as contraception, abortion, and the Equal Rights Amendment.

The writings in this section offer a glimpse into Dunn's approach to advocacy in the political arena and share examples and strategies for how Christians—as individuals and congregations—can be practitioners of a free and faithful politics and confront controversial issues. While specific suggestions are now dated in different respects, these writings contain much timeless wisdom and ethical relevance.

Lobbying Isn't a Dirty Word

James Dunn provocatively declared in a 1975 article published in the evangelical magazine Eternity *that "Every Christian should be a lobbyist." This declaration is but one example of Dunn's consistent pleading with Baptists and other Christians to be active citizens, deeply engaged in the political process. This call to practice a free and faithful politics noted that silence or non-action was really support for the status quo.*

Webster's dictionary says that lobbying is simply attempting to influence legislation. The popular image of a lobbyist is a sleazy character engaged in illegal and immoral activities to buy votes. This is not accurate or fair. Every Christian should be a lobbyist.

Democracy depends upon the participation of citizens. Without active involvement by the people, the dream of democracy can never come true. In a sense, no one can be a good Christian in a democracy without being a good lobbyist.

Common sense calls for political Christians. Most American Christians have indicated a willingness to die for freedom. Yet few are willing to live as constructive citizens working for democracy. Many of the 50 states hit an all-time low in voter turnout in the general elections of 1974. Millions of Christians did not care enough to vote.

An informal survey done by the author among 10,000 Christian college students in Texas showed that less than 10% could name their own elected representatives: two U.S. Senators, one U.S. Congressman, one state Senator, and one member of the state House of Representatives. Christian students do not even know their own public servants.

The real question is not whether Christians should be involved in working for good laws, freedom, peace, justice, and clean government. The question is how they should be involved.

Not to take a stand is to support the status quo. To accept things as they are says either that one is satisfied with the present policies and practices of government or that the risen Christ and His followers are powerless to change the world.

To fail to alarm anyone morally assures that one will remain morally asleep himself. There is no neutral ground in a living, changing democratic society. To "stay out of politics" is itself an alignment with the forces of evil, a cheap cop-out.

Sadder still is the effort by some to justify political inaction on biblical grounds. We cannot possibly expect the New Testament to have specific instructions for involvement in the political order. Those early Christians could not consider running for the Roman Senate. They were too busy running from it.

Withdrawal from the world, setting Christians apart in spiritual study, or an obsession with the end times constitute an eschatological evasion of ethical responsibility. Biblical theology clearly calls Christians to political action, to attempts to influence legislation, to lobbying.

Biblical truth must be translated into contemporary political terms. This can be done only by those who have been transformed by the Truth. If believers fail in this awesome responsibility, no one else in society is so equipped to fulfill this prophetic role.

—Reprinted with permission courtesy of the Alliance of Confessing Evangelicals.

Dealing with Controversial Issues

Throughout the 1970s, James Dunn spoke to church groups on how to address divisive issues. He emphasized that Christians should aim to "civilize controversy," making it "creative and constructive." In the presentation below, Dunn shares about how to deal with controversial issues with compassion, courtesy, and common sense.

Is it "*Dealing* with Controversial Issues" or "Dealing with *Controversial* Issues" or "Dealing with Controversial *Issues*"? Let's talk some of all three.

How one sees controversy will determine the way in which he handles it. One's basic presuppositions will determine how he deals with controversy.

One cluster of presuppositions is basically theological. These concepts are directly related to a Christian posture in regard to controversy. Let's look at a theological stance for facing controversy.

1. Man is made in God's image. According to F. J. Sheed, "The idea that man is made in the image of God is a concept of such transcendent importance that any difference between one man and another fades into nothingness by comparison." If one does believe that man is made in the image of God, then he must deal courageously with issues that affect the life of man. If one believes that man, all men, are made in the image of God, that belief will alter significantly the manner in which he deals with controversy.

2. Man is a sinner. Any biblical estimate of man includes serious consideration of man's sinful nature. Man is selfish, ego-driven, more interested in his own good than that of others. All of the institutions and organizations of society are colored by man's sinful nature. This assumption significantly affects the way in which Christians deal with controversial issues.

3. Man lives in a real world. Otherworldly religion won't get the job done. Sin, pain, evil, suffering, injustice are facts of life in our kind of world. Dr. J. M. Price used to evaluate esoteric religion with a simple phrase, "Christian Science: it's like Grape-Nuts, neither one."

William Temple insisted that Christianity is "the most materialistic of all the world's religions." He appealed to the Christian doctrine of the incarnation as evidence that God takes the stuff of life, the flesh of men, the things of this world seriously. In fact, God takes the physical and material dimensions of existence so seriously that "The Word became flesh." Controversy cannot be dismissed as unimportant by Christians who take seriously the world in which they live.

4. Christian men are God's agents. Because the church is seen as the Body of Christ, the extension of the very personality of Jesus Christ in the world today, the instrument of redemption, Christians cannot fail to deal with controversy. God was in Christ "reconciling the world unto himself." Because His was a ministry of reconciliation, our ministry is reconciliation. We serve God as we help people. The only way we do serve God is by serving people. Jesus said, "As my father hath sent me even so send I you." This kind of mission demands dealing with controversial issues.

5. Man is saved by faith, not works. God does not demand that we resolve every controversy that we encounter. He does not demand that we win every battle. He does not insist that we solve every problem we face.

We are made right with God by our dependence upon him and our commitment to him, not by works, accomplishments, or successful crusades. Since our ultimate salvation is not dependent upon our meritorious deeds, we do not need to be afraid of anything as we engage in controversy.

We may make mistakes. We may lose to overpowering forces against us. But even when we fall, are defeated, even when we do not succeed, our relationship to God remains constant and secure. With this knowledge Christians can enter controversy with a boldness not known by others.

6. Man is a free moral agent. Each of us must decide for himself about right and wrong. Each believer is a priest, relating to God independently and directly. No church or creed or hierarchy or state can tell all Baptists what they must believe. Thought control is not in our vocabulary. We as Baptists have always chosen freedom over unity when forced to make that choice. Since we allow independent action, freedom of conscience, and open expression, controversy is absolutely inevitable. Being a Baptist implies living with controversy.

Beyond the theological presuppositions directly related to dealing with controversy is a logical presupposition. If anything is important, it's bound to be controversial. We are all most defensive, opinionated, and vocal about the ideas, beliefs, and persons that we hold most dear. Why argue over something that doesn't matter? It's easy to ignore the trivial. If it's important, it's controversial.

It does not follow that everything controversial is automatically important. Man in his infinite stupidity has managed to elevate ridiculously insignificant matters to a level of great controversy. As the Russian Revolution was taking place, the church leaders in Russia were debating the length of the tassels on the bottoms of the priests' robes. In 1971, the Tennessee Baptist Convention managed to spend more than half of its business session time in debate over whether students at Carson-Newman College would be permitted to dance—on campus or across the street off the campus.

By their very nature, politics and democracy are inseparable. Democracy always involves controversy. Robert M. Hutchins said it well: "I do not think I exaggerate when I say that in a democratic society controversy is an end in itself. A university that is not controversial is not a university. A civilization in which there is no continuous controversy about important issues, speculative and practical, is on the way to totalitarianism and death. The very nature of democracy is struggle for power."

While controversy is inevitable, it is not necessarily bad. A worthy Christian goal might be to civilize controversy, to make it creative and constructive.

When one examines the current social scene, he must acknowledge that the issues we face today are many, complex, and divisive. To ignore the issues, to oversimplify them, or to fail to take a position is intellectually dishonest, morally reprehensible, and socially irresponsible. This does not minimize to any degree the difficulty that we all face in assuming our responsibility as citizens and Christians. Rather, it demands that we are informed, do our homework, study hard, and know all that we can about the problems facing society.

How do you deal with controversial issues? Dealing with controversy requires a combination of Christian compassion, everyday courtesy, practical politics, elemental psychology, and common sense.

1. Analyze. Is this issue worth your energy and concern? Since there is no way for you to fight every battle, is this battle worth fighting?

2. Prepare. God wants us to be tenderhearted, yes, but tough-minded. It's an appalling discovery to learn that most of the idealistic young who are so anxious to fight the evils of the world do not have any ammunition. Too often they fail to realize that facts, knowledge, understanding, and tough-mindedness are absolutely essential. Alfred North Whitehead said, "Not ignorance but the ignorance of ignorance is the death of knowledge."

3. Use appropriate means. Some issues demand all-out effort; others do not deserve that much attention. Don't use a cannon on a mouse. On the other hand, you probably better not use a slingshot on an elephant.

4. Innovate. Don't be trapped in the old categories. Don't accept the commonly understood alternatives to any problem. Try to find the way that's not been considered yet. "Love will find a way" is not just a silly, romantic notion.

5. Act. James 1:22 calls us to be "doers of the Word." Dietrich Bonhoeffer said, "No man can possess the Word of God for a single instant other than in the doing of it." We can't wait until all the facts are in. We must act before the issues are settled. To the best of our knowledge and with a "leap of faith," we must act now.

6. Make allowances for others. "If eating meat offends my brother" means that a sincere Christian will not take any course of action without considering its effects and impact upon others. It means that we have no right to "do our own thing" without carefully measuring the possible hurt to other persons. It's not being superior or snooty to lovingly recognize that some folks simply do not understand the situation. It's not being unkind or unchristian to know that there are those, however sincere, who are just "out of it" and others who "ain't got it and have never had it."

7. Recognize that there's not a solution for every problem. It's an American fallacy to think that every problem can be solved. It's even more futile to believe that we alone have the power to solve every problem.

8. Communicate. You may do right things with the right motive for the right people at the right time in the right place; but if you use the wrong words, you can blow it, baby. Why not say "fraternal" instead of "ecumenical," "moral" instead of "social," "progressive" instead of "liberal"? Listen to the folks around you and try to talk the language that they speak. There's no particular virtue in imposing your advanced and enlightened vocabulary upon them.

9. Be prepared for negative responses. Don't react when someone disagrees with you with surprise, dismay, hostility, or a sense of martyrdom. What do you expect? Anyone who does anything should expect opposition, reaction, resistance. It's only those who slide along never challenging the course of least resistance who fail to encounter opposition. You might need to worry if you never have any difficulty.

Dr. Joseph Fletcher has indicated that when he is accused of being "controversial," he responds affirmatively. He says, "I'm 65 years old, and I simply do not have enough time left in life to waste any of it on anything that's not controversial."

—James M. Dunn Papers, MS 632, Z. Smith Reynolds Library Special Collections and Archives, Wake Forest University, Winston-Salem NC, USA.

A Christian Lifestyle for Twentieth Century Baptists

During summer 1977, James Dunn presented the following paper before the Commission on Christian Ethics at the annual meeting of the Baptist World Alliance in Miami Beach, Florida. Here, he highlights the growing economic inequality that existed around the world and focuses on the global challenges of widespread hunger, illiteracy, inadequate housing, and lack of medical care. Dunn also offers critiques of mass consumerism in the United States and encourages Christians to recognize global interdependence and "plant the seeds of bread and justice and cultivate their growth with sacrificial, witnessing discipleship."

In his call for "nothing short of a radical new lifestyle" to "revitalize Baptists in the Twentieth Century," Dunn suggests action-oriented personal and policy prescriptions. This approach focused on specific strategies and solutions distinguishes Dunn from many Baptist ethicists of this era who were reluctant to offer applications to accompany their ethical analyses.

The following United Press International news release from the fall of 1975 puts in sharp focus the bundle of contradictions and inconsistencies in which we find ourselves as soon as we begin to discuss the lifestyle of Christians in a hungry world: "After a breakfast of fresh strawberries marinated in champagne, fish crepes with cheese sauce, scrambled eggs with chives and pecan rolls, Midwest Governors sat down to discuss the world food crisis."

The overwhelming majority of Baptists are in the wealthy northern hemisphere. One billion people have stunted bodies or damaged brains because of hunger. Most of them live in the southern half of the world. Half a billion people are actually starving and another half-billion get by on less than $75 a year.

We'd rather not be faced with these realities. There is a built-in contradiction in our profession of concern about lifestyle as we meet in this comfortable setting after having spent hundreds of dollars to get to this place.

Yet Martin Luther was right when he said, "If you preach the gospel in all aspects with the exception of the issues which deal specifically with your time you are not preaching the gospel at all." We should examine a Christian lifestyle for twentieth century Baptists . . . however self-incriminating, however uncomfortable the examination.

The "American Way of Life" could be an accurate label for the basic economic ethic of most Baptists in the world, even those who do not live in the United States of America. I believe that we should see the inherent dangers in that particular approach to life as it is compared with a Christian ethic.

The popular understanding of the American way includes certain false assumptions for personal economics, an idolatrous materialism as its fueling philosophy, and a bundle of slogans that have somehow become more precious to many Americans than the truths of Scripture.

Consider these generally accepted assumptions.

1. It is right for every family to press for a standard of living that calls for the greatest possible abundance of material things.
2. A family's standard of living is high or low depending on how many possessions they have, how expensive their cars, houses, and clothes.
3. The profit drive is an integral part of the American way of life and is not to be tampered with or questioned.
4. Every family should make all they can and own the best cars, houses, and clothes that their income will support.
5. It is acceptable for privileged people to have more than enough regardless of what happens to other people.
6. The reward for being a faithful Christian is increased prosperity. "God has really blessed our little family" often means, when translated into the language of the marketplace, "look at all the things we have."

You may add your own assumptions to this short list and make your own assessment of the validity of these assumptions. It seems that they are widely held. It also seems that they are dangerous for the believer.

One recent study indicates that "Americans . . . believe that if people are poor it's probably their own fault." The study was based on in-depth interviews in Boston and Kansas City. John Tropman, a professor at the University of Michigan who did the study, said the key is that "if the poor get what they deserve, then I'm getting what I deserve." Thinking that the poor are somehow to blame for their poverty relieves our own feelings of guilt about living well while others don't.[1]

The Scripture warns against just such an attitude. "Beware lest you say in your heart, 'My power and the might of my hand have gotten me this wealth'" (Deuteronomy 8:17).

These false assumptions about personal wealth are as American as apple pie (a dish few of the world's people have ever enjoyed). Leonard Bernstein's musical *1600 Pennsylvania Avenue* didn't last long on Broadway. I remember only one line from the one song. It stings. "If God says lovin' money is the root of all sin, Then God is un-American."

At times we try as a practical matter to minimize our wealth. Yet we are the rich.

Two-thirds of the world's people got to bed hungry. We are in the one-third who eat well.

Three-fourths of the people on earth can't really read or write. We are the literate one-fourth.

Four-fifths of the world doesn't have enough clothes. We do.

Five-sixths of the world's people have inadequate housing. The overwhelming majority of Baptists are housed adequately.

Six-sevenths of the people in the world could not get to a doctor if they needed one tonight. We are in the one-seventh who could.

By any stretch of the imagination, we are the rich. If we are the rich and if the biblical teachings have any meaning for and application to today, then the passages that apply to the rich must speak to us.

I'd rather not be the subject of those biblical passages that are aimed at the rich. But I'm afraid that I am and most of you are, too. If I take the authority of Scripture as seriously in dealing with these passages as I attempt to in applying Bible teaching to the sins of others, it's frightening. If I insist upon the abiding relevance of the ethical teachings of Jesus, then I can't escape the powerful words about wealth in the New Testament.

The philosophy that fuels the money machine in Western life is a practical materialism. It is a materialism as damning as the materialism of Communism.

Unneeded things have become the idols of this real religion that replaces Christianity. The recreational vehicle, the second house, the cars and boats and extra stuff do claim the allegiance of men's souls.

The rhetoric of the American way has become so sacred in the minds of many Christians that it is dangerous to challenge it.

The "law of supply and demand" is referred to as if it were holy writ, and the radical nature of Christian stewardship is seldom seen.

There's a modern mentality that sees loans, banking, even the whole field of economics as completely independent and autonomous. That idea is heresy. It comes from modern secularism, not from the Bible. The Lordship of Jesus Christ extends to economics.

Another common assumption is that the American consumer comes first. It's a matter of national policy. Richard Nixon was brash enough to say it, June 13, 1973. "I have made this basic decision: in allocating the products of America's farms between markets abroad and those in the United States, we must put the American consumer first." Contrast the words of John Wesley: "Any Christian who takes for himself anything more than the plain necessities of life, lives in an open, habitual denial of the Lord. He has gained riches and hell-fire.

Mad consumerism is apparently an essential ingredient of the American way. The average American teenager watches 350,000 TV commercials before he or she leaves high school. As Richard K. Taylor puts it, "In 1974, $26.5 billion went into advertising to convince us that Jesus was wrong about the abundance of possessions."

Faithful Christians continue to assert that property rights are not absolute. Carl F. H. Henry is right in asserting that the pagan Roman attitude toward private property "remains the silent presupposition of much of the free world's common practice today." It is the "Justinian view" that "derives ownership from natural right" and "defines ownership as the individual's unconditional and exclusive power over property."

Persons' rights come first. The right to eat must be recognized as basic. And as surely as faithful Christians affirm this truth, they are viewed with grave suspicion. There may be significance in the fact that the United States has developed a neutron bomb which can kill people without destroying property. Yet the life of even the most degraded person is worth more than the richest possession. It's people over property for followers of Jesus Christ.

Ronald J. Sider has written an excellent book, *Rich Christians in an Age of Hunger*. He contrasts one aspect of the American way with a New Testament ethic. "We demand that our governments foster an ever-expanding economy in order that our incomes will increase each year. We insist on more and more. If Jesus was so un-American that he considered riches dangerous, then we must ignore or reinterpret his message."[2]

It's not smart to talk about the redistribution of wealth. That's not the approved vocabulary. Yet Christians have to face up to passages like 2 Corinthians 8:13-14. "There is no question of relieving others at the cost of hardship to yourselves; it is a question of equality. At the moment your surplus meets their need, but one day your need may be met from their surplus. The aim is equality."

The "American way," then, is not the Christian lifestyle for Twentieth Century Baptists. Many real pitfalls exist for Christians who sell out to "the American way."

An effort must be made to define the Christian lifestyle over against "the American way," for having a distinct quality of life is what being a Christian is all about.

The manner of life that merits the tag "a Christian lifestyle" has purpose and values and a pattern of conduct. It is comprised of certain constructive activity and sets a different "standard of living."

A Christian's lifestyle is marked by rational acceptance of the responsibility for others taught in the Scriptures. We are our brothers' brother. "Where a man has been given much, much will be expected of him" (Luke 12:48).

Believers understand the spirit of obligation, the sense of oughtness, the responsible life. Believers can identify uncomfortably with the famous violinist Fritz Kreisler. He said, "I am constantly endeavoring to reduce my needs to the minimum. I feel morally guilty in ordering a costly meal, for it deprives someone else of a slice of bread, some child, perhaps, a bottle of milk. You know what I eat; you know what I wear. In all these years of my so-called success in music, we have not built a home for ourselves. Between it and us stand all the homeless in the world."

However idealistic that quotation may sound, it also sounds strangely like the teaching of Jesus. We can't dismiss that sort of responsibility for others as unimportant to a Christian lifestyle.

Another characteristic of the Christian lifestyle is a lengthened perspective. The stuff of Christian theology has direction, meaning, purpose, the long-look, an eschatological dimension.

The last chapter of Robert Heilbroner's *An Inquiry into the Human Prospect* is titled "What has posterity ever done for me?" It's a good question. Why should we care in the Twentieth Century about what happens in the Twenty-first Century?

Believers in Jesus Christ have the equality of hope for the future that permits, no, demands that they work at identifying with those yet unborn. The Christian has a theology of hope. God is out ahead of us beckoning us on. God is going before us as he led the children of Israel in the exodus from Egypt. A Christian lifestyle looks forward, leans forward.

Still another mark of the Christian lifestyle is the cross-life kind of caring for others . . . not simply rational obedience or theological farsightedness but genuine commitment to caring and sharing the fellowship of First Century Christians meant unconditional availability to and unlimited liability for the other brothers and sisters. This kind of mutuality is seldom seen among church members today, even among the closest friends and associates. Yet there is no doubt that the *koinonia* of the New Testament church produced just such a radical relationship of total sharing among believers.

I'm one of those who unashamedly admits that he'd like to see just a little of that kind of mutual accountability and oneness in the life of local churches today. If just a few families among us practiced that kind of love, the world would take notice.

Another distinguishing feature of the Christian lifestyle is certainly sensitivity to human need and hurt wherever it is found. It is likely that those of us who are overfed, comfortably housed, and well clothed cannot really understand what it means to watch one's own children die from starvation, but we can try. We may never really feel what others feel, but we can try to understand.

It is difficult to overestimate the importance of this sensitivity to others, this awareness of the oneness of the human family.

Possibly the most difficult characteristic of this Christian lifestyle for Twentieth Century Christians to understand is the freedom from anxiety that Jesus evidently expected of those who follow him. Those who know the Scriptures are familiar with the way Jesus urged his followers to enjoy a carefree life unburdened by anxiety over food, clothing, and possessions (Matthew 6:25-33). The joy and peace of that lifestyle has clearly been lost to most modern believers.

A certain humility should also set apart the Christian lifestyle. There is need of patience with one another. We should question our own lifestyle, not that of our neighbor.

The Christian lifestyle that is "in," chic, is not, by that very fact, authentic. We have to beware of reverse snobbery, of spiritual one-upmanship. You probably know some of the new breed of radical believers who are rich in their poverty, proud of the humble estate.

We need to remember that we are all on pilgrimage and that the Father seems to love variety. We must by all means avoid legalism and self-righteousness. This counsel against pride and judgmentalism and narrow particularism should not make us so open about lifestyles that we lack direction. We must have the courage to commit ourselves to some specific method for moving toward a more just personal lifestyle.

There is a general awareness of the need for more responsible lifestyles. Bumper stickers read "Live simply that others may simply live." The general public has seen the energy crisis, inflation, dwindling natural resources, and world hunger as adequate justification for altered lifestyles.

A Harris poll in December of 1975 indicated that 91 percent of Americans were willing to go to one meatless day a week, 92 percent would reduce paper products; 78 percent of the people polled said that they were ready to stop feeding pets all-beef foods, and 73 percent of Americans indicated that they would willingly dress in old clothes and would go along with limiting the size of homes.

Since 1975 the inevitability of altered lifestyles has become apparent. Authorities can't agree on a timetable or the exact shapes that new lifestyles will take, but there is widespread agreement that profound, involuntary changes in lifestyle are imminent.

Christians have a particularly high stake in reshaping their personal and corporate lifestyle. The world is watching to see if we care. Our very witness is at question. Senator Mark Hatfield says, "The present world food crisis may be the last chance for Western Christianity to validate itself."

Lester Brown points out that the continuous pursuit of super-affluence by some of us in a world of scarce resources can now directly affect the prospects for survival elsewhere. The statistics are familiar but still shocking. The United States citizen uses 342 times as much energy as the citizen of Ethiopia. One American draws on resources that would sustain 50 citizens of India.

Christians should not indulge in such immoral, acquisitive affluence. They must recognize global interdependence, evaluate it morally, and rectify its inequalities. They must plant the seeds of bread and justice and cultivate their growth with sacrificial, witnessing discipleship. In this recklessly over-consumptive society, they must emerge as the Salt of the earth, reflecting the Light of the world, distributing the Bread of life.

What specifically should we Christians do to escape the rat race of grasping greed? We should exemplify responsible stewardship of the world's resources by

• reducing our standard of living. Eat less (especially less grain-intensive food products), consume less (especially less energy), use less. Americans have among the most wasteful diets in the world. We eat two-to-four times as much meat as the body can use.

• restricting our reproduction. Married couples should plan to limit their families. All parents can instill in their children the importance of contributing to population control.

• growing our own gardens. A carefully managed garden just 15x20 feet can yield over $300 worth of fresh food in six months. One Miami couple recently converted their swimming pool into a garden. A *New York*

Times story of October 7, 1976, indicates that 48 percent of American households now have some sort of garden.

- learning from the example of those who have simplified their lifestyle.
- caring for your own body; exercise, rest, good dietary habits are a matter of Christian stewardship.
- reducing consumption of junk foods and totally abstaining from grain-produced alcoholic beverages.
- demonstrating our global concern by skipping at least one meal a week and contributing the money saved to the world hunger fund.
- dressing modestly. Dare we care at all about keeping up with the latest fashion?
- diminishing the use of fertilizer for non-food production purposes.
- studying and learning about the extent to which our living standards relate to world poverty and hunger.
- practicing informed Christian citizenship regarding government decisions that affect trade, aid, military spending, food policy, and overseas development.
- considering a graduated tithe as the basic pattern of Christian giving.

It is at least possible that nothing short of a radical new lifestyle can revitalize Baptists in the Twentieth Century. It is likely that the spiritual and moral health of the fellowship of Baptist believers is irrevocably, indissolubly caught up in the lifestyle question. Our wealth and the way we use it reveals who we are.

As we consider our opportunities in this era of the evangelical, an obedient simple lifestyle may be the only way to sustain religious revival. Whatever the social implications of the Christian lifestyle, the Bible puts it bluntly: "If anyone has the world's goods and sees his brothers in need, yet closes his heart against him, how does God's love abide in him? Little children, let us not love in word of speech but in deed and in truth" (1 John 3:17-18).

—James M. Dunn Papers, MS 632, Z. Smith Reynolds Library Special Collections and Archives, Wake Forest University, Winston-Salem NC, USA.

How a Pastor Relates to Politics

*In 1970, James Dunn and his colleague, Phil Strickland, published a book of essays encouraging Christians to participate in the political process and be informed citizens. At the time, Dunn was director of the Texas Baptist Christian Life Commission, and the book—*Politics: A Guidebook for Christians—*was primarily distributed in Baptist circles in the Lone Star State. However, fifteen years later, the small book would receive national attention when Rev. Jerry Falwell, founder of the Moral Majority, was pictured in* Newsweek *magazine holding a copy of the volume. Falwell claimed that his approach to politics was, in part, informed by this 1970 volume.*

Dunn often drew a sharp contrast between the free and faithful politics he preached and the political engagement approach and tactics of Falwell and the Religious Right. Yet he wholeheartedly affirmed that Falwell and other fundamentalists were correct to be engaged in public life. The following writing is the first of two chapters that Dunn contributed to Politics: A Guidebook for Christians. *In this selection, Dunn offers suggestions for how pastors can (and should) be involved in politics. He admonishes pastors not to abdicate their Christian responsibility to be active citizens. "Preachers may perform their most useful and distinctive function by translating biblical doctrines into contemporary political terms," Dunn writes.*

Can a pastor get mixed up in the politics? He is not "just another citizen." No matter how forcefully he insists upon his participation as an individual, his identity as a religious leader is inescapable.

This predicament presents both problems and opportunities. The problems center on heavy responsibilities for the past. He must exercise every caution not to abuse his special platform as pastor. He should guard against

1. being "snowed" by some "good Methodist" who is running for office,
2. determining his political position or candidate support on a single issue,
3. taking purely political positions from the pulpit,
4. becoming too indebted to or identified with one candidate or public official,
5. failing to sound a clear note on moral issues.

The opportunities peculiar to a pastor come from three sources:

1. He is generally seen as an informed opinion maker, a thought leader in the community.
2. He is known as a man of ideals, convictions, and religious standards.
3. He is largely responsible for the posture of one of the most visible and viable institutions in society, the church.

A brief consideration of each of these opportunities seems in order.

As Informed Opinion Maker

The task of keeping informed is awesome. The pastor cannot get firsthand knowledge regardless of how hard he may try. He cannot get completely objective, unbiased information on issues or candidates. He cannot spend enough time to keep abreast of the varied issues and developments with a claim on his attention.

Issues debated in the political arena are literally matters of "life or death" for God's children. Questions that finally will be decided by the political process will affect the lives of thousands of persons, each "made in God's image." Problems of society that are being faced seriously only by government will touch every citizen. According to the Scriptures, every citizen is one "for whom Christ died." When God cares so much, his servants care too.

His servant cares about all sorts of issues . . . . Keeping up with all of these is impossible! Right! But it is even more complicated than that. One must keep up with what is happening at various levels of government: city, county, state, and national. He then must know about political personalities on each level and somehow relate persons, parties, and pressure groups to the issues.

The pastor has a great obligation as an informed leader in the community. Staying informed is a big job. Here are some hints for the busy pastor.

1. Admit that you must rely on others for information upon which to base political judgments. With this admission, take care to seek information reflecting several points of view.
2. Read newspapers carefully and critically. Try to find at least one independent "opposition" paper that does not follow closely the same editorial policy as the big city daily so dependent on advertising for its life.

3. Examine more than one of the major weekly news magazines or newspapers.

4. Learn to evaluate newsletters and reports published by various special interest groups. Beware the junk mail or extremists. Sometimes they send it free. Watch out; someone is paying for it with a purpose in mind. Other times they make continuing appeals for money. Extremism is a good racket.

5. If you read the generally liberal *Christian Century*, it might be well to know what is written in the usually conservative *Christianity Today* and vice versa.

6. Listen to radio and television for the latest developments in city, county, and state politics. Political communication often must come within hours to be worth anything.

7. Gain needed perspective on issues and candidates from materials prepared by the League of Women Voters.

8. Learn about politics from the best teacher, experience. By taking part in precinct politics, paying dues, and doing a reasonable amount of volunteer work, one can gain some "inside" information available in no other way.

9. Join the PTA, a service club, or some other constructive community organization. These groups can help one keep up to date on local issues.

As a Man of Ideals

The pastor is seen as a man of ideals. He and other churchmen have a peculiar opportunity to relate Christian concepts to citizenship. Somehow the church must bridge the gap between religion and politics.

Preachers and active laymen may perform their most useful and distinctive function by translating biblical doctrines into contemporary political terms. This function can be performed only by those who have a grasp on the truths of the gospel.

Certain concepts, biblical and basic to our faith, push into politics all honest Bible practicers. It is difficult to see how one can claim to follow the New Testament as his guide if he fails to mix well his politics and religion.

Maybe he is afraid—it is not popular, never has been; that is how John the Baptist lost his head. Maybe he does not really believe that the Bible speaks to the issues of the day. Maybe he is too busy, or thinks he is, to keep up with what happens in government. Maybe he has a limited understanding of the ministry, looking to the by and by and failing God and men in the here and now, loving souls and not caring for people.

The distinctive role of the pastor is to demonstrate the application of great biblical truths to the life of his community. If he fails in this, no one else is so well equipped to serve this prophetic role.

The Bible message is clear. To apply these great themes moves every sincere Christian into active citizenship in 20th century America. Such themes as the following are the foundations of Christian political action.

Stewardship. The New Testament indicates that every blessing carries piggyback a matching responsibility. Few American Christians would deny the blessings of liberty in this land. Yet less than half of those who could vote bother to do so. Even less could be called active citizens.

Baptists have little liturgy. Baptist worship services are usually informal and free of ritual. Certain phrases are heard in Baptist prayers, however, as if they were part of an ironclad form: "We thank Thee, Lord, for freedom to worship as we see fit," "for religious liberty," "for the right to go to the church of our choice." Good for Baptists who pray thus!

Could these prayers of thanks be transposed into pledges of action? If one is sincerely grateful for the blessings of liberty, he is, in fact, promising to exercise that freedom every time he pauses to acknowledge his blessings.

If one recognizes freedom in this nation as a gift of God, then he is a steward, a trustee, of that blessing. To be a good manager, a good steward, of the liberties of this democracy, one accepts every possible citizenship responsibility. To be a good steward of one's citizenship may be more important than being a good steward of his money. After all, which is more valuable, living in a democracy or having things?

"For unto whomsoever much is given, of him shall be much required: and to whom men have committed much, of him they will ask the more" (Luke 12:48).

Love for Neighbor. It is not always easy to love one's fellow man. In rush hour traffic or supermarket lines, it is almost impossible. Most good folks would help a hungry child. Locked in their own routines, from air-conditioned job to television, to church with folks just like themselves, most good folks never even see a hungry child.

In the complexities of urban life, the biblical command to love one's neighbor becomes increasingly difficult to apply. The vast majority of white Christians seldom deal directly with those in deep need. Their parents and grandparents may have done so in a simpler style of life.

One Christian may not demonstrate love directly to many neighbors in this complicated culture. Yet, as a citizen, he may express indirectly his loving concern for others as he works for good legislation and good public servants.

The maintenance of order, dispensation of justice, advancement of safety, health and welfare, education and defense are a few of the functions of government today. In all these realms, a concerned Christian may express his loving interest in his neighbor if he knows how to work effectively in politics. "Thou shalt love thy neighbor as thyself" (Mark 12:30).

The Kingdom. Can one *pray* honestly, "Thy kingdom come on earth . . ." and fail to work for better conditions in his own home town?

Man Made in God's Image. Can a Christian *praise* the Lord and by sorry, uninformed citizenship mock the worth of "men which are made after the similitude of God"?

Lordship of Christ. Can a serious disciple of Jesus *call Him Lord* and forget His mastery over city hall, "the powers that be"?

Government Ordained of God. Can a servant of God *minister* in Jesus' name without a sense of partnership with him who is "the minister of God to thee for good"?

Witness. Can a man claim to bear witness to the truth that sets men free and refuse to tell it like it is about the county commissioners?

Reconciliation. Can Christians be afraid to try to bring warring political factions together when the very essence of their calling is labeled by the New Testament a "ministry of reconciliation"?

Incarnation. Can believers shy away from "dirty politics" when He who thought it not robbery to be equal with God "took upon him the form of a servant and was made in the likeness of man" (Philippians 2:7)?

Justice. Can churchmen ignore the machinery of justice in society when the Scripture asks, "What doth the Lord require of thee, but to do justly, and to love mercy and to walk humbly with thy God" (Micah 6:8)?

To translate these doctrines, believed so deeply, into concrete political action is certainly one of the pastor's most difficult and rewarding tasks.

As Institutional Leader

Finally, the pastor's leadership of the church as a living force in society gives him an added burden of political responsibility. He may well exercise his most significant influence as he works through the lay leaders of the church. Some insist that the pastor should train, motivate, and encourage laymen but never personally engage in political activity. Pastors generally find it difficult to lead from behind. However he conceives his role, the pastor cannot evade responsibility in the realm of politics. He must act.

If the church is to be a redemptive force in the world, it must come to terms with the realities of today's world. One of these realities is the fact that big decisions are made through the political process.

If the church would be a redemptive force in the world, it must come to a fresh appreciation of God's love for all men. One result of this will be a radical commitment to action to help people, even if that action is political. The church must move into political issues.

—Reprinted with permission courtesy of the Texas Baptist Christian Life Commission.

How to Get the Church into Politics

Below is the second of James Dunn's two essays to the 1970 edited volume Politics: A Guidebook for Christians. *This provocatively titled essay offers specific steps a church can take to ensure that its members are educated and equipped to engage in the political process. While many of these suggestions are now dated and some promote gender stereotypes, they may still serve to generate ideas for how Christians can practice a free and faithful politics that chooses civility, encourages thoughtful (even if difficult) conversations, and champions the common good. Dunn also notes the importance of formulating "a concrete plan of action." "Too often the church will speak but never do anything," he writes—an observation that still rings true nearly fifty years later.*

The local church is ideally suited to move quickly and effectively on a political plane. Churches have a ready-made opportunity for working at the task of social change. Like no other institution in society, the church can respond to moral issues facing the city, state, or nation. A church is expected to be vitally interested in the moral climate.

This is true because churchmen meet together regularly and have the basis for cooperation found only in a group of persons who know and trust one another. They have, at least generally, a common commitment to honesty, justice, and mercy. They care about people. They have through the church, even in this secular age, a respected voice in the community. They proclaim a message of redemption for all men. They take seriously citizenship responsibilities as a stewardship of God's blessings.

In several specific ways, the local church is geared for action on political issues. Here are some approaches that should not be overlooked as a church takes up its responsibility for good citizenship.

Education

An informed electorate is essential to the success of democracy. Lack of broad-based public understanding of the issues frees vested interests to have their way and lends to apathy which defeats the democratic process.

1. Study groups among youth, men, and women are made to order for studying the problems facing society. Possible solutions to poverty, racial injustice, pollution, or alcohol problems may be examined in a Christian context. Such study often leads to action.

2. Sermons still offer a teaching opportunity. A pastor fills his prophetic role as he exposes injustice and uncovers corporate sin.

3. Field trips by church-related groups can translate concern into concrete, good citizenship. A visit to the jail, to the emergency room of a busy hospital, or to a ghetto can motivate as can no printed page or spoken sermon.

4. Special programs by agencies and organizations dealing with social issues are generally available to church groups.

5. Distribution of printed materials prepared by reliable denominational or secular agencies that deal with the issues is useful.

Information

Information on current issues can be disseminated with the church in countless ways. At voter registration time or in a get-out-the-vote push, every possible channel should be used to remind church members of their opportunity. Repetition is basic to good communication. One should not overlook any of the following instruments when attempting to secure total church involvement on a particular issue like a vote to lessen limitations on liquor sales.

A. Spoken announcements in the worship services, perhaps by a layman.

B. Spoken announcements in all smaller groups: Sunday school classes, training groups, ladies' organizations, deacons' meeting, choirs, youth groups.

C. A bulletin insert or announcement in the Order of Worship.

D. Inclusion in the church calendar of important dates such as General Election day in November.

E. Posters on all church bulletin boards. (A poster contest among children or youth might stimulate interest.)

F. Reminders placed on each car in the church parking lot (may be mimeographed).

G. Interest centers with objects to draw attention to the emphasis.

H. Detailed information in the church paper or newsletter.

I. A special direct mailing to every church family.

J. Mailing developed especially for certain groups within the church—youth, men, etc.

K. Questionnaires or "worksheets" distributed to determine attitudes of church members toward the issue and the degree of individual involvement.

L. Use of the church sign or announcement board outside the church.

M. Telephone campaigns within the church membership to say, "Don't forget to vote today" or to give a similar reminder.

N. A brochure, circular, or card designed to be delivered personally as church members visit absentees and others.

Communication

Communications through the mass media constitute a realm of responsibility for the church as it faces political issues. Churchmen and committees should not bypass this kind of witness to society. The world outside the doors of the church does not know what Christians are saying about public questions. It must be said in the mass media.

1. Radio and television programs are often a regular part of a church's ministry. In times when moral issues command special attention, these channels of communication should be utilized. The church never needs to apologize for caring about people and fighting any interest that would damage human dignity or threaten human life.

2. "Talk shows" on radio and television offer a forum for all points of view. When the community or state faces critical decisions affecting the moral climate, surely pastors and other churchmen should represent a Christian perspective in the marketplace of ideas.

3. Editorials by radio or television stations may present the occasion to request "equal time." Though stations are now free to editorialize, they

must grant those who hold opposing views a fair opportunity to answer. For instance, radio or television editorials favoring looser liquor laws or supporting legalized gambling could and should be answered promptly and logically. This is done by contacting the general manager of the station and respectfully requesting the opportunity to present an answer to the station's editorial.

4. Commercial time may be purchased to tell your side of the story. Television time is expensive. Radio "spots" reach a wide audience if enough are purchased. Many short announcements (15 seconds, 30 seconds) are usually better than fewer longer "spots." In most statewide campaigns involving moral issues, denominational agencies and other organizations produce film clips and radio tapes that are available free of charge if local churches or groups of churches will purchase the broadcasting time.

5. Stories in the newspapers afford an excellent way to get the word out. How to "get press" for the cause poses a problem. One must find some "news hook" or occasion for making news. A few such "hooks" within the reach of most churches are these:

- A meeting or joint statement of community leaders, pastors, educators, professional persons, legislators, etc.
- A speech by an outsider to any church group or by the pastor to any civic group
- The organization of a committee or council for the purpose of dealing with a particular issue
- A letter sent out to a large number of persons and released to the press
- A quick answer to some public statement by the "other side"
- An exclusive statement on the issue in question made by some person of state or national prominence
- A press conference called by a well-known person in the community or a group of persons normally unlikely to be together in their thinking.

6. "Letters to the Editor" should not be minimized in an all-out effort to tell the public the truth about an issue. Certain guidelines will make the letter writing more effective.

- Letters should be short—300 to 350 words.
- Language should be clean, clear, and kind.
- A logical, factual argument should be made.

- Many different persons should write in their own words and style, since only a small percentage of letters received are printed by most newspapers.
- Letters should be signed with real names.
- Every newspaper in the area should be written, since this page in most papers has a high readership.

7. Advertising in local newspapers may be bought to make a public appeal for a moral cause. One of the easiest and most effective ways for churches to do this is the signature ad with the names of all contributors listed. Collecting a small amount of money from many different persons makes paying for the advertisement relatively easy. Obviously, the more names the better and the more widely known the better. It also makes a matter of public record the names of those who would stand to be counted for the cause involved. It is usually wise to keep the text of the advertisement simple and the list of names alphabetical.

Groups of churches may want to join in this activity. Various denominations cooperating together may make a greater impact upon the community.

Frequently, denominational agencies or other organizations developed to assist the churches will professionally produce newspaper mats or glossy prints for use by local groups. High quality artwork should be sought. Sloppy ads may actually hurt rather than help the cause.

Organization

Organization is one great strength of the church as it faces politics. With built-in organizational units, the local church does not need to engage in the time- and energy-consuming process of "getting organized."

The women's missionary organization can quickly take up a telephone campaign. Lines of communication are already established. Groups that function together regularly may be given a mailout, addressing, or telephoning assignment.

Youth groups are ideally suited for providing transportation to the polls on election day. One or two young people answering a telephone and making assignments can meet the needs of every elderly person who wants to vote. The telephone number to call for free transportation to the polls should be publicized through church mailouts beginning two weeks in advance.

Even groups of older children may be of help in distributing circulars door-to-door or handing out reminders in shopping centers. Royal Ambassadors, Girls' Auxiliaries, and Boy Scouts like to help.

Sunday school classes and other study groups may become discussion groups probing for a better understanding of the moral issue being considered. Special study material is usually available from the denomination, the League of Women Voters, and other organizations.

The men of the church should serve as a bridge from the church to the business community. They might set up a speakers' bureau and offer to provide programs for any group in the area. They could divide among them the responsibility of personal contact with every family of the church. This is a valid and helpful function for churchmen.

Church members are in practically every club and organization in the community. An important aspect of any campaign to communicate and convince involves being certain that someone is responsible for speaking to each organized segment of community life.

Some secular organizations will take a positive position on an issue at the urging of Christian members. Others will have a program on the subject. At times the best that can be done is to neutralize the collective influence of an organization.

One Chamber of Commerce in a south Texas city was on the verge of officially endorsing race track gambling in a state-wide referendum. Alert members of the Chamber created such a stir by threatening to resign from membership if such a position were taken that the move was averted. Sometimes neutralizing is the best that can be done under the circumstances.

Organizations that should be given attention, programs, and sometimes opportunity to take an official position are

- Service clubs: Lions, Rotary, Kiwanis, Optimists
- Parents and Teachers Association (PTA)
- Veterans of Foreign Wars, American Legion
- Federated Women's Clubs, Women's Study Clubs
- Masonic Order, Eastern Star, Oddfellows, Elks
- School Board, City Council or Commission, Commissioner's Court, or other county government
- Chamber of Commerce, Junior Chamber of Commerce
- Various professional or trade organizations
- Labor unions

- Gideons, United Churchwomen, and other interdenominational religious organizations
- Ministerial Alliance, Interdenominational Ministers' Union, or Council of Churches
- Racial or ethnic groups
- Other churches in the community

As churches attempt to become involved in political issues of moral consequence, they should utilize to the best advantage their present organization. Here churches have a head start on those outside the church.

Action

Action is the most important and the most neglected phase of the church's involvement in issues that are decided in the political arena. Too often the church will study a question to death and never act on it. Too often the church will speak but never do anything. Too often the church will even get organized for action and then stop short of going into battle because some dear brother objected.

Voter registration and get-out-the-vote campaigns are two of the best ways a church can begin an active citizenship program. Who can possibly object to a church insisting that her members be qualified to vote? Who could question a push toward the polls from the pulpit? Voting is minimal citizenship.

In these approaches, it cannot be said that "the church is trying to tell me how to vote." Outsiders cannot accuse the church of "building a bloc vote" or "manipulating its members."

A concrete plan of action for voter registration and get-out-the-vote is needed. No number of notices in the bulletin and no amount of eloquence in the pulpit will get folks registered to vote.

An Organizational Plan

1. Elect Citizenship Co-Chairmen. It is wise to have a man and a woman working at this task.

2. Select a group captain for every twenty church families. The group captains should be interested in citizenship, willing to spend a total of two or three hours on the telephone. They may be told that only one meeting will be required.

3. Call a meeting of all group captains to outline plans for the voter registration drive.

- In this meeting explain the purpose and importance of this endeavor.
- Distribute lists of twenty telephone numbers each to every group captain.
- Train the telephoners in what they should say as they call. They will ask if all adults in the family are registered to vote. They should be given detailed information about voter registration so they can answer any questions. Who must register? How often? May one register by mail? What is the address? Who may register for me—husband, wife? What is the deadline for voter registration?
- Instruct the group captains to offer to provide assistance such as transportation in voter registration.
- The group captain should report to the Citizenship Chairman when everyone in his group is a qualified voter.
- Keep the same organization for a get-out-the-vote drive. Captains will know those who are registered.
- Provide voter registration cards at the church at every meeting. The First Baptist Church in Texarkana, Texas, reported in 1968 that 95% of the adults in the church were prepared to vote. They used a plan much like this one.
- Devise some way to keep a progress chart on voter registration prominently displayed. Church members should feel a team consciousness in the effort for 100% citizenship participation. A thermometer, graph, or other yardstick can generate excitement.

If the church is to fulfill its redemptive function in the community, to express a corporate witness for good, to be a part of the changes that help people, it will become involved in citizenship matters. The local church is suited to work in politics and it must.

—Reprinted with permission courtesy of Texas Baptist Christian Life Commission.

Jesus and Caesar—Matthew 22:15-22

James Dunn preached the sermon below on several occasions while director of the Texas Baptist Christian Life Commission (1968–1980). In this sermon, Dunn reflects on the responsibility of Christians to render unto Caesar what is Caesar's and give to God what is God's.

It is my distinct pleasure to be with you today. May we stand in respect for the reading of God's Word. I read from Matthew 22 beginning with verse 15:

Then the Pharisees went out and laid plans to trap him in his words. They sent their disciples to him along with the Herodians. "Teacher," they said, "we know that you are a man of integrity and that you teach the way of God in accordance with the truth. You aren't swayed by others, because you pay no attention to who they are. Tell us then, what is your opinion? Is it right to pay the imperial tax to Caesar or not?" But Jesus, knowing their evil intent, said, "You hypocrites, why are you trying to trap me? Show me the coin used for paying the tax." They brought him a denarius, and he asked them, "Whose image is this? And whose inscription?" "Caesar's," they replied. Then he said to them, "So give back to Caesar what is Caesar's, and to God what is God's." When they heard this, they were amazed. So, they left him and went away.

It was a perfect trap. They were certain they had him. He would either have to be a traitor or rebel, a reactionary or a revolutionary. The Pharisees were unhappy under Rome's loyal Jews. If Jesus said "pay taxes," he would be supporting the Roman occupation forces, aiding the enemy, selling out his own people.

The Herodians were happy with things as they were. Conservative keepers of the status quo. Don't rock the boat; you might spill something that is mine. If Jesus said "do not pay taxes," he would be a rebel, an outlaw, an enemy of the state, so they set a trap. Both groups were hypocrites in two ways. First, the basic meaning of the root word for hypocrite is a mask wearer, as in Greek drama . . . pretending to be something one is not . . . they came acting, acting like honest men. But then they were hypocrites in a more serious way. They were convinced that they were pious and virtuous, blind to their actual condition. Anderson Scott sees this kind of hypocrisy as the failure to think out the practical application of one's religious principles in his relations with other men.

But the trap didn't work. Jesus asked to see a coin. Examined it. Then asked them, his testers, a question. Whose picture is here? Why, Caesar's. The very coin was used by both groups—he borrowed one from them. The currency that allowed them to carry on business was a result of Rome's rub. But more than that . . . Caesar symbolized the law and order that let life go on from day to day. He was responsible for the Pax Romana, the Peace of

Rome, the longest period of safety from rampaging warriors the Jews had ever known.

The trap didn't work because Jesus answered with a formula that sent them away "taken aback," "left them no handle." His answer staggered them. His answer suggests a formula for facing the state today. It clearly indicates a double duty for Christian citizens, a both/and approach to government and God, an as-well-as series of relationships. We're concerned with the here and now as well as the by and by; the social as well as the individual; responsibility as well as blessing; the body as well as the soul.

We apply our faith to the here and how as well as the by and by. A few years ago a political leader of men said, "We claim the earth, let the church have the hereafter." He continued to say let the church preach its gospel, stay out of politics; let the church deal with matters spiritual; it has no concern with social issues. Do you know who this man was? Adolf Hitler. But the disturbing thing is that too many Christians agree with his attitude. His very words even sound familiar. I was preaching the other day in another city, and before I had a chance to make it clear that I was quoting Hitler, I got a hearty "Amen."

Jesus said render to the ruler of the temporal order, Caesar, as well as to the Lord of eternity His due.

The Communist's phrase "an opiate of the people" is aimed at religion. It would have some truth to it if our faith were concerned only with "a gold mine in the sky some sweet day." But thank God, Christianity is vitally involved in the here and now.

Paul expressed this sensitivity to a present involvement when he reminded Timothy (1 Tim. 4:8) of the "promise of the life that now is and that which is to come."

The existentialistic philosopher did not discover the "now"— n . . . o . . . w! Listen to Paul's words from 2 Cor. 6:2 "now is the accepted time, now is the day of salvation."

Dietrich Bonhoeffer, the German martyr, commented on Jas. 1:22, "be ye doers of the word and not hearers only." He said, "It is impossible to possess the word of God for a single instant other than in the doing of it." Now is all we have to do His Will. Render unto Caesar as well as unto God.

We realize our religion in responsibility as well as in blessing. Jesus commanded "render unto"—give what you owe, pay your debt of duty to the state, fulfill your citizenship obligation. You know, every blessing brings its attendant responsibility. Luke 12:48 reminds us that "unto whomsoever much is given, of him shall much be required." Jesus saw debt to Caesar for law, order, peace, money.

I doubt if there is a church in the land today where someone will not pray "and we thank Thee our Father for freedom of worship." Had you ever thought that every time we say these words, we are solemnly swearing our acceptance of the responsibility of Christian citizenship, we are actually pledging to God our citizenship? This is especially true in a democracy. Because in a democracy the people are ultimately responsible for everything that happens. Yet we try to escape that responsibility with silly slogans.

"Dirty politics"—have you heard that expression? I wonder why we don't hear people talking about "dirty democracy." Could we have democracy without politics?

"I vote, yes, I try to be a good citizen." Ha! Someone has said that's like one asking, "Are you a Christian?" and answering, "I go to church on Easter Sunday." We have leap-year citizens just like Easter Christians.

We have not begun to be a citizen until we communicate with our legislators, study the issues, participate in politics on the local level. Certain issues face the state today that cry for an overwhelming Christian voice. We deserve whatever black days may come upon us if we continue in the sin of silence. I'm persuaded that the blood of hundreds of persons killed on the highways will be on our hands unless we try to defeat all measures that would increase consumption of alcohol, multiply outlets, and set more drunken drivers on the roads.

We see that Christianity is social as well as individual. Caesar was not only the head of the state, he was the symbol of the social order. Our Christian religion is a religion of relationships. There is no such thing as Lone Ranger religion. It is certainly true that our faith is individual, personal but not private. God made us social beings with families, wanting friends and waiting with others. Paul reminds us that we are "members one of another" (1 Cor. 12). What affects one of us affects us all.

William Temple tells of four men in a boat, out in a lake. One man with a drill began to drill a hole beneath his seat in the boat. The others protested. He replied, "It's my boat." The others begged him to stop. He said, "I'm not bothering you." He drilled the hole. The water came in. The boat sank. They all drowned. Anything that hurts and destroys others is our concern. Legislation is now being considered that would almost double liquor consumption in this state. According to the liquor industry's own figures, the per-capita consumption in liquor-by-the-drink states is 1.8

gallons annually but in package store states only 1 gallon. We do care as Christians, because no man is an island. We are a part of one another.

We know that our belief relates to the body as well as the soul. Dr. J. M. Dawson used to say the relationship of body and soul are like the coat and its lining—you can't wrinkle one without affecting the other.

Psychiatry has been telling us of the essential unity of the mind and body . . . the interaction between the physical and emotional elements of our lives. But the Bible certainly stressed a ministry to the whole man.

Tertullian said it well: Give to Caesar what is Caesar's—his image is on the coin. Give to God what is God's—His image is on the man, yourself. He doesn't want any less than you.

> —James M. Dunn Papers, MS 632, Z. Smith Reynolds Library Special Collections and Archives, Wake Forest University, Winston-Salem NC, USA.

Notes

1. *Fort Worth Star-Telegram*, 21 February 1977, 12A.

2. Ronald J. Sider, *Rich Christians in an Age of Hunger* (Downers Grove IL: InterVarsity Press, 1977) 121.

Speeches and Interviews

This section features a collection of James Dunn's speeches and interviews covering a wide range of topics like soul freedom, Baptist identity, the Religious Right, E. Y. Mullins's six axioms of religion, and "retirement" reflections on the future of church-state separation in the United States. Recurring themes, not surprisingly, include an emphasis on the necessity of religious liberty and church-state separation and Baptist identity. In speeches and interviews, Dunn encourages Baptists to remember and live into their heritage as a free and faithful people.

After Brokenness . . . Reconciliation

James Dunn gave the address below to Texas legislators in early 1979 while serving as director of the Texas Baptist Christian Life Commission. In his remarks, Dunn speaks about reconciling polarities in the political process and society and also reminds Christians of their objective to be "responsible reconcilers"—bridge builders across troubled cultural waters.

Poor ole Harry Truman was close to the essence of all politics when he said, "I'm tired of all these two-handed fellars, it's always 'on the one hand, but on the other hand.'"

We're all tempted to look for simple, easy, one-handed answers.

We don't enjoy the heated battles that have folks on the one hand fighting tooth and nail with those on the other. We'd like to be understood by our constituents who have neat, simple answers because they don't understand the question.

Most of us have some trouble making peace, making progress, getting both hands working together for the common good after a bitterly fought election.

This difficulty does not reflect upon the character or integrity of a political person. In fact, the more deeply dedicated to goals and ideals, the more sincere, the more ethically committed to practicing what one preaches, the more the agony in the aftermath.

After brokenness . . . what?

Reconciliation.

If I had a text it would be 2 Corinthians 5:18-19, which reads in part, "From first to last this has been the work of God. He has reconciled us men to himself through Christ, and he has enlisted us in this service of reconciliation" (New English Bible). Another translation reads, "we are agents of reconciliation."

The flashing lights on the tally board revealing how legislators have voted on a particular issue tell only a tiny part of the story. Imagine three green lights in a row. Three representatives have voted the same way on bill number 666. For each of them their final vote was the result of a balancing act, a trade-off, a judgment call.

For the first it was a matter of conscious compromise that finally led to a "yes." He'd cut a deal. It was expedient to cast this vote. Hey! Don't get uppity about a dirty politician who would compromise his convictions. That's what it's all about. I give a little, you give a little, we arrive at a workable solution to the seemingly insolvable. It's not altogether bad to catch a lawmaker compromising.

For the second solon, a bit more thoughtful person, her "yes" vote represented accommodation. She had evaluated carefully the ideal, the options open at this moment in the realistic political situation, and had determined that this "yes" vote was the best she could do under the circumstances, lesser evil, half-a-loaf and all that.

For the third lawmaker, compromise and accommodation are involved. More than that, he sees his vote as reconciliation. Each vote is part of a consistent pattern. Every vote maintains tension toward an ideal not yet realized. Voting is purely motivated. All religions have the common task of combating the cancers of an amoral, materialistic, success-centered world. Religion in a democracy has the added burden of maintaining a focus on what happens to individuals, considering the spiritual dimension, taking the long look, and staying ethically sensitive to justice for all.

The three votes were all the same, well, not exactly the same even though they counted in the same column.

One was a reconciling bridge-building act of faith.

Without an awareness of polarities, there can be no deliberate reconciling role. We've grown up in a world of Greek dualism. "It's gotta be this or that." Remember that ole song?

Christianity officially conquered Gnosticism in the 4th century, yet we still follow the practice of dividing all that is into opposites. With the ancient Greeks and the modern Persians whom we're having so much trouble understanding, all the cosmos is split between the forces of Light and Darkness, Good and Evil, the spiritual and the material.

Why do you think *Star Wars* was so popular?

Legislators are sorely tempted to do the same thing. The worst stereotyping, pigeonholing, and thereby dehumanizing I've ever seen is right here in the state legislature. It's handy, convenient, saves thinking. Everyone is Republican or Democrat, Urban or Rural, Liberal or Conservative.

You don't need to try to understand or think and you don't expect the other fellow to. But our day is full of paradoxes. When we try to deal with our world in these simple terms it won't work. What happens is that we get impaled on both horns of our dilemmas.

Two conflicting viewpoints may be contrary without being contradictory. I'm not saying that there are no true contradictions, no irreconcilable concepts. One must choose between democracy and dictatorship, one or the other, not both.

We can't have peace and a small war at the same time, and it's still impossible to be slightly pregnant. But most of our day-to-day work involves reconciling polarities. Sometimes the trade-offs are a clear choice between saving dollars or saving lives. Sometimes it's easy to see that we choose between doing what is popular and what is right.

But the sort of polarities of which I speak are those that need to be held in creative tension, the ones that are not so easy to see. The serious public servant has to choose between freedom and security, conserving old values and forging ahead with new ideas, protection for the individual and concern for the public good, taking the long look and meeting immediate needs, stewardship of tax dollars and putting people ahead of things.

In this session, for instance, you face the choice of what to do for thousands of AFDC (Aid to Families with Dependent Children) recipients, most of them children. It will not be easy with the present public mood to do the right thing.

Yes, Harry, it's always those two-handed people causing trouble . . . on the one hand, but on the other hand, they challenge us to be reconcilers. This audience is particularly concerned with the tension between church-state separation on one hand and the involvement of religion in politics on the other.

We refuse the formula set out in the Third Reich: "We claim this earth, let the church have the hereafter . . . let the church preach its gospel and stay out of politics." Hitler has some unwitting apostles today even in

Texas. We come close to identifying with Archbishop William Temple's view of the church's responsibility in politics. He said, "We cannot deny the existence of (the church's) power therefore we must be good stewards of it." That's extremely difficult, but the leaders of the Texas Conference of Churches have a distinguished record of responsible stewardship in public policy concerns. Listen to them carefully.

We cannot jump on the black and white bandwagon of the electronic churchmen who have belatedly taken up an involvement in politics which they, until recently, denounced. Religion at best doesn't offer a prescription for every ailment. It does offer the qualities without which there is no solution to social, political, and economic problems. Our faith offers humane goals, a passion for justice, the sustaining power to get the job done. Religion functions best when it is teaching, persuading, setting an example, holding up ideals. We are agents of reconciliation, bridges over troubled waters.

There are three basic approaches to this reconciling mission. To some degree they are determined by personality, the situation, maybe even what you had for breakfast. There are those who sit back . . . and those who leap out . . . and others who inch forward.

The ones who sit back are in danger of being thought part of the furniture by *Texas Monthly*. "Not to decide" is itself a decision, and inaction casts a vote for the forces that happen to be winning. People of faith have special problems with passivity. Failure to work for constructive change and justice says either (1) I'm satisfied with things just as they are or (2) the God whom I serve is impotent to bring about progress.

Those who leap out are in danger of being out on a limb, all alone, well known but ineffective. If the sitters-back seldom lose (nothing ventured, nothing lost), the leapers-out seldom win. They remind us of goals and dreams and ideals and in doing so make us uncomfortable and themselves unpopular.

The persons whose strategy it is to inch forward are in danger of being caught in the crossfire, homeless in the middle. The compromiser, accommodator, reconciler also finds a lonely road as a political practitioner. For the conservatives, he's too liberal. For the liberal, he's too conservative. For the ideologue, he's wishy-washy. For the wheeler-dealer, he won't stay bought. For the uninitiated, he's incomprehensible. For the old professional, he's naïve. For the dedicated person of faith, he's responsible. That's good.

Christians and Jews share the belief that all human beings are made in the image of God (Genesis 1). Through the centuries we've never completely decided exactly what that doctrine, the *imago Dei*, means. Yet there seems to be a high consensus that it means at least that mankind is capable of responding to the Creator, response-able . . . responsible.

That's our objective, then, to be responsible reconcilers, bridges, inchers-forward. After brokenness . . . reconciliation.

—James M. Dunn Papers, MS 632, Z. Smith Reynolds Library Special Collections and Archives, Wake Forest University, Winston-Salem NC, USA.

Religious Right: Wrongly Fundamental and Fundamentally Wrong

Just a few months into his tenure as executive director of the Baptist Joint Committee, James Dunn spoke before a group of mainline Protestant leaders in Washington, D.C., where he lambasted the Religious Right and offered an introspective critique of the failure of mainline churches to be effective advocates in the public square. "It's their gnostic dualism we should denounce," Dunn said of the Religious Right during the National IMPACT briefing on March 15, 1981. This speech reveals the aggressive style and bluntness that would characterize Dunn's approach to the Religious Right and the Reagan Administration throughout the 1980s.

It's not just that the Religious Right is wrongly fundamental. I'm convinced that they are fundamentally wrong.

Taking the Religious Right as a whole, generalizing in a way that is a bit unfair as all theological characterizations of groups are, the fundamentalists who have jumped from the television tube into the political pot are guilty of a classic heresy: gnostic dualism.

We of the mainline churches have had too many concerns. We can't even keep up with them. We clearly do not spend enough energy and time on many of them to make any earthly difference. The Religious Right probably has too few issues that burden their consciences, but they certainly are not guilty, as a whole, of being one-issue people.

They have oversimplified, but that's somewhat necessary for communication.

They may have violated the spirit of religious freedom, but political involvement by churches definitely doesn't deny the principle of church-state separation.

They have certainly brought politics to a popular, emotional level in many churches, and even that may not be all bad if it challenges us to get to work at appropriate citizenship. Even in our churches, apathy is rampant. Ignorance is unbounded.

It's their gnostic dualism that we should denounce. To claim to articulate the Christian position on such a range of subjects political, social, and economic is to sin presumptuously. To make sure claims while clinging to an ancient heresy is amazing. To have snowed and intimidated so many and for so long is unbelievable.

It's time for someone to say, "The Emperor has no clothes." Look for a moment at the marks of early Gnosticism:

- It had an anti-Jewish spirit.
- It was preoccupied with sex.
- It had a complex eschatology that required the initiated to interpret.
- Its cosmology required a universe dominated by a cosmic struggle between the forces of good and evil.
- It had, therefore, a very big Devil.
- It was plagued with an immoral nostalgia, out of touch with the times in longing for the past.
- It was opposed to nature, the created order.
- It assumed certainty, rational knowledge (*gnosis*=knowledge).
- For the gnostics, woman was the chief agent of the devil.

Does that doctrinal laundry list sound familiar?

It's not necessary to dwell on all the parallels between the hoary gnostics and their modern counterparts. A few points deserve attention.

Despite all disclaimers to the contrary, there is a pervasively anti-Jewish spirit among the practitioners of much of American fundamentalism. There is a "1984-ish" double speak in their claims to love the Jews.

They seem to see the Jews not as persons, but as prospects for evangelistic conquest, or, worse, as pawns in a cosmic struggle set out in their premillennial, holy-land-centered eschatology. Either reduction, to prospects or to pawns, leaves little room for love.

In the cosmology of "good guys" and "bad guys," it's a battle between Christianity and secular humanism, freedom and godless communism, the forces of light and the forces of darkness. Satan's in control. The "Statement of Purpose" from Christian Voice reminds us that "America . . . (is) under increasing attack from Satan's forces." In fact, just listening to the sermons it seems that, as with the ancient Manicheans, God and Satan are equally strong.

If cosmological considerations were abstract, we might dwell together in peace. They're not. If these citizens are of God, then their political opponents are of Satan. That's McGovern, John Buchanan, President Carter, most of us.

The Cartesian version of this dualism offers a neat division of soul-body, mind-spirit, which underlies the preoccupation with sex. I know there may be explanations more psychological than theological. That might account for the number of right-wing leaders who have themselves fallen into trouble.

The opposition to nature has historical roots in the West going back at least to a misinterpretation of the book of Genesis when it first came out. "Have dominion over the earth and subdue it" justifies in the minds of some being undertakers rather than caretakers of the created order.

Our culture has still not overcome the gnostic heresy that woman was the chief agent of the devil. We deal with it in dozens of ways, but surely one of the most blatant affronts for Christian feminism is the "keep-women-in-their-place" mentality of the Religious Right.

The assumption of certainty was the way the gnostics got their name: know-it-alls. The confidence that they know for sure the will of God has been one of the most superficially irritating and profoundly troubling traits of the Religious Right.

We wrestle. We struggle. We pray. We study. We work for years. Why, I crowded six years of seminary study into thirteen years.

The more we know about the complicated problems of economics, politics, social unrest, the more certain we are that quick fixes and simple solutions won't work. That's exactly why we have briefings like this.

Then along come small bands who terrorize the majority. There is a real danger. It's not that the vast majority will accept their views or tactics. There's less to them than meets the eye. The danger lies in the intimidation of ordinary folks, intellectual hit lists, religious guerilla warfare. The danger lies in emotional opinions overwhelming common sense, in tolerance dominating, in the dishonesty of oversimplification, in the meanness of personal attacks, in the deceit of half-truths, in the defeat of negativism, in the destruction of extremism.

Labels libel. Watch for the name-calling that follows anyone who dares to criticize the self-confident spokesman of the Religious Right.

The dogmatic, assertive, self-confidence was both the strength and the undoing of the early gnostics and others. Reinhold Niebuhr said, "The sad experiences of Christian history show how human pride and spiritual arrogance rise to new heights precisely at the point where the claims of sanctity are made without due qualifications."

This religion of easy certainty, this packaged faith, this instant spiritual maturity is with us to some degree because it has been custom made for television. Television theology is terribly black and white.

There is an obvious and logical connection between a lowest-common-denominator religion carefully crafted for television and political polemics.

The success of the electronic church has both depended upon and resulted in legitimizing the heresy of gnostic dualism.

It's understandable in a culture already predisposed to search for simple answers and ready to follow someone who knows for sure. When even the President of the United States, a born-again Christian, admitted that he didn't have all the answers.

Along come churchmen hawking salvation, promising hope, pushing a guaranteed solution. They used all the Christian-American words. They appealed to pride and patriotism. They drafted God the Almighty on our side. They designated God as the national mascot of Christian America. They told us exactly and firmly what we must do. They offered to save the nation . . . all this and heaven, too. They remind me of a modern Tetzel. Remember him? The monk selling indulgences who ticked off Martin Luther. He preached, "Consider the salvation of your souls . . . complete remission of all sins." His famous jingle: "Soon as the coin in the coffer rings, the soul from purgatory springs."

And so much money was going in the coffer of the vendor that new coins had to be minted on the spot. And look at the budgets, the tactics, the messages of the electronic entrepreneurs. It's not that hard to understand: We're afraid of grace. We try to escape from freedom. Who doesn't want an easy answer? It's only American to engage in mail-order religion. It's nice to get a guarantee for eternity. It makes sense in a free-market economy to pay for salvation. Alas, it's a religion of the misused mind.

Market research surveys told one of the popular televangelists to go easy on the charismatic evidences, tongues, healing. It wasn't selling. So he did. Deep theological commitment.

Call the 800 free-call telephone number, if you will, to make a pledge. But don't dare use it to ask for help. There's another number, one to which you pay for the call if you want counsel. One number for p-r-a-y, one number for p-r-e-y.

Now, let's stop taking on the tactics of the Religious Right, griping about their methods accusing them of political sins of which all involved citizens are guilty to some degree.

As the ACLU said in the December 9, 1980, edition of the *New York Times,* "Even those who oppose the Bill of Rights are protected by the First Amendment. The danger lies in the content of their views not their right to express them."

Let's analyze the basic presuppositions of the Religious Right and identify it as gnostic dualism: heresy.

Now after all that, we'd better be mighty careful not to fall into the ditch on the other side of the road. If those of us related to IMPACT had done our job, this peculiar political hybrid might have never appeared. To some degree, at least, they have moved into a vacuum of inaction, apathy, and ineffectiveness. The churches and synagogues of America have failed to help persons of faith become good citizens. We have not made the connection between the biblical message and the problems of our day.

We have assumed with Ted White that "there is an intelligent answer and a moral answer to the difficult problems we face, and if we search hard enough we can find the intersection of the two."

Let's acknowledge that we've not done the job that we should have done in the churches. Let's admit that we don't like to see those millions of dollars going to the TV preachers. Let's confess to our fear of a backlash of anti-clericalism that will hit us all when folks have had enough political advice from religionists. Let's not deny at least a tinge of jealousy at their effectiveness when we've worked so hard, so long, on some issues with so little evidence of success. Let's realize that we all long for certainty, a clear word, an answer that the folks in our churches can understand and accept and that we are a little threatened by that sort of clarity.

Further, maybe we need to see that the whole phenomena may have a positive outcome. This is particularly true if certain conditions are met. The burden of measuring up to these conditions is not entirely on "them." All of us who are interested in seeing "justice roll down as the waters" have a stake in meeting the critical variables.

The other night as Bill Moyers was interviewing René Dubos, Bill quoted the "Global 2000" report [on sustainable societal development] and asked what hope there is "if present trends continue." Dubos responded, "present trends never continue." I hope he's right.

Perhaps we can have a part in seeing that present trends do not continue.

If we will rightly appeal to morality in the public policy process. We will not do that in the way some of our fundamentalist cousins have, but values, principles, biblical goals and ideas are never out of date.

If we will take the Bible seriously. Martin Marty is right: "The Bible includes 500 lines against poverty for every one line against pornography. If the New Christian Right listens to the Bible and redirects its policy, America might be better off. That would split the movement and lead to some compromise but that's what politics is all about."

If in our faithfulness to the biblical message, we will be faithful to the biblical spirit, perhaps we can be reconcilers, bridge builders.

If we will be true to the biblical appeals for justice, peace, care for creation, regard for the poor, the prisoner, the oppressed, perhaps we can share those concerns with those new to the political arena.

If we'll tell the truth. There's no place in Christian citizenship for fabrications like Mr. McAteer's about the National Council of Churches' "anti-Christian Bible" or the Reverend Falwell's self-acknowledged lies about President Carter.

If we'll not put too much faith in what government can do. All of us may have been guilty of that at one time or another. We need Niebuhr's reminder that at best government offers but "proximate solutions." Yet right now some who want government off our backs are at the same time (almost in the same breath) pushing a Human Life Amendment which would be absolutely unenforceable.

Some who see the family as God's own way of doing things, written into our very nature, are appealing for laws to prop it up as if the future of the family depends upon an act of Congress.

Some who want all to pray to a boundless, omnipotent God are pleading for government sanctions to allow Him back in the classroom. What sort of God is it who is stymied by a court decision?

If we'll fight fair. We need not appeal to hate, fear, and anger. The Religious Right has reminded us all of the power of emotions. All attempts to arouse passions are not wrong. Yet we must be careful not to fall into the trap that we've seen others fall into. Mr. McAteer says, "I use shocking letters . . . . I'm appealing to instincts" (*United Methodist Reporter,* 27 February 1981).

If we'll work even harder at a broad-based awareness of political issues and responsible reporting on the process and the politicians involved. Perhaps the single most important contribution of the Religious Right has been the new awareness of the role of religion in politics, the new assessments of issues with moral and ethical dimensions, the critical reappraisal of the relationship of church and state. Journalist Norman Cousins warns, however, that "The American tradition draws a line between religious influence and religious control."

If we'll organize, mobilize, build our networks, and involve people of goodwill to express themselves through the political process.

If we'll not let the politicians manipulate and use the church. Did you see Senator Patrick Leahy's splendid column, "The Church We Love Is Being Used," in last Sunday's *Washington Post*?

A nationally known journalist friend of mine was at the now famous Religious Roundtable National Affairs Briefing last August in Dallas. He's been in the heat of the political fray for the last thirty years. He said he'd never seen so many of the old line, old right extremists under one roof at any time in his life . . . consultants, party hacks, P.R. men, errand boys for the wealthy political machinery. Suddenly born again for that evangelical gathering? Hardly!

The secular, hardline extremists have admitted to or claimed credit for the mobilization and manipulation of the Religious Right and yet they, the preachers, deny it. But wait, it's a danger that should be instructive. It could happen to anyone. Careful.

I think there's something particularly sad about the marriage of the religious community with laissez-faire, ultra-conservative politics. The cold-heartedness of economic ideology reminds me of a Charles Dickens quote: "'It's God for us all and everyone for himself,' said the elephant as she danced among the chickens."

I think of two men: one a missionary I knew. It was my first class in seminary. He was a missionary to West Africa, home on furlough, working on a seminary degree. He was sort of a hero for me. He was dealing with hunger, racism, political turmoil; he'd daringly planted his life in a difficult place, turned his back on materialism, was literally a peacemaker in a troubled, war-torn country.

The first quiz came along and he took advantage of the honor system. When the professor left the room, he took out his notes and cheated on a test over the Ten Commandments.

The other man I didn't know, but I heard about him the same time some of you did; one April afternoon on NBC Monitor radio, he came to national attention. He was a decent family man, a respectable, upstanding citizen in the community; didn't drink, didn't cheat on his wife, respected by everyone, a deacon in his church.

But that afternoon everyone learned about him because he wrapped a bullwhip around the face of a fellow deacon from a sister church who started to walk across the Edmund G. Pettus Bridge.

Seems that one crowd sees sex, drugs, alcohol, pornography as sin; the other sees materialism, militarism, racism, rape of the environment as sin.

And both may be guilty of gnostic dualism.

We don't have to choose between personal morality and social concern. If either is genuine the other is implied. Both are rooted in the same compassion for all God's children. That compassion is born of a sense of oneness with the human family.

We're in it together. We'd better make the most of it.

—James M. Dunn Papers, MS 632, Z. Smith Reynolds Library Special Collections and Archives, Wake Forest University, Winston-Salem NC, USA.

Six Simple Axioms

James Dunn was a frequent keynote speaker at Baptist denominational meetings and other Baptist gatherings throughout his ministry and especially during his tenure as executive director of the Baptist Joint Committee. In 1991, he gave the following address at a meeting of the American Baptist Churches U.S.A. In typical fashion, Dunn devoted much of his address to preaching soul freedom and lifting up E. Y. Mullins's six "axioms of religion" central to the Baptist faith.

General Secretary Weiss, I'm genuinely glad to be here, and that ain't just woofing. Woofing. I'll tell you, I'll tell you for certain, I remember . . . sometimes she was in the office next to ours in the Baptist building in Dallas. I'd come in, and just making small talk, you know, being nice, I'd ask her about her husband, Burt. I'd say, "Anna-Jo, how's Burt?" She'd say, "Compared to what?" Well, let me tell you, compared to some conventions I've been to, John Denver is right. This is almost heaven. Almost heaven,

I'll tell you. That's true. I'm not kidding you. I am genuinely glad to be here.

Norman DePuy brings a news item from Germany about a pastor who was severely reprimanded by his bishop for baptizing cats, thus implying that they'll have eternal life, which I'm sure the cats considered a singular improvement on the traditional nine. According to the January 26th *New York Times*, the Lutheran pastor was held to be, quote, "Highly theologically suspect." I should think so. But then Baptists think baptizing anything without personal faith is highly suspect. Thus, we don't baptize infants or, of course, cats and such mindless creatures who would, for Baptists, fall in the same category as infants.

The German pastor explained that he baptized those cats at the request of elderly parishioners. Now picture, if you would, baptizing a Baptist cat by immersion. Quite apart from the heresy, you'd better sedate that sucker before you go sprinkling water on him and waving your hands over him, to say nothing about dipping him under to be raised in newness of life. I think the cats would just as soon pass up heaven as be baptized by immersion, as would many people of my acquaintance, and I suspect of yours.

Many people do indeed shudder at the word "Baptist." They think of all that water and a lot of other things about us. And yet Martin Marty wrote of the Baptistification of America. He reflected upon those qualities of Baptists, on our good days, at least, those beliefs and practices of Baptists at our best that have been taken up by others. We do have, as has been said so well and eloquently by our general secretary tonight, a message that's peculiarly suited for today. It's as if our beliefs were crafted for this time and place. What is it about us that both repels and attracts? What do we see as our birthright that some see as a wart?

There is a Baptist-shaped empty place in the American head. There is a Baptist meal to satisfy the 1990s hungers. There is a picture puzzle match between the questions that we've always asked and the yearnings of our neighbors. Listen, the promise of new life in Christ, a revitalized church that we've heard spoken of so movingly this week, can hug at the heartstrings of the most jaded and cynical searcher.

For the experience-starved seeker who can't be satisfied with less than immediacy in religion, you know, a warm cozy feeling and a lot of navel gazing, ours is an experiential faith overshadowed by a transaction of grace, marked by a defining moment, a hinge in each of our histories and each of our personal stories. For the New Ager who hankers for historical connectedness and continuity, we are, in the words of the Gospel song . . . I can almost sing it but not quite . . . taught by the Bible, led by the spirit, we walk the heavenly way. You've heard it. In the great stream of witnesses from time immemorial, we're part of an unbroken line. For the victim of anomie seeking community, starved to death for that oneness of family, we're a part of a family of faith, of one blood, all nations. For the drifting and purposeless, there's direction and meaning in sharing the love of Jesus Christ.

We share many dimensions of faith with all believers, but one message is distinctively Baptist. One element holds us together and thrusts us apart. It's at the same time our best contribution and our most troublesome characteristic. What is this two-edged sword? What is both our greatest strength and one of our greatest weaknesses? Our common bond is almost surely our refusal to be bound, and our denial of any commonness. Roger Williams called it "soul liberty." Loosely translated, our most popular creed as Baptists is, in the vernacular, "Ain't nobody going to tell me what to believe."

And so we come together, every time we get together as a bunch of Baptists, to celebrate freedom. We love to quote 2 Corinthians 3:17: "Where the spirit of the Lord is, there is freedom." And we never question that we're there where the spirit of the Lord is. But soul freedom is not without form and void. It has some shape. E. Y. Mullins, who like Norm DePuy was pastor for a spell at the church at Newton's Corner, gave some shape to this Baptist bundle of beliefs that are all strung together and held together by the thin thread of freedom in his lectures before the American Baptist Education Society in St. Louis in 1905, which were later published by Judson Press in 1908 as *The Axioms of Religion.*

His six simple axioms all hinge on freedom and suggest a theology for the next century, maybe the next millennium, a message worthy of American Baptists. Now, I know Mullins could not prescribe Baptist beliefs. No one can do that. We've been reminded of that powerfully today, haven't we? No one can prescribe Baptist beliefs, but he did tellingly describe our doctrine and our ideological idiosyncrasies or, as one of my former associates called them, among Baptists, our idiosyn-crazies. Here are his six axioms.

The theological axiom: God is free. All freedom begins with God. God is holy, completely other. God is love, God is unconditioned, unconditional. God is all-powerful, all-present, all-knowing. All our freedom, then, is derived in the light of our being made somehow in the image of God. Because God is free and we replicate God, we reflect God, we bear in our very beings the image of God, we all participate in that freedom. And so this understanding of soul liberty that Roger Williams appealed to has deep, deep theological roots in the very person of God.

Then the religious axiom: every human being is free to come directly to God. So then all missions and evangelism that we've celebrated so beautifully and then again tonight are predicated upon the essentially voluntary response to the gospel. One follows Jesus Christ freely or not really. We all bear the challenge of the great commission personally and directly to go ye therefore and make disciples. Each one of us who's been born again can say, "I have found the messiah," and because we can, we must.

Each one of us individually is the world's leading authority on at least one subject—what God has done for me. No one on earth can challenge that. You are the absolute expert. No one can refute your testimony or deny your firsthand knowledge. I'm in a room tonight of the world's leading authorities on what God has done for you, for me. To what purpose is this great gift of freedom if we don't exercise our witness freely? Every human being is free to come directly to God, and, conversely, no one comes to God any other way except personally and freely.

The ecclesiological or church axiom: all believers have a right to equal privileges in the church. Baptists have historically been an equal-rights religion. Isn't that right?

We the church have real problems with explosive soul freedom, don't we? Some churches deny it, some disciple it, some creedalize it. German theologian Ernst Käsemann says,

> What gives most trouble to Christians of all epochs is neither lack of faith nor excess of criticism, it's Jesus himself. He bestows freedom so openhandedly and dangerously on those who don't know what to do with it, the church gets panic-stricken for fear of the turmoil that Jesus creates when he comes on the scene, and so it takes his freedom under its own management for the protections of the souls entrusted to it, and in order to dispense it, it doses it out when it seems necessary. Jesus' very gift of freedom is taboo.

Jesus' freedom, to us, is not always spoken of so clearly by German theologians. Sometimes I think the hymns say it better for me: "There's a wideness in God's mercy like the wideness of the sea. There's a kindness in his justice which is more than liberty. But we make his love too narrow by false limits of our own, and we magnify his strictness with a zeal he will not own." All of us need to learn the grace of acceptance, not arrogantly attempting to improve upon God's free grace.

Marty's Baptistification particularly relates to this axiom, because it includes democracy and autonomy and the priesthood of all believers and an open Bible and the right of private interpretation and the unhindered gospel and the inviolability of individual conscience—all beliefs that are traced to Baptist beginnings, as we read just a moment ago, that have now found acceptance in most American denominations. Why, Roman Catholics read the Bible for themselves, and Methodists and Presbyterians authorize local church autonomy, and all kinds of churches practice congregational democracy, a good Baptist principle.

The fourth axiom is that moral axiom: to be responsible, one must be free. No matter how thin you may slice the coin of responsible freedom, it still has two sides. Every freedom carries with it a piggybacked responsibility, and every responsibility implies a certain freedom, and so they go together indispensably, indissolubly. Freedom and responsibility are inseparable. No one's free as a bird. Only birds are free as a bird. We share, in Emil Brunner's words, the awesome burden of freedom.

That responsible freedom calls forth a stewardship. A stewardship of the creation. We're to be caretakers, not undertakers, of the environment. We dare not take second place to the politicians and the scientists in the care of the environment that God has given us. We're to be stewards of our material possessions. We must live more simply that others may simply live. Bread for the World should not simply be the name of a wonderful Christian hunger lobby; it ought to be the goal of every American Baptist.

We're called to a responsible stewardship of our citizenship. Our stewardship of influence should make the work of Bob Tiller and Carol Franklin [American Baptist leaders] in government relations easy because what they do is not dirty politics; it's calling us all to our basic responsibility. Tonight, we've once again been reminded that a good slogan like that in the denomination in which I grew up should be "Every Baptist a tither." That's a good slogan. One dear old brother in our church didn't understand it. He said, "What is this new sticker we've got up everywhere that says every Baptist a-tither?" The speaker reminded us a moment ago: we should all be volunteers. "Every Baptist a volunteer" would be a good motto. But "Every Baptist a lobbyist" because that's simply doing our Christian duty. Every Baptist a lobbyist. We are stewards of these citizenship and material blessings and environment and everything that comes our way.

Then the religio-political axiom: a free church in a free state. Some Baptists have forgotten our roots and turned away from our heritage and forsaken our tradition. We'd better not think that we're immune to the infection of civil religion. That mixing of pietism and patriotism until you can't tell the difference is pretty dangerous. It borders on nationolatry in which God becomes the national mascot. It sneaks up on you.

Now, here are some pitfalls to avoid, as seen from the pit. Listen, folks. This isn't going to be popular, and some of you are going to fuss at me tomorrow about this. But first you'll hear talk of a Christian nation and godly men. It's always men. And God's laws. Now don't forget that nations can't be Christian, only people can be Christian, and that God's laws are spiritual and never enforced by the state. "Not by might nor by power but by my spirit," says the Lord. The next step on that slippery slope toward civil religion is that diversity is denied and pluralism is seen as a bad word, and the state of government staying out of religion is called secularism, and that's made a dirty word, and public schools are seen as evil. There are people who'd much rather gripe about the public schools than do anything about it through the PTA or anything else.

Then majority rule is magnified to the very point of minority ruin. Majority rules, majority rules. I've heard that so much I've wondered if they've ever heard of the First Amendment. And history is revised to make the Founding Fathers our battery of saints. Now, don't you think that our brand of Baptists, American Baptists, are safe from this uninformed extremism? It could happen here, folks. If you want to have some early warnings, check to see how many folks in your church are paying attention to those radio and television salesmen who pitch political extremism for the buck that's in it and for the emotional buzz it'll give you.

We've got some folks who think Roger Williams is a pianist who plays "Autumn Leaves." We've got some people who don't know James Dobson from James Madison, and, let me tell you, there's a big difference. We've got some people who would take their theology for church and society from Pat Robertson instead of from Walter Rauschenbusch and that's no good.

But religious freedom is also at risk today from a Supreme Court which seems to have forgotten religious liberty and is little interested in defending it. In his *Wallace v. Jaffree* dissent, Mr. Rehnquist, now the Chief Justice, says, "The wall of separation between church and state is a metaphor based on bad history, a metaphor which has proved useless as a guide to judging. It should be frankly and explicitly abandoned." But Baptists were the ones to whom Jefferson wrote first of the wall of separation between church and state.

And Mr. Scalia, in *Oregon v. Smith*, a decision that gutted the free exercise from the First Amendment, called traditional protection for religious minorities "a luxury that we can no longer afford." He would abolish the requirement that government demonstrate a compelling state interest before meddling in religion and limiting religious liberty. Baptists don't want government intrusion. The latest voucher scheme put forth by the Department of Education [of the President George H. W. Bush administration] would be one more way of funneling public funds into private and parochial schools, and, like other such approaches, it'd be unconstitutional and regressive and unfair and discriminatory and destructive of the public schools, and divisive of the religious community and expensive and inflationary. Other than that, it might be all right.

Except that it would bring the inevitable regulations that always follow tax dollars, and Baptists have always rejected such aid and such regulation. Separation of church and state indeed. Now the Solicitor General would offer us a coercion test, whatever that means, to protect religious freedom. No longer, if this administration has its way, would a law have to have a secular purpose, neither advance nor inhibit religion, and avoid excessive church-state entanglement. I'm convinced that American Baptists will not remain silent in the face of this attempt to turn the wall of separation into one single strand of barbed wire.

Then there's the social axiom: love your neighbor as yourself. Mullins picked a pretty good source for that. Our ecumenism is based on the love that binds all believers together, but all our ecumenism rolled together is too limited a notion for this axiom. In the words of Chesterton, "We're all in a small boat on a stormy sea, and we owe each other terrible loyalty." We offer that loyalty willingly and freely and gladly. Our togetherness is free, not forced. We come together in the family of faith because we may, not because we must. With integrity, we bring our gifts to the family table, not part of a melting pot and not part of a stew or a bourguignon.

Each of these axioms that Mullins gave us, then, represent a corollary, a consequence, a component of that soul freedom that he insisted was the banner of Baptists. A God who is free, a people who freely follow, affording real freedom to every other believer, accepting the responsibility of freedom and extending it through the separation of church and state to everyone, and lovingly pursuing the liberation of all through this family of faith. That's our goal. Where the spirit of the Lord is, there is freedom. It's the freedom at the heart of our humanity, made in the image of God. It's the freedom that offers hope for eternity, the predication of all missions and evangelism. It's the freedom that gives meaning to our integrity.

That freedom, for Baptists, rests ultimately in a life-changing relationship with the living Lord. No creed or church, no pastor or priest, no book or belief, no deeds or discipline but Jesus Christ is the guarantor of our freedom, the hope of our salvation. It's Jesus.

> Not what, but Whom, I do believe
>> That in my darkest hour of need
>> Hath comfort that no mortal creed
>> To mortal man may give:—
> Not what, but Whom!
>> For Christ is more than all the creeds,
>> And his full life of gentle deeds
>> Shall all the creeds outlive.
> Not what I do believe, but Whom!
>> Who walks beside me in the gloom?
>> Who shares the burden wearisome?
>> Who all the dim way doth illume
>> And bids me look beyond the tomb
>> The larger life to live?—
> Not what I do believe,
> But Whom!
> Not what,
> But Whom!
>
> — "Credo," John Oxenham

Not what but whom.

> —James M. Dunn Papers, MS 632, Z. Smith Reynolds Library Special Collections and Archives, Wake Forest University, Winston-Salem NC, USA.

Religious Freedom Award Response

James Dunn offered this response on September 2, 1999, upon being honored by Associated Baptist Press with its Religious Freedom Award. He colorfully shares stories and remembers his eighteen years as head of the Baptist Joint Committee.

If when the books are closed, the final thirty is written, and we know how it all came out; if when we see, no longer through a dark glass, that some good has been done; if some evils have been averted and some harm avoided, it will be perfectly clear that many people have been a part of the process.

Converging circumstances counted for a lot of what's taken place.

At a farewell party for Congressman Richard Bolling of Missouri in the early Reagan years, I was whining. Fred Wertheimer of Common Cause said, "Dunn, stop complaining; our sad plight just means that we've never been more needed." I described the debaptistification of the Southern Baptist Convention to Martin Marty and he responded, "James, just remember you don't know enough to be totally pessimistic." Maybe not. It is clear that I have had the good fortune to be in the right place at the right time.

Time for the Baptist word came due and it was simply my job to say it . . . and to say it when not many others were. (I must admit here, however, that most fearless friends who were trying to get out the same sort of message didn't have a Stan Hastey, Larry Chesser, Pam Parry, or Kenny Byrd not only to turn it into news but to egg me on, say "sic 'em" to this watchdog.) Many of you in this room gutsily got out the word. That's the journalist's job.

Then, I had the incomparable blessing of having spent two years learning everything I could about Joseph Martin Dawson; did my doctoral dissertation on him in 1966, thanks to Jimmy Allen who shoved me into doing it.

I had drunk deep at the Dawson well fourteen years before anyone even mentioned my coming to the BJC. Dawson had been its first executive, 1946–1953. So for the first year or two in his chair, I just did what he did and said what he had said. It got me in trouble.

So, when y'all say nice things, and awards and unearned doctorates come my way, it seems to me as if you are giving me credit for choosing my grandfather well or picking my predecessor wisely.

But we do have some stewardship of all experience. We always need to ask, as Jeanette Holt does, "Now, what can we learn from this?" Not as some fatalist with Calvinistic certainty that God, the "heavenly computer," mixes, matches, and merges our lives like little puzzle pieces to be put in their proper places, but by looking back so that we see some other things more clearly.

They did try to do us in.

At one point the fundamentalists who set out to destroy the mission and message of the Baptist Joint Committee demanded a list of all the periodicals subscribed to by the BJC. They asked for three years of all correspondence to or from the Committee (Fat chance!). Paige Patterson, president of the Southern Baptist Convention, told the *Houston Post* (June 12, 1982) when asked about me, "There will be something done to silence him." The outrages continue: boycott Disney, target Jews, keep women submissive, beat up on gays.

One concludes, then, that to be a whistle blower on anti-Baptists trying to pass for the real thing is not for the fainthearted; no room for a fence-straddling, word-mincing, soft-spoken, pseudo-Baptist.

Stubbornness may be the most needed "gift of the Spirit." Those scriptural gifts of the Spirit are mediated to us by mere mortals. Indulge me as I catalog a few of those human shapers of this stubborn so-and-so.

Through Mother and my milkman Daddy, God sent leanliness. They helped this Depression baby put material matters in perspective. Mother, whom I never heard curse or say a dirty word, taught my sister and me that "shooey" (her word) happens. I was scrawny, sickly, but a tough little kid, the last one chosen to play on every team, the first one beat up by the bully of the month. I got even tougher in Ernest Parker Junior High, wonderfully 70 percent Hispanic. To prevent certain indignities in 9th grade P.E. classes, I bought protection from Frank Escalante and Steve Coronado by doing their algebra for them. Those other "machos" had better not mess with me, and they didn't.

Years later, Phil Strickland and I worked that demonstration plot for original sin, that laboratory for total depravity known as the Texas legislature. So I was for twelve years politically immersed in Austin working with and on people like John B. Connally and Rep. Bill Heatly, the Duke of Paducah, whose head was memorialized in the State House of Representatives as the "state rock."

Then, Foy Valentine and Jimmy Allen, great coaches, helped me see that perception is everything in politics and political effectiveness depends upon what they (the politicians) think you can deliver, but that you shouldn't lie. You don't speak for Baptists. You only speak to Baptists. When Richard

Land says, "speaking for 16 million Southern Baptists" or "most Baptists believe," as he does, he misrepresents reality.

Let's face it. All of us added together who share a passion for soul freedom make up a tiny minority even among Baptists. Our kind always has been outnumbered, likely always will be. The only authority we have is the authority of veracity. We count on truth telling and what rings true in fellow believers' innards.

That leads me to theology and the idea so passionately shared with me by Stewart Newman and Bill Estep. This Baptist belief in religious liberty is not just "doctrine," or the First Amendment, or a political elective. It is, rather, the Baptist basic: soul freedom. Each individual comes immediately to God. All vital religion is voluntary. Even God Almighty will not trample an individual's freedom to say "yes" or "no" to God.

I've come, under their tutelage and that of Dawson and Maston, to believe that there is no such thing as "'required religion" (except, of course, in some colleges), no such thing as "forced fellowship" or "coerced community." All those phrases are oxymorons, and folks who think they can force, coerce, or require them are ordinary morons.

Then T. B. Maston, my major professor, and H. Richard Niebuhr Ph.D., nudged a lot of us into the real world. He taught us that "there is nothing inherently evil about compromise unless we lose sight of the ideal," that we live with creative tension, that "the Bible is a divine-human book."

Then, there is this 8th-century prophet, Bill Moyers, born out of due season. Bill, without any doubt and as a matter of fact attested to by all sorts of authorities, is the prophetic voice of the last quarter of the 20th century. So, when Bill, my friend, indicates that he thinks the stuff I'm doing is OK, that gives me more than a smattering of confidence.

Finally, Marilyn, as uninhibited as her father, well almost. . . . She is "no respecter of persons" in the best biblical sense.

I'm really not trying to avoid responsibility for my doings in the nineteen years at the BJC but to say again when the books are closed that if we've done any good, you and those I've mentioned deserve the credit and the blame. We're in it together and we still face serious challenges.

There are Democrats, even Vice President Gore, who according to what I fervently hope was one sadly misguided foray in Georgia, would trade off the separation of church and state for a mess of Senator Ashcroft's "charitable choice" pottage. To funnel tax dollars directly into "faith-based" programs effectively neuters their first name: "Faith."

Republicans have made their first priority the passage of education vouchers, massively misled by the one church that owns 90 percent of the parochial schools. Few friends of vouchers will say the Roman Catholic Church desperate to save its schools has partnered with fundamentalist Christians seeking public money for their segregation academies: a marriage made in hell.

I was saddened by all the carrying on when a federal judge in Cleveland ruled a voucher scheme unconstitutional. Remember the Katzenjammer kids. Rollo and Hans and Otto were always into some mischief, and the last frame of the cartoon carried the same moral every week: "They brung it on themselves." They did.

Folks in both parties in Kansas, for instance, have placed a premium on ignorance for the sake of "creationism."

Then, following the flavor of the year in righteous outrage, scores of parroting preachers speak of the "clear teaching of Scripture" characterizing biblical passages that arguably might deal with homosexuality. Serious scholars suggest that violence, idolatry, prostitution, and pederasty contextually crowd those debatable verses. But there are clear teachings, not in question, condemning adultery, divorce, greed, and mistreatment of the poor, slighted by church leaders who skew the Scriptures for their own agenda.

We have a lot to do. In Chesterton's words, "We're all in small boats on a stormy sea and we owe each other a terrible loyalty."

—Reprinted with permission of the
Christian Ethics Today Foundation

Interview with *The Whitsitt Journal*

James Dunn gave a wide-ranging interview to The Whitsitt Journal, *the publication of the William H. Whitsitt Baptist Heritage Society, in 2000 following his retirement as executive director of the Baptist Joint Committee. In this interview conducted by John Finley, then senior minister of First Baptist Church, Savannah, Georgia, Dunn shares about his formative influences, reflects on his tenure at the BJC, and offers his thoughts on current and future threats to religious freedom and church-state separation. At the time of this interview, Dunn had just joined the faculty of the Wake Forest University School of Divinity as visiting professor of Christianity and public policy.*

Whitsitt Journal: What would you say have been the formative persons and experiences in your life?

James Dunn: My godly parents, William and Edith Dunn, obviously forged a set of pious presuppositions that have shaped me, served me well, and kept me in trouble most of my life. Daddy was a milkman most of his days, and Mother was a stay-at-home mom. My childhood church's minister of music, Dr. Edwin McNeely, a professor at Southwestern Seminary, was a role model in his uninhibited cussedness accompanied by his passionate personal faith. I married his only daughter forty-two years ago.

Then, my college major professor, Dr. Walter Glick, taught me to read discriminatingly and mainlined into my veins his love of history. My present dean at Wake Forest Divinity School, Bill Leonard, majored with the same man at Texas Wesleyan College, several years later. But T. B. Maston, master teacher and role model of Christian Ethics at Southwestern, mapped out and imprinted on my soul the discipline for the rest of my days.

Formative experiences must include conversion and careful nurture in a warm, wholesome church, Evans Avenue Baptist Church, Fort Worth, Texas; marriage to a deeply dedicated wife, Marilyn McNeely, December 19, 1958; and a bout with invasive melanoma in 1974 that gave me the opportunity to revise my theology and jettison the extraneous.

WJ: You stand in a long line of Texans like J. M. Dawson, E. Y. Mullins, Foy Valentine, Bill Moyers, and others who have emphasized the importance of religious liberty issues and the separation of church and state. What accounts for the strong interest and influence of Texas Baptists in this particular area?

JD: Texans and Baptists were made for each other. The frontier produced hearty people, survival of the fittest. Baptists brought an accessible, non-creedal theology, an ain't-nobody-but-Jesus going to tell me what to do ethic, and left a vast network of self-governing churches. Texas Baptists, as few others, capture the essence of what it means to be Baptist.

Roger Williams did not understand "free church" as well. E. Y. Mullins (a Texas Aggie) in *Axioms of Religion* came close to putting on paper the distinctiveness of Baptists. Two modern apologists, Bill Leonard and Bill Moyers, Texas Baptists, are infected with the ethos. Yet, maybe, like all attempts to explain God, Texas Baptist beliefs and passions are finally incomprehensible. An incarnational sally might help catch the spirit of Texas Baptists.

T. B. Maston, mentioned above and his PhDs like Foy Valentine and Jimmy R. Allen and forty-eight others took on the Baptist Zion for freedom and integrity and shook it considerably.

James H. Landes and W. F. Howard, representatives of the best of Baptist bureaucrats, understood, blessed, and funded feisty, the natural disposition of Texans.

Phil Strickland, of the Texas Baptist Christian Life Commission since 1967, has politicized, institutionalized, and made indispensable the Maston/Texas Baptist spirit.

WJ: Undoubtedly, the work of the Baptist Joint Committee on Public Affairs has had some constants which did not change while you were there, but how is its work different now than when you began in January 1981?
JD: The work of the BJC over the last twenty years became more activistic than academic; focused more on cooperation with any and all organizations that shared single-issue goals and objectives. This meant doing much of our work in single-issue coalitions (over those years working to some degree with over three hundred institutions or organizations). Because of the expertise of staff and the long history of ecumenical cooperation, many of the efforts for religious freedom were chaired or co-chaired by BJC staff. We responded to national media more than ever before and more than any other Baptist entity and narrowed, of necessity, the program assignment to strictly church-state, religious freedom issues.

WJ: What have been the proudest accomplishments during your tenure at the Baptist Joint Committee?
JD: Proudest accomplishments would include building a stellar staff; providing an opportunity for over 150 interns; offering an understandable balance between the "no establishment" and "free exercise" aspects of church-state law; leading in the passage of "Equal Access" legislation that assures public school students of free-exercise rights and leading in the defeat of the attempts to allow government to prescribe "school prayer"; helping Baptist historians like Ed Gaustad, Bill Estep, Walter B. Shurden, Everett Goodwin, Stan Hastey, Leon McBeth, and others get the true Baptist message out; organizing the Religious Liberty Council, the membership arm of the BJC; and survival, without which none of the above would have taken place.

WJ: What are the hotspots in religious liberty issues just now?

JD: The hottest of the hotspots is the serious threat of spending tax dollars for parochial purposes. Every dollar of public money (taken by force as it must be) spent for religious, "faith-based," church purposes is a blatant violation of the separation of church and state. Voucher schemes for education, "Charitable Choice" for social ministry, and county commissioners paving the church parking lot should be rejected.

WJ: During the 2000 presidential campaign, much has been made of the visit by Governor George W. Bush to Bob Jones University in the context of that institution's opposition to Roman Catholicism and interracial dating. Help us to sort out the issues involved in political candidates seeking the endorsement of various religious groups.

JD: Churches are free to endorse candidates if they choose that option. They will and should then give up their 501(c)3 status and the deduction that donors to the churches claim on their taxes. Churches can educate, inform, train in good citizenship, discuss issues, provide for candidates, even register voters. They should not endorse candidates even more for the sake of the church's witness than legal concerns.

WJ: At the height of the struggle over Solidarity in Poland, [Polish activist] Lech Walesa was asked by a reporter what he was afraid of, what kept him up at night. He answered, "I fear God, and I sleep very well at night." As you look at the landscape of church and state concerns, are there things that genuinely cause you to worry about the future?

JD: The lack of Baptist understanding of how fragile religious freedom is and the lack of Baptist understanding of our own distinctives, lacunae a plenty. Recent Baptist history with the fundamentalist takeover of denominational institutions, political embarrassments like Mr. Gingrich, Mr. Lott, Mr. Helms, and others, inappropriate engagements in the political arena (like those of the Ethics and Religious Liberty Commission of the Southern Baptist Convention) all evidence a tragic erosion of Baptist dedication to religious liberty for everyone.

And so, some otherwise right-thinking Baptists want to hunker down and resource the local church, largely forsaking public witness. Others would follow a megachurch model and deny any doctrinal identity at all. Still others would lose themselves in navel-gazing "spirituality." Oh, for the days of Baptist Training Union when we knew who we were!

WJ: In the foreword to Mark W. Witten's new book, *The Myth of Christian America*, you mention that the future of church-state relationships may be better characterized as a "barbed wire fence" than a "wall." I assume you mean that separation needs to continue but that if and when we cross that barrier we need to do so carefully?

JD: I said "bob war" until I was sixteen years old and learned it's "barbed wire." Whether we have a high and impregnable wall, a wall with doors in it, a zone, or just a barbed wire fence, we still need to keep church and state separate. Institutions of government and those of religion need some distance between them. They have different constituencies, different purposes, different funding methods, and different ways of operating. They are separate, have been, should be.

As Gardner Taylor says, church and state should be separate enough that "neither can hold the other in a bear hug."

WJ: You don't seem like a person who is ready to be put on the shelf, and a number of your friends must be asking what you plan to do now that you have retired from the BJC. How would you like to spend this next chapter of your life and what would you like to accomplish?

JD: I am happily being recycled as Professor of Christianity and Public Policy at the Divinity School of Wake Forest University. It is an exciting place to be: genuinely ecumenical, the best qualified students, great faculty colleagues. I am looking for students who will be missionaries for the best of Baptist traditions in the pluralistic culture of today.

WJ: Brent Walker and the staff of BJC seem to be nice people with enormous talent for continuing the legacy. What do you wish for them and the BJC? What kind of advice would you give them?

JD: First, I wish for the BJC of the future enough financial support to do its job well without constantly having to cut corners and hold back on travel, publications, and conferences. The money is "out there" in the hands of Baptists who believe in what the BJC does. If only those who say encouraging words would write encouraging checks, the BJC would be set free to be what it ought to be.

Then, I pray now that survival seems assured, that the BJC will do a far better job of educating Baptists about basic Baptist beliefs on religious liberty than I was able to do.

It would be grossly presumptuous for me to give the staff advice. We have worked together for ten to twenty years. They know all too well what

I think, what I pray, how I feel. They know that I trust them. Pray for the BJC.

—Reprinted with permission.

Religious Liberty as a Baptist Distinctive

James Dunn delivered the following address at the annual conference of the Texas Baptist Christian Life Commission on February 12, 2001, at Tarrytown Baptist Church in Austin, Texas. Throughout the 1990s and into the 2000s, Dunn would frequently share a version of this address when speaking at churches and denominational groups. In the aftermath of the "Battle for the Bible" that splintered the Southern Baptist Convention, Dunn understood the necessity of being an evangelist for soul freedom, seizing opportunities to preach about the theological foundations and political implications of religious liberty.

There is an unbroken chain from the historical and theological starting point for Baptists: soul freedom to religious liberty for all and its necessary corollary, separation of church and state.

See three concentric circles like the movement in water when a pebble hits a pond. The center circle is the point of impact, representing the experience of one person with the Divine, the central event of one's life, an Act of God's Grace, the immediate engagement of heaven with earth: soul freedom.

The inevitable ripple, the next circle out, represents the certain consequences of a saving faith, the moral, ethical, and social result of an individual encounter with God. Loving one's neighbor as self, doing unto others as one would be done unto, we call it religious liberty.

The third ring is as logical and theological in sequence. Because human beings are frail and fallible, limited and sinners all, because God has ordained both church and state, because their purposes, constituencies, functions, and fundings are different from each other, the separation of church and state follow as night follows day.

Baptists do not base our basic belief in church-state separation on some enlightenment theory or implied social contract. We lean not merely on the Constitution and Bill of Rights, or even on a biblical passage. We do not pretend to depend on some experiential pragmatism, claiming to have discovered that it works. *(It does, but our foundation for freedom is firmer.)*

We root our soul freedom in the very nature and person of God. We and all three religions of the book affirm the *imago Dei*, the radical idea that we are somehow "made in the image of God." We know that one major meaning of that belief is that we are able to respond to God—response-able, responsible, and free. We are wired up with a chooser and we live with the consequences of those choices.

F. J. Sheed said, "Being human is itself so vast a thing that the natural inequalities from one of us to the other are in themselves trivial." All made like God—persons and free, indeed.

There is in each of us a God-shaped empty place that can be filled only by the Divine. But it's more than a piece of a puzzle, a pattern, a cut-and-dried Calvinistic plan. It's the living energy, the dynamic dimension, the vital voluntary nature, the heart of our humanity that signals always beep-beep—made in God's Image. That's the living truth of soul freedom.

At least the idea is worth investigating that each individual has the ability to find answers in the Bible, exercise the centrality of religious liberty, hold to the sacredness of individual conscience in matters of religion, and practice the separation of church and state.

Soul Freedom

God refuses to violate one's moral nature even in order to save him. That base-line belief gets at the heart of soul freedom; it's gospel—remember the rich young ruler.

Martin Marty in a well-known article, "Baptistification Takes Over" (1983), points out that this emphasis is not new. St. Bernard in his *Treatise Concerning Grace and Free Will* wrote, "Take away free will and there remaineth nothing to be saved. Salvation is given by God alone, and it is given only to the free will." As Marty puts it, to "make Baptist" whether or not it meant joining a Baptist church "zeroed in on the key issue that modernity posed for religion: choice."

E. Y. Mullins set out in *The Axioms of Religion* (1908): the doctrine of [the] soul's competency in religion under God as the distinctive historical significance of the Baptists. We call it soul freedom.

Hear the testimonies of the scholars:

Robert Bellah (1997): "What was so important about the Baptists was the absolute centrality of religious freedom of the sacredness of individual conscience in matters of religious beliefs."

H. Wheeler Robinson: "The biblical significance of the Baptists in the right of private interpretation [of] and obedience to the Scriptures. The significance of the Baptists to the individual is soul freedom. The political significance of the Baptists is separation of church and state."

Fisher Humphreys sums up soul freedom as "the freedom, ability and responsibility of each person to respond to God for herself or himself."

Walter B. Shurden contends for the patent principle if one accepts biblical authority. The appeal of soul freedom to Baptists is anchored in "the nature of God, the nature of humanity, and the nature of faith."

Bill J. Leonard echoes: "Faith is the free response of persons to the gift of God's love. Such faith cannot be compelled by church or state."

This doctrine of soul freedom has immediate, unfiltered application to Baptist battles. Harold Bloom, America's best-known literary critic, sees "Mullins' concept of 'soul competence' destroying fundamentalism" because it "sanctions endless interpretive possibilities, the weird metaphor of a 'literal' or 'inerrant' reading totally vaporizes." Even Karl Barth told Louie Newton, "How I thank God for Mullins. [He] gave the world a mighty phrase, 'the competency of the soul.'" One cannot improve on Mullins's definitions of soul freedom: "The capacity to deal directly with God" and "The sinner's response to the Gospel message [as] an act of moral freedom."

Religious Liberty

Religious liberty, the next circle out, must follow soul freedom. It is based on the biblical view of persons. Created in the image of God, a human being is the crowning work of God's creation (bio-centrists notwithstanding). To deny freedom of conscience to any person is to debase God's creation. When anyone's religious freedom is denied, everyone's religious freedom is endangered.

George W. Truett put the concept in Victorian rhetoric that sounds strange to the ear but rings true to the soul. In his famous 1920 speech on the steps of the United States Capitol he said, "The right to private judgment is the crown jewel of humanity, and for any person or institution to dare to come between the soul and God is blasphemous impertinence and a defamation of the crown rights of the Son of God."

The Universal Declaration of Human Rights, adopted in 1948, recognizes religious liberty as an entitlement of all human beings, a human right whatever their race or nation. We claim it as the basic human right, the primary human right, the ultimate human right. That is so because through the lenses of religious liberty we know ourselves, come to understand and value others and try to figure out the world. [German philospher] Georg Jellinek argued convincingly that "freedom of conscience may be the oldest right of man, at any rate it is the most basic right of man (pre-gender free language) because it comprises all ethically conditioned action and guarantees freedom from compulsion, especially from the power of the state." Religious liberty then as the basic human right is universal in its appeal and application.

The late James Ralph Scales of Wake Forest University stressed the universal and inviolable nature of religious liberty as the basis for church-state separation. He wrote in 1976 that religious liberty is "as nearly absolute as any safeguarded by the constitutions or practiced as a natural right."

For Bloom, consequences lie far beyond Baptists or religion or even "political, socioeconomic and anthropological implications" if religious liberty is neglected. That liberty "was also the stance of John Milton and Roger Williams; if that vision abandons the United States forever, then more than our spiritual democracy will yet be threatened."

[Baptist historian] Robert Torbet also linked religious liberty directly with church-state separation. He saw "an emphasis upon the accessibility of God to all men [and women] and the free responsibility of each individual before God, hence a free church in a free state."

Separation of Church and State

This last of our irreplaceable circles coming off a pebble in a pond or a shock-sending earthquake is in separation of church and state. It is an organic part of core Baptist belief, an appendage which if amputated would bleed dry the Baptist life blood.

Only last Friday the Executive of an American Baptist state convention told me about a layman who lamented, "Why we did not just quit worrying about Baptist doctrines and be Christians?" She asked, "Like which doctrine?" and the layman replied, "Like the doctrine of church-state separation."

There are many possible explanations to this sort of misunderstanding of church-state separation. The doctrine has been so distorted, diminished, and deprecated that it's easy to see how one could arrive at that point. Yet it's not just a Baptist doctrine; separation of church and state is an indissoluble aspect of our take on the essence of Christian faith.

True, separation of church and state does not define Baptist theology, but it is a logical, inextricable, inevitable corollary of religious liberty as we know it. It is the plug which, if pulled out of our machine, the motor dies. We go no more.

So when anyone says, "Oh, I'm all for religious liberty but I really don't know about separation of church and state," I'm ready to say, "You really don't know."

Baptist soul freedom allows you to take that view; you can be that way, you have every right to say that, but it's a sign you haven't thought it out.

I must still offer you more than grudging respect and honor as a creature made in God's image of inestimable worth. I still must extend to you real freedom, not mere toleration. Beyond that I may even embrace you as a fellow believer, a part of the family of faith, a joint heir with Jesus. This is rightly far more important than any doctrine, and, since ultimate judgment is God's alone, we had all better consider and treat all professing others as if they too are Christians. But if you dismiss the separation of church and state as some irrelevant, optional teaching, I can say you are not a Baptist.

To use a T. B. Maston wordplay, I can say "to the degree that" you cannot see the coercive state as separate from the church, "to that degree" you are not a Baptist.

Walter Glick, my major professor at Texas Wesleyan College, a great Methodist layman, loved to tell of Farmer Brown's cow Maggie and how she symbolized claims of Reformers and Baptists to be the true New Testament church.

As the Reformation unfolded after a thousand years of captive Christianity, there were those who wanted to see in their credentials a historical, documented chain that linked their beliefs, their spiritual pedigree, even their ordination, link by link, all the way back to Jesus, nay, even John the Baptist. (J. M. Carroll tried that in his *Trail of Blood*.) John the Baptist baptized Jesus and also "so and so," who baptized "so and so Jr.," who in turn dunked "so and so III," who then baptized the great-grandchild of "so and so," and so on down the line to "so and so the 73rd," who baptized me. The same with ordination!

Farmer Brown lost his cow and found it down the road apiece on Dollar Bill's place. Dollar Bill said, "Okay, we will follow her tracks back to your cow lot," just like some theologians looking for tracks all the way back to the River Jordan.

Sure enough, the tracks went right down to the creek and disappeared. She had come down to the creek. But Brown insisted that she had all the markings of his Maggie the miracle milk-maker who had misplaced herself. Witnesses prevailed and Brown took Maggie home.

I contend that there is a Baptist identity. There are Baptist spots on our herd and you can tell them from the others.

There's a Thomas Helwys spot: "I'll serve the King, I'll fight for the King. I'm willing to die for the King, but the King is not Lord of the conscience. And so, that very King whose name is in the front of the favorite Baptist Bible, King James, put him to death."

There's a Roger Williams spot: "To call a nation a 'Christian Nation' may make a nation of hypocrites; but it will not make one single true believer."

There's a John Leland spot: "The fondness of magistrates to foster Christianity has done it more harm than all the persecutions ever did."

There's a Gardner Taylor spot: "We need church-state separation so that neither will ever hold the other in a bear hug."

And there's a Truett spot, and a J. M. Dawson spot, and one shaped like Maston and Estep and, yes, Newport.

So, without those spots you may be a wonderful person, maybe a devout and dedicated Christian, far closer to the Jesus model than I may ever be, but frankly, my dear, you are not a Baptist. I personally and passionately believe that Baptist Christians are an identifiable breed. One of our marks is separation of church and state. There is no doubt that there is an unbroken chain in our "Baptist bonafides" from soul freedom to religious liberty to the separation of church and state, all part of the package.

Thank God Texas Baptists are not among those so-called, semi, pseudo anti-Baptists who have turned away from our blood-bought heritage.

The proposed White House Office of Faith-Based and Community Initiatives would be a turning away from the American way in church-state relations. We have never in our nation's history had a federal office for funding religious groups. The relatively low-level people in the White House who were charged with making connections for faith groups had no "initiatives" and, more important, no budget.

This proposal by President Bush would have Madison and Jefferson spinning in their graves: five billion dollars to be funneled through churches. Mr. Bush insists that it would be done "without changing the nature of those groups." How many organizations in this real world do you know that are not shaped to some degree by their funding? And all this activism is itself set in motion by an idea.

"Charitable Choice" is a whole set of tinkerings with established law that allows government money to flow into "pervasively sectarian" organizations, mostly churches and church agencies. For years tax monies were taken and used for a range of social causes by "religiously affiliated" institutions. Since the first so-called "Charitable Choice" amendment was tacked on the Welfare-to-Work laws in 1996 by Senator John Ashcroft, it has been "Katie bar the door." Our tax dollars have been flowing freely into profoundly proselytizing programs.

This scheme is bad for the citizen. We do not know what our tax dollar is buying; there is little, in some cases no accountability on the part of the receiving spender.

It's bad for the church. He who pays the fiddler calls the tune. Ultimately there will be regulations and guidelines, must be, ought to be. And there will be reporting (pages of questions to answer) and monitoring. How's that for religious freedom?

So folks all across the political spectrum are beginning to get a little nervous about "Charitable Choice." Is it really so loving after all? How long will there be a choice?

At the very least, Baptist Christians should lead all concerned citizens in calling for extensive congressional hearings on "Charitable Choice." Surely, the Congress can do that. But then, maybe they'd rather be investigating something.

—Reprinted with permission courtesy of
the Christian Ethics Today Foundation.

Chapter 11

Sermons

James Dunn was a Baptist preacher. This is an identity that he carried with him throughout his public ministry at the Texas Baptist Christian Life Commission and the Baptist Joint Committee on Public Affairs and into "retirement" as a professor at Wake Forest University School of Divinity. In 1953, a year prior to his graduation from Texas Wesleyan College, Dunn accepted a "call" to vocational ministry, walking down the center aisle at Evans Avenue Baptist Church in Fort Worth as the congregation sang "Wherever He Leads I'll Go." He was nineteen years old. Five years later, Dunn stepped into the pulpit of Emmanuel Baptist Church in Weatherford, Texas, as the congregation's first pastor. Emmanuel began in 1958 with fifty-seven members, and when Dunn left just over three years later the new church had grown to nearly two hundred members. He baptized thirty-four new believers during this period too.

Dunn left Emmanuel to become a collegiate minister, serving as director of the Baptist Student Union at West Texas State University in Canyon. He held this position for five years until joining the Texas Baptist Christian Life Commission staff as associate director in 1966. While only a full-time pastor for a brief period, Dunn spent more Sundays in the pulpit than in the pew over the next fifty years. He was a guest preacher at hundreds of Baptist churches across the United States and was an interim pastor at several churches as well, including Ravensworth Baptist Church in the Washington, D.C., suburb of Allendale, Virginia, toward the end of his tenure at the BJC.

The sermons in this section are just a few examples of Dunn's preaching ministry, where he exposited Scripture and spoke about the importance of biblical freedom and responsibility, ethics, and putting one's faith in Jesus Christ.

God, How Can I Draw Closer to You?

As a former collegiate minister, James Dunn enjoyed speaking to students. He frequently was a guest lecturer and chapel preacher at Baptist colleges and universities in Texas and throughout the South. Dunn preached the sermon below on February 6, 1969, to students at Oklahoma Baptist University in Shawnee, Oklahoma. At the time, Dunn was beginning his second year as director of the Texas Baptist Christian Life Commission. His sermon came as part of "Christian Focus Week."

I hope Hattie McDaniel, the Negro singer, is wrong. She says you can tell whether a man is really a Christian by what he says when he wakes up in the morning. If he's really a Christian, he'll bounce out of bed and say, "Good morning, Lord!" But if there's some doubt, he'll roll over and say, "Good Lord, morning?" I have to admit, at 6:30 this morning after that dorm discussion last night, I was in the second category.

God, how can I get closer to you? I thought this was kind of unfair to be asked to come in here and then assigned a topic like that. As I wrestled with this and tried to come up with something both helpful and honest, I thought maybe we ought to ask some other questions, some prior questions.

Do I really want to get closer to God? That verse, Matthew 8:34, where Jesus tried to spell out for us rather specifically what it means to get close to God: "If any man would come after me, let him deny himself, take up his cross, and follow me daily." I'm not so sure that I really want to get closer to God. I'm not so sure, because it seems that there's a good deal of evidence in the New Testament that if I do, I'll have to subscribe to that denying of self. The modern speech translations put it a little better; they say, "say no to self." Give up all and understand that we are worth something (and I'll go along with that). But it's still a little tough for us to recognize that eternal spiritual law, "Getting by giving, and living by dying, and gaining by giving up."

And I'm not sure, if I'm going to be real honest, I'm not sure that I want to get any closer to God than I am right now. You see, there's the self-giving flow that Ron Willis referred to in his prayer, which he illustrated with this stagnant cup of coffee yesterday morning. For all our self-affirmation and recognition of our own worth, we said drawing close to God is not joyful and pleasing; it's discomforting and disturbing. When we draw closer to God we have to forget things, we have to accept responsibility, we have to acknowledge claims that God makes on our lives. The nearer we are to God, the more pain there is.

Wait a minute. I don't know if I want to get closer to God or not, if that's so. And if I really understand what Jesus was saying when he said, "If any man is going to come after me, let him deny himself and take up his cross." See, we try to grow closer to God with such terms as "I feel," or "I experience," or "I." C. S. Lewis talked about it in terms of a "tingling sensation in our gizzard." And I think Lewis may have dismissed with that definition a lot of what we call getting closer to God. "I feel," or "I think." I'll buy that.

Some folks think drawing closer to God is agreeing with him. "All right, Lord, I'll go along with that." Or perhaps it's more than just our feeling and our thinking. Maybe it's saying so. Linus and Charlie Brown come to Snoopy shivering in the snow and say, "Be of good cheer." Or "Christ is the answer," or maybe we think we're drawing closer to God when we make up our mind and sing "I have decided to follow Jesus." I wonder sometimes after we sing it and pour our hearts into it—if it's not being too sacrilegious—if God, sitting on his throne, doesn't say to himself, "So?"

What's wrong with all those, what do they have in common? "I think, I feel, I have decided, I say, I always say."

But he said, whosoever would come after me is going to have to give up all right to himself and say no to himself. And I'm not too sure that I want to draw closer to God. I'm not too sure that I want any more pain.

But you say, "I do want to draw closer to God. I understand all that and I still want to draw closer to God. How do you draw closer to God?" So, I'm going to have to ask another question: do we know what it means to draw closer to God? We talk about encounters with him, worship, taking up our cross, confrontation, radical obedience to his will, acceptance of his way, identification with Jesus Christ and his cross, fellowship with the cross. We label it worship, and in worship we attempt to draw closer to God, but do we know what it means? Do we know what worship means? Do we know what it means to meet God?

Well, Amos caught on to what it meant when he heard God saying, "I don't have any pleasure in your solemn assemblies and your offerings, and what you use to draw closer to me is a stench unto my nostrils. What I want is justice and righteousness."

Isaiah had an experience with God, a model of worship experience. When Isaiah saw the Lord in his vision, he drew close to God. But the main part of that worship experience was seeing himself as a man of unclean lips dwelling amidst a people of unclean lips. Do you know what he had to do? Before the little worship episode was over, he had to say, "Here am I."

Jeremiah tried to react to the worship of the Jews and their attempts to reach out to God. He said in one of the most mocking verses in the

Old Testament, "The temple, the temple, the temple—they think they can come to this building and get together with God." Oh, that won't work, and Jeremiah had sense enough to see this because he was close enough to God that he understood.

Raphael painted what may be one of the best commentaries on the transfiguration and worship experience that the inner circle of Peter and James and John had there. They saw God; they got closer to God than practically anyone ever does. They got so close that Peter just wanted to stay up there and build a tabernacle and settle down and live on that high closeness to God. But in the painting, painted about 1520 just before Raphael's death, he had the mountaintop experience, but he also had the episode that followed down in the valley, where the disciples couldn't even come to grips with the distraught father and his epileptic son, though they had been in the very presence of God. And the thing he was trying to say with his tremendous work of art was that the spiritual heights of a transfiguration and the depths of human need are inseparable; you can't put them on two canvases.

Well, the point is, I think maybe we look for God in the wrong places, if we're going to recognize him when we see him. The old hobos in *Waiting for Godot* saw the visitors as nonsense and missed God because of their conceptions of what his presence would be like. I think most of us can identify with Jacob, who tried to draw closer to God and who said, "Surely God is in this place, and I didn't even know it." We expect him to grasp us at worship, but he stalks the lonely streets. We expect him when we're on our knees in prayer, but he comes to us when we try to be the church. God is in and with and under and above and around all the ordinary events of life, and Alan Richardson was right, I think, when he said that the life of every man is full of the unrecognized knowledge of God, the hints of the divine presence, and that most of us never call these experiences of God by the right name, never find the proper names for the worship experiences.

Well, I think the first question we want to ask is do we really want to draw closer to God, and the second is would we know it if we did? What does it mean to draw closer to him? Martin Luther wrestled with it; he wanted to draw close to God. In his religious experience and in his history and in his day, he thought the thing to do was to go to a monastery, and so he was headed for the monastery. In a dialogue in the Broadway play that didn't last long because of all the criticism, the Broadway play *Luther*, Martin Luther says, "If life in a monastery is so easy, why aren't people beating down the walls to get in?" And his practical father said, "Martin, they're not beating down the walls to get into the monastery for those experiences because they haven't given up yet."

Maybe we're having our little monasteries. We don't call them that. Maybe we're not real sure what it means to draw closer to God. Do we act on what we already know about drawing closer to God? Or, like Lucy, do we look for a scapegoat and want all of our life and all of our relationships to be up, up, up and no downs? Like Charlie Brown, are we wishy-washy, confused from the day we were born? Like Snoopy, do we make great plans and then put them off until after supper? Or, like Linus, is there no problem so complicated that it can't be run away from? The trouble with us is that we won't listen to what the trouble with us is. Do we act on what we know about drawing closer to God?

Let's take an illustration, and it's just that—an illustration of one thing that we know. We know that we do need to share our faith with others—a verbal witness, a spoken testimony, a worded expression of our faith. We know we need to do this. We know that the call to be a Christian is the call to be a witness. We know that a non-witnessing Christian is a contradiction of terms. We know that if we have information on a human level about a murderer about to go to trial in a court of law, and to share that testimony would save a man's life, and we fail to testify—that's a highly immoral act. We can draw that over into our Christian experience to recognize that we are highly immoral when we claim to know something that would help a guy in need of the very gospel that has changed our own life, and we don't share it. We don't tell him, we don't try to communicate to him so he can understand what it means to be a Christian. We know all that, and yet what do we do?

I've even heard some this week on this campus say, "Well, I live my witness, I act out my faith." And that's been one of the thrusts of the messages of the week—action. Just living your witness, just acting out your faith, and never communicating, never verbalizing, never sharing in words what He means to you, that won't get it done.

I like Trueblood's analysis of this sophomoric attitude that says, "Well, I live my witness." What unbelievable conceit, he says, what insufferable self-righteousness. "I live my witness." Now I don't mean all those stereotyped plans, sales gimmicks, and arm-twisting techniques. I just mean sharing honestly your own experience of your relationship to the person Jesus Christ. When we deny that and fail to communicate our faith to others, we're saying, "I am capable of becoming so much like Jesus that just by looking at me, people not only will want to follow, they'll understand what it takes to follow, and they'll become Christians just by looking at me. They'll just come running over to ask me."

Insufferable conceit, unbelievable self-righteousness, said Trueblood. And I think he's right. I think it's a good illustration of a situation in which we know all we need to know about drawing closer to God, and we do in fact draw closer to him as we share him with others. What better way is there to learn something than by telling it over and over and over?

Do we want to draw closer to God? Do we know what it means to draw closer to God? And do we act on what we know already? I'm afraid not.

I like the words of George MacLeod when he said,

> I simply argue that the cross be raised again at the center of the market place as well as on the steeple of the church. I'm recovering the claim that Jesus Christ was crucified on the town garbage heap. That he was crucified on a cross between two thieves, not in a cathedral between two candles. He was crucified at the market place where it was so cosmopolitan that they wrote His title in Hebrew, Latin and Greek, that's where He was and that's what it's about, that's where the church must be, and what the church must be about.

I know that this isn't good exegesis, but I think about that verse from Matthew 9:9 when Jesus called that old publican tax collector to follow him. He saw Matthew and he said, "Come follow me." And Matthew followed him. That's what the Scripture says. Simple. Wasn't cluttered up with a whole bunch of analysis and agony. He just said, "Come follow me." Matthew didn't ask, "Where are you going, where are you going to spend the night? Wait a minute, I've got a few things. Now wait a minute, Lord, I don't know what you mean by that. Let's discuss it for a few hours. I haven't been to seminary." We clutter it up and make it so complicated. Jesus said, "Follow me," and Matthew followed him. If any man would come after me, Jesus said, let him deny himself and take up his cross and follow me."

If you would, do this with me as a prayer of confession and as an act of worship. Let's just bow our heads and say aloud together, if you will, "Lord, help me to follow you today."

—James M. Dunn Papers, MS 632, Z. Smith Reynolds Library
Special Collections and Archives, Wake Forest University,
Winston-Salem NC, USA.

Going Forth in His Presence

James Dunn preached this sermon on August 21, 1972, at a gathering of Southern Baptists at the Glorieta Baptist Conference Center in Glorieta, New Mexico.

It is plain to see that God has spoken through the men who have stood here this week. That's comforting.

But to follow Bill Pinson, Milt Hughes, Dan Blake and Doug Manning . . . that's disturbing.

A famous quotation of Ralph Waldo Emerson comforts me. He said, "The next best thing to good preaching is bad preaching. I have even more thoughts during or enduring it than at any other times." Remember that and you can't lose.

Another concept that I find interesting and comforting may be disturbing for you.

It was Kierkegaard who said it:

> The sermon is not given for the speaker's sake, that men may praise or blame him. The listener's repetition of it is what is aimed at.
>
> If the speaker has responsibility for what he says, then the listener has an equally great responsibility not to fall short in his task.
>
> In the theater the play is staged before an audience, called theatergoers. But with a sermon, God himself is the audience.
>
> The speaker is the prompter, whispering the lines.
>
> You the listeners are the actors, standing openly before God your audience. God is the critical theatergoer, the drama critic who looks on to see how the lives are spoken, how they are acted out. The customary audience is missing. The listeners are the actors. God watches to see what you'll do. (*Purity of the Heart* [New York: Harper, 1948] 180)

Like all analogies it's imperfect, but it does suggest a truth that we need to remember. God is here.

We like Jacob have had experiences when we suddenly realized, "Surely God is in this place and I knew it not."

We keep missing God's presence because we insist upon meeting him on our timetable—"now, God," "not yet, God." Or in our places—"Come here, God!" Or on or in our terms "as we are filled with the Spirit," "baptized with the Spirit," "sanctified," "separated," etc.

In Samuel Beckett's play *Waiting for Godot*, two hobos wait for Godot, who has promised to come to them. Their image of him is dramatic, spectacular, no ordinary event. As they wait, they become distressed, depressed. They consider suicide twice.

When the final curtain falls, nothing has happened

The tragedy is not that Godot did not come but that he came and they failed to recognize him.

They missed him for all their conceptions of what his presence would be.

Don't we do that?

We expect God to grasp us at worship. He stalks the lonely paths of Main Street meeting human need.

We expect God when we're on our knees in prayer. He comes to us when we stand erect and confident facing a challenge.

We expect God when we go to church. He's with us most clearly when we *are* the church. And that may be on Monday morning at 10 a.m. or at lunch on Wednesday or on Saturday night about time to go home from a date.

Alan Richardson put it well. He said, "The life of every man is full of unrecognized pieces of the knowledge of God, hints of the divine presence that we never learn to call by the right name."

Even God's hiddenness (which we often mistake for his absence) should remind us that he made us, free beings, in his image and that his apparent absence is our way of sustaining our freedom and responsibility.

He is where we haven't been yet. He waits for us to catch up. He's in and under and with and behind the ordinary events of life.

Maybe we have not seen clearly what has happened when God's children really met God face to face, knew his immediate presence.

Moses stood before the burning bush and then returned to Egypt kicking and screaming all the way to lead a revolution. He was, in fact, the first leader in organized labor, and before they left Egypt he specialized in strikes, demonstrations, and work stoppage.

Isaiah came into the very presence of God in the incident recorded in Isaiah 6. Do you remember the first thing that he thought about when the significance of the experience dawned on him? He became aware of the obscenity, the vulgarity, of his own life and the lives of those about him. He went on a sort of decency crusade.

Jeremiah had a vision of God. It got him in trouble. He started speaking out against an unpopular war. He was a dramatic demonstrator, a vigorous protestor, a conscientious objector, and it got him thrown in jail.

Amos heard the word of the Lord. It led him to start the whole consumer protection movement. He spoke out against high prices, unfair economic practices, low wages, unequal distribution of the wealth, abuse of the profit motive. Ralph Nader is a tame kitten compared to Amos.

John the Baptist baptized Jesus himself. The heavens opened up. God dramatically showed his presence. And the very next verses say, "Now after that John was put in prison." Why? For mixing religion and politics, for criticizing the government, for pointing out immorality in high places.

Saul of Tarsus had one of those face-to-face experiences with God. It produced the great apostle of love. I think we may forget that the Saul of the Damascus Road was a racist, a bigot, a hate-filled, narrow-minded fanatic of the worst sort.

In 1520, near the end of his life, Raphael painted a famous picture of the transfiguration, Peter and James and John with Jesus in a very spectacular demonstration of God's presence. But on the same canvas there is pictured the event that followed at the foot of the mountain, when those same disciples were helpless to meet human need; the epileptic son could not be healed.

Raphael insisted that both scenes be on the same canvas, that we be reminded of the heights and depths.

See! If we do not specify and confront the issues, we obscure them. God's not in the business of hiding truth.

If we do not alarm anyone morally, we ourselves remain morally asleep.

If we do not challenge and engage the forces of evil, then we contribute to the drift toward a coming human hell. God is not in that kind of apathy because he is not willing that any should perish.

Where do you find God? You find him in the lives of others all around you. It is persons who reflect God. The least, the lowliest, are "made in his image."

We see him not in theology or churches or ethics or religious art or even the Bible so much as in persons: made in his image, replicating God, snapshots of him.

You know that passage in the Sermon on the Mount that seems a bit strange: "And whosoever shall say to his brother, Raca, shall be in danger of the council: but whosoever shall say, Thou fool, shall be in danger of hell fire"? We don't understand it because we miss a figure of speech. "Raca" is an onomatopoetic expression. It sounds like its meaning. "Raca" was the sound of clearing one's throat to spit. That spitting was and is a Jewish expression of contempt. It was a dramatic way of demonstrating that the person toward whom it was directed was seen as "scum," "trash," less than human.

Jesus said no. Cut that out. All men are "made in his image," of infinite worth. You can't despise any one of his persons without it reflecting what you really think of him.

You'll find God in the lives of others.

You can find God in your own heart. Oh, not in an emotional spasm or, as C. S. Lewis puts it, in a sort of tingling around the gizzard. But you can find him personally as Pascal found him. The great French mathematician, scientist, mind above most minds, knew Jesus Christ in a personal way. At his death when his coat was examined, this testimony was found sewed in the lining over his heart: "The year of grace 1654 . . . from about half past ten until about half past twelve: First, God of Abraham, God of Isaac, God of Jacob, not of the scholars and philosophers, certitude, certitude, feeling, joy, peace, God of Jesus Christ, thy God will be my God."

Oh that I knew where I might find Him,
that I might even come before his presence
If with all your hearts, ye truly seek me,
Ye shall ever surely find me, Thus saith our God.

—James M. Dunn Papers, MS 632, Z. Smith Reynolds Library Special Collections and Archives, Wake Forest University, Winston-Salem NC, USA.

The Sin of Certainty—Mark 9:20-24

James Dunn preached the following sermon on August 24, 1997, at Ravensworth Baptist Church in Annandale, Virginia.

Our Scripture this morning is found in Mark 9, verses 20 through 24, a familiar passage to many of us:

> And they brought the boy to him. When the spirit saw him, immediately it convulsed the boy, and he fell on the ground and rolled about, foaming at the mouth. Jesus asked the father, "How long has this been happening

to him?" He said, "From childhood. It's often cast him into the fire and into the water to destroy him, but if you're able to do anything, have pity on us and help us." Jesus said to him, "If you're able, all things can be done for the one who believes." Immediately, the father of the child cried out, "I believe. Help my unbelief."

May the Lord add his blessing to this reading from his word.

He was testifying for all of us, wasn't he? "I believe. Help my unbelief." Are there any of us here who could nod and humbly acknowledge that we've been like the patient of the psychiatrist, who, when she was asked, "Do you have trouble making decisions?" responded, "Well, yes and no." Or maybe you identify as I do with Kudzu. You know, he's the gangling teenager from Bypass in our friend Doug Marlette's cartoon *Kudzu*. He has a whole lot of little set sequences that you've probably seen. There's the parrot who makes comments and the preacher who is often either at a wedding or a funeral.

Typical. Kudzu, the young, gangling, confused teenager, and the preacher were sitting on a hill, looking at a sunset, another one of their favorite spots. Kudzu said to the preacher, whose name was Will B. Dunn, "You know, preacher, I'm worried about my ambivalence." And the pastor, with a fairly typical pastoral response, he said, "There, there Kudzu. Don't be concerned. We're all ambivalent." To which Kudzu responded, "But I'm ambivalent about my ambivalence."

And we are, aren't we? Because we live in a world in which folks really want us, and we ourselves want, to be certain. We have a hankering for certainty. In this year's "Stump Sermon" of Walter B. Shurden, he talks about the craving for clarity, the hunger for exactness, the yearning for certitude, and points out that that is the very opposite of what the Bible means by faith. We sometimes set in sharp juxtaposition faith and doubt, but the opposite of doubt is not faith.

The opposite of doubt is dogmatic certainty in which there's no room for doubt and, incidentally, or maybe primarily to the point, no room for faith, because if our little bucket is so full of utter certitude, and we know that we have everything nailed down absolutely and irrevocably, and we cannot pray the honest prayer of this one who was in the face of the master himself, confronted with dramatic demonstration of power and all kinds of mystery, if we cannot pray the prayer, "Lord, I believe. Help my unbelief," then where's the room for faith? Where is there room for faith when we have it all so nailed down?

You see, that's not a question of liberalism or conservatism, or believing the Bible or not believing the Bible. Not so at all. Not all of us, hopefully, but some of us grew up listening to a preacher who said, after reading any particular verse of Scripture in its marvelous richness, "And what that means is . . . ." We grew up, many of us, with the mentality that says, "The Bible says it, and I believe it, and that settles it." It was that kind of certitude. Or if you go the other direction of the same circle of rational thought, you wind up with a sort of secular agnosticism or maybe a scientism that says, "This is what I know, and this I know. Everything else is irrelevant, not important, not significant."

And rational mechanism, arrogant dependence upon one's own capacity to have it all nailed down, brings the fundamentalist and the agnostic secularist to the same point of depending on their own little bucket of intellectual capacity, without room for mystery, without evidence of all, without the capacity for real worship, where we come to that universal prayer, "Lord, thou knowest I believe. Help my unbelief." Because he was living as really we all do, in the realm of "already, but not yet." In the realm of "as if I claim this truth, this faith, this capacity for mystery, and awe, and dependence upon thee, Lord. As if it were really mine, and I had it 100% of the time, but I know I don't."

We come, if we're really honest, to that kind of ambivalence and ambiguity that Kudzu knew, and because we do, we're ambivalent about our ambivalence. We feel a little guilty about it because we've been told we ought to have it all nailed down. Hey, now wait a minute. Don't take this too far. I love that, "To whosoever meaneth me." "This is a good old gospel foot-stomper." "Whosoever meaneth me."

Amen, and I can sing with great enthusiasm and real joy in some assurance of my faith, for I know whom I have believed and am persuaded that he is able to keep that which I've committed to him against that day (2 Tim 1:12). That's a sort of certainty, but it's a certainty born of faith, willing to risk. Certainly not in the same vein as heavy philosophical discussions about the tension between faith and reason.

Certainly, I can't see Kierkegaard singing it. "Whosoever meaneth me." Or "I know whom I have believed." But I learned, in that time in which I crowded six years of seminary work into thirteen, what Kierkegaard meant when he talked about the leap of faith, and brought that terminology, which is very existential and very experiential, into the common vocabulary of Christian folks of all sorts who, like me, could not read and comprehend fully or appreciate a whole lot of Kierkegaardian stuff. But the leap of faith,

I understand. I can identify with that, because that's the same kind of leap that this guy, with the probably epileptic son, expressed when he said, "I believe. Help my unbelief." That leap of faith.

We've got a lot to overcome because we've grown up in a world in which we hear all the time, and maybe even say, "I've always heard it said . . . ." And then we cling to that as if it were the peg post on our pilgrimage. Or "Doesn't it say in the Bible somewhere that . . . ?" And a kind of proof-texting that lets us hang on to a misinterpretation of Scripture. Or maybe, and this bothered me when I was a little kid, when a tragedy, or a sickness, or a death comes along, and the gray heads, or no-hairs among us say (Nothing personal. It either turns gray or turns loose.), "Oh, it was just God's will. It was just the way God wanted it to be."

Well, a lot of times I've wanted to scream out and say, "No way. It wasn't God's will." Because there's a lot more to human tragedy and sin and suffering and what the philosophers call "the problem of evil," than some mechanistic, Calvinistic "God's will is everything that happens." Baloney.

Yeah, or maybe we've fallen into the very American and very Western trap of interpreting the Scripture in our search for certainty, because this is all that sin of certainty that leads us into that direction, by saying, "Well, it's got to be this or that. Right or wrong. Black or white." Do you know what Jesus did when they asked him questions that would prompt the response "Well, it's either this or that"? "Do you render tribute to Caesar or not? Yes or no?" Anytime they came to him and asked him for a yes or no answer, he said, "Neither one." "Who sinned? This man or his father, or his parents?" "Whose wife will she be in the judgment?"

On and on, those trick questions. Full of them. And the world's still full of them. I got a letter this week from someone who wanted to know exactly what we believe about this or that. "It's got to be this or that." We're either with them or against them.

Jesus many times said, "Neither." And sometimes said, "Both." And sometimes took off on a tangent that didn't sound like an answer to the question. "Whose wife will she be in the judgment?" Well, he said, "There's not even going to be any marriage in the judgment." But more often than any of those responses, he said, "Let me tell you a story." And then he told a story in which there was truth, and in that truth there was the implicit, if not explicit, acknowledgment that we human beings have to live with the wheat and the tares, with the good and the bad.

With a God whose sun shines on the just and the unjust, and whose rain falls on the evil and the good. He'd tell them a story in which we'd recognize that faith is the kind of response that prays, if it's honest, "I do have faith, oh Lord. Help my lack of faith." That's what he'd do when he was encountered with "this or that." And we cannot always do it.

We're still tempted just as Eve was to want the knowledge of good and evil, and that very first sin that we have pictured in the Scripture has Eve seeking certainty. Certainty that was entitled to God alone, because she pursued the fruit of the tree of knowledge of good and evil. We are reminded, if we remember, that the Bible is indeed a divine-human book, and that the church is a divine-human institution, and that our life in Jesus Christ is a life of "I believe—help my unbelief."

And if we don't do that, we're powerfully tempted to claim more than we can deliver, for by grace you've been saved through faith, and this is not of your own doing. It's the gift of God, not the result of works, or, parenthetically, we could say, "of having it all figured out" or "utter certainty," so that no one may boast, for we are what he's made us, created in Christ Jesus for good works, which God prepared before him to be our way of life.

It's with acknowledgment of that humanity that we all enjoy and suffer, acknowledgment of that humanity that we come to him in faith, and acknowledgment of the humility that Paul, who as we all know wasn't always so humble, expressed in Romans 11, "Oh, the depth of the riches and wisdom and knowledge of God. How unsearchable are his judgments, and how inscrutable his ways. For who has known the mind of God, or who has been his counselor, or who has given a gift to him to receive a gift in return? For from him, and through him, and to him are all things, and to him be the glory forever. Amen."

It's with acknowledgment of our humanity that Paul accepts his gift of grace, which is not a package of answers. Not an almanac or an owner's manual, but grace, unmerited favor, and humility that acknowledges, in super simplicity, that we can't know it all. We humbly come to him.

When I was a little kid, Daddy worked on Sundays, and we walked to a little Presbyterian church because it's where we could go, and Mother and Dad were determined we'd be in Sunday school, and until I was about nine, we went to the little Broadway Presbyterian Church, and my mother and dad were not terribly, extensively educated. They went through all the public school they had down in Kaufman County, Texas, and then Dad went to a little business college, but they had some intuitive and spiritual insights for which I'm profoundly grateful.

I remember in that little Presbyterian church, one of the reasons Mother loved Dr. Edwin Sisserson so well as a preacher is that he was not so terribly dogmatic but could say in honesty, in identification with the kind of searching that every true believer has if they'll admit it, "Now, it seems to me . . . ," or "The best I can tell . . . ," or "In my own reading of the Scripture . . . ." You hear those qualifying phrases. Not the dogmatic utter certainty that we've experienced so many times, that troubles us so much.

After that little discourse, it seems to me, the best I can tell, in my humble opinion, on the basis of the Spirit's leadership to me, the Scripture teaches that it's in that kind of humility and acknowledgment of our own humanity, the very opposite of certainty but the very essence of taking a leap of faith, that any of us ever come to know him as Savior and Lord and Master and ruler of our lives. It was Reinhold Niebuhr who said that there's at least one moment, one moment in the life of every single true believer, when he or she said, "Here is my life." With Job, it was, "Though he slay me, I will serve him. I don't understand it, but I do give to you, Lord, my life."

Maybe there's someone here today who would, in his or her own way, or in his or her own words, say to the Lord, "Here's my life. I want to live it. Here's my life. I want to give it, serving my fellow man, doing the will of God. Here's my life. Here it is, Lord. I turn it over to you. I don't have it all figured out, but I do have enough figured out to turn it over to you. I know whom I have believed and am persuaded that he's able to keep that which I've committed to him against that day. I'm willing and ready to do that."

That one moment of utter—not nearly, not partial, not semi but total—unselfishness, according to Niebuhr, who wasn't known as an evangelist, is the moment at which we come to Christ. Could be there's someone here today. I can't offer you the utter certainty that our whole culture tends to evoke and generate, but I can promise on the strength of God's word that it seems to me he says you can pray, "Lord, I have faith. Help my un-faith." "Lord, I do believe" in the face of that miracle and mystery and power of the Lord's work in our lives.

—Published with permission courtesy of Ravensworth Baptist Church.

Grace Enfleshed—John 1:1-14

James Dunn preached the following sermon on December 7, 1997, at Ravensworth Baptist Church in Annandale, Virginia.

> In the beginning was the Word and the Word was with God, and the Word was God. He was in the beginning with God. All things came into being through him, and without him not one thing came into being. What has come into being in him was life, and the life was the light of all people. The light shines in the darkness, and the darkness did not overcome it. There was a man sent from God whose name was John. He came as a witness to testify to the light so that all might believe through him. He himself was not the light, but he came to testify to the light. The true light, which enlightens everyone, was coming into the world. He was in the world, and the world came into being through him, yet the world didn't know him. He came to what was his own. His own people didn't accept him, but to all who received him, who believed in his name, he gave the power to become children of God, who were born not of blood, or of the will of the flesh, or of the will of man, but of God, and the Word became flesh and lived among us, and we have seen his glory. The glory of a father's only son, full of grace and truth. (John 1:1-14)

I got in big trouble a couple years back on [the CNN television show] *Crossfire*, when someone said, "Dr. Dunn, do you believe in the miracles?" I said, "Well, yes. I believe in all the miracles, because I believe in the incarnation. And if indeed God came into flesh and took on human form as we believe in the Scripture we're taught that he did, all the other miracles are downhill from there."

James Dobson got in an uproar and called me a wild-eyed liberal in his newsletter, and I got phone calls, and email messages, and faxes, and harassment from a lot of people all over the country because I said all the other miracles were downhill from there. "Don't you believe in all of the miracles?" Well, yeah, but they're small peanuts compared to the incarnation.

If indeed the story we celebrate at Christmastime is true, and I believe it with all my heart, then all the rest of them are downhill from there, because if God was in Jesus Christ, seeking to reconcile the world, if God was indeed the word of God, the truth of God from the very beginning, full of grace and truth, what is water into wine and feeding 5,000? Why, it could have been, and has been since then, 5 million. Feeding 5,000 is nothing.

Dorothy Sayers likes to talk about the incarnation in these terms. Sayers said, "In the incarnation, what we have is God proving to the world that he could take his own medicine, the medicine of humanity." Or in another way, she said, "In the incarnation, when God took on flesh in the person of Jesus Christ, he was showing all of us that he could play the game by the rules he'd made."

Grace enfleshed. That's what the incarnation means. Most of us, though we may not always admit it and acknowledge it freely, have a good deal of trouble not only with the word "grace"—unmerited favor, undeserved blessing—but also with doing good and showering good things on those who don't merit it at all, who don't deserve it a bit. We have trouble with the word "grace," but we have more trouble with being graceful people ourselves. All of us do. Come on. When you get really honest about it, that's why we give gifts at Christmas. It's what the Christmas bit is all about, that God showed us in the person of Jesus Christ what grace was all about. What it means to display and dispense unmerited favor, undeserved blessing.

How in the world could God communicate to us mortals, us puny mortals, his love? His grace? His grace that is greater than all our sins? Well, when he took on flesh, when he became a human being in the person of a little baby in Bethlehem, the spiritual took on skin. A concept became concrete. Theology was suddenly tangible. All prophecy that the Jews had been listening to for years was suddenly a new person.

The remote, the distant, became suddenly near. The ideal became real. The impossible became possible. The otherworldly became as worldly as a baby who wet his swaddling clothes. The unreachable became someone you could hold, as we've just heard. The untouchable became someone you could feel with your hands. The promise of God in the flesh.

Paul Harvey tells the story of a crotchety old guy whose wife and children headed to the church on Christmas Eve. He wasn't terribly interested in the church and all this Christmas stuff. A virtual Scrooge he was. He said, "You go on. I'll stay here, read my paper, smoke my pipe, sit in front of the fire."

There was a raging blizzard. The snow was coming down. The wind was blowing, and he heard a bump, bump, bump at the big picture window and went to the window to see what the strange noise was, and it was some birds that had become lost in the storm and were banging themselves in the window and hurting themselves, and one broke a wing, and feathers flew, and they fell down in the snow, and they kept on. If he wanted to get out in the snow, he might have gone to church, but he couldn't stand that noise, or the idea that these birds were killing themselves trying to get to the warm, lighted room.

He put on his great coat and his galoshes, his hat and his gloves, and he went outside and tried to shoo them. They just kept getting more confused and continuing to bang the window. He thought, "Well . . . ." He went back in the house and got some bread and broke it up into little crumbs and pieces, and thought, "I'll lead them to the garage." And so he started throwing it down, and the bread would blow away or get lost in the snow, and the birds just kept banging the window, and trying to get in, and couldn't.

He didn't know exactly what to do, so he went back in and resigned himself to the fact that this was a real serious problem. The dumb birds didn't deserve to be saved from the snow, but he was trying anyway. He couldn't get them to save themselves in the warm, protected garage. He sat there in front of the fire, thinking a little more seriously for a change, and thought, "If I could just become a bird, then I could lead them. Shooing them wouldn't work, and enticing them with crumbs wouldn't work, but if I could . . . ."

Isn't that what they're saying happened on that first Christmas? That Jesus was in fact the one whom God became in order to lead his children, who couldn't get the point and didn't hear the message of the grace of God until someone became like them.

And so the spiritual took on skin, and the concept became concrete, and the unreachable became someone you could hold, and the untouchable became someone you could reach out and touch, and the promise of God took on flesh. That's what the incarnation is all about. God became one of us, and so we celebrate, as well we should, because God knows us, and God loves us, and God cares for us, and the grace of God is made manifest, showed off, displayed, demonstrated all over again every time we pause to remember the powerful, wonderful message of Christmas.

—Published with permission courtesy of
Ravensworth Baptist Church.

Nine-Commandment Christians—John 1:6-15

James Dunn preached the following sermon on February 15, 1998, at Ravensworth Baptist Church in Annandale, Virginia.

Hear the word of the Lord from John 1:6-15.

> There was a man sent from God, whose name was John. He came as a witness to testify to the Light so that all might believe through him. He, himself, was not the Light, but he came to testify that the Light, the true Light, which enlightens everyone, was coming into the world. He was in the world, and the world came into being through him, yet the world didn't know him. He came into what was his own, and his own people didn't accept him. But to all who received him, who believed in his name, he gave power to become children of God, who were born not of blood, or of the will of the flesh, or of the will of man, but of God. The Word became flesh and lived along us, and we've seen his glory. The glory is of a father's only son, full of grace and truth. John testified to him and cried out, "This was he, of whom I said, he who comes after me ranks ahead of me, because he was before me."

May the Lord add his blessing to this reading from his word.

You noticed that we read aloud the Ten Commandments. A friend of mine not long ago, speaking to one of his adversaries, said, "You know, you're a great nine-commandment man. You're a great nine-commandment Christian." "Nine-commandment Christian?"

He said, "Yeah, I'm not that good. I'm maybe a five- or six-commandment Christian, but you're a great nine-commandment Christian." "I don't understand what you mean." He said, "You keep forgetting that ninth one, 'Thou shall not bear false witness against thy neighbor.'"

That's a commonly broken commandment in our culture today, isn't it? "Thou shall not bear false witness."

I know the careful exegetical studies about the ninth commandment reveal it was talking more about scandal-mongering and libel and even careless gossip, or perhaps literally bearing false witness in a legal proceeding, than it was the casual failing to tell the truth. I know that's what it means. But I also know that underlying the concern of heaven expressed in the ninth commandment, "Thou shall not bear false witness against thy neighbor," is a concern about truth-telling.

As we come to the Lord's table today, in a meditation that's about the ordinary, about the routine stuff of life, about the everyday things that remind us of something more significant, we're reminded that the bread and wine, the ordinary stuff of everyday life in the world into which Jesus came—you couldn't get any more ordinary. That was cornbread and lima beans for them. That was as ordinary as you could get. That's what they lived with, bread and wine, and the most ordinary stuff of life was used of God to remind us all of the most significant relationship of life, our relationship to God.

When we start thinking about truth-telling, when we really, seriously look at truth-telling, we talk about it in different ways. The lowest level is just getting the facts right. Telling things as they are. Sometimes we may be too proud of that and too eager to just tell everything as it is. Y'all are a pretty picky crowd. Last week, I quoted Wordsworth and Shelley and I think Blake, and somebody wanted to know why I'd left Milton out.

Well, here's Milton this morning. *Aeropagitica*, his wonderful little treatise on truth-telling, and the power of truth. We're reminded in *Aeropagitica* that there is nothing virtuous about having this attitude: "Well, I don't care what anybody thinks. I just tell it as I see it. I just say what I think. I just lay all the facts out there."

No, not so necessarily meritorious. What is bad in this candid friend, according to G. K. Chesterton, is simply that he is not so candid after all. He's keeping back something—his own gloomy pleasure that he takes in saying unpleasant things. That may very well be true on the part of those who like to just tell it all. They're not really telling it all because they're not telling us that they're taking a certain fiendish delight in telling stuff they shouldn't be telling.

John Bunyan in *Pilgrim's Progress* reminded us that a man may slander or libel another with simply a raised eyebrow when the truth would do better. We have a certain level of concern about facts, but more important and more significant and more meaningful than that concern about facts is a kind of concern about the philosophy of truth-telling. Truth in its generic sense, first of all. We as Christians believe there is such a thing as truth. There are some who shrug their shoulders and imply a total and utter ethical relativism and say, "There is no truth."

Now, we're going to talk in a minute about the ultimate truth, but now I'm not talking about Jesus Christ who said, "I am the way, the truth, and the life." I'm talking rather about the fact that we recognize there is such a thing as the truth. There is a categorical understanding that you can find out truth, and Milton, again in *Aeropagitica*, has this wonderful passage in which he said, "So truth be in the field, we do injuriously, by licensing and prohibiting to misdoubt her strength. Let her, as truth and falsehood, grapple. Who ever knew truth to be put to the worse in an open and free encounter?"

We share the confidence of that early almost-Baptist Milton: that truth will out. There is such a thing as truth, and truth will be victorious. First of all, it's sort of a concern about the facts, and then it's a concern about philosophy, but ultimately, we have a concern about truth in that ultimate and final sense, in that truth is incarnational. A truth that's known only by faith, beyond the facts, which are not unimportant but can be used and misused, distorted, and used as arrows of enmity.

Beyond the philosophical understanding that there is such a thing as truth and that truth will prevail ultimately, finally, we're reminded in John 1:14 that in Jesus Christ, the Word became flesh, and the Word was full of what? Grace and truth. That's so interesting. Grace and truth.

Maybe we are not really graceful, or grace-filled, without or apart from truth. He reminds us that he is the way, the truth, and the life, or flip them around. Maybe we can't really be truthful in the highest sense, in the sense that he is truth, without God's grace. Grace and truth. Had you ever thought about that linkage? Washington, particularly when it comes to foreign affairs, is full of linkages. We're always linking. *Quid pro quos.* This for that. Bargains, deals, and trade-offs. That's the name of the game, isn't it? That's the name of the game.

In the very first chapter of the Gospel of John, we're reminded of the heavenly, divine linkage of grace and truth. Oh, we see it a lot of places in the Scripture. You know, we're reminded that we speak the truth. How? How are we reminded in Ephesians to speak the truth?

In love.

That's another linkage of grace and truth, isn't it? Speaking the truth in love. Grace and truth. Maybe we really come to know truth, with a capital T—"I am the way, the truth, and the life"—only by grace. Amazing grace. Amazing grace. Maybe we can only be graceful and grace-filled when we rest in the ultimate truth.

We come in this time that we've set aside, that he set aside, "As oft as you do this, do it in remembrance of me." In this meditation on the Lord's table, on the Lord's day, in this, the Lord's house, with you and me, the Lord's people, to mark the meaning of grace and truth, the ordinary, everyday stuff of life. The routine occurrences that require of us loving difference from a hard world that is without grace. Honest adherence to telling the truth, but telling the truth in love without a raised eyebrow.

As we come to his table today, let's look in our own lives, for the two words that marked the coming of our Lord and Savior, and that brought us to this time and this place, are so simple and so fine that they come to us every day: just truth and grace. They're yours and mine.

—Published with permission courtesy of Ravensworth Baptist Church.

It's a Matter of the Heart

James Dunn preached the following sermon on Palm Sunday, April 5, 1998, at Ravensworth Baptist Church in Annandale, Virginia.

The Upper Room was dim with candle shine as Jesus sat with the Twelve remembering and then quietly said, "There's one here whose kiss will bring betrayal by and by." They didn't look at Judas curiously, but each man murmured, "Master, is it I?" Each one looked inward. None placed the guilt on any other guest who had partaken of that generous meal. When there are hungry people on my little street, when I see tears or hear a heart's hurt cry because someone has failed to keep faith high, may I too murmur, "Master, is it I?" Each one looked inward.

That's what we think about when we think about the Last Supper. The Upper Room. "Each one looked inward." That's what I want us to do today, around that passage of Scripture that's best-known from the Upper Room, one that most of us have memorized, not because we were made to anywhere along the line but because we needed to.

You know it. In John 14:1-6, Jesus said,

> "Don't let your hearts be troubled. Believe in God. Believe also in me. In my Father's house, there are many dwelling places. If it were not so, I would have told you. I go to prepare a place for you, and if I go and prepare a place for you, I'll come again and will take you to myself, so that where I am, there you may be also, and you know the way to the place where I'm going." Thomas said to him, "Lord, we don't know where you're going. How can we know the way?" And Jesus said to him, "I am the way, the truth, and the life. No one comes to the Father except through me."

May the Lord bless this reading from his word.

It's a matter of the heart, really. This whole business of Holy Week and how we respond to it is a matter of the heart, and what troubles the heart, and how we look in our own lives; each one looks inward. Here in John 14:1-6, we have the Great Prescription from the Great Physician. What is it that troubles our hearts?

What is it that troubled their hearts in the Upper Room that day, so long ago? Well, obviously the first thing that was troubling them was the prediction of Jesus' death. All of us are uncomfortable when we start talking about death. There's the very sort of readiness to be quick to blame that we've seen when death is the subject anytime, and there's the readiness to question why. There's the readiness to steel-heartedly resolve. There's the trouble of the heart when we think of death. When we think of the death of someone close to us.

It's easy for us to get specific with illustrations here in this place. Perhaps you've had a troubled heart thinking of the imminent death of someone. Then, beyond death, there was just that terrible business of the followers having to decide what they were going to do now. They'd followed Jesus. He'd been their leader. He'd been the one who had seen to it that all their needs were met. They'd been overwhelmed with the miracles they'd seen. They'd been shocked and stunned at the way the crowds had followed him, and now suddenly the very center of their life was to be gone, and they were having to face some really tough decisions. Really tough decisions. They weren't comfortable with those tough decisions, and maybe that's where some of us are today, facing really tough decisions and not quite ready to face them. Maybe that's why our hearts are troubled.

Then there's disappointment. These very words to begin with: "Someone will betray me." They didn't know exactly what that meant, but there was profound disappointment in people, in events, in plans. All around them, there was disappointment in that Upper Room. Maybe there's someone here today; that's where we are, and that's where they were, with troubledness of heart.

Practically everyone finds themselves at one time or another somewhere on the continuum that begins with discouragement and moves to depression and winds up with despair. From discouragement to depression to despair. Who's not been there? Maybe you get off that downward slide before it becomes depression. Maybe you don't. Here Jesus' followers were. That's where they were.

That's where we are, with troubledness of heart, and Jesus gave a prescription for troubled hearts: "Don't let your hearts be troubled. You believe in God. Believe also in me."

Jesus had rebuked Peter rather severely in the last part of the thirteenth chapter of the Gospel of John when Peter said, "I'll never betray you." And Jesus said, "Before the cock crows three times, you'll betray me." "I don't want to wash your feet," Peter said. And Jesus said, "If you don't wash my feet, you're not one of mine." He'd rebuked Peter repeatedly. The rebuke of someone we love can cause us to have a troubled heart, even if it's a mild, silly, and inconsequential rebuke. None of us go out looking to be rebuked by the people we love.

Hey, we don't like to be rebuked for any little thing. You guys know the sting of rebuke when you leave the toilet seat up. We don't like to be rebuked. We do almost anything to avoid rebuke, and those of you who have been married even a year know that couples establish little patterns, little routines in all our living, to avoid the rebuke of one we love. It's not worth it, and so we learn what triggers rebuke, and we just don't do it.

Thomas and Philip said, "We don't know where you're going. How can we know the way?" They'd been with him so long. He'd told them so often, and yet here was this misunderstanding. Separation. They anticipated separation from him. You don't have to be a teenager in love to be uncomfortable with separation. Separation troubles our hearts at any time, particularly if it's a separation that's not mutually agreed upon; any separation is a cause for troubled hearts and then shattered confidence.

But it all adds up in that they were troubled by everyday things. They were troubled by the ordinary stuff that troubles us in life. They were troubled by more than just an unexpected leak in the ceiling or something at the house that doesn't work right. Their hearts were troubled by death, indecision, and disappointment. They were on the slide of discouragement, depression, and despair, in that pre-Prozac age.

I've not been on Prozac, but I know about that stuff. For me, after cancer surgery, it was Valium. Jesus' followers weren't handling this very well. They didn't even have Valium. They were moving toward the despair that Mrs. Job expressed when she said to Job, "Just curse God and die." They were troubled. They were troubled because they didn't understand. They were afraid. Their hearts were troubled. They were real people like us. They were just folks. Fishermen, tax collectors, just folks. These were the things that troubled them, and we, like them, are troubled by the same sort of stuff. I dare say that when you click through the list of things that clearly and evidently by the Scripture record itself were troubling them—death, discouragement, disappointment, shattered confidences, separation, fear, uncertainty, the rebuke of a loved one, misunderstanding—there's not one of us in this room that to some small degree, or maybe to some greater degree, don't have a little bit of trouble in our hearts about one of those things today as we sit here, but he gave them the prescription for troubled hearts, and it's the prescription for troubled hearts for us.

"Let not your heart be troubled. You believe in God. Believe also in me."

All through the years, there have been all kinds of prescriptions for troubled hearts. The British are, I think, unfairly portrayed as advising, "Just have a stiff upper lip and go at it all stoically." The Latin cultures are equally unfairly portrayed as saying, "Have a good time, and let the good times roll, and forget trouble." Some of us are quite aware that denial is not just a river in Egypt, but that we too fall into the problem of denying the things that trouble our hearts. Even as I've gone through this somber list of things that trouble our hearts, I've triggered some of you to practice that denial. "Oh, not me. Not us. I'm Christian. Not here. Not me." Hey, we've tried all the tricks. We've done all those things, and yet our hearts are troubled. How come that troubled heart?

Well, Jesus didn't just say, "Believe in God. Believe also in me." He gave directions, but then he said, "I'm not just giving you directions of how to get there. I *am* the way. I'm not going to just tell you how to go. I'm going to go with you. I am the way, the truth, and the life." He was, as some have put it, the representative "die-er." He was the representative die-er for the universe. The one who has an answer to the problem of sin, to the meaning of life, to the riddle of death—those three universal human troublers of the heart—and we believe, on his promise, that he's the one who has the answer to the problem of sin, the meaning of life, and the riddle of death.

Julius Caesar, it's said, stood before the Roman Senate and said, "If there's anything beyond death, I cannot tell." But Jesus said, "Let not your heart be troubled." He's the only one with the answer to all the great questions of life, and so I go on not knowing. I would not know if I might. I'd rather walk with Christ in the dark than walk alone in the light. I'd rather walk with him by faith than walk alone by sight.

As we come to this Holy Week, as we think about the Upper Room and the Last Supper, we're reminded of the words of Gardner Taylor, who in his most famous sermon says, "It's Friday, but Sunday is a'coming." It's Friday, but Sunday's a'coming. "Let not your heart be troubled. You believe in

God. Believe also in me." It is in that focus on the one who has the answers that we find the majesty, because he is the one worthy to say, "Let not your hearts be troubled."

We're going to sing a hymn that once again perfectly compliments the thrust of the message: "Jesus, thou joy of loving hearts, thou fount of life, thou light of men, from the blessed bliss that earth imparts, we turn unfilled to thee again."

Let's stand as we sing after the moment of reflection, and come to this hymn, which offers the opportunity, as we do in this service, for those who have never trusted Christ as Savior and Lord and accepted the fact that he is the one with the answers to the problem of sin, the meaning of life, and the riddle of death to come and accept him as Savior and Lord and say, "I trust Jesus Christ with my life and in my death. I trust Jesus Christ."

It may be that there are some here today who want to join this church, and we receive others who say, "I've already made that profession of faith another time, another place. I've been a member of a church in another situation." Or "I'm coming today having made that profession of faith to be baptized and follow Jesus in baptism in this place." When we come to that time of invitation in a moment, if he speaks to you, would you come?

—Published with permission courtesy of Ravensworth Baptist Church.

Response Able and Free

James Dunn often preached on the biblical themes of freedom and responsibility. During the early 1990s, Dunn would preach a version of this sermon when visiting Baptist churches across the United States in his role as executive director of the Baptist Joint Committee.

"Being human is itself so vast a thing that the natural inequalities from one of us to the other of us are in themselves trivial."

Those are the words of F. J. Sheed, a lay Roman Catholic theologian reflecting upon the notion that we are all made like God. That's interesting, isn't it? And scary. All the great doctrines of the church had to have a Latin name down through the years, as you know, and we talk about the doctrine of *imago Dei*, made in the image of God somehow.

I don't understand all that, but all the great religions of the book, Judaism and Islam and Christianity, affirm that we are somehow made like God, made in the image of God. Now, whatever else it means to be made in the image of God, it means at least that we are able to respond to God. However you translate the story in the first few chapters of Genesis, you can't tear the teaching out of the story, and whether you take it very literally or very liberally, the characters of Adam and Eve were somehow able to respond to God. They were "response able."

Responsible—see how we get that word. And if responsible, they were also free because freedom and responsibility are like the two sides of a coin. No matter how thin you slice it, it still has both sides. You can't divide it. Every responsibility implies a certain freedom. We're not automatons or marionettes or hand puppets. We are creatures made in the image of God. So every responsibility implies a certain freedom. And every freedom carries with it, piggyback, a responsibility. Together they go. Responsibility and freedom.

The biblical story makes it clear that we are made with choosers, deciders, the capacity to make up our own minds. And sometimes it's an awful burden, isn't it? The fact that we have to make up our own mind. We are programmed that way, to use today's terminology. We are wired for choice and for decision. Our software demands it. We can't escape it. And the slow stain of choice, all the choices that we make, the decisions of our lives color our lives, and we are shaped by those choices.

I have the notion that this idea or concept—"I've been made in the image of God and responsible and free"—this two-sided coin, is universal. It is innate. It is inherent. All of us somehow have written into, programmed into, our very being at some level, however elementary, the awareness that we are made in the image of God and responsible and free. That's the rub. That thrusts upon us tensions that we can't escape.

You remember Harry Truman who worshiped at this church saying, "I hate those two-handed fellows. They are always saying 'on the one hand but on the other hand.'" Well, I understand what he means, and you do too because every one of us has hated those two-handed fellows at one time or another, those who were constantly reminding us of the creative tensions of both hands of life.

I want us to look at them for just a moment this morning. Freedom and responsibility. Personal morality and social ethics. Intense individualism. Oh, we Baptists are great at that. "Ain't nobody gonna tell me what to believe." Intense individualism and commitment to community. I want to tell you a couple of short Texas yarns, and if you don't get the point at first, maybe you will at last.

Every year about this time they start selling the baby doll of the year. You know how that goes. Every year there are dolls that wet and cry and sleep. A few years ago they had the Cabbage Patch Kids—those ugly things—the price alone made them ugly! One year there was one that walked and there was one that felt like a real baby to touch, called a Magic Skin Doll. But one year there was one that talked. Do you remember her? You pulled a little cord in her back and she talked. What was her name? Chatty Cathy.

Well, in our extended family there was a little three-year-old who had visions of sugarplums dancing in her head. As soon as the TV commercials started, she set up a howl, and that's the right word for a Chatty Cathy. She had to have a Chatty Cathy. And there would be no story if she didn't get it, and she got it. On Christmas when we opened the presents, at the high moment, she got her Chatty Cathy. And she played with it ferociously for a little while. She had it talk as fast as it would: "I love you, I love you, I love you." And as slow as it could: "I—l-o-v-e—y-o-u." She played with it intensely for a little while, but before the mechanism even broke (you know how long that is for Christmas toys), she had put it aside, covered it up, and gone on to play with wrapping paper. Suddenly disenchanted, disinterested, uninvolved with Chatty Cathy.

I don't know, but I have the notion that what was going on was something very profound. This child had never had a course in philosophy of religion or religious psychology. She knew not the word "theology," but she had watched those television commercials, and the thing that had captured her attention was that there was a doll that was somehow like humans. It could talk—"I love you, I love you." And then she discovered that it could only say what she made it say, that it was just a dumb thing, that it was just a mechanical gimmick, and that the words were absolutely meaningless because "I love you," those three sweet words, are absolutely meaningless if they come from someone who can say nothing else. Just as all religious expression is meaningless if it is enforced and not genuine and voluntary. When she discovered that this was just a dumb toy that couldn't say anything except make the same three little noises, she became disinterested, and wrapping paper with its many colors was more interesting to her.

Let me tell you about Dee. He sort of illustrates on the same level this basic, universal, innate understanding of something deeper than we think little folks can figure out. He was a little Dennis the Menace if there ever lived one. Now Hank Ketcham has given us that term for our language, and I don't need to go into a great deal more. And I'm not being sexist or exclusive in my language—there are also Denise the Menaces, but this was a Dennis the Menace.

Tousle-headed, dirty-faced, runny-nosed, ragged jeans, scuffed shoes, little bundle of mischief. He was in the church of which I was a pastor in Weatherford, Texas, just thirty miles west of where the west begins in Fort Worth. And every Sunday, as I went to the back door of the church, as all decent self-respecting pastors everywhere do on Sunday morning to shake 'em out, here would come Dee. And instead of shaking my hand, he would haul off and kick me in the shins. Now I looked at some of those old sermons not long ago, and they were probably worthy of his critique. But I learned to do a little Texas two-step to avoid that little rascal. I probably would have forgotten him except that one Sunday when he came out he caught me by the sleeve and pulled me down to his level and hugged me around the neck. And with eyes of innocence and a voice of sincerity that they lose somewhere along the line (but when they are about four they can melt a heart of stone), he said, "Preacher, I love you."

And he stopped kicking me in the shins. He made some kind of elemental connection between what he said and what he did, what he thought and how he acted, what he believed and how he behaved. He somehow made some connection between that inner personal side and the social dimension of his religious experience, though he didn't put it in those terms. He just said, "Preacher, I love you," and stopped kicking me. And I shall forever be grateful for whatever went on in that little shin kicker's mind. His mother may have threatened him within an inch of his life if he hadn't stopped, but at least he stopped.

We, all of us, deal with a tension of freedom and responsibility because we are made to live with that dyad, with that creative tension. The best we can hope is to make it creative because we all like the kind of freedom to be what we want to be and do what we want to do, but none of us are free as a bird. Only a bird is free as a bird. We all must understand that we live with what Emil Brunner called "the awful burden of freedom."

Now that does not mean we have to be like the folks who named the church in Garrison Keillor's hometown. They called it "Our Lady of Perpetual Responsibility." That does not mean we live with that awful burden in that sense. We tend to focus so much upon responsibility sometimes that we forget the other side of the coin. We Baptists have understood that personal freedom is rooted not in the Constitution or in some Baptist doctrine. It's not even rooted in the Bible. It's rooted in the very nature and being of God.

Because we are somehow made like God, and it was God's divine intent and purpose from being the foundation of the world to make us free and responsible creatures, then we see all of the biblical teachings through that prism of personal responsibility and freedom. We affirm soul freedom and the competence of the individual before God and the right of private interpretation. We affirm the priesthood of the believer and religious liberty for others, even those whose beliefs we despise. We insist upon freedom for all to come to a religious experience on their own because we believe, at least in our Baptist heritage we have affirmed doggedly and insistently, that one makes those inward, intimate, individual commitments of faith freely or not really at all.

We understand that there is no room for coercion. That great American philosopher Peppermint Patty said to Linus, "You know, I would have been a good evangelist." And Linus said, "Why do you say that?" She said, "You know that kid who sits behind me at school?" "Yeah." "Well, I convinced him that my religion is better than his religion." "How did you do that?" said Linus. And she said, "Simple. I hit him with my lunch box."

And the reason we laugh is that we know that's no good. We make those intimate, spiritual decisions voluntarily and live with them responsibly.

But we also understand that another of those dyads is the tension between personal morality and social ethic. Here today are some friends from Texas who I haven't seen in a Baptist church in a long time, and they understand this when I say that I grew up in that tradition where we placed such an emphasis upon personal morality that we thought the only thing moral was that which was personally applicable.

You know, "I don't drink and I don't chew, and I don't go with girls that do." We had a good set of personal and moral guidelines, a long list of don'ts—so many I've forgotten a good many of them, thank the Lord. But on the other hand, we didn't have the social ethic that we should have had. We didn't understand.

We live with that tension in our Baptist family between personal morality and a social ethic. Thank God that today most of us are aware that it's not either/or but it's both/and. And we care about peace and the homeless and health care and racial justice. And we care about people, whether they bear our label and look like us or not. We understand something about a Christian social ethic that's as big as the whole world and all of humanity. Thank God that we have finally come to this posture, and yet we cannot forsake personal morality either. Because government can't do it all and the forces of social change can't do it. Ultimately, we still must bear the personal responsibility that goes with freedom.

Finally, we live with the tension between individual integrity and commitment to community. We must cling to that individual emphasis on one person at a time. We in our heritage have stood strong for soul freedom. We don't want to be part of a melting pot or a burgoo or stew and lose our identity. We know that we are personally accountable unto God, and I am not ashamed of singing "I Come to the Garden Alone" or "There is a place of quiet rest near to the heart of God," and there's a dimension of personal piety that I hope we never lose. And yet to what purpose is that individual integrity if we do not reach beyond ourselves to share in a commitment to community? And so it's not either/or. With that integrity we reach out and share. That reaching out is meaningless unless we do have the integrity and the individual commitment to bring the larger family something real and honest.

Listen to Wes Seeliger's beautiful words. He is an Episcopal minister in Houston. He says, "I have spent long hours in the intensive care waiting room watching with anguished people. Listening to urgent questions: Will my husband make it? Will my child walk again? How do you live without your companion of thirty years?"

The intensive care waiting room (and I know a lot of you have been there as I have) is different from any other place in the world. And the people who wait there are different. They can't do enough for each other. No one is rude. The distinctions of race and class and everything else melt away. One loves his wife as much as the other. And everyone understands this. Every person there pulls for world changes. Vanity and pretense vanish, and the universe is focused on the next doctor's report. And the door opens coming into that intensive care waiting room, if it will only show some improvement. Everyone there knows that loving someone else is what life is all about. Why does it take the intensive care waiting room to drive home the oneness of the human family?

G. K. Chesterton put it this way: "We are all in a small boat on a stormy sea, and we owe each other a terrible loyalty." Compassion roots itself in that solidarity. That solidarity is the full consciousness of our being a part of the human family, the deeply felt awareness that we are all made in the image of God. The knowledge that all people, however separated, are bound together by the same fragmented human condition. That solidarity lies at the very heart of the gospel because the great message of the gospel is not that God came to take away our pain but that, in Christ, he came to share those pains with us. Great things can be done where there is a community of support and awareness and oneness in Jesus Christ. Where there is an awareness that indeed we are one with him and with all who hurt.

A rock group has a video out that goes "Everybody hurts." And at the end, the message is "hold on." But for those of us who find in Jesus a spiritual strength and awareness of his presence, we have a promise that's better and surer and stronger than simply the two-word admonition, "Hold on."

Amen.

> —James M. Dunn Papers, MS 632, Z. Smith Reynolds Library Special Collections and Archives, Wake Forest University, Winston-Salem NC, USA.

Where the Spirit of the Lord Is, There Is Freedom

James Dunn preached the sermon below at Maranatha Baptist Church in Plains, Georgia, in 2001, the church home of his friend and former president, Jimmy Carter.

If you have your Bibles would you turn with me 2 Corinthians 3:12-17?

> Since then we have such a hope, we act with great boldness. Not like Moses who put a veil over his face to keep the people of Israel from gazing at the end of the glory that was being set aside, but their minds were hardened, even to this very day. When they hear the reading of the old covenant, that same veil is still there, since only in Christ is it set aside. Indeed, to this very day, whenever Moses is read, a veil lies over their minds. But when one turns to the Lord the veil is removed. Now the Lord is the Spirit and where the Spirit of the Lord is, there is freedom.

May the Lord add his blessing to this reading from God's word.

A friend of mine, Norm DuPuy, brings a news item from Germany about a pastor who was severely reprimanded by his bishop for baptizing cats, thus implying that they'd have eternal life, which I'm sure they considered a singular improvement over the traditional nine lives. According to the January 26, 1991, *New York Times*, this Lutheran pastor was held to be highly theologically suspect. Well I should think so, but then Baptists think baptizing anything without personal faith is highly suspect, and thus we don't baptize infants or of course cats.

The German pastor explained that he'd baptized these cats at the request of elderly parishioners. I can kind of imagine the scene. Can't you? Some dear older person wants to be sure that Tabby's okay for eternity. But picture baptizing a Baptist cat by immersion. Quite apart from the heresy, you'd better sedate that sucker before you go sprinkling water on him and waving hands, to say nothing of dipping him under to be raised up in newness of life. I think most cats would just as soon pass up heaven as to be baptized by immersion and called a Baptist, as would a good many people that I know who don't want to be called a Baptist.

It's been an interesting twenty years that I've just concluded, living and working in Washington. I know a lot of folks who really don't like to be called a Baptist and don't understand us very well. It is understandable that they don't understand us because of this very passage of Scripture, which we take very seriously. Where the Spirit of the Lord is, there is freedom. So people see folks who are labeled "Baptist," like many of the television entrepreneurs who call themselves Baptist, and some folks in politics who have worn the label "Baptist," and these folks have puzzled and perplexed a lot of us who also bear the same label. Folks are about as unpleasantly riled and unhappy with the notion of being called a Baptist or knowing what a Baptist is as ever in Baptist history.

At many of those meetings with folks unfamiliar with Baptists that I went to and you went to, the introduction goes something like this. "And what do you do?" "I work for Baptists on Capitol Hill." You could almost hear the snide dripping from their voice when they said, "Baptist?" I developed a quick little answer, and I say this with this message wherever I go. Not just here. I developed a quick little answer that worked. I would say, "Yes, but I'm a Jimmy Carter, Bill Moyers, Barbara Jordan kind of Baptist." You could almost hear the wheels turning. You could tell that they were catching on that there are different kinds of Baptists.

But we're not understood very well. I know all of you in the room this morning are not Baptists, but Baptists are not understood very well, partly because we do not have a neat creed, and we do not have a neat creed because of this understanding of Scripture: where the Spirit of the Lord is, there is freedom. Echoed in Galatians 5:1, it is precisely for freedom that Christ has set you free. We don't have a creed.

Now I'm doing a little theological instruction this morning. It's not heavy and it's not scary and it won't hurt anybody. But I'm distinguishing between a creed and a confession of faith. A creed is a prescription that must be filled precisely as it is issued. Like a prescription you take to the drug store. A confession of faith is a description of what we are and what we already believe. A description, not a prescription. We do not have an intellectual creed as a Baptist people. That was one of the problems Paul was dealing with in Corinthians and Galatians, because the law had become a ladder people thought they could climb to God instead of a meritocracy.

There was a head trip. They had to all believe exactly the same way. No, we do not have an intellectual creed. We're not a catechetical people. We don't have to jump through a certain set of hoops. We don't have to memorize and feed back any set of particular doctrines in order to become a Christian. We don't have an intellectual creed. We don't have a moral creed. Now this makes some folks a little nervous because I grew up in Fort Worth, Texas, and many of you have grown up in Georgia. We have a lot in common. When you ask the person on the street, what is a Baptist, they're just as likely as not to tell you what a Baptist doesn't do. "Oh, they're the ones that don't, you know, fill-in-the-blank. Dance, drink, smoke."

We have moral standards. We have moral obligations, but any Baptist worth their salt will tell you that we behave, we do right. We have moral standards because we have been saved, not in order to be saved. So we don't have a moral creed. Nor do we have a political creed. That's the European way. The European way is that there are politics and religion so mixed and intertwined that political parties take religious configurations and religions take political configurations. Thank God we do not have a political creed as Baptist Christians.

I hadn't been in Washington long when I did an interview. I say it was my first, and Marilyn reminds me it was really two interviews. My first and my last on the *700 Club* with Pat Robertson. I thought the interview had gone fairly well. I'm always nervous about television reporters and interviews, and the white lights were hot. They were so bright and right in my face, so close they could see my nose hairs. It was a grueling experience, and I got almost through, and they said, "One more question, Dr. Dunn. Do you believe it is possible for someone to be a Christian and a Democrat?"

I thought of a lot of good things to say on the way home, and it's probably a good thing I didn't think of them 'til then, but I used an answer that I think is honest and valid and true, and I said, "Well, yes I do. I think Jimmy Carter showed us that that's possible. Possible at least on the outside to be a Christian and a Democrat."

We don't have a political creed. We don't have a moral creed. We don't have an intellectual creed because where the Spirit of the Lord is, there is freedom.

So we're terribly misunderstood. It allows us to fuss and fight and divide because we have that freedom. It allows us to share the gospel with all kinds of folks and expect action because where the Spirit is, there is freedom. We don't have a creed, but we do have a confession of faith. It is the best confession of faith anyone can have. It's the most biblical. It's the most historical. It's the most accessible to anyone.

It's the most universal. It's the most memorable. It's the most dynamic and moral confession of faith because it implies far more than simply what we believe in our heads. It doesn't speak simply of the Scripture. It speaks of a vital way of life. Our confession of faith you can find all through the New Testament.

The wording is sometimes slightly different, but the message is absolutely clear. Our Baptist confession of faith is simply *Jesus Christ is Lord. Jesus Christ is Lord.* That's our confession of faith. That's the one confession of faith that all true believers anywhere in the world can and will and do say. In the many countries of the earth in which folks are labeled Christian, in some of the toughest places on earth today, that confession of faith is vital and real and dynamic and makes the difference in how they live because being Lord means that Jesus is the master, the ruler, the controller, the owner of our very lives.

Jesus Christ is Lord.

I'll tell you, a confession of faith like that will trump a creed any day. It is always better to have that living, vital, dynamic confession of faith. We're a free people who do not have a binding creed, either intellectual or moral or political. But we have a lively confession of faith. We have a coherent set of beliefs that hang together. I know some folks haven't been to BSU [Baptist Student Union] or church training and haven't learned anything about that set of beliefs, but our set of Baptist beliefs do hang together. They stem from the notion at the very beginning of being a Baptist that each one of us has immediate access to a relationship with God through Jesus Christ, not through some work scheme, not through the church, not through the preacher, but directly related to God.

There is one mediator between God and all humankind, and that one is Christ Jesus. The very idea that every individual can and does have access to God is an idea that's so radical and so transforming. It's a concept that the young generation would speak of as awesome: that every individual can relate directly to God, and out of that comes that whole set of Baptist beliefs about freedom. Because we each related directly to God, each one of us then has a right and a responsibility to study and interpret the Scripture for ourselves.

The right of immediate access to God puts upon us the wonderful obligation and opportunity, the wonderful blessing and burden of Scripture study on our own with the leadership of God's Spirit and the fellowship of believers coming to know God's word. We have the capacity, the freedom, and the responsibility to go directly to God's word. Every freedom, like the freedom to go directly to God's word, carries piggyback a responsibility rider with it. Every wonderful opportunity carries an oughtness with it. Like the two sides of a coin, you can't have one without having the other. We have the right and the responsibility of personal interpretation of Scripture.

Now if that's true, for us Baptists, each individual comes to the church on his or her own. We understand the Reformation doctrine of the priesthood of all believers, and we come to God on our own. We don't have a ruling pastor. We had a poor mistaken older pastor down in Texas a few years ago who talked about the ruling pastor. We don't have a ruling pastor. Ruling pastor is an oxymoron. If you think you're a ruling pastor, you're an ordinary moron, because you haven't met the choir, the deacons, or the women's missionary society. No, we don't have a ruling pastor. We have a democracy within the church because of the priesthood of all believers.

Beyond this local church, this church is autonomous in relationship to other Baptist churches everywhere. Every church decides for itself, sits on its own bottom, makes its own decision, charts its own course, under the leadership of God's Holy Spirit, in the fellowship of believers. We understand that. Martin Marty, probably the best-known church historian in American today, a Lutheran, wrote in 1983 in *Christianity Today* an article called "Baptistification Takes Over" in which he contended that this understanding of a personal religion, a direct relationship to God, the priesthood of all believers, democracy in the local church, and the autonomy of the local church over against other bodies, ecclesial bodies, was something that Baptists had done to America.

He wasn't necessarily bragging about it. He acknowledged that there are a lot of people who aren't too happy about it, but the Baptistification of America described by Martin Marty describes the set of coherent beliefs about freedom of worship, freedom of religion, a personal responsibility of

Bible study, the priesthood of all believers as we go out into the world, that Baptists have championed since the very beginning.

The first Baptist worthy of the name, Thomas Helwys, in 1611 wrote a little tract, 160 pages long to the king, saying, "I will pay tribute to the King. I will work for the King. I will serve in the King's armies. If need be, I'll die for the King, but the King is not the Lord of the conscience." So that king put him in Newgate prison, where he stayed for four years, and that king put to death the first Baptist in modern times. That king's name is the one in the front of a lot of our Bibles, King James, that very king.

Then Roger Williams came to this land just ten years later and planted what became the first Baptist church in America in Providence, Rhode Island. You call up there today, just dial their number, and they still answer the phone, a little snootily I think, "First Baptist America." Roger Williams reminded us that to call a nation Christian will make a nation of hypocrites but not one single true believer.

So we have insisted on this kind of freedom not only for ourselves but also for others. The first president of Harvard, Henry Dunster, was tied to a stake in Harvard Yard—that stone pillar is still there in Harvard Yard today—and he was whipped with forty lashes save one for a terrible offense in that theocratic Massachusetts Bay Colony. You know why he was whipped so brutally? For refusing to allow his infant daughter to be baptized, because he believed, as we believe, that where the Spirit of the Lord is, there is freedom, and every individual comes directly to God on their own or not at all.

As George W. Truett said, "God wants free believers and no other kind." So we have a coherent set of beliefs that hang together. We have a confession, though we don't have a creed. But more important than either or both of those added together, we as a Baptist people, who are misunderstood and who misunderstand ourselves many times, are committed to the notion that where the Spirit of the Lord is, there, right there, is freedom.

We also have a companion. It's better than a creed. Browning Ware is a friend of mine who is retired now from the First Baptist Church of Austin, Texas, and many years while he was there, he wrote a little weekly column for the *Austin American Statesman*. It's real short. This one's double-spaced and short lines and big type. It won't take long and I'd rather read it to get it exactly right than try to quote it or paraphrase it.

Here's his column:

When younger, I thought there was an answer to every problem and for a time I knew the answers. I knew about parenting until I had children. I knew about divorce until I got one. I knew about suicide until three of my closest friends took their lives in the same year. I knew about the death of a child until my child died. I'm not as impressed with answers as I once was. Answers seem so pallid and sucked dry of blood and void of life. Knowing answers seduces us into making pronouncements. I still have few friends or acquaintances who are 100% sure of most anything and are ready to make pronouncements on homosexuality and AIDS and marriage problems and teenage pregnancies and abortion and sex education or whatever else is coming down the pike, but when they get shoved into their valley of the shadow, a pronouncement is the last thing they need. A friend wrote recently, "I too get Maalox moments from all who know."

I'm discovering that wisdom and adversity replace cocksure ignorance with thoughtful, faithful uncertainty. More important and satisfying than answers with a little a, is the Answer. Thou art with me. That's what we all crave. There may or may not be answers, but the eternal one, even Jesus Christ, would like very much to be our companion, with us, and that's answer enough.

Where the Spirit of the Lord is, there, right there, is freedom. We disturb folks sometimes as Baptists because they can't carefully define us, and we may not be able to define ourselves too explicitly, but we have a confession of faith that's durable. A coherent set of beliefs that makes sense and works out in life around freedom, and a companion of the road who's with us every day we call on him to be with us. That's answer enough. Amen.

—James M. Dunn Papers, MS 632,
Z. Smith Reynolds Library Special Collections and Archives,
Wake Forest University, Winston-Salem NC, USA.

The Word Was Made Flesh

James Dunn preached the following sermon on December 29, 2002, at Ravensworth Baptist Church in Annandale, Virginia.

And the Word became flesh. The Word became flesh. So what? What does that have to do with the way we believe, with the way we think, with the way we pray, with the way we live? I think it speaks directly and powerfully to all of us, because we are indeed a paradox people. We've always dealt in what the academic calls *dyads*. The general and particular Baptist; the separate and regular Baptist; the independent and interdependent Baptist; the truth Baptist and the freedom Baptist; the sola scriptura Baptist, Scripture alone; and the sola fide Baptist, faith alone.

We have been necessarily, as a people, dialogical. We talk to each other. We've entered into tons of dialogue for hundreds of years; but worse than that or better than that, we've also been dialectical. We were dialectical before it was cool. We were dialectical before the Niebuhr boys or any of the European philosophers started talking about the dialectic. Dialectical thesis, antithesis, synthesis. Thesis: here an idea is. Here's an opposition or a reaction or a contradiction to it; and then there's a synthesis and we learn a little something. And we say, "Ah, well, I never thought about it that way."

And then that synthesis becomes the next thesis, and antithesis, and so on. We've always been that way. We Baptists have always been that way because we haven't been locked in. And we haven't been locked in because of the incarnation. The Word became flesh. What does that indeed mean for us today? Theologically, in the way we live, because our living religion shapes and forms our theology more than the other way around. But our theology then informs our living religion, and they go together. Another dialectic. Another descent and belief and growth.

Well, I want to suggest to you five words that I think are a direct result of the Word becoming flesh, of the incarnation that is the real reason we celebrate Christmas and what Christmas is all about. It's not about Santa Claus or toys. It's about God becoming flesh. And just in case you do have trouble remembering, these five words begin with P-E-D-A-L. PEDAL.

The faith then, for we Baptists who have an incarnational theology, is first of all *personal* rather than propositional. God had sent into the world his prophets. He had sent the teachings from Moses and the Ten Commandments on down. He'd sent the poets, he'd sent the martyrs, and none of it had worked. And so, as the Galatians passage we read a while ago reminded us (Gal 4:4), the word became flesh. God took on flesh in the person of Jesus Christ. You can't get any more personal than flesh and blood. We sing with the Apostle Paul, "I know whom I have believed" (2 Tim 1:12), not "I know what I have believed." I know *whom* I have believed.

It is our commitment to persons made in the image of God that fuels our passion for social justice, for Christian ministry, for evangelism, for ethical behavior. It's our commitment to persons who are made in the image of God and have flesh like the flesh that Jesus took on when he invaded humanity in the person of Jesus Christ. That's what keeps us going. Martin Luther King Jr. went to Boston and worked on a doctorate. He did so, in some significant measure, to refute the theology of Tillich, who had in King's view made theology too much a matter of words and too little a matter of experiencing the Word, Jesus Christ. Propositional theology.

There are those on the left and fundamentalists on the right who are willing to say it's what you believe that counts. Everything depends upon your interpretation of the Scripture. I know *whom* I have believed, not *what* I have believed. That roots in the very being of Jesus Christ. In a book that's now a classic definition of what it means to be a Baptist, written by an agnostic Jew, Harold Bloom, one of America's leading intellectuals today, he said that E. Y. Mullins was the Calvin or the Luther or the Wesley of Baptists because he was the definer of our creedless faith—what we believe.

Mullins is the most neglected of major American theologians, more important than Jonathan Edwards or Horace Bushnell, or even the Niebuhrs, because he formulated the faith of a major American denomination. A denomination that says it's not so much what you believe as whom and to whom you relate.

Secondly, the "e" of PEDAL. Our faith is, first of all, more personal than propositional. It's also more *experiential* than academic. It is ubiquitous. It is accessible. It is historical. It is rooted in the sound theology of being able to experience the lordship of Jesus Christ and express the simple confession that all believers anywhere in any country at any level of education or economic wealth or poverty can say: "Jesus Christ is Lord." And that means more than just an intellectual belief.

It's not just an academic notion that Jesus Christ is Lord, because when you put the word "Lord" on that affirmation of faith, you mean he's the ruler; the master; the one in charge; the driver of this little car. Jesus Christ is Lord. Our faith is more experiential than academic to some significant degree because it is an incarnational faith; Jesus took on flesh, and that's exactly what our faith does, and so it becomes experiential.

You remember the story when the man born blind was given his sight? And then they started going after this man because of that. The critics, the scholars, the religious establishment of the day said, "Is this man a prophet or not?" He tried to escape them, and so they went after his parents. And the parents got scared and they say, "Oh no. Don't ask us. Ask him." And he said to them, "Whether he is," referring to Jesus as a prophet or not, "I don't know. I know not. But one thing I do know: I was blind and now

I see" (John 9:25). That's experiential religion in a nutshell. Experience rather than primarily academics.

Next, we're *dialectical or dissenter*, and I think I'm using those words. I'm merging the descent dimension of the dialectic into dialectic or dissenters rather than some other word because ours is a faith that is incomplete, that humbly knows it needs to grow, that recognizes that we don't have it all nailed down; that we're not God; that we cannot, as some charismatic brothers and sisters like to say, "know the mind of God, and speak the language of God."

Baloney.

None of us know the mind of God. We get glimmers, but we don't have it nailed down. And this certainty, this dogmatism, is a direct affront to an incarnational theology that accepts the fact that, fleshly mortals that we are, we're not there yet. And so ours is a dissenting voice. You know, you used to sing, and I did too and I still do, "I have decided to follow Jesus." I don't see anything wrong with a little chorus. I'm not making fun of it. I certainly don't want to ruin it for anybody. "I have decided to follow Jesus. I have decided to follow Jesus." You have sung that, haven't you?

If we were going to make it theologically correct, we'd probably sing, "I have decided and decided and decided and decided and decided again; and decided again; and decided again to follow Jesus." When the Scripture, in the life of Joshua, highlights the notion that we should choose this day whom we will serve, we could, without stretching the meaning of it a bit, say we must choose *each* day whom we will serve. Isn't that right? Isn't that true to our experience?

Don't we all understand that as dissenters, we're always a little troubled, a little uneasy, a little ready to challenge and enter into the dialogue that comes out of our own limitations? Karl Barth recommended—with the Bible in one hand and the newspaper in the other—that we need to be ready to challenge corporate corruption, the rush to war, racial profiling, the rape of our natural resources, and our own admitted inadequacy.

Our faith is more personal than propositional. It's more experiential than academic. It's more dissenting or dialectic than dead letter. Set. Fixed. Inerrant. It's the same Bloom who said that the faith that Baptists know, that E. Y. Mullins set forth in actions of religion and that many Baptists have practiced, totally vaporizes an inerrant reading of Scripture because every believer has the right and responsibility of personal interpretation.

Under the leadership of God's Holy Spirit, every believer has the right and the scary responsibility. We like to say, "Oh, we have the right to private and personal interpretation under the leadership of God's spirit and the fellowship of believers, with prayer and fasting and understanding the Scripture in its context; we have the right of personal interpretation." Okay, but we also have the *responsibility* of personal interpretation, and that's kind of scary.

Our faith is also not only personal, experiential, and dialectic or dissenting but is also *active*. I love the words of Dietrich Bonhoeffer, not in his popular little book that nearly everybody's read, *The Cost of Discipleship*, but in a big fat book of his that's pretty difficult even for my seminary students that I teach: *Ethics*. *Ethics* is harder yet because he gets pretty tough. And in *Ethics*, commenting on the passage in James 1 that says, "Be ye doers of the word, not hearers only; thereby deceiving yourselves," Bonhoeffer says, "No one can possess the word of God for a single instant, other than in the doing of it."

Oh, I possess the word of God. No, that's not what he's talking about. He's talking about the Living Word. The Word that became flesh in the person of Jesus Christ. No one possesses the word of God for a single instant other than in the doing of it, because if we're merely hearers, or as James 4 reminds us, judges of the word, then we are not doers. Hearer, judge, no. But a doer of the word. Then we possess it. Our faith is active, not passive.

And finally, our faith is *lively*. Now that sounds pretty liberal, that it's lively and not simply a body of material that can be ingested. Maybe memorized. Spewed out and fed back. Taught like a catechism. But lively, squirmy, wiggly, vigorous, zipping about, going through cracks that you couldn't even imagine. Or, as the Scripture says, "Sharper than a two-edged sword, discerning, cutting even between the bone and the marrow." That's pretty tight. Lively.

Joy to the world, the Lord has come. He's given us a faith that is personal. And a faith that is experiential. We don't know all about it, but we know we were lost and now we're safe. And, dissenting or dialectical, we don't need to be afraid of the things we can't understand. In fact, there was a great little article in *Newsweek* of all places for this kind of thing last Easter. It talked about the contradictions in Jesus' legacy, and this was the way it worded it. The contradictions in Jesus' legacy are thick and epic. Contradictions, thick and epic. And then it listed a few.

In defeat, there's victory. In humility, strength. In surrender, gain. In darkness, light. All counterintuitive ideas. All apparent contradictions from a mere human reading of the concepts. All directly related to the notion that, in Jesus Christ, in the incarnation, because he took on flesh and became like us, the faith is a lively, personal, challenging, active, experiential religion. The Christmas word is "Emmanuel." God is with us. The eternal Word, capital W, of God has become flesh. Thanks be to God.

It could be, though I know nearly all of you, that there's someone who has never accepted that person Jesus Christ into your life, but you're ready to do that today. Or it could be there's someone, like some who joined just last Sunday, who wants to be a part of this fellowship of believers in this particular place. You're near here. You're going to be near here, and you need a church family; come on and join this church. Don't futz around about it, equivocate; go on and be part of a family of faith who is a group of people, a group that believes an incarnate faith. Works out in life. I know that. I recommend it to you. I know this church. I've been here a long time, off and on.

As we sing a wonderful hymn, it has very special meaning to me. The last time I saw my mother in life was in a nursing home in Abilene. And she had taken leave of most reality with Parkinson's in the very last stages. And she told me as I entered the nursing home room, "Your daddy's out there working on that old car." He was always doing something to that old car. And he'd been dead for two years. And she was out of touch with reality. But we watched the worship service of First Baptist Abilene on the tube together that morning, and when we sang this song that we're about to sing, she didn't miss a word. "All the Way My Savior Leads Me." Let's stand and sing, and if you would make a decision or a commitment to him, this is a good time to do it.

—Reprinted with permission courtesy of Ravensworth Baptist Church.

For Freedom Christ Has Set Us Free

James Dunn preached the following sermon on July 4, 2010, at Knollwood Baptist Church in Winston-Salem, North Carolina. Dunn and his wife, Marilyn, were members at Knollwood during his "retirement" years as a professor of public policy at Wake Forest University School of Divinity.

The Apostle Paul was definitely put out with the Galatian church. In perhaps the strongest words in sacred text, Paul says in Galatians 5:12—you know that passage, it's sort of softened in most translations, "I wish those who unsettled you would just castrate themselves," since they were talking about circumcision.

He was dealing with those called Judaizers, who insisted on the ritual of circumcision as essential to salvation. They taught that without the ancient Jewish rite, one could not be considered a child of God. Legalists whose descendants we still have roaming about us. The golden text for today, however, is a very positive verse. Galatians 5:1: "For freedom Christ has set us free."

The Galatian Christians had experienced the grace of God, but they were accepting the legalism, the creedal claims, of their old religion—their Jewish faith—and clinging to circumcision to make them right with God. And so in Galatians 5:6, Paul writes, "For in Christ Jesus neither circumcision nor uncircumcision counters for anything; the only thing that counts is faith working through love."

This is one of those passages that is a pivotal passage, a hinge passage. It is as sharply, penetratingly, liberatingly revelatory of the real authentic will of God for our lives as the passage in the Sermon on the Mount that says, "Ye hath said it heard of old, but I say unto you . . . ." Things are different, baby. Things have changed, and this verse puts the focus exactly where it should be. Ours is in fact an incarnational faith lived out. Faith taking on flesh with Jesus Christ at the center of it. The living Lord for all of us in that incarnational faith.

It is an incarnational theology. It's an experiential religion. We might even say *experimental* religion, because it's in those experiences of testing our faith and experiencing the grace of God that we come to know Jesus. It is a personal faith. We don't simply know what we have believed; we know *whom* we have believed, and so therein is the essence of our faith in Jesus Christ. It's not circumcision or creedalism or what we believe, what propositions we accept. It's a living relationship with the Lord.

Now, these Galatian Christians needed to hear this. As good Jews, they had understood and they had been taught that God's children were able to respond to God. The Genesis record was quite clear. Being made in the image of God means at least, whatever else it means, that we are able to respond. We are response-able and responsible.

Response-able and responsible. And if responsible, free, because it wouldn't be fair if any of us made someone responsible and then didn't let them be free to make their own choices. Certainly, God who makes us free makes us responsible. Who makes us responsible makes us free. It's like the two sides of the same coin, indissoluble.

Freedom and responsibility go together. The Galatians knew that. They'd grown up saying that. They'd grown up with it on their forehead and on their doorposts. They understood that we are all response-able—responsible and free—and because we can respond to God, we must respond. Whatever else it means to be made in the image of God, it means at least that. We wind up with the capacity for choice. Our very being demands that choice. Our hardware demands it. Our software demands it. We're wired up that way—all humankind is wired up.

The image of God in which we're all made may be marred; it may be blurred. We still have that latent image, made in the image of God, that allows us, no, demands of us that we make choices. We must make choices, and with these choices comes responsibility. We accept or we reject. We come to God and God comes to us directly.

It is for freedom that Christ has set you free. This soul freedom of which I speak is not a novel new doctrine. It is not, as some would have you believe, a liberal invention of the last century. Bernard of Clairvaux, in a very important Roman Catholic conference because they were the only ones around at that time in 1128, wrote these words: "Take away free will and there remaineth nothing to be saved. Salvation is given by God alone and is given to the free will who chooses it."

Here is theological affirmation, deep doctrinal roots, but in the American experience we celebrate today, "Freedom is found in the garden of the church, not the wilderness of the world," as Roger Williams put it.

He and Dr. John Clarke knew that the church and state had to be separate for freedom to flourish. Those early New England Baptists preached soul freedom long and loud, but they and their children stood for political freedom as well. Sam Stillman, the first pastor incidentally of the first Baptist church of Boston, preached the artillery sermon for the boys of Boston as they went off to fight in the American Revolution. He was a patriot as well as a theologian. He understood to render unto Caesar as well as render unto God.

We had a Baptist pastor of First Baptist Boston preaching the artillery sermon that said, "Go out and get them." And that was the essence of the message. Samuel Francis Smith wrote the words to "My Country Tis of Thee" when he was a twenty-two-year-old divinity school student. Have you written a hymn like "My Country Tis of Thee"? He was a divinity school student at Andover, and he took the hymn to his church in 1831, and so they sang it first on July the Fourth, 1831.

We're singing and celebrating "My Country Tis of Thee" on its 179th anniversary, this day in this church, by a young Baptist seminary student who did something worthwhile while still in seminary. Christians are dedicated to freedom, both personally and spiritually, and publicly and politically, or freedom set free. We begin the Christian life freely or not really. There is not valid forced faith. No such thing as a coerced conversion. If it's forced, if it's coerced, if it's structured and manipulated, it's phony, and if it's phony, it's not worth a thing to you.

If it's done without your free choice and consent, and you are pronounced saved, you're okay, don't believe it. Don't believe it for a minute. You must enter into that transaction. It's why Baptists have always stood for believer's baptism. For those who've made a commitment to Jesus Christ. It is for freedom that we're set free.

Roger Williams made it plain when he said, "There is no such thing as a Christian nation. To call a nation Christian may make a country full of hypocrites, but not one true believer." We come to Christ personally and freely or not at all—for freedom set free. We take up belief freely. No creeds bind us. Walter Rauschenbusch said it well for a Baptist. He said, "Baptists tolerate no creed because it's fatal to make the religious fault of one age binding for a higher age." It condemns a grownup who still thinks and talks like a child.

A creed tells you what you must believe. Our confessions of faith and church covenants report what we do believe. They are descriptive, not prescriptive, and that's the big difference between a creed and a confession of faith. We're not bound by creeds. It is for freedom that we're set free, and we don't enter into the Christian faith freely and then take up a slavery of intellect. Not so. We're free and responsible, yes, responsible. Free in faith to accept and practice God's love. For freedom we are set free.

We serve and give freely without constriction. We don't have an allotment that must be paid. We serve without deadly dull duty because we choose to serve. We serve freely. We give freely. It is for freedom that we are set free.

But politically, we also celebrate freedom. This is the Fourth of July, and you knew I'd get around to that. For freedom set free in our churches, we practice democratic polity. You have the same vote that the pastor has. Hey, young people, you have the same vote that the pastor has. He doesn't get two votes and you just get one. When you have become a part of this church, we practice democracy.

He said that in the Baptist church "our polity is approximately Christian." Approximately Christian. I guess that's the best we can do. For freedom set free; in our relationships we are free.

Brunner said that a collective, or a collection of persons without that dynamic personal freedom, is like so many pulverized briquettes of individuals, I think the kind of briquettes that are gonna be used on the grill this afternoon. That's the only way I reserved the use of the word briquette as a kid growing up, those charcoal briquettes. Rauschenbusch said that any kind of collective or collection that was called community without individual freedom to enter into it or leave it was just like so many pulverized briquettes of individuals. I like that. That's a collective, not a community.

But, with the Holy Spirit working in a community of people who have come into it voluntarily by a faith they've accepted voluntarily with a following of the Spirit of God voluntarily, it could even become more than community. It could become *koinonia*, blessed fellowship, caring, loving family of belief, but it does that only because it's for freedom that we've been set free.

And then politically, when anyone is denied religious freedom, the religious freedom of all of us is endangered that moment. We filed briefs at the Baptist Joint Committee in my years up there on behalf of the Santerians, because they were sacrificing chickens in church, and the little town of Hialeah, Florida, decided they would tell them they couldn't do that.

We filed a winning brief. The brief assured that when anyone's religious freedom is denied, however weird or bizarre, if it's not damaging other people, if it's not hurting someone, when anyone's religious freedom is denied, everyone's religious freedom is in danger at that moment. We don't need a theocracy that puts someone's god in charge, and we don't need any government that thinks any of its business is to meddle in religion.

George W. Truett was born in North Carolina, but he got to Texas and spent most of his life there. Preached for fifty years at First Baptist Dallas and was president of the Baptist World Alliance and president of the Southern Baptist Convention and the savior of Baylor, spinning in his grave nowadays. But he in Victorian rhetoric tried to get at this freedom that is set out so clearly in Galatians 5.

Now, I'm asking you for the first time in this short message to work, but work at listening to this ponderous Victorian sentence, which probably worked much better in 1910 than it does in 2010. Truett said, "The right of private judgment is the crown jewel of humanity, and for any person or institution to dare to come between the soul and God is a blasphemous impertinence and a defamation of the crown rights of the Son of God."

For any person to come between the soul and God is a blasphemous, denying God, cursing God, impertinence, too big for your britches, and a defamation of the crown rights of the Son of God. It is for freedom that Christ has set us free. Amen.

—Reprinted with permission courtesy of Knollwood Baptist Church.

Give Me Your Yearning to Breathe Free—John 8:31-36

James Dunn preached the sermon below on Religious Liberty Sunday, July 7, 2013, at the First Baptist Church in America, Providence, Rhode Island.

It's a distinct honor and a high privilege to me to be in this pulpit on this day, the 375th anniversary of the founding of this church, the First Baptist Church of America. I tell some folks, I think the office staff is just a little snooty when they answer the phone, "First Baptist America," but you can say that, and so why not? First Baptist America is OK.

In this country, we have both civil and spiritual bedrock beliefs. "We hold these truths to be self-evident, that all men are created equal, that they're endowed by their Creator with certain inalienable rights, that among these are life, liberty, and the pursuit of happiness," and then, with Genesis 1:27, we hold that we are "made in the image of God." There's no church in America more entitled than this church to try to focus on those two things at the intersection of civic life and spiritual commitment.

It's a challenge, isn't it? Sometimes these parallel principles are as hard to separate as Siamese twins.

Sometimes both beliefs are basic, and they're so basic that they're confounded and conflated. Folks don't quite distinguish between the spiritual and the secular. Sometimes patriotic truth is rooted directly in biblical revelation. Civil religion and a Christian response to events often overlap. It's a challenge to deal with the sanctity of patriotic principles without falling into the trap of nation worship and thinking that, as a nation, we are Christian.

Roger Williams, who founded this church, reminded us that we might call the whole world Christian, but doing so wouldn't make one single believer. It's a terrible challenge to start secularizing the sacred and, in doing so, lose the focus on the divine dimension. Our national birthday started this week with a celebration on the Fourth of July, an appropriate celebration. Last week we saw the Supreme Court change the game regarding marriage, and we have yet to learn how that plays out.[1]

The week before that, the United States Senate took a big step toward immigration reform.[2] The song we just heard was about as close as we have to an immigration hymn. "Give me your tired, your poor, your huddled masses, yearning to breathe free."

We don't have a better immigration song than that. So, in the last two weeks, we've had an interesting fortnight of sorting out all this sort of stuff, this sort of stuff that is terribly important for the nation, for everyone—Christian, Jew, Buddhist, Hindu, or whatever—and it's an interesting and challenging time. I must report to you, this being a Baptist church and me being a Baptist hired hand for forty years, twenty in Texas and twenty on Capitol Hill, and now, for the last fifteen, at Wake Forest University, I must report to you that the second-largest historically Baptist group, that's the newest one on the ballpark today now as a female bishop. I've talked to our church historian at Wake Forest, Bill Leonard, and he says he does not know of another CEO of a Baptist organization who is a woman, but Suzii Paynter is the newly elected executive of the Cooperative Baptist Fellowship.

It's the first time we've had a female chief executive officer of a large Baptist body. The week after Suzii was elected at the Cooperative Baptist Fellowship, the British Baptist Union, not wanting to get behind, elected a woman as chief executive officer. We Baptists don't have bishops, but it's all right to call her that. We will, since she's a first, but it's been a very busy two weeks in Baptist life, trying to figure out what we're going to do with the Supreme Court's new track they put us on regarding marriage, with the Senate's new business on immigration, in both the Court and the Congress.

We have challenges galore. There are hard questions that follow, and only with partial answers, because what do we mean when we talk about the *imago Dei*, being made in the image of God? How do we live out our lives because, and since, we are created equal? How do we live that out? How do we apply those inalienable rights that among them are life, liberty, and the pursuit of happiness?

What does that mean for our relationships? Corporately as a church and individually as persons? What does it mean for our relationship with others, who have also been granted those rights for life, liberty, and the pursuit of happiness as a part of their being created equal, and who are also, according to Scripture, made in the image of God—somehow Godlike?

I don't claim to know all that being made in God's image entails. Anybody who does, I'd sure like to talk with you right after the service. If you know what it means, fully and completely, to be made in the image of God, or if you know, as some think they do, who is made in the image of God, I still believe very much as Roger Williams did that every human is made in the image of God. It was he who challenged the wisdom of the ages regarding dealing with the Native Americans. He believed that they were made in God's image, and they were therefore valuable and free and responsible and able to make decisions for themselves, and he refused to treat them as less than fully human.

Our forebears, including Roger Williams, held tenaciously to the notion that the native peoples were created free and valuable and whole and able to decide for themselves and direct their own lives made in the image of God. Whatever else it means to be made in the image of God, it means that we as human beings are response-able—responsible. The first chapters of Genesis have the divine Creator giving instructions to human beings, with the presupposition quite clear that he, she, the divine one, understood that persons could respond to the command, to the instructions, to the very nature that he wrote into their being.

If response-able, responsible; if able to respond, responsible; and if responsible, free. Freedom and responsibility are the eternal coin of which both sides go together. We're not free unless we're responsible. We're not responsible unless we're free, and so the very idea of being made in God's image does suggest that we are free and responsible. Being made like God somehow becomes the first text in Christian anthropology.

All created equal? Not so hard to believe with all made in God's likeness, but how can we say with a straight face "created equal" when we look at the sad differences, disparities, destructiveness, hurt, pain, sin, and distortion of God's image that we see when human beings are viewed and treated like less than fully humans made in God's image? Indeed, we are equally free and equally yearning to breathe free as the Hymn of Lazarus, the immigration hymn, says.

We are equally free and equally responsible. Baptists in our formative centuries, going back to Roger Williams and others of his time, took to heart the normative words of Jesus when he said in the Scripture, "I am the way, the truth, and the life"; "You shall know the truth, and the truth shall make you free" (John 14:6; 8:32).

Baptists in our historic connotation, in our historic pursuit of the truth, in our historic proclamation of what we believe to be true, and salvific, saw truth and freedom, truth and life as indissoluble. Truth and freedom together; ye shall know the truth, Jesus said, and the truth shall make you free. The indissolubility, the oneness of truth and freedom, has been written deep into our being as Baptists. For us, personal truth is the trumping truth, the key truth, the strong truth upon which all other truths must hinge. For us, the Christian life is someone encountered, not merely something believed. Roger Williams, Calvinist though he was, was not a propositionalist who hung his whole life on theological propositions. It's primarily not what I do believe, but whom I do believe.

If Roger Williams were here today, I'm convinced that he would still be rejecting paper propositions and asking hard questions, and knowing Roger Williams as we do, and one of your members sitting here now knows him better than probably anybody in America—Stan Lemons is a Roger Williams authority—I believe he would still be rejecting propositions, asking hard questions, and refusing to shut up.

He'd be going right on, like he did then. He was called otherwise-minded. I hear that there were lots of bad things said about Williams and his crowd; recently a writer here in Providence has unearthed a "herd of heretics." That was one of their favorite terms for the folks who were members of this particular congregation.

He was called divinely mad. He was seen as having a boat with a sail that was too tall. He created a stir where he went, and with what he did, but every time I hear him, and the earlier members of this church, and perhaps the present members of this church, referred to as the *otherwise-minded*, I want to say, "Me too, me too. I'm otherwise-minded. I go along with that being otherwise-minded," and so I resonated years ago, years, I don't remember how long, twenty, thirty, maybe forty years ago, when the old commentator on CBS did a program which was a record of his travels around the country called *On the Road*.

His name was Charles Kuralt. Maybe you all remember him? Some of you are old enough to. Ah, yeah, a whole lot of you do. Charles Kuralt did a little segment on this very spot, right here, this church, and the little park across the way. He said, "The early Rhode Islander"—speaking generically of the whole crowd of Rhode Island people, but this Baptist bunch particularly—"was disrespectful and disreputable. They were always fighting about something."

Today, they put him on a pedestal, the figure atop the capitol dome. You've spotted this, haven't you? The figure atop the capitol dome is called "The Independent Man." He can see the whole state from up there, and that's probably true. He was the first to be disrespectful, and disreputable, and free. May we move and breathe and have our very being in that tradition of being, when it's appropriate, disrespectful, and disreputable if necessary, but free. Here we are, at First Baptist America. Go on and say that on the phone if you want to.

—James M. Dunn Papers, MS 632, Z. Smith Reynolds Library Special Collections and Archives, Wake Forest University, Winston-Salem NC.

Notes

1. The U.S. Supreme Court ruled in June 2013 that the Defense of Marriage Act, a federal law restricting "marriage" and "spouse" to only opposite-sex unions, was an unconstitutional violation of the civil rights of gays and lesbians. The Court held that the law interferes with the rights of states to define marriage. This landmark decision paved the way for the court's ruling in *Obergefell v. Hodges* (2015), which held that same-sex marriage is protected under the Due Process Clause and Equal Protection Clause of the Fourteenth Amendment. As a result, same-sex marriage bans in states across the nation were struck down as unconstitutional.

2. The Senate passed 68-32 legislation to overhaul U.S. immigration policy. However, the House of Representatives never held a vote.

Afterword

Working in public policy as a professional Baptist, I often ask myself, "What would Dr. Dunn say now?" The answer is always the same . . . anything he damn-well pleased.

Having gotten to know Dr. Dunn a little later in his life, I always wondered if his directness was a result of no longer caring what people thought. The speeches, columns, and sermons in this book prove that he was always blessed with the courage to say exactly what he meant, no matter the audience or consequence. It was a matter of conviction. Dr. Dunn could cut to the heart of a matter, through political talking points or pious religious jargon, to tell the truth of what was really going on and what was at stake.

I've been fortunate to have followed in his footsteps serving both the Texas Baptist Christian Life Commission and the Baptist Joint Committee. Reading this volume has been a personal reminder of the many ways I've been influenced by Dr. Dunn, by those whom he influenced, and by those who influenced him. And the timing of this book couldn't be better—his words and work, never more relevant. Baptists, and the country at large, are sorely in need of a reminder that one can be fully in favor of the separation of church and state and still expect the church to be politically engaged.

While the cultural influence of the fundamentalist movement James Dunn fought is fading fast, it is politically ascendant. In response, many pastors and church leaders would rather fly above the fray and out of the mess. Dr. Dunn called on Baptists to get messy:

> Not to take a stand in the political context is to support the status quo. To accept things as they are is to indicate either that one is satisfied with present policies, that the situation is hopeless, or that his religion has nothing relevant to say. . . . To "stay out of politics" or to assume a smugly superior pose as an independent above-it-all is itself an alignment with the forces of evil, a cheap cop-out. (85)

The words and work of Dr. Dunn have never been more relevant. In spite of potential controversy, we must engage because "withdrawal from the world is a time-tested denial of religious realism, an evasion of ethical responsibility. Biblical truth must be fleshed out, incarnate" (83). Just as he wrote decades ago,

> The issues we face today are many, complex, and divisive. To ignore the issues, to oversimplify them, or to fail to take a position is intellectually dishonest, morally reprehensible, and socially irresponsible. This does not minimize to any degree the difficulty that we all face in assuming our responsibility as citizens and Christians. (228)

Failure to engage due to complexity or controversy gives those consequences too much power to stifle our faith and silence our witness. Staying silent is not only a cop-out, I believe it also endangers the future of the Church. From his time as campus minister at West Texas State University to his final position at Wake Forest School of Divinity, Dr. Dunn engaged and inspired young people. In an age when many faith leaders are bemoaning the loss of young people in the church, that next generation is wondering if the Church has anything powerful or even relevant to say in our times. Rather than just fondly remembering the cantankerous Texan and some of the crazy things he said, reading this collection of his words and writings and following his plea might spark a revival.

In Dr. Weaver's book, we are reminded not only of Dr. Dunn's love and devotion to soul freedom, but also his love of neighbor. This love drove his advocacy because "the biblical understanding of love involves far more than sentiment. Caring for one's neighbor in concrete terms requires engagement with the political process because politics affects so vastly every nook and cranny of life" (75). For Dr. Dunn, soul freedom was always paired with responsibility in order to avoid "cowboy Christianity" and "Lone Ranger religion."

The call to engagement is not easy, but worth it. Dr. Dunn reminds us that

> since our salvation is not dependent upon our meritorious deeds, we do not need to be afraid of anything as we engage in controversy. We may make mistakes. We may lose to overpowering forces against us. But even when we fall, are defeated, even when we do not succeed, our relationship to God remains constant and secure. With this knowledge Christians can enter controversy with a boldness not known by others. (227)

Were he with us today, Dr. Dunn would likely be shaking that bony finger in many faces and he'd surely have some choice words for the state of our politics. I think he'd also have a word of encouragement and urge us all to "Think well, be true to the Bible, love people, dare to act, and work hard. 'Unto whomsoever much is given, of him shall be much required'" (219).

—Stephen K. Reeves
Associate Coordinator of Partnerships and Advocacy
Cooperative Baptist Fellowship
Decatur, Georgia

About the Editor

Aaron Douglas Weaver has served as communications director of the Cooperative Baptist Fellowship in Atlanta, Georgia, since 2013. He is the editor of *fellowship!* magazine and oversees media strategies and digital and print communications. He received his MA in church-state studies and PhD in religion and politics from Baylor University, where he focused on faith-based advocacy and religion and the First Amendment. His dissertation examined the environmental ethics and political advocacy of Southern Baptists and American Baptists over the past fifty years.

Weaver is the author of *James M. Dunn and Soul Freedom* (Smyth & Helwys Publishing, 2011) and the editor of *CBF at 25: Stories of the Cooperative Baptist Fellowship* (Nurturing Faith Publishing, 2016) and *Different and Distinctive but Nevertheless Baptist: A History of Northminster Baptist Church* (Mercer University Press, 2018). He is also the author of numerous journal articles as well as a regular contributor to popular digital publications and news outlets including Baptist News Global, Patheos, EthicsDaily.com, and Christian Ethics Today among others. He is a past board member of the Baptist History & Heritage Society and serves on the Commission on Creation Care and the Commission on Baptist Heritage and Identity of the Baptist World Alliance.

Weaver and his wife, Alexis, have two children, Oliver (age 6) and Miriam (age 4). They reside in Tucker, Georgia, where they are members of Smoke Rise Baptist Church.

www.ingramcontent.com/pod-product-compliance
Lightning Source LLC
Chambersburg PA
CBHW071236160426
43196CB00009B/1082